Rev. Arthur Drewitz

Tradition and Testament:
Essays in Honor of Charles Lee Feinberg

Tradition and Testament:
Essays in Honor of Charles Lee Feinberg

Edited by
John S. Feinberg
and
Paul D. Feinberg

MOODY PRESS
CHICAGO

© 1981 by
THE MOODY BIBLE INSTITUTE
OF CHICAGO

Library of Congress Cataloging in Publication Data
Main entry under title:

Tradition and testament.

Includes bibliographical references and indexes.
1. Bible. O.T.—Criticism, interpretation, etc.
—Addresses, essays, lectures. 2. Feinberg, Charles
Lee—Addresses, essays, lectures. I. Feinberg,
Charles Lee. II. Feinberg, John S., 1946–
III. Feinberg, Paul D.
BS1192.T69   221.6   81-11223
ISBN 0-8024-2544-5   AACR2

Printed in the United States of America

Contents

Part I
HERMENEUTICAL AND THEOLOGICAL

Part II
EXEGETICAL

Part III
TEXTUAL AND LINGUISTIC

Part IV
INTEGRATIVE

Preface

Most people love and appreciate their father and think he is quite special. What is rather unusual is to have a father who is so illustrious that those who know him agree that he is indeed an unusually gifted person. Charles Lee Feinberg is such a person. As a scholar, man of God, counselor, and friend his life and ministry have marked the lives of many people. Not the least of those who have benefitted are his children. As loving sons who are extremely proud and appreciative of our father, we asked ourselves how we could possibly express our thanks in a tangible way. Obviously, there is no adequate way for any child to reflect all his appreciation for his parents, but we wanted to express our gratitude to our father in at least some measure. It was decided that an appropriate way of honoring our father would be to bring together a collection of scholarly essays on various topics concerning the Old Testament he so totally loves and so masterfully understands. Thus was born the idea for this *festschrift,* and it is with much thanks to God for giving this unique servant to His church that we are delighted to present these essays in honor of Charles Lee Feinberg.

As you read this volume's personal comments about Charles Feinberg, you will see him through the eyes of several who have known him in various relationships and situations. However, none of them has had the privilege of knowing him as father and it is in that regard that we want to pay tribute to him. There are many ways in which we as sons have been influenced by his life, but probably his greatest influence has come in terms of his example of godly Christian living. As we grew up, it was always clear to us that he had an intense love for God. The person of God and the Word of God were always central in his life and in our home. His habit of daily, lengthy, personal Bible reading made a deep and lasting impression on all of us. Moreover, his passion to serve his Lord by serving others made it unequivocally clear that the Bible verse from Joshua 24:15 ("As for me and my house, we will serve the Lord") hanging on a plaque in our living room was much more than just words. Such an atmosphere in the home is bound to mark the children, and indeed, it did. It is not accidental that we have spent our adult lives actively involved in full-time Christian service and that our sister, Lois, has always played an active role in the local church and its related ministries. Although our parents never forced any of us into any ministry, it would indeed be correct to recognize that their godly example was used by the Lord to lead us into His service.

Most who know of our father think of him as a scholar, and certainly, he is. Often, outsiders think that we must have learned Hebrew and Greek just from living in his home. Even though we never had lectures in Hebrew exegesis or theology at the dinner table, our parents made certain that we knew enough both to be saved and well-informed in the faith. Beyond that, though, Dad's example of personal commitment to studying the Word of God and to producing excellent scholarship about the Word served both as a model and a motivation to us.

In all of those respects we greatly appreciate him, but we also thank God for his role in our lives as father and friend. Some children look for a father to be merely a pal, but God knows that they need more than that. They need wise guidance, a godly example of Christian manhood, a firm but loving hand of discipline, and encouragement during times of difficulty and defeat. In short, they need a *father*. God has been most gracious to us in giving us such a man as the head of our home. As we grew, it was always reassuring to know that Dad not only loved us deeply, but he also understood us extremely well. When we needed advice or encouragement, he was always there to give just the appropriate word. One of the greatest sources of encouragement was his habit of showing his confidence in us by granting us as much independence as we could possibly handle (sometimes even more than we could handle). Such confidence engendered a sense of responsibility on our part, as well as a genuine feeling of trust in his concern for our total welfare and development.

Although we believe that our father has been unusually good in all the above-mentioned respects, we also recognize that his life and ministry could never have been so effective in our lives and in the lives of others without the ministry of our mother. Dad often had to be away from home in ministry, and we know that it was a tremendous help to him to know that the care of his home and children were left in the capable hands of his loving wife. Without her constant devotion to God and the ministry, her complete confidence in and encouragement of her husband, and her godly example and tireless work in the home, neither his ministry nor the development of us as children would have been what they were.

Believing that by honoring those who love Jesus Christ we honor Christ Himself, we are proud to present this volume of essays to Charles Lee Feinberg. Though the nature of a *festschrift* is such that the chapters tend to be of varying topics, we have been able to group them into several broad categories: (1) hermeneutical and theological, (2) exegetical, (3) textual and linguistic, and (4) integrative. In addition to discussing themes of import for Old Testament theology, articles in the first section raise different perspectives on key issues of hermeneutical approach to Scripture. The second section focuses on the careful exegesis of key Old Testament passages. Though they are all of theological import, the particular approaches taken by the authors are more exegetical-theological in nature than are the approaches of the chapters in the preceding section. The third section deals with matters relating to textual critical issues and to the very understanding of the grammar of Hebrew. All three of these sections deal with matters that are internal to the text of Scripture. The fourth section handles matters that go beyond the immediate text of the Old Testament to other disciplines. We have labeled the section integrative in that the essays involve matters of interaction between those disciplines and Scripture. We believe that these four sections and the articles in them reflect many of the foci of our dad's research, teaching, and ministry.

Many people are involved in producing a volume such as this. We would like to express our gratitude to them for their invaluable help: first, to our wives, Patricia and Iris, for their constant help and encouragement; second, to the outstanding scholars who contributed to this volume. All have known our father personally—as students, colleagues in teaching and preaching ministries, all as friends. We think it worthy of note that each person we initially contacted accepted our invitation to write for this volume. We believe that this is a most positive reflection on Dad's influence and on their graciousness as Christian scholars and gentlemen. Third, we thank Moody Press for approval and help in this project. We extend special thanks to David Douglass and Charles Phelps. Finally, Ms. Sherry Kull and Mrs. Ruth Wolf, deserve recognition for graciously giving of their time to type manuscripts and correspondence. To all of these we express our genuine appreciation.

It is our sincere desire that these essays will prove to be effective tools of ministry and instruction in the lives of those who read them. We know they rightly honor our father. It is our ultimate desire that this project would bring glory to the Lord and Savior whom we all love and serve!

John S. Feinberg
Paul D. Feinberg

A Tribute to Charles Lee Feinberg

It has been my privilege to know Dr. Feinberg since 1948. Since then we have been very closely associated in the work and progress of Biola College and Talbot Theological Seminary. I am writing about him as I have known him and worked with him and loved him in the Lord during the past decades. He came to Biola as one of the Torrey Bible Conference speakers in 1947. At that time we were developing a theological program at Biola that ultimately led to the graduate school—Talbot Theological Seminary. Dr. Talbot and I conferred with Dr. Feinberg concerning the possibility of his coming to Biola to head up the theological program we were developing and enlarging. Through a series of circumstances, he was led to accept the invitation and began teaching in 1948.

As I think back on those days, I am amazed at the patience that he showed in connection with the development of the program and also in connection with the early years of Talbot Theological Seminary. As we endeavored to build the curriculum and obtain a suitable faculty, there were comparatively few students who were even interested in coming to this school. He must have experienced keen discouragement, many, many times, wondering if he had done the right thing in leaving a most success-ful position in another seminary and coming to what looked to be a rather bleak situation at Biola. But he never let on that he was the least bit discouraged. He always gave the impression that everything was going very nicely and that things were going to be picking up and we would be moving along in a comparatively short time.

I will never cease to be thankful for his loyal support in connection with the slow development of the seminary work. During these years that it has been my privilege to know him, he has been as true a friend as I could possibly have. Never once has he spoken harshly to me concerning events or ideas that surely must have given him a great deal of concern. His friendship has meant more than I could ever tell during this entire period of time.

And then I think of Dr. Feinberg as a scholar. He has two earned doctorates, years of study for the rabbinate, and years of individual and intensive study of the Word of God as well as in related (and many nonrelated) areas. He is truly "a walking Bible encyclopedia." His knowledge of the Scripture is phenomenal. For a number of years, we participated in a panel discussion program on the Biola Hour—a radio program that has been sponsored by Biola for almost fifty years. His ability to pull from memory just the right verse or verses to answer a question constantly amazed us. I consider him one of the greatest living authorities on the Bible and the Lord of whom it speaks. I heard him say on one occasion that his goal is to read through the Bible four times a year. The knowledge of the Word that he evidences in his conversation demonstrates this fact of his life. His mind is full of Bible passages and Bible truths.

He is also a great prayer warrior. Untold hours of prayer have gone to the throne of grace on behalf of Biola and the seminary and on behalf of the hundreds of graduates who have gone out from this sacred place into all parts of the world to minister to those in spiritual need. We all love to hear him pray. His prayers are extraordinarily beautiful. The vast storehouse of Scripture upon which he draws contains something appropriate for any set of circumstances. A volume of his prayers would be a most worthwhile contribution to the great body of Christian truth.

He has quite a sense of humor. I have been with him on several tours to the Holy Land. He is constantly ready with a quip or anecdote or a good story to keep the crowd alive and interested during long and otherwise tiresome trips from one part of the Holy Land to another. But his humor was never at the expense of another person in the group. He downgraded himself, but never anyone else.

There have been many references to his Holy Land trips. He was always very respectful toward the official tour guides. But when the guide was not lecturing, he would inevitably listen to Dr. Feinberg's conversation with other members of the tour group and would soon learn that Dr. Feinberg knew more about a given place or circumstance than the guide himself. On a number of occasions after the guide had finished his discourse, he would ask if Dr. Feinberg had anything to add. This was always asked with the greatest respect for his knowledge. I know of no one with whom I would rather visit the Holy Land than Dr. Feinberg. He has a wealth of information concerning the Holy Land—its past, present, and future.

Probably one of the most outstanding attributes of this great man of God is his defense of the faith. To him, the Word of God is inerrant. He is quick to discern heresy or any deviation from the straightforward truths of the Word of God. He was quite young during the days of the modernist-fundamentalist controversy in the 1920s and early 1930s. Nevertheless, he was quick to discern the errors of the modernism of that era. He took his stand squarely upon the great fundamentals of the faith, and he proclaimed them with a thoroughness and vigor that was refreshing. He also kept abreast of the theological trends of the 1970s, and it is encouraging to listen to him speak concerning the current liberalism, pointing out its fallacies and weaknesses, and then bringing in the great truths in the Word of God.

The list of the translators of the *New American Standard Bible* has never been published, but it is quite a well-known fact that Dr. Feinberg contributed in a most significant way toward its translation.

He has a trip-hammer mind, and it frequently expresses itself in his very rapid speech and conversation. It appears that his mind is always a sentence or two or three ahead of what he is saying.

I thank God for the privilege of being a co-worker with Dr. Feinberg in the program at Biola College and Talbot Theological Seminary. His influence will be felt upon the school and upon the lives of hundreds of young men who have gone out from these sacred halls into the service of the Lord for a long, long time to come. In his retirement years, he may rest from some of his labors, but his works are following him to the ends of the earth.

Samuel H. Sutherland
President Emeritus
Biola College
LaMirada, California

Years at Dallas Theological Seminary

When Charles Lee Feinberg arrived on the campus of Dallas Theological Seminary in the fall of 1931, he was the envy of his classmates. He had already earned an A.B. from the University of Pittsburgh in three years of study. The achievement that was of special interest to his fellow classmates was his skill in the Hebrew language. Having studied Hebrew from boyhood, he read it more fluently than his teachers at the seminary and accordingly was excused from all required Hebrew courses.

In less than three years he earned the Bachelor of Theology and the Master of Theology degrees, graduating in May 1934 with an A-plus average and a major in Old Testament. One year later he had completed the course to the coveted Doctor of Theology degree.

He wrote his doctoral dissertation, "Premillennialism or Amillennialism" (after compiling his research materials), in one month. He is probably the only graduate of Dallas Theological Seminary who earned Bachelor's, Master's, and Doctor's degrees in less than four years. That course usually requires six or seven years for the average student. His dissertation was published and has enjoyed wide sales due to its systematic and biblical presentation of premillennialism as opposed to amillennialism. This was the first of many books.

In addition to completing his doctoral work in less than a year, he served as acting professor of church history during his period of doctoral study (1934–35). He then was called to serve as professor of Semitics and Old Testament, beginning his work in the fall of 1935 and continuing until 1948. During his Dallas years he also served the Cumberland Presbyterian Church as pastor from 1936 to 1940.

Not content with simply teaching in the classroom, he pursued graduate work at Southern Methodist University, where he earned an M.A. in 1943. Then with a two-year leave of absence he went to Johns Hopkins University where he received his Doctor of Philosophy degree in Semitics. Returning to Dallas, he remained for the next three years serving ably on the faculty until he was called to the professorship of Old Testament at the Los Angeles Biblical Theological Seminary, which later became Talbot Seminary.

On the Dallas campus Dr. Feinberg was respected for his thorough scholarship, for his unquestioned orthodoxy, for his deep insight into the Scriptures of the Old Testament and New Testament, and for his intimate knowledge of Hebrew, which allowed him to read at sight any portion of the Old Testament, and his acquaintanceship with Jewish customs served to enrich his theological scholarship.

Almost from the beginning of his student days he excelled as a pulpiteer and was in demand across the country as an expository teacher of unusual depth and breadth.

In 1935 he was married to Ann Priscilla Fraiman, a fellow Hebrew Christian. The Lord blessed their marriage with three children—Paul David in August 1938, Lois Anne in September 1940, and John Samuel in April 1946.

As one of the most illustrious Dallas Seminary alumni, Dr. Feinberg has distinguished himself as scholar, linguist, expositor, teacher, and lecturer. He was recognized on the fiftieth anniversary of Dallas Seminary and gave the commencement chapel address.

On the occasion of this Festschrift, his Dallas colleagues and friends salute him for what he is—a Christian scholar of tremendous gift and labors. His effective ministry to his students and to the general public will bear fruit for another generation.

John F. Walvoord
President
Dallas Theological Seminary
Dallas, Texas

With All Thy Mind

"Thou shalt love the Lord thy God . . . with all thy mind" (Matt. 22:37). We have all experienced the blessings of sharing the intellectual and spiritual fruits of great minds—our teachers and the authors of our books. Some of us have had the privilege of being a friend to one who not only has a great mind but who is a great soul.

Charles Lee Feinberg has been that mind, teacher, and spiritual blessing to me. I have never known another man who so earnestly loves the Lord with all of his mind. To me he is like the apostle Paul—one who has a brilliant mind, but whose brilliance is eclipsed by his love for the Lord Jesus Christ.

In a very real sense Dr. Feinberg's intellect is a natural gift of God. He was born into an orthodox Jewish home, and his parents nurtured this gift. Like Saul of Tarsus and Timothy of Lystra, he learned the Holy Scriptures as a child. He grew up in Pittsburgh, a university city. Dr. Feinberg "neglected not" God's gift. He nurtured it, trained it, and disciplined it.

I shall never forget my first visit to Las Vegas. Dr. Feinberg and I were speaking at a prophetic conference in a local church. I planned to arrive early so that I could do some sight-seeing. Since Dr. Feinberg was staying at the same motel, I stopped by to invite him to go sight-seeing with me.

But when he opened his door, I looked inside and thought, "No sight-seeing now." He had been working. There were books on his desk, on the chairs, and on his bed. One of my teachers once told of a simple German peasant who wrote over his door, "Dante, Moliere, and Shakespeare live here." When Dr. Feinberg invited me in I discovered that not only Dante, Moliere, and Shakespeare lived with him, but so did Moses, David, Jeremiah, Isaiah, and Paul. They all were in his room, and so was the One of whom they wrote, the Lord Jesus Christ!

Dean Farrar in his splendid *Life of St. Paul* wrote, "Paul knew his Old Testament so well that his sentences are constantly moulded by its rhythm and his thoughts are incessantly coloured by its expression."

Dr. Charles Feinberg has had an advantage over the apostle. He has not only the Old Testament but also the New Testament. Read his books—his very language is molded by the Scriptures. Attend his lectures—how he teaches the Bible by quoting the Scriptures!

Oh, yes, Dante, Moliere and Shakespeare are also there. But they take second place, because to Dr. Feinberg the light of human inspiration is a tiny lesser light.

To Dr. Charles Lee Feinberg the Scriptures, all the Scriptures, are the infallible Word of God. The Holy Spirit has enlightened and heightened the gift of his intellect, so he finds and proclaims the Lord Jesus Christ in the classroom, in the pulpit, in his writings, and in his life.

Dr. Feinberg has added a new standard of excellence to evangelical scholarship. He does not tolerate anything less than excellence. He cannot, because he loves the Lord with all his heart.

But even his great intellect is overshadowed by another gift. I have called his intellect a natural gift of God. He enjoyed that gift before he became a believer in the Lord Jesus Christ. But Dr. Feinberg's chief characteristic is not his mind; it is his heart of love. This is part of the fruit of the Spirit, not a natural gift. Fifty years ago Charles Lee Feinberg found the Lord Jesus Christ at the Pittsburgh branch of the American Board of Missions to the Jews. The brilliant young rabbinic student was overwhelmed by the love of the Lord Jesus Christ. When he met the Lord, Charles Lee Feinberg fell in love with Him. This has been the passion of his life. One cannot listen to him teach or preach, or read his writings, without realizing this truth—he loves the Lord with all of his heart as well as his mind.

Dr. Feinberg is a great theologian. Do not make any mistake about it—his theology is deep, but it is not just a theology of the head. It is the passion of his heart. The incarnation is not just a fact in history; Dr. Feinberg loves and walks with and serves his incarnate Lord.

Since Dr. Feinberg loves the Lord Jesus Christ, he loves the same people our Lord loves. As the Lord wept over the lost sheep of Israel's house, so Dr. Feinberg weeps. This century has not seen a greater proponent of the cause of Jewish missions than Charles Lee Feinberg. To him, Romans 9, 10, and 11 are not just printed in ink in his Bible. They are written and engraved on his heart—"I could wish myself accursed from Christ for my kinsmen according to the flesh. . . . My heart's desire and prayer to God for Israel is that they might be saved."

Dr. Feinberg takes "to the Jew first" of Romans 1:16 very literally. But, he loves *all* people whom our Lord loves. He not only loves them, he ministers to them. As a teacher, as a preacher, his love and gifts have been expended in teaching all of the Scriptures to the entire church of Christ. His students, trained by him to the same standard of excellence he maintains for himself, preach the unsearchable riches of the Lord Jesus Christ all over the world to all men everywhere.

Finally, Charles Lee Feinberg loves the American Board of Missions to the Jews. Christians at the Mission prayed for him before he heard the gospel. There he heard the gospel and accepted his Lord. For fifty years we have been joyously laboring together for the Lord.

Daniel Fuchs
Chairman, Board of Directors
American Board of Missions to the Jews

Biographical Sketch
of
CHARLES LEE FEINBERG
A.M., Th.M., Th.D., Ph.D.

Dean Emeritus, Professor Emeritus of Semitics and Old Testament Talbot Theological Seminary

PERSONAL DATA:
—Born and reared in Pittsburgh, Pennsylvania, in an orthodox Jewish home
—Studied Hebrew and related subjects for fourteen years preparatory to the rabbinate
—Converted to Christ in the fall of 1930
—Married Anne Priscilla Fraiman, 1935
—Children: Paul, (spouse, Iris, nee Taylor), Lois (spouse, Albert Gonzenbach), John (spouse, Patricia, nee Buecher)
—Grandchildren: Eden, Aaron, Sarah, Paul, Joel, Josiah, Jonathan
ACADEMIC DATA:
—Graduate, Hebrew Institute of Pittsburgh, 1927
—Graduate, University of Pittsburgh, 1929: A.B. degree with honors
—Graduate, Dallas Theological Seminary:
    Th.B. and Th.M. in 1934, both magna cum laude
    Th.D. in 1935 with summa cum laude
—Summer Session, Columbia University, 1938
—Graduate, Southern Methodist University, 1943: A.M. in Old Testament
—Graduate Scholarship, The Johns Hopkins University, 1944–45

—Graduate, The Johns Hopkins University, 1945: Ph.D. in Archaeology and Semitic Languages
—Fellow by Courtesy, University of Southern California, 1949-50
AFFILIATIONS DATA:
—Member (Charter), Evangelical Theological Society
—Member, The Society of Biblical Literature and Exegesis
—Member (Associate), American Schools of Oriental Research at Jerusalem and Baghdad
—Member, National Association of Professors of Hebrew
—Member, Phi Alpha Theta, National Honorary History Fraternity
—Member, Eumatheia, National Honorary Scholastic Fraternity
—Member, The Association of Honor Graduates, University of Pittsburgh
—Fellow, Philosophical Society of Great Britain
MISSIONARY DATA:
—Former president, Iran Interior Mission, Kermanshah, Iran (now merged with International Missions)
—Home missionary, Detroit, Michigan, and Brooklyn, New York, under American Board of Missions to the Jews, Inc.
BOARD OF REFERENCE DATA:
—International Missions; Hindustan Bible Institute; Mission to the Migrants; American Board of Missions to the Jews; South Side Witness to Israel (Chicago); Ceylon and India General Mission (now International Christian Fellowship); Utah Bible Mission, Inc.; Long Island Messianic Witness; The Missionary Dentist, Inc.; Israel's Hope, Inc.; Illinois Bible Church Mission; Mid-America Mission; Far Eastern Gospel Crusade; Gospel Missionary Union; International Council on Biblical Inerrancy; Mid-South Bible College, Memphis, Tennessee; Christian Embassy, Washington, D.C.
BROADCASTING DATA:
—Codirector, Hebrew Christian Testimony Broadcast, Dallas, Texas, 1935-43
—Director, The Messianic Hour Broadcast, Los Angeles, California, 1951-72
—Biola Hour Broadcast, Los Angeles, California, 1948-79
—Bible Teacher, New Standard for Living, 1979—
PASTORAL DATA:
—Pastor, First Cumberland Presbyterian Church, Dallas, Texas, 1936-40
—Pastor, Jewish Department, Church of the Open Door and Biola, Inc., 1948-53
—Pastor, Stanton Community Church, Stanton, California, 1953-55

—Supply Pastor, in Memphis, Texas; Tyler, Texas; Fort Worth, Texas; Pasadena, California

PROFESSIONAL OR VOCATIONAL DATA:

—Instructor in church history at Dallas Theological Seminary, 1934-35

—Professor of Semitics and Old Testament, Dallas Theological Seminary, 1935-48

—Bible Conference Speaker throughout the United States of America; parts of Canada; Japan; South Africa; Rhodesia; South Pacific; Israel

—Listed in *Who's Who in the Clergy; Who's Who in the Americas; Dictionary of International Biography* (London); *Who's Who in Religion*

—Lecturer for 1953, Griffith-Thomas Memorial Lectureship, Dallas Theological Seminary

—Lecturer for 1954, Lyman Stewart Memorial Lectureship, Talbot Theological Seminary

—Lecturer for 1959, Rehfeldt Theological Lectures, Midwest Bible College, St. Louis, Missouri; and same lectureship, Calvary Bible College, Kansas City, Missouri, 1973

—Lecturer for 1959, Bueermann-Champion Lecture Foundation, Western Conservative Baptist Theological Seminary, Portland, Oregon

—Lecturer for 1964, Louis S. Bauman Memorial Lectures, Grace Theological Seminary, Winona Lake, Indiana

—Alumni Lecturer, Grace Theological Seminary, 1978

—Visiting professor, Institute of Holy Land Studies, Mt. Zion, Jerusalem, Spring, 1978

—Member, Scofield Reference Bible Revision Committee

—Member, Scripture Translation Committee, Lockman Foundation

—Visiting Bible lecturer, Dallas Theological Seminary, 1959-69

—Professor of Old Testament, Los Angeles Bible Theological Seminary, 1948-52

—President, Emeth Publications, Inc.; President, Ministry in Tape

—Translation consultant for Lockman Foundation, Tokyo, Japan, 1964

—Summer Research, Bodleian Library, Oxford University (Oxford, England), 1964

—Participant, Jerusalem Conference on Biblical Prophecy, Jerusalm, Israel, 1971

—Dean, professor of Semitics and Old Testament, Talbot Theological Seminary, 1952-75

—Dean emeritus, professor of Semitics and Old Testament, Talbot Theological Seminary, 1975-79

—Preacher, Twenty-Fifth Anniversary, South Africa Jews Society, Summer, 1975
—Lecturer, Pretoria University; Wits University; Natal University; Rhodes University; Capetown University; Stellen-bosch University, South Africa, Summer, 1975
—Ministry in New Zealand and Australia, Summer, 1978
—Adjunct professor, Semitics and Old Testament, Talbot Theological Seminary, 1979—

LITERARY DATA:
—Author:
  Premillennialism or Amillennialism? (3d ed. title, *Millennialism: The Two Major Views,* 1980)
  The Sabbath and the Lord's Day
  Minor Prophets (5 volumes; now in one)
  God Remembers
  Israel in the Last Days
  Ezekiel, The Glory of the Lord
  Is the Virgin Birth in the Old Testament?
  Israel in the Spotlight (3d ed. title, *Israel: Center of History and Revelation,* 1980)
—Editor:
  Talbot Theological Seminary Bulletin (1953–1975)
  The Fundamentals for Today
  Focus on Prophecy
  Prophecy and the Seventies
  Prophetic Truth Unfolding Today
  Jesus the King is Coming
—Contributor of many articles to:
  Bibliotheca Sacra
  The Chosen People
  King's Business
  Jewish Perspective
  Moody Monthly
  Seek
  Union Gospel Press publications and other periodicals. . .
—Contributor of articles to:
  IVCF Bible Dictionary
  Wycliffe Bible Encyclopedia
  Wycliffe Bible Commentary
  Zondervan Pictorial Bible Encyclopedia

Part I
HERMENEUTICAL AND THEOLOGICAL

1

A Canonical Process Approach to the Psalms

Bruce K. Waltke

BRUCE K. WALTKE *(M.A., Ph.D., Harvard University; Th.M., Th.D., Dallas Theological Seminary) is professor of Old Testament at Regent College, Vancouver, British Columbia.*

Dr. Charles Lee Feinberg is one of our Lord's rare and precious gifts to His church. He uniquely brings to the proclamation of Jesus as Messiah those strengths of his commitment to the Christian faith, his many spiritual gifts, his Jewish heritage, and his studies with W. F. Albright. As I thought about offering a small token of my affection and appreciation for Dr. Feinberg, who preceded me in the teaching of Semitic languages and Old Testament exegesis at Dallas Theological Seminary, it seemed fitting that it pertain to the proclamation of Jesus as Messiah and to the exegesis of the Old Testament.

Throughout the history of the church, Christians have found meaning and significance in the Old Testament in the conviction that the Old Testament foretold an age of salvation to come, and that this age had come with the advent of Jesus of Nazareth. That conviction that the Old Testament promised an age of salvation, including a regenerated people under a restored king of the Davidic line, is based solidly on the teaching of the New Testament. For example, Peter said in his Temple sermon: "Indeed, all the prophets from Samuel on, as many as have spoken, have foretold these days" (Acts 3:24; see also 1 Pet. 1:10-11).

The writers of the New Testament saw Jesus as the fulfillment of prophecies not only in the prophetic literature *sensu stricto,* but also in specific statements in the book of Psalms that they treated as though they belonged to the prophetic literary genre. The early church, for example, regarded the sufferings of Christ at the hands of Herod and Pontius Pilate as the fulfillment of Psalm 2:1–2 in precisely the same way as they saw His death on the cross as the fulfillment of Isaiah 53. After rehearsing the psalm,

> Why do the nations rage
>   and the peoples plot in vain?
> The kings of the earth take their stand
>   and the rulers gather together
> against the Lord and against his Anointed One,

they concluded: "Indeed Herod and Pontius Pilate met together with the Gentiles and the people of Israel in this city to conspire against your holy servant Jesus, whom you anointed. They did what your power and will had decided beforehand should happen" (Acts 4:27–28). At Pentecost, Peter regarded Psalms 16 and 110 to be just as prophetic as Joel 2 and used all three texts indiscriminately to prove that God predicted Jesus' death, resurrection, ascension, and the pouring out of His Spirit.

But since the apostolic era, the church has not agreed about the extent and the nature of the psalms that speak of Jesus Christ. Those who employ the allegorical method of imposing Christian doctrine upon the psalms without considering their meaning and significance to the audiences for whom they were originally composed have tended to see Jesus in almost every verse of every psalm. Augustine, who dominated all subsequent interpretations of the Psalter in the Western church, was never surpassed in seeing Christ everywhere. According to Augustine, our method of interpretation should be "Him first, Him last, Him midst and without end."[1] Thus, for example, he says that the blessed man of Psalm 1 "is to be understood of our Lord Jesus Christ."[2] Adhering to the same approach, Bonaventure commented on Psalm 3:5,

> I laid me down and slept
>   and rose again:
>   for the LORD sustained me,

"Our blessed LORD is speaking. He laid him down in the sepulchre. He slept His sleep of three days; He rose up again on the third day from the dead."[3]

Those scholars, on the other hand, who reject the unrestrained Alexandrian method of interpretation and who opt instead for the Antiochian principle that every passage has only one literal, historical meaning, have tended to minimize the messianic element in the psalm. Those employing this approach, which is the most widely accredited method among Protestants, can be classified further into three broad categories: the precritical or noncritical expositors, the literary-historical critics who deny any real predictions, and the literary-historical critics who see the psalms cited in the New Testament with reference to Jesus as containing both direct prophecies and indirect prefigurements of Christ.

The precritical or noncritical expositors—represented by such writers as E. W. Hengstenberg,[4] A. C. Gaebelein,[5] David Baron,[6] David Cooper,[7] and the late J. B. Payne[8]—tend to limit the number of messianic psalms to the approximately fifteen psalms cited in the New Testament with respect to Jesus Christ, and they regard them as direct prophecies of Christ. J. B. Payne divided these psalms into two groups: those that predict the Messiah in His glory (Psalms 2, 8, 45, 72, 89, 110) and those that foretell His passions (Psalms 16, 22, 40, 41, 69, 109).

But most scholars today disdain an approach that ignores a psalm's historical context and meaning. Noncritical scholars by their "prooftexting" actually discredit the claims of Jesus in the eyes of literary and historical critics.

The literary and historical critics who deny there is any real prediction in the Psalter explain the messianic element in the psalms, which they limit to statements about an ideal, future son of David, as reflections of the natural and nationalistic aspirations of the late postexilic Jewish community who hoped for the return of the Davidic political conditions. Wellhausen wrote: "The theocratic or messianic hope was the hope that the conditions of David's times might return." Moreover, for him prophecies are "not predictions . . . but announcements of aims."[9] Most recently R. E. Clements continued to show Wellhausen's influence when he wrote: "The main essential of the 'messianic' hope was . . . derived from the expectation of the restoration of the Davidic family to the kingship of a renewed Israel after the Babylonian exile."[10] He then added: "We find that not one of the texts which the New Testament appeals to in support of such a hope can, from a strictly historical-critical point of view, be held originally to have been intended in the way in which it was later taken. . . . Yet, in spite of this certainty about their original meaning, it is precisely these texts which have formed the seedbed of the messianic hope."[11]

Whereas the noncritical approach tends to discredit the messianic claims of Christ by its neglect of history, this approach discredits the New Testament by untying, or at least loosening, the bond connecting the New Testament with the original meaning of the Old Testament.

The literary-historical critics who see the messianic psalms pertaining to the sufferings and the glories of the Christ as containing real predictions and indirect prefigurements of Jesus, reject both the Montanistic theory of inspiration, which represented the biblical writers as passive instruments of the divine Spirit, and the attack upon the credibility of the New Testament witness. These men insist on the literal, historical sense as the only proper sense, but they recognize that the psalms contain real predictions in that they present an ideal that was only partially real in ancient Israel, but which became actual in the life of Christ. C. A. Briggs put it this way: "The psalms embraced the vision of a reality beyond the impression of the senses, a vision which guided Israel to an ever deeper understanding of the reality."[12] H. H. Rowley found the vision of a king whose kingdom would extend to "the ends of the earth" (Psalm 2:8), whose "divine throne [is] for ever and ever" (Psalm 45:6[7]), and who would "live while the sun endures, and as long as the moon, throughout all generations" (Psalm 72:5) went beyond pious optimism or flattering hyperbole. He wrote, "While they may have been royal psalms, used in the royal rites of the Temple, they were also 'messianic.' They held before the king the ideal king both as his inspiration and guide for the present, and as the hope of the future."[13]

Franz Delitzsch,[14] followed closely by Kirkpatrick,[15] analyzed the messianic psalms into five classes: (1) typical, that is, psalms that refer primarily to the circumstances of the time but which God also intended to prefigure some feature in the life of Christ (see Psalms 34; 69); (2) typico-prophetic psalms, not only were the sufferings of the psalmist typical of Christ's sufferings, but the records of them were so molded by the Spirit of God as to predict the sufferings of Christ even in circumstantial details (see Psalms 22; 40); (3) Jehovic psalms, that is, those that prepared men's minds for God's incarnation in this world and his victory over evil (Psalms 18; 50; 58; 93; 96-98); (4) indirectly messianic psalms, those that pertained to David's seed and thus indirectly to Jesus Christ as the son of David (see Psalms 45; 72); and (5) purely predictive (Psalm 110). Concerning this last reference Delitzsch wrote: "Among all the Davidic psalms there is only a single one viz. Ps cx, in which David . . . looks forth into the future of his seed and has the Messiah definitely before his mind."[16]

But while this approach maintains a balance between history and prophecy, yet it fails to give a consistent and comprehensive method for identifying the messianic element in the psalms. For the most part these expositors limit the typical element in the psalms to those cited in the New Testament, because apparently they are afraid of allowing the typical method of interpretation to degenerate into the unrestrained allegorical method. But this method cannot adequately explain why, for example, the New Testament (John 2:17) cites Psalm 69:9, "zeal for your house consumes me," as a reference to Christ but not Psalm 3:1, "How many are my foes." In all fairness, it seems as though the writers of the New Testament are not attempting to identify and limit the psalms that prefigure Christ but rather are assuming that the Psalter as a whole has Jesus Christ in view and that this should be the normative way of interpreting the psalms.

I conclude, therefore, that both the nonhistorical and undisciplined allegorical method of interpreting the psalms and the Antiochian principle of allowing but one historical meaning that may carry with it typical significance are inadequate hermeneutical principles for the interpretation of the psalms. In place of these methods, therefore, I would like to argue for a canonical process approach in interpreting the psalms, an approach that does justice both to the historical significance(s) of the psalms and to their messianic significance. Indeed, I shall argue that from a literary and historical point of view, we should understand that the human subject of the psalms—whether it be the blessed man of Psalm 1, the one proclaiming himself the son of God in Psalm 2, the suffering petitioner in Psalms 3-7, the son of man in Psalm 8—is Jesus Christ.

By the canonical process approach I mean the recognition that the text's intention became deeper and clearer as the parameters of the canon were expanded. Just as redemption itself has a progressive history, so also older texts in the canon underwent a correlative progressive perception of meaning as they became part of a growing canonical literature.

My indebtedness to Childs'[17] canonical approach is obvious. But I distinguish the approach advocated here from his, especially as he represents it in *Introduction to the Old Testament as Scripture* (1979), in at least these three ways:

1. Childs does not clearly distinguish the stage of literary activity in the development of the text from changes that take place through scribal activity on the text. This is due to the fact that he has no clear definition of inspiration. But by the "canonical process approach" I have in mind that development of the text and canon that took place under the Spirit's inspiration in contrast to those changes that took place through scribal copying.

2. Childs reckons with tracing the development of the tradition through historical criticism, another term he does not define, though recognizing that all too often the procedure is arbitrary and as such leads to inconclusive and nugatory results. One of the frequent presuppositions underlying historical criticism is the denial of supernatural activity as a cause effecting an event. Childs allows the possibility of a divorce between

Israel's religious history and the canonical witness to that history. By canonical process I have no such division in mind and clearly affirm God's supernatural intervention in Israel's history.

3. Childs lays emphasis on the authority of the Jewish text achieved at about A.D. 100. I lay emphasis on the meaning of the Hebrew Scriptures within the context of the New Testament.

In contrast to canonical criticism—represented also in the writings of J. Sanders[18] and R. E. Clements[19]—according to which the ancient texts were reworked in the progressive development of the canon in such a way that they may have lost their original historical significance, the canonical process approach holds that the original authorial intention was not changed in the progressive development of the canon but deepened and clarified. I agree with Childs' emphasis on the unity of the text and the value of rhetorical criticism, and with his minimizing the recovery of original literary unities apart from their canonical form, but I would emphasize that canonical texts in their earlier stages in the progressively developing canon were just as accurate, authoritative, and inspired as they are in their final literary contexts.

The canonical process approach is similar to the approach known as *sensus plenior* in that it recognizes that further revelation brought to light a text's fuller or deeper significance, but it differs from that approach in several ways.

First of all, in contrast to the normal sense of *sensus plenior* that God intended a fuller meaning in a text than that intended by the human author,[20] the canonical process approach does not divorce the human authorial intention from the divine intention. According to the canonical approach, the original poets presented their subjects in ideal forms, that is, in prayer and in praise fully acceptable to God. Progressive revelation, however, fleshed out this vision and made more clear the exact shape of the ideals always pregnant in the vision.

Second, *sensus plenior,* although insisting that the text's true historical significance was always present in the mind of God, tends toward an allegorical method of interpretation by regarding later writers as winning meanings from the text quite apart from their historical use and significance. By contrast, the canonical process approach underscores the continuity of a text's meaning throughout sacred history along with recognizing that further revelation won for the earlier text a deeper and clearer meaning.

And third, the canonical process approach consciously recognizes and represents the distinct stages in that winning of the clearer and deeper significance of older texts through the discernment of the stages in the development of the canon rather than viewing the New Testament writers as "supernaturally" discovering the fuller, divine meaning of the text.

In the case of the Psalms we can identify at least four distinct advances in the meaning and significance of many specific psalms, and the exegete must keep these four stages in view in his interpretation of them. We can liken the four stages to four lookout points on a mountain. From each successively higher vantage point the vista becomes more full or complete. So also in the four successive stages of the canonical approach to these psalms the text's significance becomes more and more complete and at the last stage the fullest meaning of the text is finally won.

The four distinct points in the progressive perception and revelation of the text occasioned by the enlarging of the canon are: (1) the meaning of the psalm to the original poet, (2) its meaning in the earlier collections of psalms associated with the First Temple, (3) its meaning in the final and complete Old Testament canon associated with the Second Temple, and its meaning in the full canon of the Bible including the New Testament with its presentation of Jesus as the Christ.

I was surprised recently in rereading Delitzsch's commentary on the Psalms to discover that he had come to a similar position almost a century ago. He wrote:

> The expositor of the Psalms can place himself on the standpoint of the poet, or the standpoint of the Old Testament church, or the standpoint of the church of the present dispensation—a primary condition of exegetical progress is the keeping of these three standpoints distinct, and, in accordance, therewith, the distinguishing between the two Testaments, and in general between different steps in the development of the revelation, and in the perception of the plan of redemption.[21]

Unfortunately, however, Delitzsch too sharply distinguished the standpoints and failed to recognize the genetic and organic connection between them in the development of the revelation. But in recognizing three distinct stages in the revelation he anticipated my own awareness of the need for identifying stages in the progress of revelation and apprehension of many psalms.

This canonical process approach to the interpretation of the Psalms rests on at least four convictions.[22]

First, it assumes that the people of God throughout history are united by a common knowledge and faith (certainty in the knowledge). Although the community's knowledge is expanded during the time that the canon is taking shape, the former knowledge and faith is not changing. To preserve the "givenness" of its faith, Israel was instructed to remember her heritage both by recital and ritual at the Passover and Firstfruits festivals in the spring and at the Tabernacles festival in the fall (Exod. 12:26-27; 23:14-17; Deut. 16:1-17; 26:1-11; 31:10-13). Moreover, the people of God preserved other tokens of their history by preserving relics such as an omer of manna (Exod. 16:32) and by erecting memorials such as the stones at Gilgal (Josh. 4:20-24). From the call of Abraham to the close of the Old Testament era, each succeeding generation passed on its common faith by circumcising its male infant. In short, each succeeding generation of the believing community was shaped by its unchanging past history, and the knowledge added to it was consistent with that heritage. This is one reason we can confidently say that the progressive revelation by clearer perceptions of earlier texts was an organic and genetic unity.

Second, this approach accepts the biblical witness that God is the ultimate author of the progressively developing canon. He inspired elect individuals to add to that revelation already received through their own unique experiences with God in the progress of sacred history. Because of that common, divine inspiration we have further reason for affirming the continuity in the progressive revelation and grasping of the canonical literature. Moreover, because God is the author of the whole Bible, any piece of literature within it must be studied in the light of its whole literary context.

Third, this approach rests on the conviction that as the canon developed, lesser and earlier representations were combined to form greater units that are more meaningful than their component parts. Therefore, the full meaning of an earlier and smaller text cannot be gained without interpreting it in the light of the entire Bible.

Finally, this approach presupposes that the canon closed with the addition of the last book of the New Testament. Thus the received Scriptures constitute the final literary framework within which any given text must be interpreted.

Now that we have broadly sketched the canonical process approach with its four organically connected stages of interpretation and the four convictions that undergird it, let me now apply the approach to the Psalms.

First of all, we ask what the psalm meant to the original poet. Here it is important to note that the human subject of most of the psalms is a king. Two lines of evidence lead to this unmistakable conclusion: the external evidence of the so-called superscriptions and the internal evidence of the psalms themselves. The Masoretic text identifies King David as the author, and presumably the human subject, of seventy-three psalms; the LXX attributes eighty-four psalms to him.

There are many good reasons for accepting Gesenius-Kautsch-Cowley's (par. 129 c) contention that the preposition l^e in the phrase $l^ed\bar{a}wid$ in these headings designates authorship even as in Arabic, and that the phrase accordingly should be translated "by David." First, many Old Testament traditions from both the pre-Exilic and post-Exilic periods present David as a composer and a promoter of Israel's psalmody. In the book of Samuel, for example, it is claimed for the psalm numbered as Psalm 18 in the English version that "David sang to the LORD the words of this song" (2 Sam. 22:1). The same statement is found in the heading to Psalm 18 after the phrase לְדָוִד ($l^e d\bar{a}wid$). Moreover, the superscriptions of fourteen psalms specify the incident in David's life that prompted him to write the psalm. The Chronicler claims that David assigned the Levites to various musical guilds in order to beautify the Mosaic ritual with music and associates David with Israel's psalmody (1 Chron. 16:1-43).[23] Then too, one of Israel's earliest writing prophets complained that the men of the Northern Kingdom whiled away their time strumming on their harps like David (Amos 6:5). The same persuasion regarding Davidic authorship persists in both the early Jewish tradition and the New Testament. Ben Sirach (c. 190 B.C.) put the tradition into poetry: "In all that he [David] did he gave thanks to the Holy One, the Most High, with ascription of glory; he sang praise with all his heart, and he loved his maker" (Eccl. 47:8-9; cf. Josephus, *Contra Apion* VII:305-06). The New Testament cites David as the author of Psalms 2, 16, 32, 69, 109, 110. In the case of the last reference, Jesus identified the Messiah as greater than David on the assumption that David wrote it (Matt. 22:43-44). There is no need to chronicle the numerous contributors to this orthodox opinion after the close of the canon.

Furthermore, the literature from the Ancient Near East tends more and more to support this unanimous biblical and ancient tradition by pointing to the antiquity of the Psalms. H. Gunkel demonstrated that Israel's hymns closely parallel in their forms the hymns of ancient Egypt and Mesopotamia.[24] Parallel Sumerian hymns contain musical notations as unintelligible to Sumeriologists as the musical notations in the Psalter are unintelligible to Hebraists.[25] S. Mowinckel has demonstrated from internal evidence that the psalms were sung in the cultus of the First Temple,[26] and M. Dahood backed up his conclusion with linguistic evidence from the Ugaritic texts, though he marred his work by overextending the argument.[27]

In addition to the evidence of the superscriptions that King David is the author of about half the Psalter, and presumably the human subject of these psalms, there is the internal evidence of the psalms themselves. None disputes the form-critical researches of H. Gunkel that Psalms 2,

18, 20, 21, 45, 72, 89, 101, 110, 132, 144 are royal psalms. But more significantly John Eaton[28] has followed up the work of H. Gunkel, S. Mowinckel, and others in showing that the supplicator in the so-called psalms of lament (c. fifty psalms) is also a king. Eaton wrote,

> Gunkel identifies the following. All nations attend to the psalmist's thanksgiving (Pss. 18:50; 57:10; 138:1, 4; 119:46). His deliverance has vast repercussions (22:28f.). He invokes a world-judgment to rectify his cause (7:7, 9; 56:8; 59:6; 59:9; cf. 43:1). He depicts himself as victorious over the nations through God's intervention (118:10-12). He confronts armies (3:7; 27:3; 55:22; 56:2f.; 59:6; 72:4; 109:3; 120:7; 140:3, 8). He is like a bull raising horns in triumph (92:11).
>
> To these items from Gunkel . . . we may add considerably. The speaker vows continual psalmody. He stands out before the vast festal congregation (22:33, 26; 40:10f.). His head is raised on high. . . . His glory receives special mention. . . . He is blessed with superabundant life. . . . His designations of God as his helper are often related to warfare. . . . Enemies, military and national in character, aim at him personally rather than at his country and people.[29]

We conclude, therefore, that transcending the various types of psalms so laboriously analyzed and classified by Gunkel stands the more significant fact that in the original composition the king is the human subject of the psalms, whether they be lament, acknowledgment, praise, or belonging to various other types of psalms.[30] Furthermore, we must bear in mind that the king is presented idealistically and prays to God and praises Him through the inspiration of God's Spirit.

We now move to the second standpoint in our canonical approach to the Psalms by asking the question, What did these psalms mean in their earlier canonical collections mentioned in such passages as 2 Chronicles 29:30 and Psalm 72:20 and used in connection with the worship of the First Temple? Here too we come to the conclusion that the living king continued to be understood as the human subject of many of these songs of praise and petition.

In the first place, the Davidic covenant, alluded to several times in the Psalms (most especially Psalm 89), provides us with a firm basis for the conviction that the individual in view in many psalms was the son of David. According to this covenant, God promised David a son whose house and kingdom would endure forever before God and whose throne would be established forever (2 Sam. 7:12-16). In the light of such a promise it would be most surprising if David did not intend his many and varied types of royal psalms to be used by and for the house of David at the house of the LORD. Almost certainly these royal psalms had a royal significance in Israel's cultus.

Second, those scholars sensitive to the extensive royal interpretation of the psalms universally recognize that the king represented the people. Mowinckel wrote, "All that concerned him and his cause also concerned the people; nothing which happened to him was a purely private affair."[31] It would be utterly foreign to the culture of preexilic Israel to suppose that the psalms were democratized in their interpretation. Such an interpretation would be appropriate for texts in our democratic, twentieth-century Western societies, but it would be unthinkable during the monarchy in preexilic Israel.

Third, we believe the living king was understood to be the human subject of most psalms, because in the Ancient Near Eastern literature the king was the patron of the foreign cults (exactly as is the case in Israel) and was the subject of numerous hymns. Gunkel noted that the extant prayers and laments of the Mesopotamian kings are "extraordinarily numerous."[32] Why, then, should we think that Israel would have reinterpreted the psalms at this early period in Israel's history as a reference to the common man or some other individual than the son of David? Directly reinforcing this argument is the universal recognition among students of Ancient Near Eastern languages and literatures that the king played a central role in the religions of the Ancient Near East.[33]

Fourth, it is sufficiently clear that in many psalms not ascribed to David the king is the human subject of the psalm. For example, in Psalm 44, associated with the sons of Korah, is it not most likely that the king represents the defeated army of Israel in prayer before God? Who is a more likely candidate than the king as the speaker of the line, "I do not trust in my bow, my sword does not save me" (v. 6)? It is also instructive to note that in this psalm, as in many others, there is a fluid interchange between the plural pronoun "we" and the singular pronoun "I." This psalm begins, for example, "We have heard with our ears . . . our fathers have told us that you did in their days" followed by "You are my King and my God who decrees victories for Jacob" (v. 4). This change can best be explained on the assumption that the human subject is the king representing the people. In short, although the psalm is assigned to the sons of Korah, the human subject is a king. Does not this also suggest that other psalms not assigned to David were composed for Israel's king?

Fifth, Birkeland[34] has shown that in many psalms the enemies are Israel's international political enemies and that this indicates, as Kraus[35] also argued, that the individual subject is a king.

We conclude, therefore, that most psalms had a royal significance in their cultic use at the First Temple.

Now it is important to note that each living successor to David's throne was clothed in the large, magificent, purple mantle of the messianic vision attached to the House of David. Each king became the son of God through his anointing with Yahweh's Spirit. Of these historical kings Ringren wrote: "The king is Anointed of Yahweh, he is set up by him and proclaimed his son, he shall maintain right and righteousness in the country, he conveys to his people divine blessings, rain and fertility, he defeats in divine power all enemies, he rules over the whole world, and his throne shall stand eternally."[36] We should also add that ideally he also suffers on behalf of the kingdom of God and wrestles with God in prayer in accordance with the divine imperative: "Ask of me [my son], and I will give the nations as your inheritance" (Psalm 2:8). H. Gressman[37] pointed out that Israel's association of the reigning monarch with messianic significance found its counterpart in Egypt where the pharaoh was also associated with messianic expectations. But none of David's successors up to the time of the Captivity had shoulders broad enough to fill this ideal mantle that was laid upon him at his coronation as Yahweh's king over Israel.

We conclude, then, that the many types of psalms composed for the First Temple and used in it and constituting a part of Israel's canonical literature had a messianic meaning and significance that none of David's successors satisfied up to the time that the house of the LORD was destroyed and the House of David was deported to Babylon.

A third vantage point in interpreting the psalms is gained by now asking the question, What did these royal psalms mean to the editors who gave the Old Testament canon its received shape and substance? Or, to put the matter another way, What do these psalms mean in the broader context of the Old Testament canon compiled during the postexilic period, probably between 400 B.C. and 200 B.C?

Haggai makes it sufficiently clear that the exiles who returned from the Captivity continued to associate the living House of David with the messianic hope. This perception of the matter inherited from the preexilic period is apparent in the LORD's address to the House of David through Haggai:

Tell Zerubbabel governor of Judah that I will shake the heavens and the earth. I will overturn royal thrones and shatter the power of the foreign kingdoms. I will overthrow chariots and their drivers; horses and their riders will fall, each by the sword of his brother. "On that day," declares the LORD Almighty, "I'll take you, my servant Zerubbabel son of Shealtiel," declares the LORD, "and I will make you like my signet ring, for I have chosen you," declares the LORD Almighty.

In sum, the two institutions—the House of David and the house of the LORD—providing Israel with its greatest sense of continuity were revived at the beginning of the postexilic era.

But Zerubbabel and apparently his descendants continued to fall short of the messianic expectation laid upon them, and by about a century later the last of the Old Testament canonical prophets, Malachi, projected the vision of Israel's golden age, when the LORD would come to His people with healing in His wings, to an age beyond his own temporal horizon and on into the eschatological future. Thus, when the Old Testament canon closed, no son of David was sitting on Yahweh's throne, and no living scion of David's line was associated with that hope. Accordingly, we may safely conclude that the royal psalms in the final shape of the Old Testament canon must have been interpreted prophetically precisely as we found them interpreted in the New Testament. This prophetic interpretation of these old texts is not a reinterpretation of them away from their original, authorial meaning; rather, it is a more precise interpretation of them in the light of the historical realities. Aage Bentzen noted, "It must, however, be acknowledged that the difference between the 'cultic' and the 'eschatological' interpretations of the Enthronement [sic; royal] Psalms is not very great."[38] If one keeps in mind the genetic and organic unity in the progressive apprehension of these psalms, the following statement by R. E. Clements might prove helpful:

From the point of view of the messianic interpretation of certain psalms it appears most probable that the same stimulus towards a new dimension of interpretation has been felt. It is in fact possible that those editors who incorporated into the Psalter the texts of royal psalms, which must have appeared obsolete at a time when Judah had no king, do so out of a genuine hope that Israel would again need them. In this case, a dimension of hope was present in the act of retaining compositions which the contemporary political scene made inapplicable in their original sense [sic]. The formation of the canon, therefore, must have had its own part to play in projecting the ideas and images associated with the kingship into the future.[39]

The intertestamental literature and the New Testament make clear, however, that the royal dimension of the lament psalms became lost during this period of time, and thus Israel lost sight of a suffering Messiah. Perhaps these psalms now become democratized in the synagogues and interpreted as references to Everyman, as Mowinckel theorized.[40] But that was not their original meaning and significance, and Jesus had to correct Israel's understanding back to their original intention. In brief, the New Testament does not impose a new meaning on these old psalms but wins back for them their original and true significance. We cannot be sure how the editors who compiled the final form of the Old Testament interpreted the lament psalms. It seems plausible to me to suppose that they continued to understand them according to their original meaning. I draw that conclusion on the basis that the progressive development of the canon is a genetic and organic unity, on the recognition that later prophecies, such as Isaiah 53, made it abundantly clear that the one to be exalted by Yahweh over all the nations must suffer and die, and on the certainty that the protoevangelium was understood as a reference to the suffering and triumph of the Messiah over Satan.

Thus we conclude that at this third stage in the development of the canon, the psalms continued to have a royal and messianic significance, but they now carried a predictive meaning as well. Israel must now wait in hope for a future son of David worthy to pray and sing these psalms.

With the advent of Jesus Christ this hope was satisfied. Accordingly, within the literary context of the New Testament the psalms find their final and full meaning and perception. From this fourth and highest vantage point we win the full significance of the psalms. Jesus of Nazareth, son of David and Son of God, fulfills these psalms. Those elements in each psalm presenting the king as anything less than ideal, such as his confession of sins, are the historical eggshells from the preexilic period when the psalms were used for Israel's less than ideal kings.

We conclude, then, that the Psalms are ultimately the prayers of Jesus Christ, Son of God. He alone is worthy to pray the ideal vision of a king suffering for righteousness and emerging victorious over the hosts of evil. As the corporate head of the church, he represents the believers in these prayers. Moreover, Christians, as sons of God and as royal priests, can rightly pray these prayers along with their representative Head. Dietrich Bonhoeffer also reached the conclusion that Jesus Christ is the one praying in the psalter. "The Psalter," he wrote, "is the prayer book of Jesus Christ in the truest sense of the word."[41]

NOTES

1. J. M. Neale and R. F. Littledale, *A Commentary on the Psalms: From Primitive and Mediaeval Writers* (London: John Masters, 1884), p. 77.
2. Saint Augustine, *Expositions on the Book of Psalms,* A Select Library of the Nicene and Post-Nicene Fathers of the Christian Church, Philip Schaff, ed. 8 vols. (New York: Christian Literature Co., 1888)8:1.
3. Neale and Littledale, p. 107.
4. E. W. Hengstenberg, *Christology of the Old Testament* (Grand Rapids: Kregel, 1828, 1970).

5. Arno C. Gaebelein, *The Jewish Question* (New York: Our Hope, 1912).
6. David Baron, *Types, Psalms and Prophecies,* Amer. ed. (New York: Amer. Bd. of Missions to Jews, 1948, 1907).
7. David Cooper, *Messiah: His First Coming Scheduled* (Los Angeles: Biblical Research Soc., 1939).
8. J. B. Payne, "Psalms," in *Zondervan's Pictorial Encyclopedia of the Bible,* Merrill C. Tenney, ed. (Grand Rapids: Zondervan, 1975), pp. 940-43.
9. Julius Wellhausen, *Prolegomena to the History of Israel* (Edinburgh: A. & C. Black, 1885), p. 415. See also G. R. Berry, "Messianic Predictions," JBL (1926):232-38.
10. Ronald E. Clements, *Old Testament Theology: A Fresh Approach* (London: Marshall, Morgan and Scott, 1978), p. 150.
11. Ibid.
12. Charles Augustus Briggs, *Messianic Prophecy* (New York: Scribner's, 1886), p. 63.
13. Harold Henry Rowley, *The Faith of Israel* (Philadelphia, Westminster, 1957), p. 192.
14. Franz Delitzsch, *Biblical Commentary on the Psalms,* trans. Francis Bolton (Grand Rapids: Eerdmans, 1952), pp. 68-71.
15. A. F. Kirkpatrick, *The Book of Psalms* (Cambridge: Cambridge U., 1916), pp. lxxvi-lxxxv.
16. Delitzsch, p. 66.
17. Brevard S. Childs, *Biblical Theology in Crisis* (Philadelphia: Westminster, 1970).
18. James Sanders, *Torah and Canon* (Philadelphia: Fortress, 1972).
19. Clements, p. 150.
20. Raymond E. Brown defined *sensus plenior* as: "that additional, deeper meaning, intended by God but not clearly intended by the human author, which is seen to exist in the words of a Biblical text (or group of texts, or even a whole book) when they are studied in the light of further revelation or development in the understanding of revelation." Cited by William Sanford LaSor, "The *Sensus Plenior* and Biblical Interpretation," in *Scripture, Traditional Interpretation,* eds. W. W. Gasque and W. S. LaSor (Grand Rapids: Eerdmans, 1978), p. 270.
21. Delitzsch, p. 64.
22. I am partially indebted here to Adolf Schlatter, "The Theology of the New Testament and Dogmatics," in *The Nature of New Testament Theology,* ed. Robert Morgan (London: SCM, 1973), pp. 117-66.
23. W. F. Albright (*Archaeology and the Religion of Israel* (Baltimore: Johns Hopkins, 1953, pp. 125-26) and H. Ringgren (*Theological Dictionary of the Old Testament,* 3:164) also connect David with Israel's psalmody.
24. Herman Gunkel, *Einleitung in die Psalmen* (completed by Begrich [Gottingen: Vandenhoeck & Ruprecht, 1933]).
25. Samuel Noah Kramer, *The Sumerians* (Chicago: U. of Chicago, 1963), p. 207.
26. Sigmund Mowinckel, *The Psalms in Israel's Worship,* 2 vols. (New York: Abingdon, 1962).
27. Mitchell Dahood, *Psalms I* (New York: Doubleday, 1966).
28. John H. Eaton, *Kingship and the Psalms* (London: SCM, 1976).
29. Ibid., pp. 23-24.
30. Although I have argued here that לְדָוִד (*l^e dāwid*) means "by David," other proposed interpretations of the phrase do not undermine the thesis that the

original composition had an ideal king in view. Mowinckel (1:77f; 2:98–100) argued that *dawidum* originally meant a chief or king, especially among seminomadic groups. Elsewhere he argued ("Psalm Criticism Between 1900 and 1935" *Vetus Testamentum* 5 [1955]:18) that the phrase meant "destined for the (cultic) use of David" (= the reigning king). D. R. Ap-Thomas ("Saul's 'Uncle,'" *Vetus Testamentum* 11 [1961]:244f) also read *dwd* as a title of office, more specifically "deputy, ruler, governor." Eissfeldt (*Old Testament Introduction* [1965] p. 451) interpreted the phrase "in praise of David's exploits." Dalglish (*Psalm Fifty-One* [Leiden: E. J. Brill, 1962], p. 240) interpreted the preposition *l* more vaguely "of David." Accordingly, it could mean: "a collection belonging to David," a psalm "for David," etc. (I am indebted here to my student Gordon Brubacher, who is writing a thesis on the structure of Psalm 68, for bringing these references together.)

31. Mowinckel, 1:42–61.
32. Gunkel, *Einleitung,* p. 161. Mowinckel makes the same observation: "All this points to the fact that in Israel, as in Babylonia and Egypt, the psalms ... were originally intended, not for all and sundry, but for the king and the great" (Mowinckel, 1:77).
33. For a critique of Mowinckel's notion of an annual enthronement festival for Yahweh, of the myth and ritual school, and of the comparative phenomenology approach of the Uppsala school, see my forthcoming article "Israel, Religion of," in *The New International Standard Bible Encyclopedia,* II.
34. H. Birkeland, *The Evildoers in the Psalms* (Oslo: I. Kommisjon has J. Dybwad, 1955), pp. 12ff.
35. H. J. Kraus, *Psalmen,* 1 (Neukirchen: Neukirchen Verlag, 1961): 40–53 (Excursus 2).
36. Helmer Ringgren, *The Messiah in the Old Testament* (Chicago: Allenson, 1956), p. 20.
37. Hugo Gressman, *Der Messias* (Gottingen: Vandenhoeck & Ruprecht, 1929), pp. 1–7, 415–23.
38. Aage Bentzen, *King and Messiah* (London: Lutterworth, 1955), p. 37.
39. Clements, p. 151.
40. Mowinckel, 1:78–80.
41. Dietrich Bonhoeffer, *Life Together,* trans. John W. Doberstein (New York: Harper and Brothers, 1954), p. 46.

2

The Abolition of the Old Order and Establishment of the New: Psalm 40:6-8 and Hebrews 10:5-10

Walter C. Kaiser, Jr.

WALTER C. KAISER, JR. (B.D., Wheaton Graduate School; M.A., Ph.D., Brandeis University) is dean and professor of Old Testament and Semitic languages at Trinity Evangelical Divinity School, Deerfield, Illinois.

Psalm 40 belongs to that unique group of four psalms (Psalms 40, 50, 51, and 69) that appears to depreciate the sacrifices prescribed in the Levitical legislation of the Torah. Yet this was the psalm that the writer of Hebrews used to authenticate four major points as he concluded his Christological[1] argument: (1) The law was only a shadow (*skia*) of the true reality (*eikōn*) of salvation in Christ; (2) the plurality of sacrifices demanded by Mosaic law is to be strikingly contrasted with the single unique sacrifice of Christ; (3) the repeated sacrifices are admittedly ineffective in and of themselves in forgiving and removing sin; and (4) the Mosaic ritual law is abolished so that another order might be established in Christ.[2] In the entire New Testament, only Hebrews 10:5-7 uses Psalm 40:6-8.[3]

INTRODUCTION

THE ISSUES

It is clear that the New Testament writer cited this passage to demonstrate that the psalmist had in some way anticipated both the coming of the Messiah and the abolition of the Mosaic ceremonial legislation. But

19

such major claims touch on some of the most sensitive issues in the whole curriculum of theology.

It is as if the writer wished to settle once and for all the question of continuity and discontinuity between the Old and New Testaments in one fell swoop. Does the psalmist point directly to the heart of this issue with his contrast between sacrifices and obedience? Did that distinction point to the removal of the first order of things and the establishment of the second in Christ?

And if that problem appears to be too broad in its implications for theology, what are we to say about the writer of Hebrews finding Christ and His perfect sacrifice in Psalm 40:6-8? By what legitimate and reasonable method of exegesis can the psalmist's words be made to bear such heavy freight? Of whom were these verses written originally? Was David their author? What possible meaning could these words have had in their original Old Testament context? How can a Messianic prediction be reconciled with the psalmist's admission of sin in verse 11? In this admission he certainly was not a type or an "earnest" of the Messiah. Furthermore, how important is it to recognize the LXX text, which prefers "body" for the Hebrew MT of "ears"? Is this a deliberate distortion of the actual text in order to make an otherwise shaky case?

Each of these questions takes us to the heart of evangelical theology and to the hermeneutical debate about the method of New Testament writers in citing the Old Testament. So difficult are many of these questions, that some have gloomily concluded as did S. R. Driver:

> It must be obvious that the Psalm, in its original intention, has no reference to Christ: it is some Old Testament saint, not Christ, who declares that it is his delight to do God's will; hence 'I am come' in v.7 cannot refer to the Incarnation: if further proof were needed, it would be found in v.12, where the Psalmist speaks of his 'iniquities,' which, except by most strained and unnatural exegesis, can be understood only of the iniquities which he has himself committed. It is, of course, perfectly true that parts of the Psalm are appropriate to Christ, and might well have been taken up by Him upon His lips . . . [but] a possible *application* of a Psalm is no guide to its *interpretation,* and cannot determine its original intention. Rather, the author of the Epistle to the Hebrews puts vv.6-8a into Christ's mouth, not because the Psalm as a whole refers to Him, but because . . . these verses are, in the words of the [then] present Dean of Ely a 'fitting expression of the purpose of His life,' and of His perfect conformity to His Father's will. And so the Psalm is suitably appointed in the Anglican Church as one of the proper Psalms for Good Friday.[4]

But can such an "application" have any force, especially in a passage that seeks to establish an argument, when it is not based on a fair interpretation as originally intended by the psalmist? Why cite words which in their original intention have no reference to Christ even if it is only by way of appropriating and applying them? Would such a line of argumentation be convincing to any knowledgeable Jew? It is difficult to understand how this type of citation could be of any evidential or practical value for a frame of mind that might wish to resist such wholesale supplanting of traditional values and convictions. The situation is as F. S. Sampson has described it:

> This passage presents one of the most vexed questions among interpreters, both as to the propriety of the Apostle's reference to this Psalm to the Messiah and as to his adoption of the erroneous translation of the LXX.[5]

It will be the contention of this essay not only that the logic and argumentation is fair, but also that it is consistent with the original intention of the psalmist. We offer this essay in gratitude to God for the gifted life and fruitful ministry of Professor Charles L. Feinberg.

THE AUTHOR OF PSALM 40

The psalm begins with a heading that we believe to be as original[6] as the body of the psalm: "To the chief musician, a Psalm of David."

Most modern commentators such as Briggs[7] prefer to place this psalm in the postexilic era. Usually their arguments are built around alleged reminiscences of the language of Jeremiah and Isaiah, in that order, because of their own systems of late dating. The psalmist's reference to the "pit of destruction" (bôr shā ôn) and "miry clay" (tît hayyāwēn) in Psalm 40:2 [Heb., 3] is usually compared with Jeremiah's experience in the "mire" (tît) and "pit" (bôr) in Jeremiah 38:6. Yet such terminology also appears in Psalm 28:1 and 30:3 [Heb., 4].

Likewise, these same scholars find a dependence on the preexilic prophets for the psalmist's contrast between sacrifice and obedience (see Isa. 1:11ff.; Hos. 6:6; Amos 5:22; Mic. 6:6; and Psalm 40:6-8 [Heb., 7-9]). Yet, once again it could be successfully argued that if the psalmist needed a biblical precedent for this truth, he could easily have appealed to 1 Samuel 15:22. Certainly, the Davidic psalms, Psalms 32 and 51, reflect the same theology, which places a premium on the priority of a right relationship to God as the basis for any successful sacrifice to Him. Even the very Torah that set forth the ceremonial law itself insisted on the primacy of obedience and a personal response of faith and love to God as a condition for pleasing God with one's ritual and worship; a fact that shines with special clarity in Exodus 15:26 and Deuteronomy 10:12, 20.

Even the reference to an inward law of the heart (Psalm 40:8 [Heb., 9]) need not point to Jeremiah's new covenant or Ezekiel's new heart and new spirit, for David also used it in his psalm, Psalm 37:31.

Thus, all of the alleged evidences[8] fail to show direct dependence; instead, they build a case for a shared informing theology in which many of the writers show an obvious awareness of the others' contributions. Seldom can it be demonstrated, however, that that literary and religious heritage appeared *after* the Davidic period. Consequently, from this standpoint, no case can be made against a Davidic authorship. Too many biblical scholars, from all theological persuasions, are far too skeptical about what a divinely inspired penman could or could not have known at any given period in the Old Testament.

Thus, judged both on internal grounds and external circumstances, it is best to accept the ancient witness in the title of this psalm as the best clue to its authorship, at least until sufficient evidence is forthcoming to the contrary—in the event that some may still be unpersuaded that the psalm titles are an authentic part of the text, as we have argued for here.

THE UNITY OF PSALM 40

Usually Psalm 40 is understood as consisting of two parts which differ widely in tone, character, and type. The first part (vv. 1-11 [Heb., 12]) is epitomized by thanksgiving and gratitude for deliverance; the second part (vv. 12-17 [Heb., 13-18]) ends with a lament in which the psalmist prays for a speedy deliverance from his foes. Many interpreters find this association of grand success (1-11) with great disaster (12-17) so troublesome that they believe it only fair to hold that the psalm is a composite of two earlier pieces.[9]

Such tension is not an unresolvable dilemma. As both Wieser[10] and Mowinckel[11] have argued, thanksgiving for past deliverance is the basis for the expected deliverance from the psalmist's present difficulty.

Of course, it is true that the second division appears with very slight textual variations as a separate psalm: Psalm 70. As Carl B. Moll has argued:

> ... this does not prove that two songs originally different have been subsequently united ... , or that the unity can be maintained only by the supposition that the poet speaks in the name of Israel ... , or the pious members of the people ... Still less can it be shown, that Ps. 1xx. was the original, and that it is here imitated and attached as a prayer to a Psalm

of thanksgiving . . . There are rather in Ps. lxx. many signs of its being a fragment. This portion of Ps. xl. moreover might very easily and properly, owing to its character, have been separated for the special use of the congregation. . . .[12]

Thus we think it almost certain that Psalm 40 in its entirety is the original and that the lament was subsequently isolated and given an independent form in Psalm 70. Perowne[13] adds three additional reasons for maintaining the unity of this psalm. (1) The two parts are found together in all MSS and ancient versions. (2) It is easier to explain the textual variations in Psalm 70 on the supposition that it was detached from Psalm 40 than on the reverse hypothesis. (3) There is a play in the second half of Psalm 40 on the words appearing in the first half (e.g., "be pleased" [v. 13] with "thy pleasure," omitted in Psalm 70 [v. 8]; "let them be struck" [v. 15] is weakened in Psalm 70:3 to "let them return"). Most significant of all, however, is the fact that "vs. 12 is not a natural ending to the Psalm, and [it] seems to require a prayer to follow it."[14] So we conclude that there are sufficient reasons for maintaining the unity and the originality of this psalm.

THE BACKGROUND AND CONTENT OF PSALM 40

No one can say for sure what the circumstances were when David composed this psalm. Some have suggested that it was written at the time of his flight from his son Absalom. Nevertheless, as is the case with so many psalms, the contents of the psalm are so clear that "if we did know [the historical background], we should hardly understand the Psalm better."[15]

The psalmist began Psalm 40 by describing a past[16] danger[17] he had experienced and God's rescuing him after he had patiently waited on the Lord (v. 1 [Heb., 2]). So grave had been the situation that he was like a person sinking into a miry pit. But he had been rescued and placed on a solid rock (v. 2 [Heb., 3]). This evidence of God's grace elicited from the psalmist a "new song"[18] of gratitude and praise for the encouragement of all who trust in the Lord (v. 3 [Heb., 4]). Such a people the psalmist pronounced happy (v. 4 [Heb., 5]). This forms the transition to his mention of the incalculable multiplicity of the Lord's miraculous works and his incomparable plans for the believing community (v. 5 [Heb., 6]).

What adequate response can the psalmist then make for such unbounded goodness from God? Surely, God can best be thanked, not by external ritual offerings (v. 6 [Heb., 7]), but instead by voluntary obedience to do that will of God, which is written in the roll of the book. This the psalmist will do; he is ready and delighted to do what is written for him (vv. 7-8 [Heb., 8-9]). Thus, he openly proclaimed God's goodness toward him in the great congregation (vv. 9-10).

But then the psalmist prayed for the continuance of this divine protection (v. 11 [Heb., 12]). Additional causes of danger had arisen, some as a result of his own transgressions (v. 12 [Heb., 13]). Therefore, he prayed that God would once again hasten to his aid (v. 13 [Heb., 14]) and put his foes to shame (v. 14 [Heb., 15]) for all of the scorn they had heaped on him (v. 15 [Heb., 16]). Consequently, all who love the Lord are to rejoice and praise Him (v. 16 [Heb., 17]) even though at the time the psalmist was poor and needy; yet he believed and prayed that God's assistance would come very shortly (v. 17 [Heb., 18]).

INTERPRETATION OF PSALM 40:6–8 [HEB., 7–9]

Very few commentators on this psalm have addressed its main point and purpose as well as C. von Orelli. His key assertion is worth repeating here:

['Then I said, "Behold, I come . . ."'' etc.] applies to the writer's resolve to place himself, his own person, completely at God's disposal. As the servant, when his lord calls him, says *hinnēnî* (1 Sam. iii.4), so here the delivered saint: 'Lo, I am come to do what Thou wishest.' How he knows the Lord's wish the further sentence tells: 'In the book-roll it is written concerning me; there it is prescribed to me what I have to do' (2 Kings xxii.13). For the rest, this sentence gives the impression that it is an eminent personage who speaks thus (which is already evident from ver. 3), nay, one of whom the book of the divine law specifically treats. It is a king, so we must conclude, one whose conduct was there specially described, not merely in 'the law of the king' (Deut. xvii.14ff.), but in all that is said in the Torah respecting government and judgment. Ps. li. 17 would naturally suggest David himself, where the latter has spoken in similar terms of the value of sacrifice, in exact correspondence with the great principle . . . [of] 1 Sam. xv.22f. . . .[19]

But such a view, no matter how accurate, raises a most important and preliminary question: what are the principles for interpreting messianic psalms?

PRINCIPLES FOR INTERPRETING MESSIANIC PSALMS

In 1852, John Brown[20] set forth two principles for the correct interpretation of Messianic passages in the Psalms. His first principle was "that passages in the Psalms, which in the New Testament are expressly represented as predictions of the Messiah, are to be considered as having been originally intended to be so, and are to be interpreted accordingly."[21] In his development of this principle, he expanded it to also include what he could have called another principle: "If the *speaker* in a psalm, or if the *subject* of a psalm, is obviously the same from the beginning to the end, and if a portion of such a psalm is, in the New Testament expressly referred to the Messiah, the whole is to be considered as applicable to him."[22]

Brown's second principle is "that when, in the Psalms we meet with descriptions of a perfection of character and conduct—a depth and complication of suffering—a suddenness and completeness of deliverance—a height of dignity, and an extent of dominion, to which we can find no adequate correspondence in David, or in any of the great and good men commemorated in the Jewish history,—we are warranted to hold that they refer to the Messiah."[23]

Helpful as these interpretive principles may be for a Christian audience living in the post-Old Testament era, they are not satisfying as precise *exegetical* principles, i.e., those principles which are *drawn from the Old Testament text itself*. Instead, to be very precise, Brown's first principle smacks of eisegesis in that it lays over the text a meaning subsequently derived from a later text; thus, technically it can be faulted.[24] It certainly runs into trouble when it is expanded so as to embrace the entire psalm—witness verse 12 of Psalm 40. An interpreter must resort to enormous hermeneutical gymnastics to avoid saying that Messiah confesses his own iniquities in verse 12. Furthermore, the second principle is too ambiguous to be of any real help. Must every sudden deliverance of any type be interpreted to be a deliverance of Messiah? No, Brown should have stated it differently.

W. M. MacKay[25] initially gains a much better perspective by asking whether the psalms rank as historical or prophetical writings; i.e., to appropriate the question of the Ethiopian eunuch in Acts 8, "Of whom does the psalmist speak, or himself, or some other man?" MacKay decides that the psalmist speaks of someone other than himself, since approximately one hundred psalms employ the first person singular, which should not be arbitrarily assigned to two or more different persons in different parts of the same discourse. What is more, the Holy Spirit has already applied several of these first person singular references to Christ in the New Testament;[26] therefore, the speaker may be presumed to be the same in all of these psalms. MacKay also lays down as a rule that whenever "a passage in a psalm is not completely true regarding David, then it does not apply to David."[27]

But both these interpreters miss exactly what Willis J. Beecher pointed out: "Most of [the psalmist's predictions] should not be regarded as disconnected predictions, but as shoots from a common stem—the common stem being the body of connected messianic promise-history."[28] Beecher went on in the same place to acknowledge that many of these psalms have a "certain quality of universalness" that can be understood as "direct forecasts of a coming personal Messiah." Thus the original setting of the psalm occasionally could be left out of the account without seriously jeopardizing the basic meaning. Yet he correctly argued that a more satisfactory and consistent meaning could be obtained if it were linked with the designated men and accumulating doctrine of promise. The psalmists, like the prophets, usually employed promise phraseology that had already accompanied the original statement of the promise in the preceeding eras. Thus, they frequently used amplification of existing promises as the basis for disclosing additional revelation (e.g., Psalm 89 expands on 2 Sam. 7).

In some of these psalms, however, there is something new. It is the idea that some suffering may not only be for the benefit of others; some calamities that the current representative of the coming man of promise or that the whole nation as the people of promise suffer are connected with their mission as the channel of blessing for all the nations of the earth. Prominent among such psalms are Psalm 22 and the psalm under investigation here, Psalm 40.

What then are the internal clues in Psalm 40 that indicate that the psalmist as the vehicle of revelation is aware that what he now says and does relates more to his office and function as the current representative in a long series of fulfillments of that coming man of promise? There are seven words[29] in Psalm 40 located strategically both before and after verses 6–8 so as to tie these key words into the context. But more than that, they also signal David's awareness that the present inspired words elicited by a past deliverance are of more than personal or passing interest.

In verse 5 [Heb., 6], David praised God not only for his numerous wonderful miraculous deeds, but more important for our purposes here, for "your plans" (*maḥsh^{e}bōtèka*) towards him and all Israel (*ēlênû*, "to us"). It is interesting that Psalm 33:10–11, which likewise called for a "new song" (Psalm 33:3 = 40:3 [Heb., 4]), had highlighted the eternal plan of God[30] for all peoples and times against the backdrop of the frustrated plans of the nations. This word is also used later of the divine plan for specific nations in Jeremiah 29:11 and 51:29 and is expanded by other synonyms elsewhere. It must be concluded that when David praised God for "his plans" towards *all Israel,* especially when only he, David, had been rescued, he was deliberately showing his cognizance of his own place in that promise-plan.

Such an understanding is strengthened by his employment of six more words in verses 9-11 [Heb., 10-12]. The words of verses 6-8 David proclaimed more accurately, "heralded as good news" (*biśśartî*, v. 10) in the great congregation. This term is the exact equivalent of the New Testament *kerussō* and *euangelizō*, to herald the good news of the gospel. David's good news was basically about God's maintenance of His covenant promises in His acts of deliverance (*ṣidqātkā*, v. 11), His reliability (*'ĕmûnātkā*, v. 11), His work of delivering the nation (*tᵉshû'ātkā*, v. 11), and most impressive of all God's lovingkindness or grace and love as evidenced by His covenant (*ḥasdᵉkā*, and *'ămittᵉkā*, v. 12). This final combination of "grace and truth" was a strong reminder of the very character of God as first announced in His "name" (Exod. 34:6) when he forgave Israel for the golden calf fiasco. These were catchwords that signaled that more was underfoot in this public praise than a testimony to God for a rather private and personal escape. Instead it had communal, indeed, worldwide implications; it was another link in God's promise-plan.

If we have heard David properly, as he and the Spirit of God indeed intended to be understood, then we are now ready to tackle verses 6-8, which had brought such an "evangelical" delight to David as he announced them "in the great congregation."[31]

SACRIFICE AND OBEDIENCE

1 Samuel 15:22 is the first passage that had formally set forth the principle that sacrifices in and of themselves were worthless unless they were offered out of a heart right with God. Yet, this truth was already implicit in the contrast between Cain's and Abel's sacrifices in Genesis 4. Moreover, the same requirement was explicitly laid down in Leviticus 16:29, 31; that is, that each Israelite who expected to be forgiven of "all" his sins had to truly repent, "afflict [his] soul." Only then could one of the most persistent phrases in the Levitical sacrificial instructions be pronounced over such individuals: "And he shall be forgiven" (Lev. 1:4; 4:20, 26, 31, 35; 5:10, 16; 16:20-22).[32]

Thus, the psalmist was not rejecting sacrifices as such any more than were the prophets who followed him Isa. 1:11-18; 66:3; Jer. 7:21-23; Hos. 6:6; Amos 5:21; Mic. 6:6-8). These same sentiments appear elsewhere in the Psalms (50:8, 14; 51:16 [Heb., 18]; 69:30-31 [Heb., 31-32] and Proverbs (15:8; 21:3) not to mention Exodus 15:26; Deuteromy 10:12, 20; and 1 Samuel 15:22. Sabourin labels the form of the psalmist's statement "dialectical negation,"[33] i.e., the ceremonial practice is held in tension until the ethical and spiritual preparation for the performance of that practice is met. The effect is to speak in a proverbial form: "I do not desire this so much as I desire that," or "without this there is no that." It is the language of priorities. What is the use of having this (sacrifices) without that (a prior heart of obedience)?[34]

Neither does there appear that any special emphasis is placed on the four words for sacrifice. It may be indeed, as many commentators suggest, that the offerings are named in respect to: (1) their material, *zebah*, animal offering, and *minḥāh*, cereal offering including perhaps *mesek*, wine, and (2) their purpose, *ʿōlâ*, to obtain the divine favor, and, *ḥaṭṭāʾt*, to turn away the divine wrath.[35]

Between these two pairs of sacrificial terms in parallel stichs is the middle clause: "ears you have dug for me." Initially, this unique biblical phrase suggests the well-known custom of boring a slave's right ear to denote the slave's voluntary dedication of himself in perpetual service to his master (Exod. 21:6 and Deut. 15:17). But this otherwise suggestive explanation has two serious drawbacks: (1) the technical word for bore is not *kārâ*, "to dig," but *rāṣaʿ*, "to bore" (Exod. 21:6), and (2) only one ear was bored, not both[36] "ears" (*ʾoznayim*), as in this verse.[37]

In addition to Psalm 40:6, *kārâ* is used fourteen times in the Old Testament. These may be tabulated as follows:

"to dig" a pit (eight usages)
Exod. 21:33
Psalms 7:16
   57:7
   94:13
   119:85
Prov. 26:27
Jer. 18:20
   18:22

"to dig" a well (two usages)
Gen. 26:25
Num. 21:18

"to dig" a grave or tomb (two usages)
Gen. 50:5
2 Chron. 16:14

"to dig up" evil (one usage)
Prov. 16:27

"to prepare" a feast (one usage)
2 King 6:23

Thus, the meaning "to dig" is well established, even though the LXX *katērtizō* "to prepare," may be explained by the 2 Kings 6:23 usage. The phrase then refers to the fact that the instruments for obedience, the ears, were made by God (cf. Psalm 94:9: "He who planted the ear. . . ."). Thus the ability to obey has been given by God. Perhaps the phrase may be compared with a later development of a similar concept in the prophets, "to *open* the ear" (Isa. 48:8; 50:4-5) or the earlier form "to *uncover* the ear" (1 Sam. 9:15; 20:2, 12, 13; 22:8, 17; Job 33:16; 36:10, 15). Thus, in effect, one part of the body (the one that receives the command and word of God) is put for the whole body in a *pars pro toto* [part for the whole][38] argument. Significantly, the prophet Jeremiah complains, "Lo, [Israel's] ears are closed (*'ărēlâ*) so they cannot hear, the word of the Lord is offensive to them; they find no pleasure (*ḥāpēṣ*) in it" (Jer. 6:10). But David in Psalm 40 instead "delights" to do God's will (vs. 8 [Heb., 9]).

THE PRESCRIPTIONS OF THE BOOK AND THE WORK OF THE MAN OF PROMISE

Instead of connecting verse 7 [Heb., 8] in a temporal sequence, the psalmist emphasized the internal connection between the declaration of the preceeding verse and this one. "Then," verse 7, marks the consequence of the announced obedience which he had contrasted with mere ritualistic offering of sacrifices.

But what form was that expression of obedience to take? David now placed himself at God's service: "Behold, I come [or] have come." His very first words were those of a servant who presented himself at the beck and call of his master (cf. Num. 22:38; 2 Sam. 19:21; or Isa. 6:9).

What he came to do, however, is that which was written of (or concerning, for, about) him in the roll of the book (v. 7 [Heb., 8]). Certainly, this clause is not to be regarded as a parenthetical remark, since the infinitive "to do your will" in verse 8 [Heb., 9] cannot serve as the object of "I come" because it has its own verb. Accordingly, the function of the *bet*, ("in, with," etc.) before *mᵉgillat sēper*, "roll of the book," becomes as crucial for exegesis as the *'ālāy* "of, concerning, about, or for me"—all in verse 7 [Heb., 8].

The phrase *'ālāy* "for, upon, concerning, about me" is not to be taken as meaning "*upon* me" as if it were parallel to the clause in verse 8 [Heb., 9], "and your law is my (inmost) heart," for the heart hardly has "a *roll* of the book" written on it. Therefore, the preposition points to the one respecting whom the Word of God was written. It was a word written for David. The combination of this verb and preposition (*kātûb*) occurs also in 2 Kings 22:13, except that there the words of the book prescribed Israel's duty: "because our fathers did not listen to the words of this book to do according to all which is written for [or concerning] us" (*kᵉkol-hakkātûb 'ālēnû*). The preposition, *'al* in Psalm 40:8 [Heb., 9] denotes the object of the contents: David. Similarly ʿal functions as the object of prophecy in 1 Kings 22:8 yitnabbēʾ ʿālay and Isa. 1:1, ḥāzâ ʿal.[39]

Where then did David find a word concerning himself? "In a roll of a book." The absence of the Hebrew article appears to emphasize the fact that it was written.[40] The preposition Bet with verbs of motion like "come" usually carry the sense of accompaniment, "with";[41] yet the usage here appears to be more elliptical[42] in that the verb of motion is less intimately tied to this clause than is usually the case. Therefore, we believe it is the preposition of location, "in."

What book then was this? The exact phrase "roll of a book" appears in Jeremiah 36:2, 4 and Ezekiel 2:9, while "roll" alone appears in Jeremiah 36:6; Ezekiel 3:1-3; Zechariah 5:1-2; Ezra 6:2 (Aramaic). Some would wish to restrict David's reference to the lex regia, the law of the king found in Deuteronomy 17:14-20. But it is better to understand the reference to be all of the written will of God to the extent that it was available to David in his day: the Torah i.e., the five books of Moses and perhaps part of Samuel's composition or some of the earlier prophets such as Joshua, Judges, Ruth (just then released?) and parts of 1 Samuel.[43]

It would be extremely helpful to be able to decide if this psalm were written before or after Nathan's disclosure that Yahweh would make David's line the continuation of the patriarchal promise (2 Sam. 7). Unfortunately, we know of no way to determine this. But we can show that David in Psalm 40 shows awareness that he was a man about whom the Scriptures were written (v. 7) and that he employed catch phrases that were becoming household terms for the promise. Individually the arguments are not terribly moving, but collectively they force us to conclude that the obedience mentioned by David has to do with a new office and function he had as the current installment in God's coming man of promise.

Verse 8 [Heb., 9] completes the psalmist's statement. He delights (ḥāpēṣ, see v. 6 [Heb., 7]) to do God's "will," in this passage (rāṣôn), similar to the word for God's "plan," although it stresses the aspect of pleasure and favor connected with that plan. In fact, the law of God is in the "innermost parts" of his being (betôk mēʿāy), (cf. Isa. 16:11; Jer. 31:20). That God's Torah should be written on the heart was already indicated in Deuteronomy 6:6, Psalm 37:31, and later on in Proverbs 3:3; 7:3. According to Jeremiah 31:33, the law of God would be implanted in the heart of all God's people as a characteristic of the era of the new covenant; however, already in the Old Testament era this was true at least to some degree: "A people in whose heart is my law" (ʿam tôrātî belibbām, Isa. 51:7).

We conclude that in Psalm 40 the psalmist presents to God an obedient spirit, willing to go and do all that is written about himself. He carries in his person and in each favored descendant all that God is going to do for all the nations of the earth. What had been written thus far in Scripture about the coming Messiah and His work was written, in effect, about David, so far as he and his generation were concerned. He, David, delighted to do every bit of what he found written therein, for God had also dug out his ears, as it were, and had given him a willing heart and mind. Such a spirit was more to be desired than all the false religiosity of compounded ritual upon ritual. Such also, especially in light of David's most recent deliverance from danger and in light of all of God's past acts and His all-encompassing plan with so many aspects of His thought, was the substance of the good news that he would herald forth in the midst of God's gathered congregation.

HEBREWS 10:5-10 AND CONCLUSION

THE GREEK TEXT

The variants from the Hebrew Masoretic Text in the Greek LXX (=Psalm 39:7-9*a*) are: (1) the appearance of *sōma*, "body," instead of the expected *ōtia*, "ears," for Hebrew *'oznayim;* (2) the Hebrew, Vaticanus, and Sinaiticus LXX have singular "burnt offering," Alexandrinus LXX and Heb. 10:6 uses the plural "burnt offerings"; (3) the Hebrew *shā'al* "to require" is accurately rendered by Vaticanus *ētēsas,* and nearly so in a variant *ezētēsas* in Sinaiticus and Alexandrinus, but Hebrews 10:6 has *eudokēsas,* "take pleasure in"[44]; (4) by omitting *eboulēthēn*, the writer to the Hebrews is able to connect "I come" directly to the phrase "to do your will" (a fact further emphasized by placing "your will" at the end of the quotation).[45]

None of these variants is harmful to the truth-intention of the psalmist. The use of "body" for "ear" is, as we have already argued, a case of the whole being used for the part.[46] In this case the translator opted for the culturally meaningful dynamic-equivalent. The use of the plural "burnt offerings" is hardly worth noticing except as it sheds light on the lines of textual dependence. Again, in the third variant, the writer might have been pressed into using a different verb than "require" since he had just argued in Heb. 9:12-19 that God had commanded the sacrifices of goats and bulls. The final variant developed when the writer to the Hebrews stopped short of *eboulēthen* (LXX, Psalm 39:9) and thus the infinitive became the object of "Behold, I come." Since this textual change did not affect the overall meaning of the psalmist, the writer to the Hebrews adopted this shorter quotation, even though from twentieth-century rules on style and procedures for citing quotes it could be faulted.

THE ARGUMENT OF THE WRITER TO THE HEBREWS

Since Psalm 40 is quoted only once in the New Testament, it certainly does not lend credence to Rendel Harris's hypothesis[47] that the New Testament writers tended to draw from a list of proof texts known as *testimonia* rather than drawing directly from the Old Testament and its context. More important than that discussion is the one concerning the exegetical practices of the writer to the Hebrews.

Was this writer guilty of using homiletical midrash[48] in Psalm 40 where the original setting was either forgotten or considered irrelevant and thus was blithely applied to Jesus? Or, as Kistemaker suggested, did he use a *pesher* type of exegesis,[49] according to which the psalmist delivered a mystery (a *raz*) for which he had no explanation, but which only a much later *pesher* could unlock.

Frankly, neither suggestion offers any satisfaction or textual demonstration. Instead of finding that the scriptural exegesis of Hebrews was fantastic, Alexandrian, or even Philonic, G. B. Caird opined that it was "one of the earliest and most successful attempts to define the relation between the Old and New Testaments, and that a large part of the value of the book is to be found in the method of exegesis which was formerly dismissed with contempt."[50] This, we believe, is closer to the real facts as we have seen them in these two passages.

If our understanding of the psalmist's words is even close to what he had intended to say under the inspiration of the Holy Spirit, then it will come as very little surprise to read the argument of Hebrews 10:5-10. What had been a shadow under David became a complete reality finally in Christ's incarnation and substitutionary atonement. David was a true model of the final reality because of the gracious calling and appointment of God. History could reflect this kind of scheme (shadow and reality) solely because of the all-embracing divine plan and divine designation to the office and function of promise, and not because of a Platonic (?) tradition that tended to bifurcate reality into earthly and heavenly divisions.

When we turn to the question of sacrifices, it must be noticed immediately that nowhere in the Old Testament was it ever claimed that the blood of bulls and goats could or ever did take away anyone's sin. What part, then, did those sacrifices play? Did they have any kind of efficacy?

The answer is that if sacrifices were offered out of a heart of contrition and obedience to God, then on the basis of the word of a faithful God these sacrifices were *subjectively* efficacious. Invariably, the word pronounced with such an offering was, "And he shall be forgiven." Thus, the offerer did receive relief from the penalty and memory of his sins.

Nevertheless, this sin had not yet been cared for *objectively*.[51] Certainly the principle of substitution was clear by now, but these sacrificial victims were animals, not people. Moreover, the matter was never settled, for sacrifice followed upon sacrifice. Something was missing. Therefore, there was a "passing over" (*paresis*, Rom. 3:25) the sins of the Old Testament on the basis of God's declared word until He himself could provide His own final substitute as a true, but sinless, man.

How then does the writer to the Hebrews employ Psalm 40 in Hebrews 10:8–10? His argument falls into two parts: (1) v. 8, the "above" *anōteron* with the quote from Psalm 40:6 [Heb. 7] being repeated and (2) v. 9 "then he said" with the quote of Psalm 40:7 [Heb. 8], deleting, however, the clause "in the volume of the book it is written concerning me." Simply put, he sees in the first quotation the abolishment of the old order and in the second the establishment of the new.

Has he played fair with the text of Psalms? We believe he has. The permanency of obedience of the man (whether it begins with his hearing [ears] or results in the use of his whole body) is correctly set off against sacrifices that at best could only mirror or symbolize that prerequisite obedience. Thus the one act (that is, obedience) had to be enduring and permanent while the other exuded forms of obsolesence and temporary usefulness. Clearly, God desired one as being more basic and foundational than the other.

The new order would focus on that man of promise who would always delight to to the will of God. Even though David's obedience and especially his office and person pointed to one who was to come, only Christ fulfilled every aspect of this future hope. Furthermore, if the writer of Hebrews was himself aware and thought his readers might also recall the whole quotation from Psalm 40 with its additional clause about the law of God being in man's innermost being, then he also thereby called for the new covenant era when God's law would be unmistakenly engraved on all His people's hearts.

What then was removed in the first order? The Old Testament? No, it was the ceremonial law that was removed. But that same law carried a warning from the day it had been given to Israel that it was only the model, a copy (e.g., Exod. 25:9, 40; 26:30, "pattern"); the real was yet to come. Hence, no one should have been alarmed at this word of abolishment.

Most important, the writer to the Hebrews does not build his argument on the *sōma* clause of the LXX. In fact, he simply ignores it when he restates and comments on Psalm 40:6 [Heb. 7]. True, Hebrews 10:10 does almost incidentally introduce "the offering of the *body* of Jesus Christ once for all," but he does not refer this usage back to the psalmist. Thus, those interpreters are mistaken who make the *sōma*, "body," clause the key to the writer's use of this psalm. Those who focus on the clause about the "roll of the book" being written concerning him are also mistaken. Neither clause is used in his exposition. While the second (i.e., "roll of the book") may have been a reason that the psalmist initially went to this passage to make the connection he did, it cannot be used as a part of his main contention and argument since he made no direct use of it. Instead of the contrast[52] in Hebrews 10 between the Levitical system (10:1-4) and the free surrender of the body of Christ (10:5-10), it is a contrast between the death of an animal, which has no way of entering into the meaning of what is happening (10:1-4), and the perfect obedience of Jesus for which act He specifically came into this world (10:5-10): "I have come to do thy will."

Psalm 40:6-8 contains fewer messianic clues and less promise phraseology than other messianic passages (e.g., Psalm 2, 22, 72, 89, or 110), but patient attendance on the text will reveal that the writer to the Hebrews was on strong exegetical grounds. Meanwhile, it is not necessary to make David's confession of his iniquities (v. 12) somehow fit the Messiah without impugning his sinlessness. But most important of all, Psalm 40 teaches us that the advent of the man of promise was deliberately designed by God to supplement, and in the case of the sacrificial order, to supersede it.

NOTES

1. The epistle's main Christological section is found in Heb. 7:1—10:18.
2. I am indebted to Theodore G. Stylianopoulos ("Shadow and Reality: Reflections on Hebrews 10:1-18," in *The Green Orthodox Theological Review* 17[1972]: 216) for the general formulation of these four points.
3. I am indebted to T. Allan Armstrong, "The Use of Psalm 40 in Hebrews 10" (MA thesis, Trinity Evangelical Divinity School, 1975) for this conclusion. He surveyed four additional references listed in the second edition of The United Bible Societies' Greek text, viz., Luke 7:19 (Psalm 40:7), Eph. 5:2 (Psalm 40:6) and Rev. 5:9, 14:3 (Psalm 40:3), but found them unconvincing.
4. S. R. Driver, "The Method of Studying the Psalter," *Expositor,* Seventh Series 52(1910): pp. 356-57. (Italics are his.)
5. F. S. Sampson, *A Critical Commentary on the Epistle to the Hebrews* (New York: Carter, 1866), p. 369. My student Stuart Erdenberg pointed out this reference to me.
6. Sigmund Mowinckel, *The Psalms in Israel's Worship,* trans. D. R. Ap-Thomas, (Nashville: Abingdon, 1967), 2:98-101, is one of the most recent studies on the authenticity of the Davidic headings in these psalms. He concludes that these are all late titles, but he notes on p. 99, n. 52, that only in a half dozen or so of the seventy-three Davidic psalms do we have no MS or contradictory MS evidence. We conclude that the case for Davidic authorship in Psalm 40, since it is not in this list, is secure and as old as the text. See also

Robert Dick Wilson, "The Headings of the Psalms," *Princeton Theological Review* 24(1926): 353-95.

7. Charles Augustus Briggs, *A Critical and Exegetical Commentary on the Book of Psalms,* 2 vols., International Critical Commentary (New York: Scribner's, 1906), 1:351.
8. Briggs also lists Isa. 41:5 (v. 4), Isa. 55:8, 9 (v. 6) and Psalm 22:26 (vv. 10-11), *Psalms,* 1:351. The old commentator Ewald believed that the prominence given to the roll of the book in v. 7 was enough to link this psalm with the time of Josiah's reformation, but the Mosaic Deut. 17:14-20 could serve just as well as a source for this idea if need be.
9. See Mitchell Dahood, *The Psalms: Introduction, Translation, and Notes,* 3 vols., The Anchor Bible (Garden City: Doubleday, 1966) 1:245; and Thomas Kelly Cheyne, *The Christian Use of the Psalms* (London: Isbister, 1899), p. 125. I owe this last reference to Terry Armstrong.
10. Artur Weiser, *The Psalms: A Commentary,* The Old Testament Library, trans. Herbert Hartwell (Philadelphia: Westminster, n.d.), p. 334.
11. Mowinckel, 2:74.
12. Carl Bernhard Moll, *The Psalms,* Lange's Commentary (New York: Scribner, Armstrong & Co., 1872), pp. 270-71.
13. J. J. Stewart Perowne, *The Book of Psalms,* 2 vols. reprint of 4th ed. (Grand Rapids: Zondervan, 1966), 1:332.
14. Driver, p. 355.
15. Driver, p. 348. Franz Delitzsch, *Commentary on the Epistle to the Hebrews,* vol. 2, reprint (Minneapolis: Klock & Klock, 1978) p. 150, places Psalm 40 in the time of Saul's persecution of David. This appears to be too early.
16. Driver, p. 355, has a fine note: "Vv. 2-3 cannot synchronize with V. 12: if the unity of the Psalm is to be preserved, v.2f. must describe the danger from which the Psalmist was delivered in the past, and v. 12 the fresh troubles which have fallen upon him since. Observe how a single word in P.B.V., A.V., R. V. obscures this. '*Hath* put' in v. 3 suggests what has just occurred, and so is in contradiction with v. 12: we require aorists throughout vv. 1-3: what is described in these verses is then thrown entirely into the past: v. 12 describes what is happening in the present; and the two parts of the Psalm become perfectly consistent."
17. The danger could have been a sickness, persecution, exile, bodily harm, or a threatened political revolution.
18. On the theology of a "new song," see Psalms 33:3; 96:1; 98:1; 144:9; 149:1; and Isa. 42:10.
19. C. von Orelli, *The O.T. Prophecy of the Consummation of God's Kingdom Traced in Its Historical Development* (Edinburgh: T. & T. Clark, 1889), p. 178.
20. John Brown, *The Sufferings and Glories of the Messiah,* reprint (Byron Center, Mich: Sovereign Grace Publishers, 1970), pp. 26-30.
21. Ibid., p. 26.
22. Ibid., p. 27. Italics mine.
23. Ibid., p. 27.
24. See our recent discussions on the proper and improper use of "The Analogy of Faith," especially as an *exegetical* tool in W. C. Kaiser, Jr., "The Single Intent of Scripture," *Evangelical Roots,* ed. Kenneth Kantzer (Nashville: Nelson, 1978), pp. 139-40; idem, "Meanings from God's Message: Matters for Interpretation," *Christianity Today* 22 (5 October 1979): 30-33.

25. W. M. MacKay, "Messiah in the Psalms," *Evangelical Quarterly* 11(1939): 153–64.

26. MacKay, pp. 160–61, goes on to find "seven unchallengeable references covering ten psalms which Christ takes authoritatively to Himself," viz., Psalm 41 (= John 13:18); Psalm 82 (= John 10:35); Psalm 118:22 (= Matt. 21:42; Acts 4:11; Eph. 2:20); Psalm 118:26 (= Matt. 21:9); Psalm 31:5 (= Luke 23:46) (a Psalm that is parallel to passages in Psalm 18, 25, 69, and 102); and Psalm 2 (=Rev. 2:26; 12:5; 19:15; Acts 4:25, 13:33; Heb. 1:5; 5:5). J. Barton Payne, *Encyclopedia of Biblical Prophecy* (New York: Harper & Row, 1973), pp. 258–60 finds "13 definitely Messianic psalms": Psalms 8:3–8; 72:6–17; 89:3–4, 26, 28–29, 34–37; 109:6–19; 132:12b; 45:6–7; 102: 25–27; 110:1–7; 2:1–12; 16:10; 22:1–31; 40:6–8: and 69:25. He has grouped them according to third person, second person, or first person pronoun usage respectively.

27. MacKay, p. 162.

28. Willis J. Beecher, *The Prophets and the Promise,* reprint (Grand Rapids: Baker, 1963), p. 244.

29. As pointed out by my student, Wayne Werner.

30. See Walter C. Kaiser, Jr., *Toward an Old Testament Theology* (Grand Rapids: Zondervan, 1978), pp. 29–32, for further discussion on a single cosmopolitan plan of God.

31. Also in Psalms 22:25; 35:18.

32. The old, but false, definitions for "witting" and "unwitting" sins must now be reexamined, for "all" sins were pardonable, except high rebellion or blasphemy against God and His Word (Num. 15:27–36). See W. C. Kaiser, *Toward an Old Testament Theology,* pp. 117–19.

33. Leopold Sabourin, *The Psalms: Their Origin and Meaning,* 2. vols. (New York: Society of St. Paul, 1969), 2:48.

34. Terry Armstrong found an older commentator, Benjamin Weiss, *New Translation, Exposition and Chronological Arrangement of the Book of Psalms* (Edinburgh: Oliphant, 1858) p. 429, who tried to solve this tension by contrasting *hāpas* with *rāṣôn.* But the exercise is both unnecessary and unconvincing—as if one word meant God's chief desire and the other just His wish apart from ranking it primary or secondary. Furthermore, the other parallel word used here is *shā'al,* "to require."

35. So Moll, p. 272; A. F. Kirkpatrick, *The Book of Psalms* (Cambridge: U. Press, 1906), p. 210.

36. Ancient interpreters are most arbitrary when they apply the plural of ears to the *active* and *passive* obedience of Christ or that Christ offered himself for a congregation composed of two parts: Jews and Gentiles. So reports Moll, p. 272.

37. Note the NIV has opted for this translation: "my ears you have pierced."

38. The writer to the Hebrews following the LXX will just reverse this same process and express it by a *totum pro parte* argument by using "body" instead of ears.

39. E. W. Hengstenberg, *Commentary on the Psalms,* trans. P. Fairbairn and J. Thomson, 3 vols. (Edinburgh: T & T Clark, 1846), 2:72 decides against the messianic view of this passage (which he had held to earlier, see E. W. Hengstenberg, *Christology of the Old Testament,* abridged by T. K. Arnold, reprint (Grand Rapids: Kregel, 1970), pp. 90–93, because of this expression which he translated "to write *over* me" in the sense of prescribing. He pointed

to Josh. 1:7 and 1 Kings 2:3 as convincing reasons. But this is strange, since the terminology used there is nothing like that used in Psalm 40. He should have retained his earlier view and substantiated it with better exegesis than appears in his earlier *Christology*.

40. Kirkpatrick, p. 211. He compares Hos. 8:12.
41. E. Kautzsch, *Gesenius' Hebrew Grammar,* ed., A. E. Cowley, 2d ed. (Oxford: Clarendon, 1910), p. 380.
42. Note the NIV rendering: "Here I am, I have come—it is written about me in the scroll."
43. David L. Cooper, *Messiah: His First Coming Scheduled* (Los Angeles, Biblical Research Society, 1939), p. 187, felt David quoted from the "Roll of the Book." Thus Cooper concluded, "Evidently there was a primitive revelation given originally by the Lord for a definite and specific purpose.... When it had served its purpose, the Lord caused it to pass out of circulation." There is no need to create an Old Testament "Q source," however, for the reference is not a citation which is no longer in existence.
44. A word paralleled in Psalm 50:18 and found in LXX[2013] Boh. Sad. See Kenneth J. Thomas, "The Old Testament Citations in Hebrews," *New Testament Studies* 11(1964-65): 314.
45. So Thomas, p. 314.
46. This common figure of speech is known as synecdoche. According to T. Armstrong, John DeWitt (*The Psalms: A New Translation with Introductory Essay and Notes* [New York: A. D. F. Randolph & Co., 1891], p. 108) was the first to make this suggestion in recent times. Many have followed him since then.
47. For a criticism of Harris's view, see C. H. Dodd, *According to the Scriptures* (London: Nisbet, 1952), p. 26, and Simon Kistemaker, *The Psalm Citations in the Epistle to the Hebrews* (Amsterdam: Wed. G. Van Soest N.V., 1961), p. 9.
48. The idea belongs to George Wesley Buchanan, *To the Hebrews,* Anchor Bible (Garden City: Doubleday, 1972), p. xxi.
49. Kistemaker, *Psalm Citations,* 88. Cf. Richard N. Longenecker, *Biblical Exegesis in the Apostolic Period* (Grand Rapids: Eerdmans, 1975), pp. 70-75.
50. G. B. Caird, "The Exegetical Method of the Epistle to the Hebrews," *Canadian Journal of Theology,* 5 (1959): 45, as cited by Longenecker, p. 172.
51. This distinction between subjective and objective efficacy I owe to Hobart Freeman, "The Problem of Efficacy of Old Testament Sacrifices," *Bulletin of the Evangelical Theological Society* 5(1962): 73-79, 90.
52. See the very penetrating and thoughtful presentation of the views of Calvin, Barnes, Westcott, Nairne, Bruce, Montefiore, Morris, Moffatt, and V. Taylor in T. Allan Armstrong, pp. 59-67.

3

Salvation in the Old Testament

John S. Feinberg

JOHN S. FEINBERG (M.A., Ph.D., University of Chicago; M. Div., Talbot Theological Seminary: Th.M., Trinity Evangelical Divinity School) is professor of systematic theology at Liberty Baptist Seminary, Lynchburg, Virginia.

What does the Bible teach about salvation? Ask this question of most people, and they will respond with their understanding of the New Testament's teaching on salvation. One can search for hours and find little written about salvation in the Old Testament. Biblical theologians tend to discuss it more often than systematic theologians, but neither group devotes much attention to it. Moreover, if one were to peruse course outlines for most classes taught in seminaries or Bible colleges in soteriology, he would find that the question of salvation in the Old Testament receives little or no treatment whatsoever.

If it is difficult to find discussions on the Old Testament's approach to the broad theme of salvation, it is even harder to find treatments of the Old Testament's perspective on the specific matter of salvation of the individual. Although there are studies of such topics as corporate election and national salvation (especially when the topic is physical deliverance from some kind of bondage or evil),[1] it seems that theologians and exegetes have tended to shy away from a consideration of the Old Testament teaching about how an individual was to acquire spiritual salvation. Why this should be so is not entirely clear. Perhaps it has stemmed at least partially from a feeling, on the one hand, that the Old Testament really says nothing different than the New on the matter of personal salvation.

Or perhaps it stems from a fear that what the Old Testament teaches about salvation is so radically different from the teaching of the New Testament that close attention to it would only serve to confuse us about God's manner of dealing with personal salvation, and might even lead us to the theologically damaging conclusion that God has been inconsistent in regard to the matter of salvation.

In view of these considerations, I suggest that the study of salvation in the Old Testament is more urgently needed, and it is my intention to consider several issues related to the Old Testament's teaching about the spiritual salvation of the individual. Obviously, it would be impossible in a study of this length to cover every relevant aspect of Old Testament teaching, but I should like to address three main topics. First, I want to consider the method of salvation. Does Scripture teach more than one way of salvation—an Old Testament and a New Testament way? This matter is of interest not only from the standpoint of coming to a proper understanding of scriptural teaching, but also because many have thought that dispensationalism involves or even necessitates a commitment to multiple ways of salvation. What I shall argue in regard to the first issue is that neither the approach of Scripture nor that of dispensationalism *necessitates* holding to multiple methods of salvation. Second, I want to discuss the implementation of salvation. To say that Scripture teaches only one way of salvation is not to specify what it is or how it has been implemented at various times in history, especially during Old Testament times. Third, I want to consider the relationship of Old Testament sacrifices to Christ's sacrifice and to discuss as well the exact *soteriological* function of sacrifices in the Old Testament system. Involved in the discussion of the function of the sacrifices will be a treatment of their efficacy, especially in view of the statement in Hebrews 10:4 that "not all the blood of bulls and goats could take away sin."*

THE METHOD OF SALVATION

How many ways of salvation does Scripture teach? Reading various theologians, one might initially assume that the question is a waste of time, for all seem to assert that Scripture teaches only one way of salvation operative in all economies and at all times. For example, after presenting opposing viewpoints, Hodge emphatically argues:

---

*In the process of preparing this study I have been greatly aided by discussions and interaction with Duane Dunham, Paul Feinberg, Robert Hughes, and Bruce Ware. I want to express my appreciation for their help.

In opposition to these different views the common doctrine of the Church has ever been, that the plan of salvation has been the same from the beginning. There is the same promise of deliverance from the evils of the apostasy, the same Reedeemer, the same condition required for participation in the blessings of redemption, and the same complete salvation for all who embrace the offers of divine mercy.[2]

Likewise, Payne argues that in spite of some difference, the doctrine of regeneration is taught in the Old Testament as well as in the New. He explains:

> This definition of regeneration as being "in Christ" by no means, how- ever, eliminates the doctrine of the new birth from the Old Testament. There is but one, unified testament, God's sole plan of salvation, through which Christ offers a redemption that is equally effective for the saints of both dispensations. Christ states that Abraham, in the patriarchal period, rejoiced to see His day, "And he saw it, and was glad" (John 8:56). Jesus was the Mediator of the older testament, as well as the newer (Heb. 9:15); and, since it is true that no man cometh unto the Father but by Him (John 14:6) and yet, since the saints of the older dispensation did indeed come to the father (Ps. 73:24), they must have been made perfect *in Him* (Heb. 11:40).[3]

Examples such as the preceding could be proliferated seemingly ad in finitum, but of course, if that is the case, is it even worthwhile to ask the question about how many ways Scripture teaches? The question is important because there are many who *think* there is much disagreement over the issue. Many nondispensational writers (such as Hodge and Payne, quoted above), who hold to one method of salvation, have accused dispensationalists of teaching multiple ways of salvation. They assume that since the dispensationalist consistently differentiates between God's program for Israel and His program for the church, since he emphasizes that God institutes different economies with men at various times, and especially since the dispensationalist claims there are significant dif- ferences between the dispensation called law and the dispensation called grace (even the labels of the dispensations supposedly tip us off to dif- ferent methods of salvation), the dispensationalist must hold that Scrip- ture teaches multiple ways of salvation. For example, Daniel Fuller, after quoting the old Scofield Reference Bible, concludes:

> Hence Dispensationalism, as expounded by one of its foremost sys- tematizers, teaches two ways of salvation: that during the era of law,

obedience to it was a condition of salvation, whereas during the age of grace, salvation comes simply through faith in Christ.[4]

Payne does not put the matter quite so bluntly as Fuller, but as he reasserts the unity of God's redemptive plan throughout Scripture, the message in regard to dispensationalism is the same as Fuller's. Payne writes:

More serious, however, than its misapplication of particular prophecies, is what amounts to dispensationalism's repudiation of the whole, unified redemptive plan of God in human history. Indeed, the normative truthfulness of the older testament of the past is dependent upon its essential identity with, and fulfillment in, the newer testament of the present and the future. Correspondingly, the blessing for the modern Church, as this is contained in the Old Testament, can be appropriated by today's saints only when they accept their own equation, as the Israel of God, with that ancient Israel to whom God extended His testamental promises. It thus becomes apparent that a comprehensive understanding of God's gracious purpose—which has been one and the same from Genesis 3:15, right on through to the closing chapters of Revelation—lies contingent upon the Christian's recognition of one cross, one testament, one faith, and one Church throughout all history.[5]

These citations level devastating attacks at dispensationalism, especially if dispensationalists in fact hold multiple methods of salvation, whereas Scripture teaches one method. As a matter of fact, dispensationalists (older and contemporary) do hold that Scripture teaches only one way of salvation. In all honesty, however, it must be admitted that statements made by certain dispensationalists in the past appeared to teach multiple ways of salvation. That such careless statements did not reflect the full thinking of those theologians (as can be seen from other statements they made) seems to have escaped many critics of dispensationalism. One such unguarded statement, however, appeared in the old Scofield Reference Bible:

As a dispensation, grace begins with the death and resurrection of Christ (Rom. 3:24-26; 4:24, 25). The point of testing is no longer legal obedience as the condition of salvation, but acceptance or rejection of Christ, with good works as a fruit of salvation.[6]

Fuller (see above) cites this as evidence that Scofield taught multiple ways of salvation, one by law and one by grace. Certainly, such a statement would appear to be problematic. What seems to be equally problematic, however, is that Fuller never quotes the Scofield Reference Bible when it states that "law neither justifies a sinner nor sanctifies a believer."[7] Fuller went on to claim that although some dispensationalists hold to the view that Scripture teaches only one way of salvation, he claimed that it was a new trend in dispensationalism and not really consistent with its basic line of thought.[8] Fuller was at least willing to admit that dispensationalists make statements contrary to the multiple methods position. But he still thought that this was merely a new development in dispensationalism. Many critics of dispensationalism have not even bothered to mention such statements as those cited by Fuller. Charles Ryrie in *Dispensationalism Today* has presented ample evidence that older as well as more recent dispensationalists in fact hold to only one way of salvation being taught in Scripture.[9] It is truly unfortunate that in spite of all the ink that has been spilled on the subject, the commonly held caricature of dispensationalism (perhaps even held by some uninformed who claim to be dispensationalists themselves) is that it is committed to and even necessitates the notion that Scripture teaches multiple ways of salvation. The old *Scofield Reference Bible* is cited as proof, and that is supposed to settle the matter. Of course, it is equally important to note what the *New Scofield Reference Bible* (the work of many dispensationalists) says. Writers such as Payne (*Theology of the Older Testament*) and Fuller (*The Hermeneutics of Dispensationalism*) can hardly be faulted for not taking it into account in their works, since the *New Scofield Reference Bible* was published after their works were completed. However, some changes have been made. The comment concerning the inability of law to justify has not been removed from the notes on Galatians 3. Moreover, the objectionable comments on law and grace have been totally removed from the notes on John 1. In their place we read the following:

In its fullness, grace began with the ministry of Christ involving His death and resurrection, for He came to die for sinners (Jn. 1:17; Mt. 11:28-30; 16:21; 20:28; Rom. 3:24-26; 4:24-25). Under the former dispensation, law was shown to be powerless to secure righteousness and life for a sinful race (Gal. 3:21-22). Prior to the cross man's salvation was through faith (Gen. 15:6; Rom. 4:3), being grounded on Christ's atoning sacrifice, viewed anticipatively by God . . .; now it is clearly revealed that salvation and righteousness are received by faith in the crucified and resurrected Savior..., with holiness of life and good works following as the fruit of salvation....[10]

Certainly, the above statement reflects dispensational thinking, but it also clearly speaks of a unified method of salvation—by grace through faith.

Though this discussion of what dispensationalists claim is interesting (especially to a dispensationalist who holds to only one method of salvation), it would seem that there is a much more important question to be asked and answered. The question of greater significance is whether dispensationalism as a system necessitates holding a view of multiple ways of salvation. A description of what dispensationalists hold is one thing, but a much more important question is whether the system is consistent with a single method of salvation view, a multiple method of salvation view, or both. In other words, what position could a dispensationalist hold without contradicting his system on the matter of the ways of salvation? This is a significant question because the underlying assumption in the attacks of Fuller, Payne, and others, is not just that dispensationalists hold multiple ways of salvation, but that the system demands such a view. The complaint, then, is not so much against what dispensationalists are thought to believe as what the logic of the system purportedly demands.

Does dispensationalism as a system demand adherence to multiple ways of salvation? In order to understand the logic of dispensationalism, it is necessary first to specify its essence. The next task is to determine what sort of position(s) on the method of salvation would fit such a system. Specifying the essence of dispensationalism is not at all easy. A starting point, however, is Ryrie's suggestion. According to Ryrie, there are three necessary conditions of dispensationalism: (1) the distinction between Israel and the church, (2) the usage of a system of literal hermeneutics, and (3) the belief that the underlying purpose of God in the world is to produce his glory.[11] Ryrie is saying that whatever other views a dispensationalist holds, those three conditions mark him off as a dispensationalist.

Although Ryrie's suggestions are indeed helpful, I am not convinced that they present an accurate picture. It would seem unfair to assume that nondispensationalist theologians never distinguish between Israel and the church, never use literal hermeneutics, and do not recognize the glory of God as His purpose in history. It would be better to say that the dispensationalist *consistently* makes these emphases, whereas the nondispensationalist does not.

PRINCIPLES OF DISPENSATIONALISM

The matter of hermeneutics is the crucial issue for dispensationalism. For example, one who consistently uses literal hermeneutics will be on his way to distinguish consistently between Israel and the church and to focus on God's glory as His underlying purpose. In other words, consistent literal hermeneutics (as the dispensationalist understands such her-memeutics) seems to be foundational to dispensationalism. But many nondispensationalists make two claims that call into question the dispensationalists' claim to being practitioners of sound hermeneutics. (1) They claim that they consistently use literal hermeneutics. (2) They claim that dispensationalists do not consistently interpret literally, for they admit that Scripture contains figures of speech and attempt to interpret such figures. Although a full-scale discourse on hermeneutics is beyond the purpose of this study, I think that these issues are important enough to warrant some consideration.

Many nondispensationalists claim that they consistently interpret literally. But their understanding of how literal hermeneutics operates is different. In particular, they argue that literal interpretation demands that many of the Old Testament references to Israel are to be understood as typological of the church. Consequently, even on a literal interpretation, given the principle of typology that dispensationalists certainly accept, many of the Old Testament references to Israel are to be interpreted as referring to the church. After all, they argue, this was the method of many a New Testament writer. So how can nondispensationalists be blamed for doing the same? An example of this sort of thing appears in Ladd's work when he writes:

The fact is that the New Testament frequently interprets Old Testament prophecies in a way *not suggested by the Old Testament context*.

Let us take first a very simple illustration. Matthew 2:15 quotes from Hosea 11:1 to prove from Scripture that Jesus must come from Egypt. This, however, is not what the prophecy means in the Old Testament. Hosea says, "When Israel was a child, I loved him, and out of Egypt I called my son." In Hosea this is not a prophecy at all but a historical affirmation that God had called Israel out of Egypt in the Exodus. However, Matthew recognizes Jesus to be God's greater son and deliberately turns a historical statement into a prophecy. This is a principle which runs throughout biblical prophecy. *The Old Testament is reinterpreted* in light of the Christ event. . . .

The main point in the preceding section is that many Old Testament passages which applied in their historical setting to literal Israel have in the New Testament been applied to the church. What does all this have to do with the question of the millennium? Just this: The Old Testament did not clearly foresee how its own prophecies were to be fulfilled. They were fulfilled in ways quite unforeseen by the Old Testament itself and unexpected by the Jews. With regard to the first coming of Christ, *the Old Testament is interpreted by the New Testament.*

Here is the basic watershed between a dispensational and a nondispensational theology. Dispensationalism forms its eschatology by a literal interpretation of the Old Testament and then fits the New Testament into it. A nondispensational eschatology forms its theology from the explicit teaching of the New Testament.[12]

The last paragraph of Ladd's statement is crucial to the discussion. If one operates as Ladd suggests for the reasons he suggests, one can, it seems, legitimately claim to be using literal hermeneutics. However, it seems that what ultimately generates such a procedure of interpretation as suggested by Ladd is a misunderstanding of the nature of typology (whether Ladd, in fact, makes such an error is beyond my knowledge, but it would seem that the difficulty I shall mention is reflected in the thinking of many nondispensationalists). Undoubtedly, the cases cited by Ladd and others are Old Testament types of something in the New Testament. The problem stems from thinking that, just because we understand the relation of the Old Testament type to its New Testament antitype, either the Old Testament figure has no meaning other than the meaning of the antitype in the New Testament, or the meaning of the type in its own context is simply to be neglected. The point about typology is that the Old Testament type must retain its own meaning in its own context, even though it simultaneously foreshadows its antitype in the New Testament and even has a different meaning in the New Testament context. For example, Joseph may be seen as a type of Christ, which is not to say that the story of Joseph has no importance on its own apart from its relation to Christ. As a matter of fact, neglecting the integrity of the Old Testament meaning of Joseph undermines the basis for the type/antitype relation between Joseph and Christ. The failure of nondispensational interpretation at this point, then, is that its view of typology (a misunderstanding of typology, that is), ignores or minimizes the meaning of the Old Testament event or person in its own setting, just because it takes on another meaning in a New Testament context.

The fact that a type must retain its distinctive meanings in both the Old Testament and New Testament contexts is perhaps never so clearly seen as in the case of Hosea 11:1/Matthew 2:15, an example Ladd gives to prove that Old Testament passages are reinterpreted in the New Testament. Ladd is unquestionably right about Hosea 11:1 being given a new meaning in Matthew 2:15. What is problematic is that we are given the impression that the meaning of Hosea 11:1 in Hosea 11:1 either becomes the meaning given it in Matthew 2:15, or the meaning of Hosea 11:1 in its context is to be neglected. This really becomes problematic when one recognizes that Hosea 11:1 refers to a past historical event. In the case of Joel 2/Acts 2, one could argue (though incorrectly) that since Joel 2 was yet future to Joel when he wrote it, it must be understood exclusively in terms of Acts 2. However, Hosea 11 presents a different kind of case in that the event referred to in Hosea 11:1 (the Exodus) was already a historical fact at the time Hosea wrote. Therefore, even though the passage is to be seen as typical of Christ, and even though Matthew makes that typological connection, the meaning of Hosea 11:1 in its own context must not be ignored, for the sake of the type/antitype relation and because the passage had a historical referent when Hosea wrote it. The matter of typology can be summarized as follows: (1) a type must have meaning in its own context; (2) the meaning of the type in its own context is essential for a type/antitype relationship (otherwise we have an example of a parable or perhaps an allegory, but not an example of typology); and (3) ignoring items 1 and 2 threatens the very integrity of the Old Testament. The problem that arises from nondispensational approaches to typology is that they seem to neglect items 1 and 2, at best, and deny them, at worst. Consequently, whether one begins with the New Testament and goes to the Old Testament, or vice versa, should not make a bit of difference in one's interpretation of the Old Testament as long as one properly understands the implications of typology. The nondispensationalist may indeed be trying to interpret Scripture in a consistently literal way, but as long as he incorporates a faulty approach to typology, his understanding of and application of literal hermeneutics is problematic.

The claim that dispensationalists actually interpret figuratively on occasion is definitely erroneous. The error stems from neglecting to distinguish between figurative language (e.g., figures of speech) and interpreting figuratively. The former refers to certain phenomena of language itself, whereas the latter refers to a method of interpreting those or any phenomena of language. To interpret figuratively means to decide the meaning of a word or sentence without paying close attention to the denotative or connotative meaning of the words involved, without heeding the demands of context, or without paying attention to grammatical considerations. Literal interpretation, on the other hand, seeks to come to the meaning which is demanded by the denotative and/or connotative meaning of the words under consideration, by the context and by grammar. The one

who interprets literally must always be able to justify his interpretation on
the grounds of the phenomena within the context. A figurative interpretation is tied only loosely to the context. Consequently, we can say that either
figures of speech or nonfigurative language may be interpreted figuratively or literally. Recognizing that language contains figures of speech
does not indicate that an exegete interprets figuratively.

The keys to determining whether or not one is a dispensationalist rest
in hermeneutical, ecclesiological, and eschatological issues, not soteriology. Obviously, the distinction between Israel and the church is of crucial
import for both eschatology and ecclesiology. I do not, however, see any
soteriological position that is inherent to and thus necessitated by dispensationalism. Thus, the question of whether dispensationalism necessitates a multiple methods of salvation view, or a single way of salvation
position is irrelevant. Soteriology is not the determinative area for dispensationalism. For example, if one consistently distinguishes between
Israel and the church and applies that distinction throughout his
ecclesiology and eschatology, will he be forced to hold any particular view
on the methods of salvation issue? It would seem that distinguishing
between Israel and the church could fit either a single or multiple method
view. One could, without contradicting his system, claim that God has in
general two separate programs for the two distinct groups. But He saves
both groups by one method of salvation. On the other hand, one could also
claim, without contradicting his own position, that God not only works
with two separate groups, but that He saves them in different ways.
Concerning the glory of God issue, it would seem that the notion of God's
purpose ultimately being His glory fits with either view. One way of
salvation for all will bring glory to God. But then multiple ways would
not have to bring God disgrace.

Notice that at this point I am not speaking about what Scripture actually teaches. My concern is to focus on the intrinsic ideas of dispensationalism and to ask what a dispensationalist could hold without
contradicting his position, even if Scripture does not teach something
that he could hold. As for the matter of hermeneutics, it should also be
obvious that literal hermeneutics, as I have described them, would lead
one to hold multiple ways of salvation, if Scripture, interpreted literally,
demanded such. Such hermeneutics would lead one to hold a single way of
salvation, if Scripture, interpreted literally, demanded such. As a result, I
must reiterate that there is nothing intrinsic to dispensationalism's hermeneutics that necessitates either a single or multiple methods view. I
know there are critics of dispensationalism who would disagree, but I
think they are reacting to what they think dispensationalists hold, rather
than to the logic of the system itself. The point is that neither a dis-

pensationalist's hermeneutics nor any doctrinal views he has gained from exegesis of Scripture commit him to holding a multiple or single method view of salvation. Before the dispensationalist does a detailed study of the text of Scripture, it is not inevitable that he will come to any particular view on the method of salvation.

In the preceding discussion, we demonstrated to be invalid the charge that a dispensationalist must hold one or the other view regarding single or multiple methods of salvation. However, that does not answer the question of what a dispensationalist *should* hold. Obviously, what he should hold is whatever Scripture actually teaches, regardless of what positions could be made to fit with his system. That being the case, what should he hold? Given what Scripture actually says, it would seem that a dispensationalist should hold to multiple methods of salvation if and only if Scripture, when interpreted according to literal hermeneutics as the dispensationalist understands such, teaches such a view. In view of the comments in Galatians 3:11 about the law, and in view of Hebrews 11, which teaches that Old Testament saints were saved by faith, it would seem that a dispensationalist should not hold that more than one method of salvation is taught in Scripture. Of course, the dispensationalist may be inconsistent in his hermeneutics, and in that case a multiple methods view would be understandable (but wrong). However, if he interprets Scripture by the method his system tells him to use, then he will not in fact hold to multiple methods of salvation. Happily, most dispensationalists, for whatever reason, do hold that only one way of salvation is taught in Scripture. To that view I also subscribe.

Having come to this point, we have indeed accomplished much. We have established that (1) it is the consensus of both dispensationalists and nondispensationalists that Scripture teaches only one method of salvation, that (2) dispensationalism as a system, contrary to the views of some, does not necessitate multiple methods of salvation, even though it could fit such a position, that (3) dispensationalism also fits with a single method of salvation view, and that (4) a dispensationalist, to be consistent with his foundational principle, should hold that only one method of salvation is taught in Scripture.

But what is that one method of salvation? There are many differing opinions on that subject. The disagreement does not lie in the matter of whether salvation is by faith or works. Dispensationalists and nondispensationalists agree that it is by faith. Hebrews 11 lists the great Old Testament heroes of the faith and indicates that they were saved by faith. Moreover, as one studies the list, it becomes obvious that those included represent different stages in the progress of God's revelation concerning himself and His plan of salvation. Both dispensational and nondispensational interpreters agree that in all ages God had graciously required of man faith, not works. Oehler states the matter nicely when he writes:

> The *law*, by always pointing back *to God's electing grace*, and onward to God's just retribution, as the foundation of the righteousness of the law, presupposes *faith, i.e.* such a *trusting submission to the covenant God* as was exhibited in *Abraham's* believing adherence to the Divine promise. This is in conformity with that fundamental declaration, Gen. xv. 6, "He believed in the Lord, and He counted it to him for righteousness".... Accordingly the requirement of faith runs through the entire Old Testament. The leading of Israel, from the time of its deliverance out of Egypt, Ex. iv. 31, xiv. 31, comp. especially Deut. i. 32, ix. 23, and many other passages, rests entirely on faith. But in proportion as its Divine election seemed to human apprehension thwarted, and the promise of redemption forfeited, by the apostasy of the nation and the judgments thereby incurred, the more emphatically is it asserted how all-important *faith* was, as the root of all righteousness, and the condition on which the blessing was to be obtained.[13]

Faith, then, is recognized by all as requisite for salvation. But faith in what or whom? At this point opinions diverge. That divergence does not fall neatly along the lines of dispensationalism versus nondispensationalism. Even those working within the same broad system of theology do not entirely agree on this matter. But there is a nondispensational approach that has many affinities to other nondispensational positions (though not identical to all such positions).

The position of Charles Hodge on this issue is most helpful, for he not only claims that faith is the key, but he also explains in detail what the revealed content of faith is at all times. Hodge begins by explaining that in all dispensations, Jesus Christ is the Redeemer. He writes:

> It is no less clear that the Redeemer is the same under all dispensations. He who was predicted as the seed of the woman, as the seed of Abraham, the Son of David, the Branch, the Servant of the Lord, the Prince of Peace, is our Lord, Jesus Christ, the Son of God, God manifest in the flesh. He, therefore, from the beginning has been held up as the hope of the world, the SALVATOR HOMINUM.[14]

Hodge's statement is most interesting. On the one hand, I can agree with parts of it, for in a certain sense which I shall mention, I hold that, indeed, Christ is the Redeemer at all times. On the other hand, it is another thing to say that Jesus Christ is the One who from the beginning "has been held up as the hope of the world." If Hodge means nothing more than that Christ's work is the ground of redemption for all ages, I have no problems. If, on the other hand, the statement means that Jesus Christ has literally been the revealed content presented to men from the very beginning, I have tremendous problems. It is definitely debatable as to how much understanding there was of the full import of the prophecies about the Messiah or how much the truth about Christ's coming redemptive work was involved in the presentation of the gospel in the Old Testament. What does not seem to be the case is that men consciously believed in *Jesus* Christ, for we do not find until the New Testament the explicitly stated revelation that Jesus of Nazareth is the long-awaited Christ. Although it is always possible that the Holy Spirit could have revealed the truth about *Jesus* to an eager seeker, it seems to overlook the progress of revelation to say that knowledge of Jesus was universally or even widely known in Old Testament times. Consequently, when Hodge specifies the content of faith, he goes too far. He writes:

As the same promise was made to those who lived before the advent which is now made to us in the gospel, as the same Redeemer was revealed to them who is presented as the object of faith to us, it of necessity follows that the condition, or terms of salvation, was the same then as now. It was not mere faith or trust in God, or simply piety, which was required, but faith in the promised Redeemer, or faith in the promise of redemption through the Messiah.[15]

Although I would not want to deny that God revealed as early as Genesis 3:15 that One would come to take care of the sin problem, I find it very hard to accept the notion that the promise of redemption through Jesus Christ was so clearly understood or so exclusively held to be the sole revealed content of God's method for handling sin, as Hodge seems to think. It seems that those who hold this view are so concerned to uphold the unity of God's redemptive program that they do not entirely do justice to the truth of the progress of revelation. Moreover, if there were no other way to uphold the unity of God's redemptive work, I suspect I would be drawn to this view, but as I shall point out, there seems to be a satisfactory way to uphold the unity of redemption without weakening the truth of progressive revelation.

Some might object that Old Testament believers obviously knew the truth about Christ, in light of passages like 1 Peter 1:11–12 and Hebrews 11:13. At the outset, let me make two points. First, I am not denying that God *could* have revealed the truth about Jesus to Old Testament saints. But I doubt that He did on any widespread basis. The passages in question do not state that He did. Second, even if someone like Hodge is correct, and even if the dispensationalist agrees with Hodge, I do not see that such an eventuality would necessitate abandoning dispensationalism. Since dispensationalism is not about whether Christ was the revealed content of faith in the Old Testament, a dispensationalist can certainly hold that He was, without having to surrender his dispensationalism.

Now, what does 1 Peter 1:10–12 actually say? According to verse 11, the Old Testament prophets wanted to know what the Holy Spirit was revealing about the kind of time (*poion kairon*) it would be and the kind of events there would be (*tina*), when the Holy Spirit informed them of the sufferings of the Messiah. What is obvious from this verse is that Old Testament saints did know about a coming suffering Savior. No one disagrees that such information was available. But it seems erroneous to conclude on the basis of this passage that they knew that Jesus of Nazareth would be that suffering Messiah. In verse 12 we are told that in response to their questions, the prophets learned essentially that the time of fulfillment was not their own time. They were prophesying of things that would occur in the lifetime of others. Certainly, there is no statement to the effect that they were or were not informed that the Messiah would be Jesus of Nazareth. They may have been so informed, but 1 Peter 1:10–12 neither proves nor disproves that. Arguments from silence are consistent with everything and consequently prove nothing.

When we turn to Hebrews 11:13, we find a similar case to that of 1 Peter 1:10–12. The verse speaks of many Old Testament saints who, through the time of Abraham, died without seeing the promises of God fulfilled, though they were aware of those promises. Considering the promises made through the time of Abraham, it becomes clear that God had revealed that some day a redeemer would come to put away sin. It is not stated that the redeemer would be Jesus of Nazareth. Consequently, it would be entirely possible for the saint to see the promises, as verse 13 says, and still not know about Jesus. It would also be *possible* that he had been told about Jesus. But Hebrews 11:13 does not say whether these saints in fact did or did not know about Jesus of Nazareth. Again, the argument from silence is inconclusive.

In summarizing this matter, Payne's comments are helpful in gaining a proper perspective of the issue. Payne writes, "Union with Christ is the only way of salvation; and 'Christ in you, the hope of glory,' was a 'mystery' that was hidden to the Old Testament saints (Col. 1:27) only in respect to the exact knowledge of the Savior's Person, and not in respect to its practical efficacy."[16] Though I cannot fully agree with Payne's perspective on the relation of union with Christ to the Old Testament saint, I agree with his comments about knowledge of Jesus in the Old Testament.

The basic objection to a position like Hodge's is that it does not seem to pay adequate attention to the implications of progressive revelation. Consequently, the Old Testament saint seems to be granted more revelation and more understanding of revelation than Scripture seems to indicate he actually had.

THE IMPLEMENTATION OF SALVATION

Is it possible to give proper weight to the progress of revelation without fragmenting the redemptive plan of God to the point of claiming that God operates according to multiple ways of salvation? I should like to argue that a commitment to allowing the truth of progressive revelation to hold its full weight does not necessitate a subscription to multiple methods of salvation. In order to support this claim, I shall present what I take to be God's one method of salvation, operative throughout Scripture. At the outset, it would seem to be crucially important to understand that though God always uses the same method of saving men (the point which preserves unity of redemption and of the redeemed), what He reveals about that method is progressively amplified and necessitates changes in the way the believer expresses the fact that he has appropriated God's one method of salvation (the points that allow for the diversity demanded by progressive revelation). The full import of this statement will be understood as I unfold what I take to be God's method of salvation.

In attempting to set forth God's plan of salvation, it is essential to recognize initially that at all times in history salvation must begin with God's gracious activity. Paul's statement in Ephesians 2:8 that "by grace are ye saved," is true of every believer, regardless of the dispensation in which he lives. The major reason that salvation must be a result of God's gracious activity lies in the condition of man. God demands absolute righteousness of any creature who would be saved. But no one except Christ ever met such standards (Psalm 14:3; Rom. 3:10-12). The problem is complicated by the fact that not only is no one righteous, but that no one even has the ability to live a perfectly righteous life (John. 1:13; 3:5; 6:44; 8:34; Rom. 7:18, 24; 8:7, 8; 2 Cor. 3:5; Eph. 2:1, 8-10; Heb. 11:6). Given man's inability to do right in God's eyes (man's problem ever since the Fall), if God were to deal with men in strict justice alone, no one would be saved. Thus, since God has chosen to save men, He extends divine grace toward them. The ways in which such grace expresses itself may vary at different times, but what is constant is that God's method of salvation is always a grace method, never a works method.

God works, then, in a gracious way to save people. But how does He express that grace? In other words, what specific gracious thing(s) has God done to save men? In order to understand God's gracious dealings in saving men, it would seem helpful to make and explain some key distinctions.[17] I should like to distinguish between the basis, or ground, of salvation, the requirement for salvation, the ultimate content of salvation, the specific revealed content of salvation to be accepted, and the believer's expression of his salvation. The first three are constant throughout all dispensations, whereas the latter two change. This approach, as we shall see, allows for unity of salvation without ignoring the progress of revelation and God's different administering orders for the world. It should also be noted that the first item deals with the objective work of God which provides and pays for salvation so that it is available to be offered, whereas the latter four focus on items involved in the subjective application of salvation to the believer and his life as a believer.

BASIS, OR GROUND, OF SALVATION

God has graciously acted in an objective way so that man can be saved. What He has done constitutes the basis, or ground, of salvation. In other words, because of this act, God can extend salvation to men at all times. The basis of salvation is nothing other than God's gracious provision of the death of Christ. The reason that Christ's death must be the basis is stated in Leviticus 17:11, according to which blood must be shed, if there is to be atonement for sin (cf. Heb. 9:22). But not just any blood fully and finally removes sin. If so, one could argue that the blood of sacrificial animals fully and completely removes sin. However, the writer of Hebrews explicitly states that the blood of bulls and goats could not take away sin, for only the blood of Christ could do that (Heb. 10:4ff.). The implications of this verse for the significance of Old Testament sacrifices will be discussed more fully later. At this point, suffice it to say that the verse implies that animal sacrifices could not in any dispensation be the ultimate basis for God's removal of sin. Moreover, there is no indication whatsoever in Scripture that the blood of a human being would atone for sin. Therefore, since God demands the shedding of blood for removing sin, and since no human or animal blood will suffice to atone for sin fully, the ultimate ground, or basis, upon which God can offer salvation at any time in history has to be the sacrifice of Christ.

Christ's sacrifice is the ground, but what does that involve? First, it does *not* mean that at all times in human history the death of Jesus Christ was already a historical fact. Though God decreed the event prior to history, it still had to be accomplished within history. It did not become a historical fact until it actually occurred. Second, claiming that Christ's death is the ground of salvation does *not* mean that at all times in history God had revealed that the death of Jesus of Nazareth is the sole basis for granting salvation. It is most unlikely that anyone knew that before His advent. Progressive revelation must be given its due. What is meant by saying that Christ's death is the ground of salvation is that from God's perspective, the sacrifice of Christ is the objective act on the grounds of which God offers salvation in any age. In trying to understand how this can be so before the event occurs historically, we must distinguish between God's perspective and man's. God has known about Christ's death from all eternity. Since He decreed it, it was an accomplished fact in His thinking long before it was an accomplished fact in history. Because God knows that the deed will be done (since He decreed it), and because He sees all of history (including the completed work of Christ) at once, God can grant man salvation, even before the sacrifice is performed in history. There could never have been a time in human history when God would learn that He had been mistaken about the fact that Christ would sacrifice Himself for sin. Although there is no past, present, or future for God, He, as an omniscient being, cannot help but know what is past, present, and future for the creatures He has made. Thus, God always sees Christ's work as an accomplished fact. But before it was done within history God knew that the death of Jesus Christ had not been accomplished in history. Man, limited by his human perspective, did not know about the atoning work of Jesus Christ until God revealed it and then accomplished it within human history.

In sum, in order to gain a proper perspective on this matter, one must avoid two mistakes, both of which involve confusing God's perspective with man's. The first error is thinking that God neither knows nor sees any more than we do. The people of the Old Testament era did not know that *Jesus* was the Messiah, that *Jesus* would die, and that His death would be the basis of salvation. But that is not to say that God did not know. God did know at all times that Christ's death was as good as accomplished. Consequently, He could grant salvation on the basis of it. The second error comes from assuming that because God understood the full import of the death of Jesus and granted salvation on the basis of it, everyone in the Old Testament also must have had that information and must have understood it. I see no reason that God's knowledge and man's must have coincided on this issue before Jesus. I see no indication that at all times God's and man's knowledge of these matters totally coincided.

REQUIREMENT OF SALVATION

This refers to what is required of man in order for him to be saved (although God enables man to do what he does). It does not refer to what

God must do either objectively or in the subjective application process in order for man to be saved. Scripture is very clear that no one is saved by attempting to perform a good act in his own power. In fact, no one on his own is capable of an act that is righteous in God's eyes (Psalm 14:3; Rom. 3:10-12). It is certainly doubtful that even Adam, before the Fall, totally on his own without any divine enablement was capable of performing any act of moral good in God's eyes. When Adam did act on his own, he committed the first sin (Gen. 3). Not only is it futile to attempt to gain salvation by good works in general, but as Scripture teaches clearly even complete adherence to the Mosaic law (difficult as that would be) would not justify anyone (Gal. 2:16; 3:11). Performance of religious rites simply for the sake of the rite will not save anyone, for God desires something else (Psalm 51:16-17). According to Scripture, the sole requirement for salvation is that man exercise faith in the provision that God has revealed. Faith is not to be considered a meritorious work on man's part, for Scripture affirms everywhere that faith, as all of salvation, is God's gift to man (Eph. 2:8; Rom. 6:23; 2 Tim. 2:9). There is no question that faith is clearly taught as the sole requirement for salvation in the New Testament. Equally clear is the message that faith was the only prerequisite during Old Testament times. Even if one were to miss that point from a study of the Old Testament, he could hardly miss the explicit teaching in Hebrews 11 on what men in the Old Testament period did to be saved. God always requires that man respond in faith to whatever He reveals concerning salvation.

ULTIMATE CONTENT OF SALVATION

Scripture is very clear about this matter. The ultimate object of faith in any and every age is God Himself. The ultimate issue at any time in history is whether a man will take God at His word and exercise faith in the provision for salvation which God reveals. The message of Hebrews 11 is again instructive, for it repeatedly emphasizes that each hero of faith did what he did because of his faith in God (cf. Rom. 4:3). Moreover, it is interesting to note that the prophets do not call the backslidden people to return to the sacrificial system or even to a renewed belief in the promises of God. Instead, the plea is to return to God (Jer. 3:1, 12, 14, 22; 4:1; Ezek. 33:11; Hos. 12:6; 14:1; Joel 2:12 are examples of the prevalence of this message in the prophets).[18] Clearly, whatever religious rites, good works, and so on a person might begin or resume, and whatever promises he might reaffirm, the repentant sinner was ultimately turning or returning to God. In all times, He is the ultimate object of faith. Even today when we ask men to believe in Jesus Christ as their personal savior, we are asking for an ultimate commitment to God. He is the one who has revealed that salvation is available through faith in Christ. Moreover, a rejection of Christ constitutes a refusal to believe God's word about Christ; it is a rejection of God Himself.

SPECIFIC REVEALED CONTENT OF SALVATION

All the items discussed so far have remained constant as the dispensations changed. But not everything in regard to salvation is constant. It seems clear that the specific revealed content to be believed changes at various times in history. One may believe that at all times men have believed in Jesus of Nazareth, the Christ, for salvation. But still he cannot deny that at various times God has given more information than previously specified about that Christ. For the one who does not hold that men at all times have consciously known about and believed in Jesus, the conclusion that the specific revealed content changes is especially clear. There are several key points in connection with this matter.

First, it is important to remember that since in each economy the content is what God has revealed, belief in the content for that age is belief in the ultimate object of faith, God. The believer is ultimately trusting God when he responds positively to the truth for his dispensation: believing in the promises (age of promise), agreeing that God will forgive and cleanse the sin of the one who in faith offers sacrifice (age of law), or placing his faith and trust in Jesus as Savior (age of grace). Thus, it is not, for example, the performance of the sacrifices or a belief in the sacrificial system per se that saved someone living under the Mosaic law. Instead, what saved a person then was a commitment to the God who had revealed that sin was to be expiated through sacrifices made in faith that God would give atonement. Therefore, in agreeing to respond positively to the specific content for any given age, the believer was ultimately responding to the God who revealed the content. Romans 4:3, for example, says that Abraham believed God, and it was counted to him for righteousness. Of course, someone might respond, "He believed the promises, didn't he?" Certainly, he did, but the point is that in doing so, he was believing the God who gave the promises.

The second point about the content of revealed truth is especially important. The content of faith is cumulative throughout Scripture. This should not seem strange in view of progressive revelation, but nonetheless, it needs explanation. There must be a message at all times (a gospel, so to speak) which tells men about God and His plan for salvation and urges them to respond. From the beginning through the time of the law, the information that God had revealed about salvation (information that could have been put into a message, even if it never was in terms of all it involved) was cumulative as revelation progressed. This means that an individual was not to ignore whatever God had said about Himself and His method of salvation in previous ages. (The amplification of revelation might require that man express his faith in different ways. However, that is a different matter that I shall discuss shortly.)

Thus whatever God has presented to be believed in one age may be amplified and/or supplemented in another age, but it is not canceled. For example, the person responding in faith for salvation under the Mosaic law is also responding to the God of the promises to Abraham, the God of the Exodus, the God of the Noahic covenant. Consequently, the believer living in the time of the Mosaic law is not to ignore that a reason for believing in God is that he has given certain promises to Abraham that are also applicable to the one under law. He may emphasize in his thinking what God has done for Israel most recently, but whatever God had said and done previously is not unimportant. All are reasons for faith. Even if the believer did not understand that he was committing himself to the God who had done all these things and revealed all these things about Himself in the past, nonetheless, he was making a commitment to such a God. It makes no sense to say that someone living in the time of Abraham, for example, believed the content of the promises, but that nothing else God had ever said was part of the content. Moreover, Galatians 3:12ff. states clearly that the promises that Abraham believed were not and could not be annulled just because God revealed the law to Israel (Gal. 3:16–17). These are just some examples in support of my contention that the content of faith during the Old Testament times was cumulative.

The advent of the age of grace maintains a certain continuity. What the Old Testament pointed toward is fulfilled in Christ. When a person believes in Christ as Savior, he is committing himself (whether or not he recognizes it) to the God who brought Israel out of Egypt and the God who gave the Mosaic law. It is the same God, and thus, the specific content of faith can be seen to be cumulative throughout the whole of Scripture. The emphasis in the age of grace is, of course, on what God has done through Christ. In fact, the gospel message may not even include a comment about what God had done for Israel in the past. However, since what God has done through Christ is the culmination of what He had done and said previously, the believer during the age of grace is committing himself to the God of the promises, the God of the Exodus, the God of the Mosaic law, and the God and Father of our Lord Jesus Christ, even if the believer, when he responds, does not understand that, since the emphasis of the message is on Christ.

An example of a message that included a rehearsal of all God had done in the past is Stephen's speech (Acts 7). Granted, the speech was an indictment against his listeners. But the indictment is so strong because

Stephen appeals over and over to what God had done for Israel through-out history and to Israel's refusal to believe him. Stephen completes his indictment by pointing to the fact that this same God whom Israel had rejected has now sent Christ. Just as they should have trusted God in the past but did not, so they were in Stephen's time rejecting God and His Messiah. Stephen's speech met a negative response. Nonetheless, the cumulative emphasis of his speech seems most instructive in regard to the matter before us.

OLD TESTAMENT SACRIFICES

In order to understand the idea of cumulative content more fully, we must know what that content was. Two broad strands run throughout the Old Testament content presented to man as the reason for placing faith in God.

First, the entire Old Testament (viewed as comprising several dis-pensations or not viewed dispensationally at all) teaches that blood sac-rifice is of utmost importance in order for man to maintain a right stand-ing before God. (The exact soteriological relevance of these sacrifices will be discussed later.) This teaching appears before Leviticus 17:11. As early as Genesis 3:15, it is seen that someone must die in order ultimately to defeat sin. The theme of sacrifice is continued in Genesis 3:21. God cov-ered Adam and Eve with animal skins. Obviously, animals had been killed to provide this covering. In Genesis 4, Abel's blood sacrifice was acceptable to God, whereas Cain's offering was not. It seems that Cain demonstrated disbelief in refusing to bring a blood sacrifice. In view of Genesis 3:21, the information about blood sacrifice would have been available to Cain. He chose to ignore it and thereby expressed his rejec-tion of God and of his method of coming to Himself. During the time of Noah (Gen. 8:20), sacrifices were still important. God did not abrogate that revelation. Certainly, during the time of Abraham, sacrifices were of crucial importance in man's relation to God. We see Abraham sacrificing to God on various occasions (e.g., Gen. 12:7-8; 13:3-4). The Abrahamic covenant itself was ratified with Abraham as God passed among the pieces of the sacrifice on the altar (Gen. 15). In subjecting Abraham to the ultimate test of his faith, God requested him to sacrifice his son Isaac (Gen. 22, a passage that beautifully prefigures Christ's sacrifice). When God redeemed Israel from Egypt, a lamb was slain, and its blood was applied to the doorposts of the houses. Clearly, during the age of promise, sacrifices were significant. With the giving of the Mosaic law, sacrifices were still important. The system of sacrifices became more elaborate, as the kinds of sacrifices to be given and the uses of such sacrifices were delineated. Finally, during the time of law it became more clearly evident that a person would have to be sacrificed for sin (Isa. 53; Dan. 9:24-26). God's suffering servant, the promised Messiah, would have to die for the sins of His people (cf. Dan. 9:24-26—commentators generally agree that in order for the things mentioned in verse 24 to be accomplished, Messiah the prince would be cut off, as mentioned in verse 26).

In addition to the theme of sacrifice, there is the theme of promises. Some promises concern salvation from sin and thus overlap the theme of sacrifice. Others are of a national, political, and social nature. Walter Kaiser has argued that the theological center of the Old Testament canon is the notion of promise.[19] One can hardly read Kaiser's work and not be convinced that the concept of promise is crucially important for the whole of Old Testament life.

Thus we see that in each period of the Old Testament economy, the specific content revealed for men to believe involved truths about sacrifices and promises. The change of dispensations did not abrogate existing promises but rather supplemented and amplified them. Passages such as Genesis 3:15-16, Genesis 9 (Noahic covenant), Genesis 12 and 15 (Abrahamic covenant), Deuteronomy 28-30 (Palestinian covenant), 2 Samuel 7 (Davidic covenant), and Jeremiah 31 (New Covenant) show that even though dispensations changed, God did not abrogate His promises. He amplified and clarified them.

Promises were not only important in terms of believing that in the future God would do what He promised. They were also important from the standpoint of past fulfillment. The ways God had demonstrated His faithfulness in the past formed a basis for trust in Him for salvation and for fulfillment of promises in the future. Paul states very clearly that the giving of the law did not nullify the promises made to Abraham (Gal. 3:16-17). God's revelation concerning His promises is cumulative.

The specific content to be believed, then, was cumulative, and it was composed of two major components: sacrifice and promise.[20] The believing Jew, therefore, whether he understood what he was doing or not, was committing himself to the God of the promises, the God who had faithfully formed the nation of Israel and brought her out of Egypt and into the land, and the God who had revealed all along that sin could be atoned for by means of blood sacrifice. This is what it means to say that the content of faith in the Old Testament is cumulative. The person who committed himself in faith to that God, and all that He had revealed about His saving and keeping power, was saved.

But only since the time of Jesus Christ has the revealed content to be believed coincided entirely with the basis, or ground, of faith. During the age of grace, God has revealed the fulness of salvation through the shed blood of Jesus Christ (the basis of salvation in any age). Neither God's acts in history nor His revelation concerning His acts had given man the complete content about Christ. We must be careful not to think that during the Old Testament economy it was necessary to accept the content over and over again to be saved. For example, one might think that since during Old Testament times a sacrifice was required for each sin, the person was being saved with each sacrifice. As we shall see, such a view is a misunderstanding of the function of Old Testament sacrifices as well as a confusion of the requirement for salvation with the expression of faith that a saved person would make. Moreover, merely doing sacrifices never justified anyone. What did justify the repentant sinner was a one-time commitment to the God who had revealed that sin was to be atoned for by blood sacrifice (as well as whatever else He revealed for that economy). The Old Testament believer might fall out of fellowship with the Lord and need to return to Him, but there does not seem to be an indication that once a person was saved he could lose that salvation and needed to be saved over again.

BELIEVER'S EXPRESSION OF SALVATION

Just as the specific content of faith changes as revelation progresses (the content is cumulative), so there is an aspect of change in regard to the fifth element of salvation, the believer's expression of his salvation. It is crucially important not to confuse this element with the requirement for salvation. The requirement (faith) confronts a *nonbeliever* as he contemplates God's message of salvation. The specific expression of faith confronts the *believer* as he contemplates how he is to live out the salvation he has already been given. It is his way of responding to God in obedience as evidence that he has already believed.

The believer's expression of faith must take into consideration at any given point in history three kinds of elements. First, elements that are constant, such as the moral law. Since the moral law reflects the nature of an unchanging God, it, too, is always binding. Thus, at all times, a believer is to express the fact that he is saved by adhering to the moral law. Such adherence will not save him, but it will provide evidence that he already has met the requirement of salvation. Second, in any given age, there seem to be elements that conclude with a given age. A good example of this is the bringing of animal sacrifices. Through the time of the Mosaic law, the offering of such sacrifices was important as the believer expressed his trust in God. However, with the advent of the age of grace, the believer no longer expresses his devotion to God through bringing animal sacrifices. There are ways by which he can receive cleansing from sin as a believer and express his devotion to God, but animal sacrifice is not one of them. Finally, there are items in the believer's expression of his faith that commence in a given age. For example, in the age of grace the believer can express his obedience to the Savior through observance of the Lord's Supper and baptism. Before the age of grace, such expressions of faith were not open to the believer.

A final point in regard to the expression of faith is simply to reiterate that though it may change from one age to another, it does not entail a change in God's one method of saving men. How could it, since it has nothing to do with what God and the nonbeliever do in order to bring the nonbeliever to the point of (in New Testament terms) conversion, regeneration, and justification?

In the previous pages, I have suggested what I take to be God's one method of salvation as taught by all of Scripture. Even the items that vary from one dispensation to the next (specific revealed content of faith and expression of faith) do not necessitate multiple ways of salvation. Moreover, it seems obvious that one could hold the kind of position I have espoused and remain a consistent dispensationalist. Nothing mentioned seems to contradict anything essential to dispensationalism.

Our discussion so far has stressed the unity in God's method of salvation. But is anything different (besides the items mentioned) about being a believer in Old Testament times, as opposed to New Testament times? Certainly the method of salvation is the same, but is everything else equal as well? This question is important for a proper understanding not only of the two testaments, but also for a proper conception of the distinctions between biblical Judaism and biblical Christianity. Moreover, in specifying the differences between the two, we want to be careful not to contradict what has just been presented, that is, we do not want to derive differences that will necessitate multiple ways of salvation, since it has already been argued that God uses only one way. What, then, seem to be the key differences?

The first and obvious difference is that the content of faith presented to the believer and the expression of his faith differ, as has been noted.

Second, the believer's relation to the law has changed (an aspect of the change particularly involved in the expression of his faith). The Mosaic system distinguishes between the moral law, the ceremonial law (rules and regulations regarding clean or unclean, as well as the whole sacrificial system and all the regulations about the Tabernacle, for example), and the civil law (application of the moral law to certain features of Israel's community life).[21] But the New Testament believer in Jesus Christ is no longer under the civil law or the ceremonial law. God's standards of morality do not change. The two testaments take different approaches toward obedience to the law. Put simply (perhaps too simply), the Old Testament approach can be characterized as "do and you shall live," whereas in the New Testament the approach seems to be "you are; therefore, do." But the oft-heard comment that in the New Testament believers keep the law out of love, obviously implying that Old Testament believers kept it out of obligation, is not consistent with passages such as Psalm 119: 16, 35, 47, 70, 77, 92, 143, 174, which speak of delight in the commandments of the Lord.

Third, the New Testament believer receives a much greater enablement for obedience to God in virtue of the indwelling Holy Spirit. The Old Testament speaks of the Holy Spirit coming upon a person for a special enduement of power for a particular task (e.g., the case of Saul as recorded in 1 Sam. 10:6; 11:6; and 18:12; the case of craftsmen working on the Tabernacle as noted in Exod. 31:1-11; Micah as recorded in Mic. 3:8; the seventy elders as recorded in Num. 11:16-17, 24-30; and in the cases of some of Israel's judges as seen in Judg. 3:10; 6:34; 11:29; 13:25; 14:6, 19; 15:14). But there is no mention of the indwelling of the Holy Spirit, as found in the New Testament (Rom. 8:9, 11; 1 Cor. 3:16; 2 Tim. 1:14; 1 John 3:24).[22]

Fourth, the 'εν Χριστῷ (en christō) relationship, union of the believer with Christ, is part and parcel of the New Testament believer's salvation, whereas that relationship does not pertain to salvation of an Old Testament saint. Such union with Christ is accomplished by means of the ministry of the Holy Spirit whereby He baptizes the believer into the Body of Christ (1 Cor. 12:13). But the Holy Spirit did not begin to perform that ministry until the day of Pentecost (Acts 2).

Finally, though there was forgiveness for sin in both the Old and the New Testaments,[23] sin was only fully and finally paid for when Christ made His sacrifice. This point is fully developed and explained below.

SOTERIOLOGICAL FUNCTION OF OLD TESTAMENT SACRIFICES

At this point, I should like to consider the function of the sacrificial system in the Old Testament. In particular, I am interested in clarifying the soteriological function of Old Testament sacrifices.

The Mosaic system of sacrifices is very complex, and it is not always easy to distinguish the meaning and function of the various sacrifices. Nonetheless, for our purposes it would seem possible to clarify at least some of the different offerings that Scripture mentions. First, there is the עֹלָה ('ōlâ) or burnt offering (Lev. 1; 6:8-13). Payne suggests that this offering was the "continual burnt offering" (mentioned in Exod. 29:38-42) and that it symbolized the idea of complete and continuous atonement and consecration.[25] Second, the מִנְחָה (minhâ) or meal offering (Lev. 2; 6:14-23) symbolized especially the devotion of one's person and property to the Lord.[26] Third, there is the category of offerings designated as peace offerings (Lev. 3; 7). Three offerings fall under this category, i.e., the thank offering, the vow, and the freewill offering. Oehler distinguishes the three as follows:

> The זֶבַח תּוֹדָה [*zebaḥ tôdâ*] being offered without having been previously promised for some benefit received, and thus referring to a favor not already supplicated . . . , was the highest among the שְׁלָמִים [*shelāmîm*]. The vow, נֶדֶר [*neder*], on the contrary, is a promised offering usually presented *after the reception* of some benefit previously entreated; yet the one making a promise might connect an offering immediately with his prayer, and it would fall under this species; but the נֶדֶר [*neder*] always refers to something distinctly prayed for. And lastly, the נְדָבָה [*nedābâ*] is every free gift for which there was no other occasion than the will of the offerer, whom his heart impelled to show his thankful sense of all the blessings which the goodness of God had bestowed on him.[27]

The final three offerings are the sin, guilt, and trespass offerings. The precise distinction between the three is a matter of debate, a debate that lies beyond the scope and purpose of this study. Suffice it to say, these are the offerings that deal specifically with atoning for sin.[28]

What does the Mosaic system teach about the meaning of these sacrifices? In other words, how are they to be understood? What is their purpose? Unfortunately, there is no unanimity in regard to the meaning of sacrifices. In examining this topic, we shall consider it from two distinct perspectives, (1) that of the idea behind the sacrifice, and (2) that of the relation between the sacrifice and the sacrificer.

The idea behind sacrifice. Here there is indeed no unanimity. Oehler is helpful in speaking of the basic idea of pre-Mosaic sacrifice, although our main concern is with the Mosaic system. He claims the ideas of expiation and atonement are not the most significant ideas behind pre-Mosaic sacrifices (although they are hinted at). Oehler writes:

> The pre-Mosaic offerings had the signification of *thank-offerings and offerings of supplication,* though a propitiatory element is connected with the burnt-offering (first mentioned Gen. viii. 20) lying in the רֵיחַ נִיחֹחַ [*rêaḥ nîḥōḥ*] (literally, odor of satisfaction), through which the sacrifice has an appeasing effect, see ver. 21. Offerings for atonement, in the strict sense, are not mentioned in the Old Testament before the introduction of the Mosaic sacrificial law. The book of Job, too, which brings before us the customs of the age of the patriarchs, represents, in chap. i. 5, xlii. 8, the presenting of burnt-offerings for sin

committed, and avoids the term כִּפֶּר [*kipper*], which denotes *expiation* in the terminology of Mosaic sacrifice (giving, instead, the more general term קִדַּשׁ [*qiddash*]).[29]

According to Oehler, the offerings were not expiatory in the strict sense because "an *expiatory offering,* in the strict sense, presupposes the revelation of divine holiness in the law, and the entrance of the people into covenant relation with the holy God."[30] But it would seem that expiation in the strict sense is not part of pre-Mosaic sacrifices. Nonetheless, expiation is present in some sense, as even Oehler's evidence indicates. Of course, he is also correct in pointing out the significance of thanksgiving and supplication in many of the offerings.

J. Barton Payne delineates four different approaches to sacrifice, and rejects the first three. First, some of a liberal persuasion have suggested that sacrifice was intended to be a meal, nourishing the deity (cf. Gen. 8:20). As Payne suggests, this theory does not square with Old Testament teachings, for among other things, Psalm 50:9–13 and Isaiah 40:16 indicate that God has no need of sacrifices for any purposes.[31] Second, there are those who understand Old Testament sacrifices as gifts. Payne points, for example, to Vos's claim that the two main ends served by sacrifice are expiation and consecration.[32] Payne claims that although there is an element of truth in this conception, it does not explain the necessity for blood. It is estrangement from God that necessitates blood, not the desire to consecrate oneself.[33] It is interesting that Payne does not focus on the fact that Vos specifies both expiation and consecration. He restricts his comments solely to the matter of consecration. Third, the Canaanites viewed sacrifice as a means of communion with deity. Such communion was specifically physical, i.e., they considered themselves to be eating the blood of the deity, for example. As Payne accurately responds, "Though Scripture surely believes in communion with God (Exod. 24:11), this blessed communion transpires in a moral and spiritual sphere only. It arises, moreover, as a result of the sacrifice, not as the explanation by which to account for the sacrifice."[34] Finally, Payne argues that the correct explanation of the matter is that sacrifices were propitiatory, or atoning.[35] It seems to me that all of the notions of expiation, propitiation, and consecration are involved in sacrifices. That the sacrifices were atoning can hardly be denied. The kinds of sacrifices required necessitate that atonement for sin was one of the ideas behind sacrifices. Reflection on the kinds of sacrifices (peace offerings, for example) suggests that the ideas of consecration and worship are involved as well.

But why could such sacrifices atone? As Elliott notes, sacrifices per se, apart from underlying spiritual motivation, could not bring atonement.

Jeremiah's complaints against sacrifice (Jer. 7:21-26) are to be interpreted not as teaching that sacrifice and the sacrificial system have no
value, but that without a repentant and obedient heart, the offering of a
sacrifice is worthless from the standpoint of atonement.[36] God never has
been and never will be satisfied with mere ritual.

The relation between the sacrifice and the sacrificer. Again, we find
varying interpretations. This is especially true in the case of those sacrifices given in order to make atonement for sin. Vos outlines three basic
theories in relation to the matter of the offerer's relation to the offering.
First, he outlines what might be called the "no theory" theory. According
to this view, held by many of the Wellhausen school of criticism, neither
the Old Testament in general nor the law in particular present any coherent, consistent theory of sacrifice.[37] The second view is what Vos calls
the purely symbolical theory. According to this theory, the process of
sacrifice portrays certain things that must be done to the offerer and will
be done. Consequently, this view holds that what must take place is
entirely internal or subjective to man. As Vos states, this interpretation
of the sacrifices sees them much along the same lines as do the moral and
governmental theories of the atonement in relation to Christ's sacrifice.[38]
The final theory is the symbolico-vicarious theory. In comparing it to the
purely symbolic theory, Vos writes:

> If the latter assumes that the further steps continue to portray what
> will be done within man to modify this, the symbolico-vicarious theory
> presupposes the recognition by ritual itself that nothing can be done in
> man himself with the proper effect, and that, therefore, a substitute
> must take his place. All the successive acts of the ritual apply to this
> substitute, not to the offerer. It becomes something done, to be sure, for
> the benefit of the offerer, but done outside of him. It will thus be seen,
> that the objectivity and the vicariousness of the process go together. On
> the same principle adoption of the purely symbolical theory carries
> with itself exclusion of the vicarious element and of the objectivity.[39]

The third of these theories is clearly supported by such passages as
Genesis 22:13; Leviticus 1:4; 16:21-22; 17:11; 19:20, 21; and Numbers
6:11. In spite of such evidence, however, Gerrish claims that the substitution theory cannot be upheld. What is clear, according to Gerrish, is that
"the offering is one with which the worshipper can by faith *identify himself,* not so much an offering which bears his punishment *in his stead.*"[40]
Thus, Gerrish holds that the theory presented is representative, not substitutionary. Although it is true that the offerer is identifying himself

with the sacrifice, it would also seem clear that the sacrifice is given in his place. Such passages as those mentioned above would seem to confirm this point.

The Old Testament teaching on sacrifices seems to indicate that the sacrifices included four basic functions or usages.

First, the sacrifices served a governmental or theocratic function. (Obviously, before the time of Moses no such function was served.) This function corresponds to the civil part of the law. Under the Mosaic system, the Israelite was related to God by physical birth as a Jew through the theocracy. God was the ruler in Israel. Even when Israel had kings or judges, God was still the ultimate ruler. Consequently, when a person sinned, such sin affected not only his relation to the one who saved him (God), but also to the one who was the ruler in Israel (God). Thus, sin was a governmental as well as a spiritual matter. As a result, the purpose of offering was not merely to restore one's relationship with his God, but to insure his right standing within the theocracy. The kinds of sacrifices that were most relevant to this were the sin, guilt, and trespass offerings. In addition, sacrifices seem on at least two occasions to have played a "political function" in that they were offered as the country prepared for or was in the midst of a war (1 Sam. 7:9ff.; 13:8ff.). The type of sacrifices most relevant to this were those not used specifically for atoning for sin (the broad category of sacrifices that Payne calls sweet savor sacrifices). If someone committed a sin that became a civil issue, he could be restored to his rightful place theocratically or governmentally by bringing sacrifices. However, by bringing such sacrifices, he did not automatically give indication of spiritual salvation or restoration at all. His sacrifice, if done without repentance toward God, might meet the external requirements for restoration to the community, but it need not be anything more. It might serve a purely civil function. Consequently, the theocratic or governmental use of the sacrifices carried no particular soteriological implications and no particular relationship to the sacrifice of Christ, other than a typological one.

A second function of the sacrifices in the Old Testament was a typological function. Sacrifices at all times during the Old Testament had this function. Hebrews 10:1, speaking of the Mosaic law and its sacrifices, says that the law is not the image (εἰκων, *eikōn*), that is, the exact representation, of what was to come, but it was a shadow (σκιά, *skia*) of it. In contrasting the meaning of the two words Wescott writes:

The words contain one of the very few illustrations which are taken from art in the N.T. The 'shadow' is the dark outlined figure cast by the object—as in the legend of the origin of the bas-relief—contrasted with the complete representation [εἰϰων, *eikōn*] produced by the help of colour and solid mass.[41]

Bringing meaning of the words out of the realm of art and into the context of our discussion, we can see how the figure of the Old Testament sacrifices being a shadow actually carries the idea of their being a foreshadowing of something to come. Given this kind of language, the writer of Hebrews seems to be stating that the Old Testament sacrifices were a type of what was to come in Christ's sacrifice.

It is important to distinguish between the typological truth present in the Old Testament sacrifices and the degree of understanding of the typological truth possessed by the Old Testament believer. Even though it must be granted that sacrifices from the time of Adam prefigured the sacrifice of Jesus Christ, it is moot as to how many people during Old Testament times understood all of this. As revelation progressed, more information was given so that in the sacrifices one could discern a prefiguring of a Messiah who would be sacrificed, even if no one (unlikely) in fact ever did fully understand that typology. The point is that although the Old Testament sacrifices were invested with typological significance, there is no warrant to say that the individual by bringing such sacrifices was showing that he placed his faith and trust in Jesus Christ, or even necessarily in a coming Messiah, for salvation. He may have understood that they pointed to a Messiah. However, from the standpoint of what God had revealed, as I have argued throughout, it seems most difficult to accept the notion that the Old Testament believer perceived that the sacrifices pointed to Jesus of Nazareth. The second point in regard to the typological function of the sacrifices is that even though they foreshadowed Christ's sacrifice by type, the typological nature per se of the sacrifices neither saved nor cleansed anyone. In other words, the typological function of the sacrifices was just that, typological; it was not soteriological.

A third function of the sacrifices was their role in worship. Obviously, by bringing a sacrifice for atonement (a non-sweet-savor sacrifice) and thereby agreeing with God's revealed means for handling sin, the believer was performing an act that brought glory to God. However, those sacrifices (sweet-savor sacrifices) that were not brought in order to secure atonement for sin, seem to be involved in the act of simply worshiping one's God (Lev. 2:2, 9—grain offering; Lev. 3—peace offering; 1 Sam. 1:3—example of an occasion on which worship and sacrifice are connected). Obviously, such sacrifices did not necessarily have any soteriological function. As to their relationship to Christ's sacrifice,

Payne has sketched some of the ways in which these sacrifices have foreshadowed Christ and the believer's relation to Him.[42]

A fourth function of the sacrifices was their role in soteriology, or their soteriological function. In regard to this matter, there are many pitfalls to be avoided. First, the sacrificial system in the Old Testament has a relation to the initial reception of salvation (what in New Testament terminology would be referred to as the point of justification), but it is not what many might think it is. It is clear that merely performing sacrifices never saved anyone. In fact, even if the sacrifices were offered in faith with a repentant heart, the public offering aspect of the sacrifice itself did not give the offerer salvation. As we have already seen, the sacrifices were part of the ceremonial aspect of the law. As Paul says in Romans 3:20, no one is justified by doing the works of the law. If the sacrifices *qua* sacrifices did not justify (whether given with a repentant heart or not), what, then, was their relation to a person coming to salvation? In accepting the God of Israel for personal salvation, the believer was not committing himself to the sacrifices for salvation, but to the God who had revealed that such sacrifices were to be the means of handling sin. The natural *outworking* of such saving faith in God was the performance of the sacrifices in believing faith, since God had said that He would cleanse the sin of the one who brought such sacrifices.

Although the Old Testament sacrifices had a relation to justification, their main function, soteriologically speaking, was in the sanctification process. Certainly, the sacrifices that were brought in worship of God or in consecration of the individual (sweet-savor sacrifices) would strengthen the believer's relationship with God. However, offering sacrifices in believing faith also brought cleansing from sin and the restoration of fellowship with God. Performing substitutionary and expiatory sacrifices seems to be more involved with cleansing the sin of a believer than with bringing a person to salvation. Job, when he offered a sacrifice for cleansing (Job 42:7-9), was obviously saved at the time he gave the sacrifice (the Old Testament abounds with such examples). The expiatory sacrifices, then, seem to be primarily involved with the sanctification process rather than having a soteriological function.

Again, we must recognize that merely giving sacrifices, without a repentant heart and a believing attitude that God would forgive, would not suffice to atone (Ps. 40:6-10; 51:10, 16ff.; Isa. 1:11-15; Micah 6:6-8). The case of Job is most helpful in this respect as well. Before Job offered the sacrifice, he had already repented of his sin in dust and ashes. A comparison of sanctification in the Old and New Testaments would show that when the New Testament believer sins, in order to restore fellowship with the Lord he must receive cleansing from the sin. In order to continue to grow, he must confess his sin in believing faith that on the basis of Christ's sacrifice God will cleanse him from sin (1 John 1:9). The Old Testament believer also confessed his sin, but in addition, he brought in believing faith a sacrifice, since God had revealed that sin would be handled in that way. Before Christ's sacrifice, the public offering had to accompany the repentance of the believer. Once the all-sufficient sacrifice of Christ had been made, the repentant believer need not give another sacrifice in order to have cleansing.

When sacrifices were presented with repentant faith, did the offerer actually receive forgiveness at that time? The Old Testament clearly teaches that sacrifices brought in repentant faith did result in God's forgiveness being granted, as seen in Leviticus 1:4; 4:26-31; 16:20-22; 17:11; Psalms 25, 32, 51, 103, 130; Isaiah 1:18; Ezekiel 18:22 in the Old Testament and Hebrews 9:13 in the New Testament.[43] This stands in clear opposition to the idea that the Old Testament teaches that unintentional sins could be atoned for and forgiven, whereas intentional sins (sins committed "with a high hand") could not be forgiven.[44] Careful study of the Old Testament does not support such a claim. Kaiser put the matter well when he wrote:

> How many sins could be atoned by such a system in Israel? All sins of weakness or rashness were capable of being atoned whether they were done knowingly or unwittingly. Leviticus specifically affirmed that the trespass offering was for sins such as lying, theft, fraud, perjury, or debauchery (Lev. 6:1-7). And on the great day of Atonement (Yom Kippur), "all" the sins of "all" Israel of "all" who had truly repented ("afflicted their souls" [Lev. 16:16, 21, 29, 31]) were forgiven. Indeed the most persistent phrase in the Levitical sacrificial instructions was the assurance: "And he shall be forgiven" (Lev. 1:4; 4:20, 26, 31, 35; 5:10, 16; 16:20-22). Therefore, the old but false distinction between witting, i.e., "sins done with a high hand," and unwitting, i.e., as it was explained, sins done in ignorance of what the law said on the matter, was unwarranted. The unwitting sins בִּשְׁגָגָה (bishᵉgāgâh), or better still, sins "in error," involved all sin which sprang from the weakness of flesh and blood. But the sin of Numbers 15:27-36, the sin of a "high hand" בְּיָד רָמָה (bᵉyād rāmâ), was plainly that of rebellion against God and His Word. . . . This is what the NT calls blasphemy against the Holy Spirit or the unpardonable sin. It was high treason and revolt against God with the upraised, clenched fist: a picket against heaven! But this was not to be put in the same class as sins of murder, adultery, or the like. Treason or blasphemy against God was much more serious. Rather, it attacked God Himself.[45]

Israel repeatedly rebelled against God and went after strange gods. Such sin certainly was not unintentional. Nonetheless, the constant message of the prophets to the people is to return unto the Lord. Why would God urge the people to return to Himself for forgiveness and restoration if atonement for their sin was an impossibility?[46]

Thus we see that the sacrificial system was useful in the sanctification process, and that the one who offered sacrifices in believing faith did receive forgiveness. As a matter of fact, at that time offering sacrifices was crucial to retaining a right relationship with God. As Hobart Freeman has so aptly written:

> ... sacrifice was not to the Hebrew some crude, temporary, and merely typical institution, nor a substitute for that dispensation until better things were provided by revelation, but as will be shown, *sacrifice was then the only sufficient means of remaining in harmonious relation to God. It was adequate for the period in which God intended it should serve.* This is not the same as saying Levitical sacrifice was on an equal with the sacrifice of Christ, nor that the blood of bulls and goats could, from God's side, take away sins: but it is recognizing the reality of the divine institution of Mosaic worship, and looking, as too often Old Testament interpreters fail to do, at sacrifice from the viewpoint of the Hebrew in the Old Testament dispensation. Sacrifice, to the pious Hebrew, was not something unimportant, or simply a perfunctory ritual, but it was an important element in his *moral obedience to the revealed will of God.*[47]

So, it can be demonstrated that Old Testament sacrifices did result in forgiveness of sin. Someone might then suggest, "Let's continue the sacrificial system now. It would suffice for sin, wouldn't it? In fact, it's as efficacious as Christ's sacrifice, isn't it?" The answer is that although sacrifices were once the means for maintaining a harmonious relation to God, continuing such sacrifices would mistake the relation of those sacrifices to Christ's sacrifice and miss the importance of Christ's sacrifice. The answers to the imagined questions show something of the soteriological relation of Old Testament sacrifices to Christ's sacrifice.

There are several important aspects to the relation of the Old Testament sacrifices to Christ's sacrifice. First, Scripture is very clear that the system of the law, including the sacrifices, is superceded and done away with by the sacrifice of Christ (cf. Gal. 3:24-25; the book of Hebrews). Second, as we have seen, Old Testament sacrifices actually covered sin and assured the believer of cleansing and forgiveness. However, it was the sacrifice of Christ that actually once and for all removed the sin (Heb.

9:13; 10:4, 11–14). If Old Testament sacrifices had actually made a full and final objective payment for sins so as to remove them totally, then it could not be said that Christ's sacrifice paid for such sin. Of course, that would contradict the fact that Scripture teaches that Christ's sacrifice did pay for the sins of all men (Heb. 2:9; 7:27; 10:10; Rom. 6:10; 1 Pet. 3:18). In fact, such a position would even contradict a passage in the Old Testament itself, i.e., Isaiah 53:6. If all sins in the Old Testament economy are completely removed by animal sacrifice, then it makes no sense for an Old Testament prophet to write that the Lord laid on Him (the Messiah) the iniquity of us all. Even if one refused to interpret the passage messianically and chose to see it fulfilled in Israel, for example (that is, one claims that "him" is Israel), the passage still would make no sense if sin in the Old Testament were ultimately being removed by animal sacrifice. Because Christ's sacrifice was not the first act in human history does not mean that its efficacy does not extend to every sinful act of history. Old Testament sacrifices were, so to speak, the down payment for sin, whereas Christ's sacrifice was the full and final payment. Why, once the sacrifice of Christ pays the debt in full owed for sin, continue to make "down payments" on sin? The sacrificial system must be done away with.

The Old Testament sacrifices pointed to (typological function) the sacrifice of Christ, which would fully handle sin (even if the Jew did not understand the typology of the sacrifices). On the ground of His sacrifice to which the Old Testament sacrifices pointed, the Old Testament believer who in repentant faith brought a sacrifice could be assured that God would cover, cleanse, and forgive such sin (soteriological function). But the objective deed, from God's standpoint, that would completely pay for and remove sin was only offered on Calvary.

Another reason that Old Testament sacrifices are not to be continued is that we can see that the scope of the respective sacrifices greatly differs. Under the Old Testament system, the general rule was that when a sacrifice for sin was made, sin was actually forgiven, but only the sin for which the sacrifice was made was expiated. Of course, the sacrifice made on the Day of Atonement covered more than just one sin, but even so, it did not cover all sin of all time. On the contrary, the word of Scripture in regard to Christ's sacrifice is that it is all-inclusive, once for all, never to be repeated (Heb. 10:12, 14). Certainly, if Christ's one sacrifice pays for all sin, there is no need to go back to Old Testament sacrifices. What could they possibly add, since Christ's sacrifice already provides atonement for *all* sin?

There are many misunderstandings and seeming contradictions about the subject of Old Testament sacrifices. Someone might state that everything that has been said is contradicted by Hebrews 10:4: "It is impossible for the blood of bulls and goats to take away sins." Moreover, the problem seems to become more complicated by Hebrews 9:13, which indicates that the blood of bulls and goats did cleanse from sin. There seems to be a tremendous contradiction between the two passages as well as with the content of the preceding discussion. The seriousness of the problem can be seen in that one could incorrectly assume that Hebrews 10:4 means that no one in the Old Testament period was actually saved, that Old Testament believers had to await the sacrifice of Christ before their faith was actually "validated," when they became saved (even though dead), or that there really was no forgiveness of sin when it was repented of. These problems can be resolved by a proper understanding of the verses and concepts involved.

First, Hebrews 9:13 does not relate to internal cleansing and forgiveness from sin. As Westcott notes, the verse is actually referring to "the ceremonial purity which enabled the Jew to enjoy the full privileges of his covenant worship and fellowship with the external Church of God."[48] With the exception of the comments about the "Church of God" I find myself in full agreement. In fact, verse 14 contrasts Christ's sacrifice with that of bulls and goats and shows that His sacrifice gives internal cleansing, whereas that of bulls and goats is, according to verse 13, relevant to external cleansing (ceremonial cleansing). Of course, Hebrews 10:1-4, refers primarily, if not exclusively, to internal cleansing from sin. Therefore, Hebrews 9:13 and 10:1-4 cannot be in contradiction, because they are not referring to the same kind of cleansing for the same purpose.

Though Hebrews 9:13 does not refer to internal cleansing from sin, it is incorrect to assume that sacrifices in the Old Testament were relevant to ceremonial cleansing only, and thus did not really bring forgiveness of sin. We have already examined many passages from the Old Testament that indicate there was internal cleansing and forgiveness from sin. Moreover, Hebrews 10:4 seems to be talking in its context not about external, ceremonial matters, but internal matters. But, by resolving the apparent contradiction between Hebrews 9:13 and 10:4, we have not removed the problem altogether.

A final resolution to this difficulty seems to be possible only in the light of two crucial distinctions. The first is the distinction between the provision of atonement (the objective work of God) and the application of the atonement (the subjective work of God). The second is the distinction between the forgiveness and the removal of sin. In regard to the first distinction, in order for a person to be saved, two conditions are necessary: (1) someone must provide and pay for the basis of that salvation, and (2) someone must take the salvation that has been purchased and apply it to the sinner in need of salvation. The former aspect, providing and paying for the salvation is called the objective aspect of God's atoning work. It is what He had to do as a basis for offering and applying salvation to any specific person. It is a work that is performed externally to all subjects (persons), and in that respect it is called "objective." When the objective work has been performed, salvation is potentially available to the sinner. The basis for salvation has been provided, so that it is possible to be saved. However, just because salvation is provided does not mean that anyone is in fact saved. The actualization of that salvation in the life of the individual can only come when God has applied that salvation to the person. Since this aspect of salvation is done within the life of the person (subject), it is called the subjective aspect of salvation.

In regard to the difference between removal of sin and forgiveness of sin, we can say, using the terminology set forth above, that the removal of sin refers to the payment for sin, the objective aspect of salvation. On the other hand, forgiveness comes when God applies salvation to the subject or cleanses him from sin. Thus, it refers to the subjective side of salvation. That there is a genuine distinction should be clear in that one can objectively pay for sin's removal even if no one applies that salvation to himself, whereas no one's sins are actually forgiven until he subjectively applies what has been provided for him objectively. Moreover, it is possible to cover (through partial objective payment via animal sacrifice) and forgive a sin without completely objectively paying for and removing it.

With those two distinctions in mind, we can resolve our problem. In Hebrews 10:4 the writer states that the blood of bulls and goats cannot remove sin; it does not state that when such sacrifices were given, there was no forgiveness. The testimony of the Old Testament is that there was forgiveness when sacrifices were given in faith. The point, then, must be that mere animal sacrifices, though acts external (objective) to the sinner, could never from God's perspective take care of the objective dimensions of the atonement. Only Christ's objective work could provide the full and final payment for salvation from sin and make it potentially available (we can now see better why the sacrifice of Christ had to be at all times the objective basis, or ground, for salvation). Thus, Old Testament sacrifices could only in type foreshadow His sacrifice. They could not pay for sin so as to remove it; only the sacrifice of Christ could do that. However, that did not mean that the sacrifices were totally worthless, for there was still the subjective side of salvation (in addition, the sacrifices gave a "down payment" on sin—objective function), that is, the need for application of the atonement and, in particular, for forgiveness. On the basis of the believer's trust in the revealed content for faith for his particular age, God could and did subjectively apply salvation and forgiveness to the repentant sinner. Thus, the problem can be resolved. When the objective work of a sacrifice was given, it could not fully and finally pay for sin (the provision of atonement). Hebrews 10:4 is upheld. Nonetheless, since it had been given in faith and obedience to what God had revealed for that age, God could and did grant the sinner forgiveness (subjective side of salvation) on the ultimate grounds of Christ's sacrifice, which would someday be given. All the Old Testament comments about forgiveness of sin can be upheld. In fact, it would seem that this resolution does the most justice to all the verses involved. We do not conclude that Old Testament sacrifices had the same amount or kind of efficacy as did the sacrifice of Christ, but neither do we derive the unwarranted conclusion that during Old Testament times no one was saved or no one's sins were cleansed and forgiven.[49]

This study, then, has investigated some key issues pertaining to the topic of salvation in the Old Testament. As we reflect upon the unity and the diversity within God's gracious plan of salvation for all time, we can only repeat what Paul said as he reflected on the mercy of God, "Oh, the depth of the riches both of the wisdom and knowledge of God! How unsearchable are His judgments and unfathomable His ways! . . . For from Him and through Him and to Him are all things. To Him be the glory forever. Amen" (Rom. 11:33, 36).

NOTES

1. James K. Zink, "Salvation in the Old Testament: A Central Theme," *Encounter* 25 (Autumn 1964):407. Zink explains that the term "salvation" has three basic meanings in the Old Testament: (1) national salvation in the sense of protection from foes and deliverance from exile, (2) individual salvation from the results of sin, deliverance from enemies, disease, and trouble, and (3) eschatological salvation from sin issuing in a richer life in communion with God in the present world and in the afterlife.
2. Charles Hodge, *Systematic Theology,* (London: James Clarke, 1960), 2:367.
3. J. Barton Payne, *The Theology of the Older Testament* (Grand Rapids: Zondervan, 1962), p. 241. See also pp. 72-74.
4. Daniel P. Fuller, "The Hermeneutics of Dispensationalism" (Th.D. diss., Northern Baptist Theological Seminary, 1957), pp. 144-45. See also pp. 151 and 144-81.
5. Payne, pp. 467-68. See also J. Barton Payne, *The Imminent Appearing of Christ* (Grand Rapids: Eerdmans, 1962), pp. 31-32, for a more blatant statement on this issue.
6. C. I. Scofield, ed., *Scofield Reference Bible* (New York: Oxford U. Press, 1945), p. 1115.
7. Ibid., p. 1245.
8. Fuller, pp. 153ff.
9. Charles C. Ryrie, *Dispensationalism Today* (Chicago: Moody, 1965), pp. 113-16.

10. E. Schuyler English, ed., *New Scofield Reference Bible* (New York: Oxford U. Press, 1967), p. 1124.
11. Ryrie, pp. 44–46.
12. George E. Ladd, "Historic Premillennialism," in *The Meaning of the Millennium: Four Views,* ed. Robert G. Clouse (Downers Grove, Ill.: Inter-Varsity, 1977), pp. 20–21, 27.
13. Gustav F. Oehler, *Theology of the Old Testament,* reprint (Minneapolis: Klock & Klock, 1978) p. 459.
14. Hodge, p. 370.
15. Ibid., pp. 371–72. See also Payne, *Theology of the Older Testament,* p. 241, and Hodge, p. 372, who writes, "The Apostle proves that the specific promise which was the object of the faith of the patriarch was the promise of redemption through Christ. That promise they were required to believe; and that the true people of God did believe."
16. Payne, *Imminent Appearing,* p. 128.
17. The basic format is suggested in Ryrie, pp. 123–26. However, I am modifying and amplifying it. The fifth element in this series and some aspects of its amplification were suggested to me by Paul D. Feinberg.
18. Snaith points out that in the Old Testament God is portrayed as the savior; see Norman H. Snaith, *The Distinctive Ideas of the Old Testament* (New York: Schocken, 1975), pp. 85–86. For the concept of God as the object of faith, see also Henry McKeating, "Divine Forgiveness in the Psalms," *Scottish Journal of Theology* 18 (March 1965):78.
19. Walter C. Kaiser, Jr., *Toward an Old Testament Theology* (Grand Rapids: Zondervan, 1978), pp. 20–40. Kaiser elaborates this theme throughout the book.
20. God's ethical standards, of course, run throughout the whole Old Testament, but they give man an awareness of God's standards and man's own failure. They are not per se part of the content to be believed as one trusts God for salvation.
21. Kaiser, pp. 114–18.
22. Oehler, p. 462.
23. I shall elaborate this point in the following portion of the chapter.
24. It would also be appropriate to note that in the New Testament the eternal destiny of the believer is stated much more clearly than in the Old Testament. Redemption of the whole person, including his body, and glorification of the believer indeed are stresses in the New Testament that are seldom mentioned in the Old Testament. This does not mean, though, that Old Testament believers are not to be resurrected and glorified. This is simply to point out a difference in amount and content of information available in the Old Testament as opposed to the New Testament, not a difference in the final status of the Old Testament saint.
25. Payne, *Theology of the Older Testament,* p. 386.
26. Ibid.
27. Oehler, p. 288.
28. For discussions of the distinctions see Oehler, pp. 300–303; Payne, *Theology of the Older Testament,* pp. 386ff.; Norman H. Snaith, "The Sin-Offering and the Guilt-Offering," *Vetus Testamentum* 15 (January 1965); and Geerhardus Vos, *Biblical Theology* (Grand Rapids: Eerdmans, 1968), pp. 188–89.
29. Oehler, p. 263.

30. Ibid.
31. Payne, *Theology of the Older Testament,* p. 382.
32. Geerhardus Vos, *Biblical Theology* (Grand Rapids: Eerdmans, 1968), p. 173.
33. Payne, *Theology of the Older Testament,* pp. 382-83.
34. Ibid., p. 383.
35. Ibid.
36. Ralph H. Elliott, "Atonement in the Old Testament," *Review and Expositor* 59 (January 1962):15.
37. Vos, p. 177.
38. Ibid., pp. 176-77.
39. Ibid., p. 177.
40. Brian A. Gerrish, "Atonement and 'Saving Faith'," *Theology Today* 17 (July 1960):188.
41. B. F. Westcott, *The Epistle to the Hebrews* (Grand Rapids: Eerdmans, 1967), p. 304.
42. Payne, *Theology of the Older Testament,* pp. 385-88.
43. See McKeating article. See also Elliott, p. 25, on the idea of the suffering servant's sacrifice bringing forgiveness.
44. See Hobart Freeman, "The Problem of Efficacy of Old Testament Sacrifices," *Bulletin of Evangelical Theological Society* 5 (1962):74 for explanation of three views concerning the efficacy of Old Testament sacrifices.
45. Kaiser, pp. 117-18.
46. Snaith, "Distinctive Ideas," pp. 84-85. Snaith shows that God forgives in spite of Israel's sin of rebellion.
47. Freeman, p. 73.
48. Westcott, p. 261. See also p. 260.
49. I was greatly aided in coming to my resolution of this problem by the comments of Kaiser, p. 118, and Freeman, pp. 76-77.

4

The Theology of the Balaam Oracles

Ronald B. Allen

RONALD B. ALLEN *(Th.M., Th.D., Dallas Theological Seminary) is profes-sor of Old Testament language and exegesis at Western Conservative Bap-tist Seminary, Portland, Oregon.*

This essay is presented with warm appreciation to Dr. Charles Lee Feinberg, a man whose love for the Lord Jesus Christ, the Scriptures of God, and the people of Israel is a continuing model for other students of the Old Testament. His particular affection for the prophetic portions of Scripture prompts this study on the oracles of a most improbable prophet.

INTRODUCTION

Ronald M. Hals begins his monograph *The Theology of the Book of Ruth* by facing a credibility problem head-on: "The first reaction to the title, 'The Theology of the Book of Ruth' is quite likely a doubt as to the importance, or even the existence, of any such theology."[1] An initial response to the title "The Theology of the Balaam Oracles," might be similar to that imagined by Hals regarding his theme. Nonetheless, as we shall see, a careful study of the Balaam story shows it to be not only a remarkably well-written and enjoyable story, but also one rich in theological content and import.

THE SETTING OF THE NARRATIVE

Our initial task will be to survey the outlines of the story of Balaam (Numbers 22-24) in context. Numbers 22 begins with the Israelites having recently defeated the Amorite kings Sihon and Og, rulers of Heshbon and Bashan, respectively.

In two quick assaults Israel had conquered the Transjordan north of the kingdom of Moab and was now encamped in the plains of Moab, opposite Jericho. The presence of this formidable foe within its borders brought terror to Moab. The intensity of Moab's fear is expressed with considerable feeling in Numbers 22:3.

> So Moab was in fear because of the people, for they were numerous; and Moab felt a sickening dread before the Israelites.[2]

In one sense Moab's fear of Israel was quite unnecessary, although Moab could not have known it at the time. Yahweh had charged Israel not to take so much as the space of a footprint (עַד מִדְרַךְ כַּף־רָגֶל *'ad midrak kap rāgel*) of land from that nation. Yahweh had granted Mount Seir to Esau and He had given Ar to Moab—an expression of His sovereignty over the nations (Deut. 2:4-9). Deuteronomy 2:9 states Israel's lack of claim to the land of Moab in absolute terms:

> And Yahweh said to me,
> Do not show hostility to Moab,
> and do not engage in war with them;
> for I will not give you any part of its land as a possession,
> for I have given Ar to the descendants of Lot as a possession.

This significant passage reminds us that Israel, though under God's blessing, was restricted by divine limits. Yahweh is sovereign over all of Israel's acts.

There is another level, however, on which the sickening fear Moab felt for Israel was fully in keeping with the divine economy; in fact it may be said to be a fulfillment of prophecy. We read in Deuteronomy 2:25:

> This day I will begin to put the dread of you and the fear of you
> on the faces of the peoples under all the heavens,
> who, whenever they may hear report of you,
> will quiver and writhe in terror before you.[3]

The fear that Moab felt was accentuated by the news of the defeat by Israel of the Amorite kings to the north of Moab, that is, Sihon and Og (Num. 21:21-35; cf. Deut. 2:26-3:11). This put Moab in an especially difficult position, for the newly conquered lands had formerly belonged to

Moab. Numbers 21:26 indicates such, as it states that Heshbon, the capi-
tal city of Sihon, had been wrested by the Amorites from a former
Moabite king (perhaps Zippor, the father of Balak). Hence, the taunt song
of Numbers 21:27–30 (NASB) was especially galling to Moab:

> Therefore those who use proverbs say,
> "Come to Heshbon! Let it be built!
> So let the city of Sihon be established.
> For a fire went forth from Heshbon,
> A flame from the town of Sihon,
> It devoured Ar of Moab,
> The dominant heights of the Arnon.[4]
> Woe to you, O Moab!
> You are ruined, O people of Chemosh!
> He has given his sons as fugitives,
> And his daughters into captivity,
> To an Amorite king, Sihon.
> But we have cast them down,
> Heshbon is ruined as far as Dibon,
> Then we have laid waste, even to Nophah,
> Which reaches to Medeba."

As van Zyl indicates, the singing of this song may well have been a
principal cause for Moab's excruciating dread of Israel. He states, "In this
song we can therefore ascertain a primary cause for the king of Moab's
summoning Balaam."[5] In a similar way, Geikie summarizes:

> Moab had never relinquished the hope of winning back from the Amo-
> rites the lands taken by them for a time. But the appearance of Israel as
> a new owner, by right of conquest, seemed to cloud their prospect, and
> substitute another victorious people as the wrongful holders of the
> territory they still counted theirs.
>
> The position of Moab was, indeed, in every way full of alarm. Already
> stripped of more than half its territory, it seemed now in danger of
> losing the rest. Zippor—"The Bird," father of Balak, the reigning king—
> had lost his life in the battle with Sihon, which had cost him also the
> greater and richer part of his kingdom. Seeing the utter overthrow of
> the Amorites, the conquerors of his own people, Balak, in "sore dis-
> tress," sent messengers to the elders of Midian, a related tribe, urging
> them, in a figure well suited to a pastoral race, to come to his help, else
> "this people will lick up all round us, as the ox licketh up the grass of
> the field."[6]

Such then is the setting for the narrative: the sickening dread that Moab felt toward the people of Israel. Despair seized the nation, and that despair led to a desperate act—an appeal to supernatural power, the power of the curse.

A SUMMARY OF THE NARRATIVE

Balak, king of Moab, believed there was no military means by which he might conquer the Hebrew forces. Hence, he turned to the supernatural means of the effective curse. He consulted with the Midianite elders and then, with their advice guiding him, sent for an internationally known soothsayer to curse the armies of Israel. This was predicated on the belief in the power of the spoken word, as was prevalent in the Ancient Near East. The diviner with the remarkable reputation was Balaam.

Chapter 22 relates the story of the call of Balaam from his home, some four hundred miles distant, and the vacillations and equivocations of the prophet. At first God refused permission for Balaam to go. By stalling and by other deceitful means, however, Balaam rejected the directive will of Yahweh and opted for His permissive will. All the while, he was induced by offers of magnificent remuneration.

During his trip by donkey to Moab, there occurred the famous encounter between Balaam and the Angel of Yahweh, and the even more famous incident of the talking donkey. The Angel sent Balaam on his way, but only after sternly warning him that he was to speak only the word that Yahweh would tell him (v. 35). Balaam and Balak then met, and began their preparations for the intended curse on the people of Yahweh.

In chapters 23 and 24 of Numbers we have the actual oracles of the pagan soothsayer, who was under the control and the inspiration of the Spirit of God. After cultic acts of preparation, Balaam began to curse Israel. Then, to his utter amazement, and to Balak's stunned chagrin, only blessing came forth. There was a series of attempts to curse Israel, with only the blessings coming forth. Balaam found it impossible to curse whom God had not cursed. Finally, in an act "entirely beyond his control he spoke one final word, one of the most glorious prophecies in the Old Testament" (Num. 24:17, NASB)[7]:

I see him, but not now;
I behold him, but not near;
A star shall come forth from Jacob,
And a scepter shall rise from Israel,

And shall crush through the forehead of Moab,
And tear down all the sons of Sheth.

Subsequent to these oracles, Balaam tried a new tack. What he had
been unable to do by cursing, he managed to do by more subtle means.
Chapter 25 of Numbers relates the infamous incident when the men of
Israel "yoked themselves to Baal Peor" (Num. 25:3), giving rise to the
severe anger of Yahweh, which resulted in a judgment of plague in which
some twenty-four thousand were killed. Only after the act of zeal by
Phinehas, the son of Eleazar, was the anger of Yahweh stayed. This priest
stabbed a copulating couple with his spear (vv. 7-8). The names of the
offending couple are given: Zimri the Jew and Cozbi the Midianitess.
The citation of the names seems to lend even more severity to the
aggravated picture. Why their names? Perhaps to record for all time
that "this was the first contact with the immoral fertility cults of Canaan,
the very essence of which was sexual aberration of all kinds."[8] This
is an issue of history and theology of great moment.

Finally there is the account in Numbers 31 of the holy war with Midian in which Balaam was killed (Num. 31:8, 16). There is in this chapter
a summary of Balaam's involvement in the incident of Numbers 25,
where the name "Balaam" did not appear (Num. 31: 15b-18, NASB):

Have you spared all the women? Behold, these caused the sons of Israel,
through the counsel of Balaam, to trespass against Yahweh in the
matter of Peor, so the plague was among the congregation of Yahweh.
Now therefore kill every male among the little ones, and kill every
woman who have known man intimately. But all the little girls who
have not known man intimately, spare for yourselves.

With this sketch of the events before us, we may now move to a consideration of the theology of the narrative.

THE *HEILSGESCHICHTE* OF THE BALAAM ORACLES

Many contemporary Old Testament theologians have seen in the
Balaam narrative what might be termed the quintessence of the theology
of the Pentateuch. I share their enthusiasm concerning this magnificent
corpus, even with all of its bristling problems. Such ebullient remarks,
however, must be evaluated on the basis of sound methodology in theological discipline. When the term *Heilsgeschichte* is used by the biblicist, it
may not be used to develop truth apart from historical reality. But rather

it is used to give expression to the truth being taught within that historical reality.[9]

THE BLESSING OF YAHWEH

The specific contribution of the Balaam incident to Old Testament
theology appears to be its graphic development of the concept of Yahweh's
blessing of Israel. The story is an unexpected event. It appears to be an
extended excursus on the theme of blessing, but an excursus acted out in
the arena of human history. The setting, the personae, the conflicts, and
the very subject matter all contribute to one of the most eloquent expositions of Yahweh's deep and abiding relationship with His people Israel.

That these events are recorded at such length in the book of Numbers is
remarkable, and not only for reasons of the question of authorship.[10] The
book of Numbers does not present the people of Israel in a very favorable
light. In many respects the book of Numbers is a tragic account of Israel's
rebellion and unbelief in failing to living up to God's expectations for her.

The murmuring motif that begins in chapter 11 develops as the action
progresses to include the entire population. Time after time the people of
God showed themselves disloyal to and discontented with His suzerainty.
Time after time the grumbling and sinning people provoked Yahweh to
anger against them. The record of the places in which Israel camped is a
grim recital of the judgments of God on those who rebelled against His
rule. Some of those names include: Taberah ("a burning"), Numbers 11:3;
Kibroth-hattaavah ("the graves of greediness"), Numbers 11:34; and
Kadesh-Barnea, the scene of unbelief that cost a generation its promise of
the land of Canaan, Numbers 13-14.

The thirty-eight years of Israel's existence that are chronicled in this
book are, for the most part, years of silence. These are years of silence
occasioned by the sheer monotony of wandering in a forbidding wilderness, waiting for a generation to die. These were years of burials—one
dreadful burial after another. For the most part, the only relief from the
monotony of wandering and waiting is the record of a new sin and its
consequence. Sins of impatience, jealousy, murmuring and apostasy—
such constitute the action of the book. The rebellion of Korah (Num. 16),
the jealousy of Miriam and Aaron (Num. 12), and even the failure of
Moses (Num. 20) are recorded.

Hence, when the reader comes to Numbers 22:1 and reads that Israel
has finally reached the shores of the Jordan River and is encamped across
from the land of promise, the questions might well arise, is this indeed
the people of promise? Does this nation really have a unique relationship
to the God of the universe? Is Israel really the chosen people?

The answers to those questions come in a most unexpected manner.

The reader is taken to the enemy camp and is given an inside view of the machinations of Israel's foes in their attempts to destroy the nation. The threat of Israel is felt to be so great to Moab that that nation turns to a superstitious and supernatural means to attempt to ward off the enemy. The resort to which Moab turns is the curse. And then God breaks in. Yahweh, the God of Israel, confronts an internationally-known pagan diviner in his homeland, far removed from the people of Israel. Yahweh, the God who spoke to Moses, now speaks to a heathen mantic prophet. Yahweh, the God of patriarchs, breaks into the dealings of a power play on the part of unbelievers in the realm of the occult. And God says, "You shall not curse the people, for they are blessed" (Num. 22:12).[11]

The fact of Israel's blessing by Yahweh is the major theme in the *Heilsgeschichte* of this pericope. Israel is blessed by Yahweh from of old. Balaam, the pagan prophet, attempts to reverse the curse to earn his mantic fee, but is frustrated at every turn. Yahweh's blessing on His people is irrevocable. Demonic powers have no sway; supernatural means are ineffective; pagan acts are useless in the face of the objective reality of the blessing of Israel.

The institution of Israel's blessing is to be found in Yahweh's choice of the primal patriarch, Abraham, as described in Genesis 12. It seems to be nearly impossible to overestimate the seminal significance of the Abrahamic covenant in Old Testament theology. At the very beginning God's intent for this new people was made quite clear. To Abraham He said, "I will bless you" (Gen. 12:2). The Balaam story may be regarded as a frontal attack by Satan on the foundational blessing of God's people—a frontal attack that was countered and defeated by the intervention of Yahweh Himself.

As Mowinckel observed,[12] the theme of the oracles may be stated in a *nuce:* "Blessed is everyone who blesses you, and cursed is everyone who curses you" (Num. 24:9). This is a strong reminder of the original words of the Abrahamic covenant (Gen. 12:3):

And I will bless those who bless you,
but the one who curses you I will curse.
And in you all the families of the earth shall be blessed.

The history of the Jewish people is replete with examples of attempts to curse and destroy them. But the Balaam incident seems to be the test case for the objective reality of the blessing of Israel.

As Habel observed respecting the events of Numbers 25,[13] the story of Numbers 22-24 is also a record of no peccadillo. An attempt was made at a direct, studied, and frontal attack on the blessing of God's people. But those who wished to curse Israel found themselves cursed. Israel's blessing is unique (Num. 23:7-10); it is based on her unique relationship to Yahweh (Num. 23:18-24); it is absolute (Num. 24:3-9); and it has an ultimate fulfillment in her Deliverer from all enemies (24:15-19). The enemies of Israel, present and future, are under the curse they wished had been placed on her (Num. 24:20-24).[14]

Furthermore, Numbers 23:10b suggests the futile desire by Balaam to participate in the blessing of Israel:[15]

Let me die the death of the upright!
O that my glorious future could be like his!

Now this is marvelous. He who came to curse Israel asks to join Israel in her blessing. The irony of this verse seems to surpass even that of the donkey narrative. This verse seems to be a statement of futility. Balaam is unable to affect the people of Israel with a curse. Rather than curse them, he is used by God to bless them, and then he utters the forlorn hope to join Israel in her blessing. However, his death was in fact in the enemy camp (Num. 31:8, 16).

The major thrust of the Balaam oracles centers on Israel's blessing. Israel's blessing is unique, because it is rooted in the character of her unique God. Despite Israel's many failures in the years of wilderness wanderings, God is still faithful to His people. Despite their many rejections of His leading and the several denials made of His goodness, He still leads, and He remains good to Israel. God has blessed Israel, and God is at work in Israel (Num. 23:23). Attempts to curse Israel are quite ineffective.

THE ATTRIBUTES OF YAHWEH

In addition to the emphasis on the blessing of Israel, the *Heilsgeschichte* of our pericope concerns the revelation of the attributes of the person of Yahweh, the source of blessing.[16] It would be an error to try to find in the oracles of Balaam a complete catalogue of the attributes of God. Rather, it is the purpose of this section to stress those attributes of the divine Being that are presented and implied by our text. Moreover, an attempt will not be made to group the attributes of Yahweh along classical lines (personal as against constitutional, absolute as against relative, communicable as against incommunicable). In short, the approach is that of the exegete, with a view to presentation of the major emphases.

A further limitation is felt by the writer, and this is the problem one always faces in trying to "define" God. For even when one has said all that he can say about the sublime Person of Yahweh, he realizes that he has not said enough. In the final analysis, all descriptions taken together do not exhaust what we mean by "God." R. T. France writes:

> He is not an academic proposition. The Bible provides us with no defini-
> tion of the word "God"—it cannot, because, as Pascal said, "Dieu defini,
> d'est Dieu fini." A God who is susceptible to the static delineation of
> cold philosophy, or even of a rigid dogmatic theology, is not the
> dynamic God of the Bible. God is known by His words and His acts, not
> by abstract speculation. To try to tie Him down with human definitions
> is idolatry; and it is idolatry which draws out some of the most superbly
> scathing mockery of the Old Testament.[17]

With these limitations in mind we may now turn to the attributes emphasized in our text.

The incomparability of Yahweh. In the introduction by A. van Selms
to the book by C. J. Labuschagne, *The Incomparability of Yahweh in the
Old Testament,* we find a rather sad remark:

> As far as the present author is aware, Dr. Labuschagne's book is the
> first monograph to appear on the subject of Yahweh's incomparability
> in the Old Testament. It is most remarkable, in view of the abundance
> of Old Testament texts which bear witness of Yahweh's incomparabil-
> ity, that this subject up till now has not been treated in any separate
> study.[18]

Van Selms proceeds to remark that the reason for the relative neglect
of God's incomparability lies in its negative aspect. Against that, however, he avers that "it should be clear from the first that the testimony of
this negative quality is the human expression for an all-transcendent
positive intensity of being."[19]

Whereas our passage does not contain the standard formulae for expressing the incomparability of Yahweh as delineated in the treatise by
Labuschagne, the theme of His incomparability forms one of the substructural premises from which the whole receives its unified meaning.[20]

I have argued that Balaam is best seen not in the context of "false
versus true prophets," as has been debated so often in the history of
exegesis,[21] but as outside the proper realm of biblical prophecy. He is
neither a false prophet nor a true prophet in the usual sense of those
terms. Those words are usually used as value judgments within the cultus of Israel and within the context of revealed religion. Balaam is best

understood as a pagan who unwittingly steps into the focus of the drama of the people of Israel and their God, and finds himself totally overwhelmed by what happens to him.[22]

It is in Balaam's reaction to Yahweh's use of him that the substructural postulate of the incomparability of Yahweh is demonstrated. Yahweh, the God of Israel, is totally unlike anything or anyone Balaam had ever encountered or ever imagined. Balaam was a trafficker in the spirit world, a craftsman with the supernatural. It would not be reading too much into his character to see him as more than a clairvoyant, as fully in the context of idolatry in its demonic aspects.[23]

Whatever Balaam's experience had been in the past vis-á-vis the spirit world, we recognize that he knows that he is up against Someone totally different from all of his experience when he confronts Yahweh. This is a means of teaching the reader about the uniqueness of the God of Israel. Be it known, the Balaam oracles seem to be saying, that the God of Israel is incomparable. Truly the psalmist praises Yahweh when he writes (Psalm 113:4-5):

> High above the nations is Yahweh!
> Over all the heavens is His glory!
> Who may be compared to Yahweh our God,
> Who is enthroned on high?[24]

In the first oracle we read of Balaam extolling the uniqueness of the people of God (Num. 23:9):

> When from the top of the mountains I see him,
> And from the hills I gaze at him;
> Look! A people that dwells alone,
> And among the nations it is not reckoned!

How are we to understand the difference of the people of God from all other nations? Certainly not in the sense of race.[25] Nor does the Bible allow us to regard this difference in terms of Israel's own self-worth.

This passage in itself, and in the larger context, never allows even Israel to take center stage. The genuine theological truth presented in the testimony to the uniqueness of Israel is the fact that Israel was related to the incomparable Yahweh. It is only because Yahweh is beyond compare that His people become distinct. As Labuschagne states, the incomparability of Israel was never to be taken as a "laudatory ascription to an arrogant and self-glorifying nationalism," nor was it "an expression of religious chauvinism." Rather, he argues:

Our investigation has brought to light that a unique position among the nations was given to Israel as a result of her election by Yahweh. Within the scope of her election Israel was called to practice an *imitatio Dei,* not only by obeying the commandment "You shall be holy, for I Yahweh am holy" (Lev. 20:26), but especially because, through her very existence in the world, her *imitatio Dei* became manifest. As her God was a 'Single One' among the gods, so Israel was a 'single one' among the nations; as her God was incomparable among the gods, so Israel was incomparable among the nations. Israel owed her incomparability not to herself, but to Yahweh, who mercifully elected and entered into communion with her—Yahweh the incomparable God, of whom Israel has confessed since His intervention in her history and still confesses this very day: יהוה מִי כָמוֹךְ [*yhwh mî kāmôkā*].[26]

It may be stated with conviction that one strong emphasis within the Balaam corpus is the assertion of the incomparability of Yahweh.

The sovereignty of Yahweh. Perhaps related to and growing out of the incomparability of Yahweh is the stress in the Balaam oracles on the absolute sovereignty of Yahweh. Indeed, this is stressed throughout the account. Yahweh's choice of Israel is rooted in His sovereignty. Yahweh's blessing of Israel comes from His sovereignty. Yahweh's use of Balaam, yes, and even of the donkey, are expressions of His sovereignty. In all His acts there is the patent demonstration of His essence: Yahweh is sovereign.

On this excellence of the divine Person, John Bright writes:

Equally prominent is Israel's understanding of the sovereign and exclusive lordship of Yahweh over His people of the demands that He has laid upon them and the response that He expects of them if they are to continue in His favor: in short, that whole understanding of reality that expressed itself in the concept of covenant. This again was a primitive feature in Israel's faith.[27]

Van Imschoot speaks on the issue of the sovereignty of Yahweh in this fashion:

Yahweh, without doubt, who chose Israel from all the nations (Ex 19:5; Am 3:2) and concluded an alliance with them and with their ancestors (Ex 24:8; Gn 15:8; 17:1, etc.) bound Himself to protect His people in a very special way, on condition, however, that in exchange they observe the stipulations of the moral and religious order which Yahweh had imposed on them (Ex 19:5; 24:3; Dt 11:13-17, 26-32; 26:17-19; 28:1-68). But since the covenant is an act of pure benevolence on God's part (Am 9:7; Is 11:1; Jer 31:3; Ez 16:3-14; Dt 7:7-9; 10:15), it does not violate the rights of any other people and is not contrary to God's justice; it is uniquely an act of Yahweh's sovereignty, "who shows favor to whom He shows favor" (Ex 33:19), that is to say, He grants favors to those whom He wishes.[28]

Yahweh's sovereignty relative to Israel is seen in His mighty acts on her behalf. But it is also seen in the pithy statement in Numbers 23:21, "The shout of a King is among them." It is in the ascription of this title to Yahweh that His sovereignty is manifest. Further, it is unfortunate that Numbers 24:23b is customarily regarded as hopelessly corrupt.[29] For it would seem that in fact this verse is a climax to the sevenfold oracle pattern.[30] As translated by the *New American Standard Bible* this verse reads, "Alas, who can live except God has ordained it?" Those words do not need to be reconstructed; they need to be believed. Yahweh is sovereign. This verse seems to put into capsule form His sovereignty.

The Immutability of Yahweh. Another basic attribute of Yahweh that is stressed throughout the Balaam oracles is immutability; He changes not. Some have imagined a conflict in chapter 22 that would suggest that God does in fact change. Noth, for example, says that if the connection of the chapter is left as it stands, the anger of Yahweh in 22:22 would be "an act of irresponsible despotism on God's part."[31]

Such a charge, however, is based on faulty presuppositions concerning the text and a seemingly naive approach to the complexities of human nature.[32] Were there not the question of source analysis, it is doubtful whether such a conflict in the activity of God would have been suggested. To maintain a proper view of God, Noth seems to suggest, one has to have a low view of the text. Yet it is only from the text that we ever learned a pure and lofty view of God in the first place.

Noth's charge also betrays what seems to be a naive approach to human nature. He wants to read the story of Balaam as though Balaam were less complex than the figure that the text presents. Balaam is no stick figure in this account. In the shifting personality of Balaam lies the reason for God's anger. Balaam says one thing with his lips but thinks another in his heart. The anger of God in chapter 22 is to be found because of the sinful nature of Balaam, not in a low view of Deity. Yahweh's immutability is not affected by this chapter.

On the contrary, the immutability of Yahweh is stated with precision in Numbers 23:19:

God is not a man, that He is able to lie,
Nor is He a son of man that He is able to change.
Has He said, and will He not do it?
Or has He spoken and will He not confirm it?[33]

Balaam is used as a foil for God. Balaam is constantly shifting, prevaricating, equivocating, changing—and he is himself the prime example of the distinction between God and man.

One of the effective pedagogical devices found in the Scriptures is that of contrast and comparison. Witness, for example, the contrast and comparison implicit in the linking together of chapters 38 and 39 of the book of Genesis. So it is here. Balaam is the contrast to Yahweh as Judah is the contrast to his brother Joseph (as we will see later). Further, Balaam is used by Yahweh to state the distinction: God is utterly distinct from man in that God is unable to lie. He is unable to deviate from His purpose. He is in fact, immutable. The Mighty One is different from man; that which He has spoken He has bound Himself to fulfill and to accomplish.

Van Imschoot has discussed this major truth:

God is immutable in His being and also in His will: "He does not call back His words" (Is 31:2). He has spoken and has not repented. He has resolved and has not gone back on His word (Jer 4:28). "The heavens shall vanish like smoke, and the earth shall be worn away like a garment, and the inhabitants thereof shall perish (like gnats); but My salvation will be forever and My justice shall not fail" (Is 51:6; cf. 51:8). If Israel was not consumed because of its faults, it is because "Yahweh does not change" (Mal 3:6). This means that He is constant in His plans of salvation, because He is "the eternal rock" of His people.[34]

The problem of the repentance of God in this connection is more apparent than real. There are, of course, passages that speak of the repentance of God in anthropopathic terms, even as Van Imschoot lists.[35] But the teaching of Numbers 23:19 is of a different order. The word *repent* in this verse is parallel to the word *lie,* and in this context is colored in tone by that very association. There are times when the Old Testament writers speak in anthropopathic terms of God "repenting." But the repentance of God is never tantamount to falsehood on His part. The concept of the truth of Yahweh is related to immutability, as this verse insists.[36]

Since God is truth, He does not lie; in fact, He cannot lie. He is immutable.

The Love of Yahweh. That the love of Yahweh for Israel is part of the

Heilsgeschichte of the Balaam pericope is made explicit in the following verse:

> But Yahweh your God was not willing to listen to Balaam, rather Yahweh your God turned the curse into a blessing for you because Yahweh your God loves you. [Deut. 23:5; (Heb. 6)]

The love of Yahweh for Israel is closely aligned to His incomparability, as may be seen in Deuteronomy 4:31–40. The latter passage is a significant parallel to the Balaam account, because it is roughly contemporaneous with the Balaam episode on chronological grounds. When Balaam and Balak were plotting the cursing of Israel, Moses was instructing the people of God within the camp concerning God's love for them and concerning His incomparable relationship to them. That splendid text reads:

> For Yahweh your God is a compassionate God:[37]
>   He will never abandon you;
>   He will never exterminate you;
>   And He will never forget the covenant with
>   your fathers which He swore to them.
> Indeed, ask, if you will, concerning the former days,
>   those days which were before you;
>   Ask even from the day when God created man on earth,
>   Ask even from one end of the heavens to another:
> Has anything like this great thing ever happened?
> Has anything corresponding to it ever even been heard?
>   That a people actually heard the voice of a god,
>   speaking from the midst of the fire—even as you
>   have heard—and survived?
> Or, has a god ever attempted to go to take for himself a
> nation from the midst of another nation,
>   by means of trials,
>   and signs,
>   and wonders,
>   and war,
>   and by means of a strong hand and an outstretched arm,
>   and with great terrors—
>   corresponding to all which Yahweh your God has done
>   for you in Egypt, before your eyes?
> *You* were made to see in order that you might experience

that Yahweh is the genuine God:
There is absolutely none besides Him!

From the heavens He made you hear His voice to instruct you,
And on earth He caused you to see His great fire,
And you heard His words from the midst of the fire:

Simply because He loves your fathers,
   And He made His choice in his seed after him;
   And He personally brought you out from Egypt,
   by means of His great strength—
dispossessing before you nations mightier and
      vaster than you,
   in order to cause you to enter,
   and to give to you their land as an inheritance,
      even today!

So know today,
And bring it to your heart:

That Yahweh is the genuine God
   in the heavens above,
   and on the earth below:
      None other exists!

So guard His statutes and His commandments which
I am giving to you today,
   in order that it may go well with you,
   and for your children after you,
   and in order that you may stretch out your days
   on the land which Yahweh your God is about to
   give to you in perpetuity.

This magnificent text seems to be the commentary from within as to the significance of the Balaam oracles, which were from without the camp. In this passage there is an extraordinary emphasis on the love God has for His people and the incomparable nature of His person and His acts on behalf of His own. The uniqueness of Israel, which is related by Moses in Deuteronomy 4 and by Balaam in Numbers 23, is not something inherent in her as a people. It is rather an absolutely unparalleled relationship with Yahweh. One might go back to the beginning of man's existence to ask whether such a thing has ever been, and one might search the universe from one end to another to find a parallel. Since the beginning of time, there has been nothing to compare with God's relationship to His own.

The reason is stated by Moses. It is based on Yahweh's love for the patriarchs: "He loves your fathers" (Deut. 4:37). That the verb *'āhab* is to be translated as present tense seems correct in that it is an emotive word used in the speech of an eternal God. Moreover, God's purpose for His people is stated quite emphatically. He desired Israel to know experientially that Yahweh is the genuine God. No other exists. This stress on the incomparability of Yahweh is here linked to God's love for His people.

Moses thus explains a large part of the *Heilsgeschichte* of the Balaam passages when he tells Israel that Yahweh was acting in her behalf out of His great love (Deut. 23:6). Further, God's love is related to His incomparability (Deut. 4:31-40). Moreover, the latter passage introduces us to the mighty acts of Yahweh for His own—further elements in the *Heilsgeschichte* of the Balaam pericope.

THE RIGHTEOUS ACTS OF YAHWEH

We are indebted to Micah for explaining the Balaam story as a part of the righteous acts of Yahweh (Mic. 6:5):

> My people, remember
> What Balak king of Moab counseled
> And what Balaam son of Beor answered him;
> From Shittim to Gilgal,
>   In order to know the righteous acts of Yahweh.[38]

This too is a major element in the *Heilsgeschichte* of the Balaam pericope. "The God who acts" is a fitting theme for theological consideration.[39] Some scholars, however, have said that the acts of God, rather than the words of God, are His means of revelation. That sets the acts and the words of God in opposition, the acts alone conveying revelation. Such is a false methodology, as is demonstrated amply by the Balaam incident. The God of the Bible is ever presented as the God who acts *and* the God who speaks. The Balaam narrative blends the acts and the words of God into an inseparable unity. One cannot, on sound methodological grounds, extricate one without doing violence to the other.[40]

We may now look briefly at the righteous acts of Yahweh in the Balaam story.

His acts and the spoken word. The ancient belief in the spoken word is described by van Imschoot:

> For the ancients and the uncivilized the word is not simply the expression of a thought or of a will; it is something concrete, something existing and active, and is, so to say, charged with the force of the soul

of the one who pronounces it. The pronounced word does not only subsist in the conscience of the one who pronounced it and in the one who heard it, it exists in itself and acts just as such a concrete force would act.[41]

This is the cultural background of the events of Numbers 22. Balak did not know for sure if his resort to the supernatural use of the curse would avail. We may observe the use of the word *perhaps* (*'ûlay*) in Numbers 22:6. But this was his desperate attempt to try to escape what he thought was impending doom.

Nevertheless, as Kaufmann states, this pagan view of the efficacy of the spoken word is to be contrasted to the word spoken by Yahweh. The word of Yahweh is efficacious, not on the level of a magical (or demonic) sense, but as the expression of His sovereign will:

> In pagan thought blessings and curses are a variety of incantations; they are regarded as automatically effective, and—since the gods also use and are affected by them—transcendentally potent. YHWH neither uses nor is affected by incantations. He acts by the word; but that this is no more than an expression of his will is indicated by the fact that he never uses fixed words or formulas, as do Ormazd or Brahma. His utterances simply say what he wills at a given moment: "Let there be light . . . Let there be a firmament."[42]

If the attempt to curse Israel had been a merely magical act, Israel would have had nothing to fear, of course. If, however, the appeal was to demonic powers (viewed as the gods of the nations), the situation would have been more serious. Yahweh sovereignly moved in His own mysterious way to frustrate the futile attempt of a petty pagan king to vent his fear, as an object lesson for Israel and as a polemic against paganism. It is in this context that the relatively large amount of space given to the Balaam materials in proportion to the period of time covered in the book of Numbers is justified.

The polemical nature of some sections of the Old Testament is gaining recognition as of importance to the theology of the mighty acts of God. For example, it is on the basis of polemics that Leah Bronner has demonstrated the credibility and the purposefulness of the mighty acts of Yahweh in the stories of Elijah and Elisha.[43]

In Yahweh's intervention in the Balaam story there is an attack on paganism that Israel should have taken to heart. The dynamic presence of Yahweh, the God of Israel, is of infinitely more worth than the spoken word of the enemies of Israel from without the camp. How could one trust in the power of the spoken word of paganism when Yahweh had intervened and overruled in the Balaam incident? How could an Israelite place his trust in the gods of the nations when Yahweh, the God of Israel, had acted in his behalf?

His acts and the donkey story. A second area in which the righteous acts of Yahweh are displayed in the Balaam pericope concerns the donkey incident of Numbers 22. As viewed by many scholars, there are two major difficulties with the donkey section. The first difficulty concerns the relationship of this incident to the pericope as a whole. The second concerns the nature of the miracle.

Whereas many scholars have dismissed the donkey story as not contributing anything to the story, Mowinckel and von Pákozdy have noted that the donkey story functions as an action-slowing and tension-developing element.[44] It is incorrect to state that no advance is made by the use of the story. Comparison may be made with the Joseph story (Gen. 37–50). Use of the device of repetition in the Joseph chapters may be compared to the thrice-repeated attempt of the Angel of Yahweh to frustrate the advance of Balaam. For example, there is the repetition in the dreams of Joseph in Genesis 37:5–10 (giving him the derisive sobriquet "that dreamer"). There are also repetitions of dreams in Genesis 40–41.

But perhaps the most informative parallel to our account is the so-called "intrusion" of chapter 38 into the midst of the Joseph story. Remarks similar to those made concerning Numbers 22 are applied in this case as well. Genesis 37:36 relates that Joseph was sold to Potiphar, an officer of Pharaoh. Genesis 39:1 is a restatement of that incident. Hence, chapter 38 might be said to "add nothing at all to the story." There is no advance in our knowledge of Joseph.

The careful reader, however, finds in Genesis 38 a vital element for the understanding of Joseph's character, even though his name is not mentioned. By contrast with the apostate acts of his older brother Judah the righteousness of Joseph is set in relief. Judah reached such a spiritual nadir that he was forced to admit that his Canaanite daughter-in-law demonstrated a righteousness higher than his, when she acted incestuously in the guise of a ritual cultic prostitute (Gen. 38:26). This is then the bold and graphic setting for the acts of Joseph in chapter 39 when daily (יוֹם יוֹם, *yôm yôm*) he was confronted with attempts of his master's wife to seduce him (Gen. 39:9), yet refused to compromise himself or his God. The contrast with Judah is heightened, considering that he was a free agent in the land of promise, whereas Joseph was a slave in a land of curse.

To regard Genesis 38 as an "unnecessary intrusion" into the story of Joseph is to miss the point of the literature at hand. The same may be said respecting the story of the donkey and the Angel in Numbers 22. Further, other examples are not lacking in great literature of all ages. Chapter 32 "Cetology," of *Moby Dick* by Herman Melville "does not advance the story," but is an integral and essential element of the whole.

We agree with Goldberg that deleting the donkey story from the narrative would deprive the text of its most beautiful point. He writes:

Dieses ganze Stück ist bei allem Ernst doch voll beissendem Spott: Der blinde Seher wird der sehenden Eselin gegenübergestellt. Selbst deren Mund könnte Gott öffnen—nur um etwas zu sagen, bedarf er Bileams nicht. Eben darin erweist sich Bileam als die Verkehrung des Propheten seines Zeitalters, des Moses. Dieser war nicht nur Seher, einer, zu dem Gott von Angesicht zu Angesicht redet, sondern ein Fürsprecher seines Volkes. Ihn konnte man nicht mit Geschenken zu irgendeinem Geschäft des Segnens oder des Fluchens holen, ihm wurde niemals Ehrung angetragen. Vielmehr lietete er sein Volk und trug dessen Last trotz all der Unbill, die er erfahren musstc.[45]

The narrative is one of studied ridicule. We see the prophet Balaam as a blind seer, seeing less than the dumb animal. In the graphic representation of Balaam pitted against the donkey, we also see a more important contrast, as Goldberg avers: the contrast of Balaam and Moses. The long shadow of Moses falls across the pages of the Balaam story even though Moses is never named. Certainly a Hebrew reader of the account of Balaam's folly in the donkey incident would be compelled to contrast the foolishness of Balaam with the magnificent image of Moses. Moses spoke face to face with God. Balaam was a blind "seer" instructed by the mouth of a dumb beast.

What then is the purpose of the donkey incident apart from the function of slowing the drama and increasing the tension? The purpose seems to be polemical. Many have observed the humor in the contrast of the seer and his donkey. It could not be more stunning, more devastating. This is the penultimate in polemics against paganism. It is well known that the ass has been depicted from the earliest times as a subject of stupidity and contrariness.[46] Whether that reputation is deserved or not, it is a common enough element in wisdom literature to form the setting for the polemics against the powers of Balaam. Further, in the contrast between Balaam and Moses, there is, of course, the contrast between the respective deities. The incident of the donkey of Balaam is thus best regarded as a satirical attack on paganism. It is not to be deleted without the loss of the "best part."

We may now turn to the second difficulty of the story, the nature of the miracle. The question of the miraculous brings immediately to the fore the distinction between the naturalist and the supernaturalist, a discussion ably treated by C. S. Lewis in his work on miracles.[47] Lewis states that "the difficulties of the unbeliever do not begin with questions about this or that particular miracle; they begin much further back."[48] Nevertheless, even the supernaturalist limits the kinds of miracles that are admitted. Lewis writes, "It by no means follows from Supernaturalism that Miracles of any sort do in fact occur."[49] Some miracles are more difficult for the supernaturalist to accept than others, e.g., Balaam's talking donkey.

A century ago Samuel Cox wrote, "It is rational to believe in miracles, but it is not easy to believe in *all* the miracles recorded in the Old Testament Scriptures" [his emphasis].[50] The same writer continues:

> It is rational to believe in miracles, then, if we believe in God and in any revelation of his will to men. But to believe in some miracles is not to believe in all miracles; and, obviously, some of the miracles recorded in the Old Testament make a very large and heavy demand on our faith; none of them, perhaps, a larger and heavier demand than this, that "the dumb ass speaking with man's voice forbad the madness of the prophet" [2 Pet. 2:16].[51]

Since only in the realm of fable do animals speak in human voices, most moderns regard the speech of the donkey as an example of the fabulous, the fairy tale.[52] Moriarty avers, "We only deceive ourselves if we think that the sacred writer really believed that an ass at one time complained to its owner."[53] Supposed mythical parallels are found in classical literature—parallels suggesting the same type of fabulous genre. One example is the speech of Xanthus to Achilles:

> Then fleet Xanthus answered from under the yoke—for white-armed Hera had endowed him with human speech—and he bowed his head till his mane touched the ground as it hung down from under the yokeband. "Dread Achilles," said he, "we will indeed save you now, but the day of your death is near, and the blame will not be ours, for it will be heaven and stern fate that will destroy you. Neither was it through any sloth or slackness on our part that the Trojans stripped Patroclus of his armor. It was the mighty god whom lovely Leto bore that slew him as he fought among the foremost, and vouchsafed a triumph to Hector. We two can fly as swiftly as Zephyrus who they say is fleetest of all winds; nevertheless it is your doom to fall by the hand of a man and of a god."

When he had thus said the Erinyes stayed his speech, and Achilles answered him in great sadness, saying, "Why, O Xanthus, do you thus foretell my death? You need not do so, for I well know that I am to fall here, far from my dear father and mother; none the more, however, shall I stay my hand till I have given the Trojans their fill of fighting."
So saying, with a loud cry he drove his horses to the front.[54]

Others, not wishing to attribute legend, fable, or fairy tale to the biblical text, have argued that the miracle was internal and subjective rather than external and objective. Maimonides, for example, suggested that the event was a dream vision, which Balaam had at night.[55] There is no indication in the text that the event was a dream vision, however. Perhaps the strongest defense of the internal viewpoint was given by Hengstenberg in his major treatise on Balaam. Hengstenberg was a supernaturalist, but he argued that the incident of the donkey's speech was a miracle internal to Balaam rather than external (in the donkey).[56] Beek also internalized the story by saying that the speaking of the ass was Balaam's bad conscience.[57]

The proper starting point, however, is the text itself, not in our philosophical difficulties with a concept. The text quite simply relates the event as an objective, external phenomenon. Noth is clear and to the point:

The ass's ability to speak, with which may be compared the speaking of the serpent in Gen. 3. 1ff., is not an element that is particularly stressed or even necessary; it is, however, an integral part of the narrative and is attributed to a miracle on the part of Yahweh (v. 28a) which indicates how directly and unusually Yahweh acted in this affair of blessing or curse for Israel.[58]

The biblical text says, "Yahweh opened the mouth of the donkey and she said to Balaam . . ." (Num. 22:28a). The plain wording of this passage seems decisive. If one were to take the ass cum grano salis, how would one then regard the Angel of Yahweh, who is the more important figure in the story? May He also be dismissed with a laugh as simple naivete on the part of the writer? If the speech of the donkey is regarded as an internal phenomenon, is the appearance of the Angel of Yahweh (a theophany) also to be regarded as internal?
As Unger insists, "The case of the speaking ass is an instance of the omnipotence of God, and is not to be explained away by unbelief."[59] The speaking of the ass is demanded by the wording of the Old Testament and

is confirmed in explicit terms in the New Testament. Peter writes, "For a dumb donkey, speaking with a voice of a man, restrained the madness of the prophet" (2 Pet. 2:16).

A rather remarkable phenomenon respecting New Testament citations of Old Testament passages has been observed by some scholars. It seems that some of the most perplexing data of the Old Testament are the very elements seized upon by the New Testament writers and exploited for their contributions to our knowledge of the acts of God. Allis observes:

> It is most instructive and illuminating to study the New Testament use of passages which modern scholars would regard as myth, legend or folklore and seek to "demythologize," in order to find in them some element of truth which the modern mind can regard as profitable. The appeal to the account of the creation of women (Gen. 2:12f.) by Paul (I Cor. 11:8; I Tim. 2:13), to a primitive monogamy (Gen. 2:23f.) by Jesus (Matt. 19:5), to the flood by Jesus (Matt. 23:37f.) and by Peter (I Peter 3:20; 2 Peter 2:5), to the brazen serpent (Num. 21:8) by Jesus (John 3:14), *to the speaking ass (Num. 22:28) by Peter* (2 Peter 2:16), to Jonah in the belly of the great fish (Jonah 2:1) by Jesus (Matt. 12:40), illustrate the striking difference between the two methods of interpretation. What the one treats as difficulties to be gotten rid of, the other appeals to as significant evidences of God's activity in human affairs [Emphasis added.].[60]

The speech of the donkey is thus to be regarded as a genuine element in the righteous acts of Yahweh. Yet we should view this miracle in some perspective and not attempt to make more of it than the text does. In the Numbers account the emphasis should not be placed unduly on the donkey. Theology is ever about God. We must not let the strange zoology divert the spotlight from the central theology. Respecting this issue Vischer states:

> Assuredly [Israel seems to have forsaken its blessing]—yet nevertheless (and this is the miracle of God's faithfulness, which is incomparably more wonderful than the fact that Balaam's ass opens its mouth to speak), the LORD transforms the curse in the mouth of Balaam into blessing. Despite all Israel's infidelity the blessing of Abraham and the blessing of Jacob remain.[61]

We should not, therefore, make more of the speech of the donkey than is made by the text. As miracles go, this is a rather minor item. Far too often the incredulous naturalist sidetracks the pressured believer into a prolonged defense of relatively minor miracles such as Jonah's fish and Balaam's donkey. But that only diverts attention from the issue that is of supreme import: the miracle of the resurrection of the Lord Jesus Christ.[62]

If, in fact, Christ has risen from the dead (1 Cor. 15:3-8), then God's use of Balaam's donkey for a moment is of minor significance. Compared with the resurrection of our Lord, the donkey's speech is but a rough common stone beside a lustrous diamond. Conversely, if Christ is not risen from the grave, the gift of intelligent speech to all the animals of creation could not assuage the despair that would result to the broken believer. For, "if Christ has not been raised, then our preaching is vain, your faith also is vain" (1 Cor. 15:14).

The miracle of the donkey must also be seen in the perspective of the power of God. We ever live with a restricted view of God. We need to have our minds expanded by the liberating Word of God (John 8:32). Job's description of the vast power of God demonstrated in His creation and control of the universe is unparalleled in graphic sweep and majestic impact (Job 26). Yet, in view of all we know of God's mighty acts, Job (26:14) has to conclude:

Look! These are just the fringes of His ways;
And what faint whisper we hear of Him!
But His mighty thunder—who could attend?

Surely one who refuses the possibility of God's using a lowly creature in whatever way He so desires has a rather petty view of the One whom universes are unable to contain.

The miracle is not only possible, it is purposeful. If God wished to use an animal in His dealings with a pagan, superstitious mantic, so be it. There is poetic justice in this act. Balaam the *bārū* was experienced in seeking vague indications of the will of the gods through examining the viscera of animals as well as the movements of the creatures.[63]

Before God revealed Himself to Balaam in the person of the Angel of Yahweh, He first "got his attention" in this dramatic fashion. Balaam the "seer" could not see what even the donkey saw. Balaam had to learn from a donkey before he could learn from God. What a graphic tool for polemics against the superstitions of the East. How wonderfully well it fit the occasion. Balaam's ass was no Xanthus, however. There was no majestic prophecy coming from the animal's mouth, only the words that an animal might speak if given the chance. The prophecies came through the voice of one stranger than a donkey—they came from the pagan mantic Balaam himself. And all of those events, the opening of the mouth of the donkey and the opening of the mouth (and eyes) of the mantic—all are among the righteous acts of Yahweh (Mic. 6:5).

His acts as the Deliverer. A third major area in which the righteous acts of Yahweh are demonstrated in the Balaam story relates to Yahweh as the Deliverer of His people. Yahweh's mighty acts are seen respecting the spoken word and the donkey incident, as displayed above. But they are portrayed more excellently within the oracle corpus in terms of the deliverance of His people.

There are three tense spheres in the concept of God's acts of deliverance for His own, each contributing significantly to the *Heilsgeschichte* of our corpus. God's past acts of deliverance center on the Exodus from the land of Egypt. There is a sense in which it may be said that the Exodus was the central event in the history of Israel before the advent of the Messiah. It may be seen as corresponding for the Old Testament believer to the meaning of the death and resurrection of Christ for the New Testament believer. This was the demonstration of Yahweh's deliverance and redemption of His people.

Numbers 23:22 reads:

> God is bringing them out of Egypt;
> He is for him as the horns of the aurochs!

Similarly, Numbers 24:8a reads:

> God is bringing him out of Egypt;
> He is for him as the horns of the aurochs![64]

God is Israel's Deliverer. It is significant that in these two parallel verses the verbs are participles. Whereas the act of the deliverance from Egypt was in the past, the event of forty years' standing still had not culminated when Balaam uttered these words. The deliverance from Egypt was still being effected in that the people were not yet in the land of promise.

The vivid image of the horns of the aurochs brings to the fore the supernatural acts and mighty displays of Yahweh's power on behalf of Israel in the Exodus event. Lehman writes:

> The Exodus account of Israel's deliverance from Egypt gave special emphasis to the supernatural workings of God. A casual study of these references [Ex. 3:20; 4:2-9, 21; 6:6, 7; 7:3, 9-12; 8:19; 9:15; 14:22, 31; 15:8, 11; 34:10; Ps. 78:42-51] reveals a vocabulary which unequivocally

asserts the demonstration of miraculous power. This vocabulary includes such words as *wonders, signs, miracles, mighty acts,* and *powers.* These words most aptly describe the ten plagues, the dividing of the Red Sea, the giving of manna, and the supplying to them water from the rock.[65]

Certainly, there can be no question but that the Exodus is central to the righteous acts of Yahweh.

The second sphere, anticipated above, is Yahweh's acts of deliverance in the time present to the oracles. The totality of the Balaam narrative bears witness to this factor. More specifically, within the oracles there is emphasis on Yahweh's present acts in delivering Israel.

Numbers 23:21*b* reads:

Yahweh his God is with him!
And the battle cry of a King is in him!

The astounding fact confronted by Balaam was that Yahweh was personally at work in Israel. Yahweh had settled among His own and had become their resident King. That was the grand purpose of the Exodus, as is stated so nicely in Psalm 114:1-2:

When Israel went forth from Egypt,
The House of Jacob from a people of incomprehensible
speech,
Judah became His sanctuary,
Israel His dominion.

God's purpose in delivering Israel was to have a people in whom He might dwell and over whom He might have dominion. Balaam and the psalmist were given similar insights into the intent of the Exodus. The one whom God delivers He wishes to indwell; and the one whom God indwells, He desires to rule. Amazingly, Balaam was the first to be given the revelation that Yahweh was the King of His people Israel.[66]

God was at work in Israel. Balaam was led by the Spirit to say (Num. 23:23):

Now it must be said for Jacob,
And for Israel—What God has done![67]

The third time sphere of the deliverance of Israel by the righteous acts of Yahweh is the future, from the perspective of the events in Numbers.

Such is found in Numbers 24:8c–e:

> He will devour the nations, His enemies,
> And their bones He will crush,
> And their arrows He will shatter.

Since Israel is animated by the power of God, all opposition to her must be futile.

But Balaam's most striking prophecy is contained in his fourth oracle, as the mighty acts of Yahweh as Deliverer have their climax (Num. 24:17):

> I see Him, but not now,
> I behold Him, but not near,
> A star shall march out from Jacob,
> And a scepter shall rise from Israel—
> And shall crush the temples of Moab,
> Even tear down all the sons of Sheth.[68]

Israel had experienced Yahweh's deliverance in the past and was experiencing His deliverance in the present. But the grandest expression relates to the coming of Israel's future Deliverer. He will be like star and scepter in His royalty and will bring victory over the enemies of His people. That this passage refers to the Messiah is remarkable.[69] This is one of the grandest prophecies of Messiah in the Pentateuch, and it comes from the mouth of a pagan, unrelated to the promise. Such unexpectedness drives one to remember such verses as Isaiah 55:8:

> My thoughts are not your thoughts,
> Neither are your ways my ways, says Yahweh.

The remaining oracles (the rest of IV, plus V, VI, and VII)[70] detail in broad sweep the future acts of Yahweh in the deliverance of His people. Those who have cursed Israel are themselves cursed in direct fulfillment of the primal blessing accorded the patriarchs from the time of Abraham. Israel is blessed. This fact was told to Balaam upon the occasion of his first flirtation with the elders of Moab and Midian (Num. 22:12):

> And God said to Balaam,
> "Do not go with them;
> You shall not curse the people;
> *For they are blessed*" (italics added).

The coming Deliverer forms the *Heils* of the *Heilsgeschichte*. Certainly the later prophets of Israel, particularly Isaiah, were to be given more detailed and complete revelation concerning the coming One. But the revelation given to Balaam is significant and stunning.[71]

We may note briefly as well, that the Deliverer works deliverance for His own, and hence, destruction for His enemies. With the blessing comes a curse—a curse on those who are in opposition to the blessing (Num. 24:9).

Blessed is everyone who blesses you,
And cursed is everyone who curses you.

SUMMARY

We began this section with a consideration of the development of Yahweh's blessing being the specific contribution of the Balaam incident to Old Testament theology. The blessing vouchsafed Abraham was under attack in the machinations of Balak and Balaam. God used the incident to display to Israel and to the nations His sovereign purpose in conferring His absolute blessing on His people.

A second major element to the *Heilsgeschichte* of the pericope concerns those things said and implied concerning the source of blessing, Israel's God. Properly considered, this concerns the name and appellatives of Yahweh,[72] as well as His attributes. Those attributes that are given special attention in the pericope include Yahweh's incomparability, His sovereignty, His immutability, and His love.

A third element considered was the display of the righteous acts of Yahweh. Among those acts given emphasis were God's actions related to the spoken word, His acts and the donkey story, and His acts as the Deliverer.

In this section we have attempted to center attention on the Person and acts of Yahweh, for He is the true center (*Mitte*) of Old Testament theology.[73]

We need not say that within the Balaam oracles there is to be found every element of the theology of the Pentateuch. Creation, for example, is a major omission. But we may suggest that the oracles are indeed a summarization, even the quintessence of Yahweh's relationship to Israel. That the mediator of this revelation was outside the congregation of Israel, without the blessing of Israel, and apart from the God of Israel, is remarkable.

Throughout the account we sense polemics. There is a polemic in Balaam's name,[74] in the donkey episode, and in the event as a whole. Not only is God teaching something about Israel, He is also teaching something about those who are outside of Israel. The folly of attempting to come to the will of God through mantic means is everywhere demonstrated in unforgettable terms. The most celebrated diviner of all is powerless before the God of Israel.

There is a sense in which we may compare God's use of Balaam with His use of Cyrus. Cyrus was sovereignly ordained as an instrument of Yahweh, and this fact was revealed long before his birth. Cyrus is termed by Yahweh "My shepherd" (Isa. 44:28), and even "His anointed" (Isa. 45:1). Yahweh's purpose in His use of Cyrus is stated fully by Isaiah ben Amoz (Isa. 45:3b-5):

> In order that you may know that it is I,
> Yahweh the God of Israel who calls you by name.
> For the sake of My servant Jacob,
> And Israel My chosen;
> I have even called you by name,
> I give you a title even though you do not know Me.
> I am Yahweh and there is no other;
> Apart from Me there is no God:
> I will gird you though you have not known Me.

Yahweh is sovereign. He uses whom He pleases, how He wills, for His own glory. Yahweh is incomparable; none may be compared to Him. Yahweh is irrevocably bound to His people by His own gracious desire. Israel is blessed, and Yahweh the God of glory guarantees this blessing for all time.

With Balaam, with Cyrus, with Moses, with Isaiah—with all those who know anything about our God, we may exclaim:

יהוה מִי כָמוֹךָ! (yhwh mî kāmôkā).

AN APOLOGETIC: BALAAM AND THE WORD

God sovereignly used Balaam, a pagan mantic, to communicate His Word. This has profound implications for the present crisis in the church regarding the issue of the inspiration and inerrancy of the Scriptures. Our shelves are heavy with works touching the issue of inspiration and its corollaries. But the writer is unaware that the role of Balaam has had its proper due respecting this issue.

Many hold the *a priori* assumption that since God used men to record His revelation, His word (though perfect in its source) was necessarily corrupted in its transmission through fallible men. Perhaps one of the most original and instructive illustrations of this point of view is given by Brunner. J. R. C. Perkin writes:

> Emil Brunner has a brilliant illustration about the Bible in *Our Faith*. He says it is possible to buy a record with the trade name of "His Master's Voice," and be told that if you play it you will hear the master, Caruso's voice. So you will, or at least you will hear a record of it; but there will be other noises as well. The needle may scratch the record, and it is possible to concentrate so fiercely on the scratching that the effect of the master's voice is completely lost on you. Perhaps we may extend the illustration a little to complete the picture. If the needle does scratch slightly, there is not too much to worry about, but if the scratching is really bad, there is no point in saying that it is a good record; far better admit that the master's voice can be heard despite the recording.[75]

In our age of high fidelity, stereophonic (and quadraphonic) sound, the suggestion of a scratchy needle on an old-fashioned 78-RPM recording is quite apt. But it is appropriate as an illustration of the phenomenon of biblical authority only if Balaam is forgotten.

For in the figure of Balaam we have the negation of Brunner's illustration. If we were to catalogue the men and women who were used by God in transmitting His revelation, we would not be able to find one less likely than Balaam. He is the least probable of the prophets. His character flaws are so manifest that he was denounced, even excoriated, by three different writers of the New Testament as the paradigm of the false teacher. He was not a part of Israelite prophetism, in the strict sense, nor was he a believer in the God of Israel, in a saving sense. Balaam died as an enemy of Israel in the enemy camp—hostile to the end toward the people blessed of God.

Knowing our own weaknesses, we may grant the possibility of flaws in the personal lives of the greatest of the prophets (excepting only our impeccable Lord). But in the case of Balaam it is difficult to find anything right.

Nevertheless, when Balaam spoke the Word of God, he spoke just that: *the Word of God*. The corrupted nature of Balaam *left no scratch* on the record of the Word of God. Note again the insistence throughout the narrative on the fact that Balaam *could not alter* the words God gave him.

Numbers 22:20,
"But only the word which I speak to you shall you do."

Numbers 22:39,
"The word that God puts in my mouth, that I will speak."
Numbers 23:3,
"Perhaps Yahweh will come to me, and whatever He
shows me I will tell you."
Numbers 23:5,
Then Yahweh put a word in Balaam's mouth and said,
"Return to Balak, and you shall speak thus."
Numbers 23:12,
"Must I not be careful to speak what Yahweh
puts in my mouth?"
Numbers 23:16,
Then Yahweh met Balaam and put a word in his mouth
and said,
"Return to Balak, and thus you shall speak."
Numbers 23:17,
And Balak said to him,
"What has Yahweh spoken?"
Numbers 23:26,
"Did I not tell you, whatever Yahweh speaks, that
I must do?"
Numbers 24:2,
And the Spirit of God came upon him.
Numbers 24:4,
The oracle of him who hears the words of God,
Who sees the vision of Shaddai.
Numbers 24:12-13,
"Did I not tell your messengers . . .
I could not do anything contrary to the mouth of Yahweh,
either good or bad, of my own heart.
What Yahweh speaks, that I will speak?"
Numbers 24:16,
The oracle of him who hears the words of God,
And knows the knowledge of the Most High,
And sees the vision of Shaddai.

This list of verses within the brief compass of three chapters is impressive. An observable phenomenon in Scripture is the employment of repetition for emphasis. The intent of this pericope respecting Balaam's relationship to the Word of God is stressed so highly, one wonders how it might be missed. Moreover, we are dealing not only with the explicit statements of the text, but also with the underlying substructure as well.

Charles C. Ryrie has written: "Theological substructure is just as valid proof of any doctrine as explicit statements, and no discipline in all the realm of theological studies reveals theological substructure as Biblical Theology does."[76] The point seems quite clear: Even a wicked individual causes no scratch on the record of his Master's voice, when the Master is using him in a sovereign manner.

Now, this is not a retreat to a supposed dictation theory (if there ever was such). The personality of Balaam is evident in word choice, in parallel synonyms, in meter, in form and structure. But his personality causes *no scratch*. Although he was a polytheist, the oracles are monotheistic. Even though he was engaging in mantic acts awaiting his revelation, his oracles betray none of the foolishness of the East. Despite his hatred of Israel (manifested in the events of Numbers 25), his oracles could not be more favorable to the descendants of Jacob. There is no scratch. Look where one might within the oracle corpus—the fidelity is the highest, the sound is pure. Listen again to his unwilling testimony (Num. 24:13):

I could not do anything contrary to the mouth of Yahweh,
either good or bad! of my own heart.

The inerrant character of the Word of God is not endangered by the corruption of man; it is firmly rooted in the character of God. This too is the testimony of Balaam (Num. 23:19):

God is not a man that He is able to lie,
Nor a son of man that He is able to change.

Yahweh has bound His Word to His character. "The master's voice" in this instance is the voice of a Master whose sound will be heard aright. And the story of the ever-enigmatic Balaam, with all of its bristling problems, may well be one of the strongest contextual and substructural arguments for the inerrancy of the Scriptures of God.

AN APPLICATION: BALAAM AND THE MINISTRY

A final word concerns the relationship Balaam bears on the issue of the Christian ministry. It is sometimes said that God never uses an unclean vessel. But remember Balaam. Perhaps it might better be said that God rarely uses unclean vessels.

This factor may indicate that our success syndrome is wrongly directed. A given minister of God's Word may have blessing and success simply because God is honoring His Word and not necessarily because He is honoring the messenger.

The fate of a Balaam is beyond comprehension. Perhaps the Balaam of the Numbers account will not be the only one who died in the enemy camp, having never been related to the God whose Word he communicated to others. Many others may say, "Lord, Lord," whom the Lord never knew. The story of Balaam tells us a great deal about our God. It also places a mirror before us. We must view ourselves.

NOTES

1. Ronald M. Hals, *The Theology of the Book of Ruth,* Facet Books, Biblical Series, no. 23. (Philadelphia: Fortress, 1969), p. 1.
2. Unless otherwise identified, all translations of the Bible in this paper are my own. Rabbi Samson Raphael Hirsch speaks of the repulsive and sickening dread Moab had for Israel in The Pentateuch Translated and Explained, vol. 4, trans. Isaac Levy, *Numbers,* 2d rev. ed. (London: L. Honig, 1964), p. 390.
3. Compare Exodus 23:27.
4. The phrase אַרְנֹ֖ן בָּמֹ֥ות בַּעֲלֵ֛י (*ba'ălê bāmôt 'arnôn*) is difficult to interpret. The RSV renders, "the lords of the heights of the Arnon"; the Torah reads, "the lords of Bamoth of the Arnon."
5. A. H. van Zyl, *The Moabites.* Praetoria Oriental Series, ed. A. van Selms (Leiden: E. J. Brill, 1960), 3: 7. Van Zyl discusses this passage at some length (pp. 8-10), arguing against critical reconstructions that would have the song refer to the defeat of Mesha, king of Moab, by Omri, king of Israel. The latter is argued by Bruno Baentsch, *Exodus-Leviticus-Numeri.* Hand-kommentar zum Alten Testament, ed. W. Nowack (Göttingen: Vandenhoeck und Ruprecht, 1903), p. 584. Van Zyl states, "To transfer this incident to the period of king Mesha conflicts with the historical context of this poem and there is no reason to doubt the historicity of this context" (p. 9). George Buchanan Gray is quite vague on the significance of this poem: "The one thing that is clear is that the poem celebrates a victory over Moab. Everything else is more or less uncertain." *A Critical and Exegetical Commentary on Numbers.* ICC (New York: Scribner's, 1903), p. 300.

Van Zyl's conclusion is that "the author of this pericope cited it to magnify the Israelite victory over Sihon. Thus this song was transformed by the Israelites into a mocking song, by which they demonstrated their own superiority over the Moabites. Perhaps we may suggest that this song was originally intended to be an Amorite mocking song, sung by their מֹשְׁלִים (*moshlîm*) after they had defeated the Moabites. This may be indicated by the sarcastic invitation to Moab to return to the recently destroyed city of Heshbon and to rebuild it. In ancient times the mocking song played a prominent part in warfare. This interpretation of the song conforms to its context, and it does not require inherent alterations of the text. By re-using this Amorite mocking song directed against the Moabites, the Israelites by implication uttered a threat against Moab. Thus they urged the king of Moab to acquire the help of Balaam" (*The Moabites,* p. 10).

It is to be observed further that chapter 21 of Numbers makes use of other older material, i.e., the quotation from the Book of the Wars of the Lord (vv. 14-15) and the Song of the Well (vv. 17-18). The use of the taunt song of verses 27-30 is only one element in a larger collection.

6. For a more detailed presentation of the difficulties than this cited from Cunningham Geikie, *Old Testament Characters* (New York: James Pott, 1897), pp. 112-13, consult Yohanan Aharoni, *The Land of the Bible: A Historical Geography,* trans. A. F. Rainey (Philadelphia: Westminster, 1967), pp. 184-92. Aharoni sees two traditions with entirely different conditions in Numbers 21 as against Numbers 33. He does state, however, that "already during the reign of the first Moabite King, Sihon, the King of Heshbon, carried out a sweeping campaign and conquered all of the Mishor as far as the Arnon. Heshbon, which had managed to hold its own against Moabite pressure, finally fell before the stormy attack of the Israelite tribes who then assumed for themselves the privilege of taking over all of its land as far as the Arnon.... Henceforth, the Arnon was the traditional border for the Israelite tribes in eastern Transjordan. On the other hand, the Moabites considered this an encroachment on their land. The pressure of their expansion was always directed northwards, and in different periods they succeeded in restoring this region to themselves as far as Medeba on the border of Heshbon and sometimes as far as the southern end of the eastern Jordan Valley, which was known even in Israelite tradition by the name 'the plains of Moab'" (p. 189).

Noth relates the victory song of Numbers 21:27-30 to the "extension of the land holdings of the tribe of Gad" Martin, Noth, *The Old Testament World,* trans. Victor I. Gruhn (Philadelphia: Fortress, 1966), p. 75. In this view, Noth is relating the victory song of Numbers 21 to the events of Numbers 32:28-36. For a brief survey of the geography and history of Moab, see William H. Morton, "Moab, Moabites," in *The Biblical World: A Dictionary of Biblical Archaeology,* ed. Charles F. Pfeiffer (London: Pickering & Inglis, 1966), pp. 392-96.

7. Eugene H. Merrill, *An Historical Survey of the Old Testament* (Nutley, N.J.: Craig, 1966), p. 125.

8. Ibid., p. 27.

9. The way in which many writers employ the term *Heilsgeschichte* today calls for some caution in its use. Yet the term may be very serviceable when it is employed according to the guidelines of Johann Christian Konrad von Hofmann (1810-1877). It was he who gave this term its classic expression. See the sympathetic exposition of von Hofmann's contribution by Hans-Joachim Kraus in *Die Biblische Theologie: Ihre Geschichte und Problematik* (Neukirchen-Vluyn: Neukirchener Verlag, 1970), pp. 247-53. I have developed these concepts in an unpublished paper presented to the Evangelical Theological Society (meeting at the Reformed Theological Seminary, Jackson, Miss., 30 December 1975), entitled: "Is There *Heil* for *Heilsgeschichte?*"

10. Since Moses is neither an observer nor a participant in the Balaam story, there has long been a question as to how this narrative could have come to Israel. The famous Talmud citation Baba Bathra 14*b*-15*a* reads: "Moses wrote his own book and the section concerning Balaam, and Job." The inclusion of the words, "the section concerning Balaam," would indicate that this was a matter of concern among the ancients as well.

Hengstenberg suggested that Balaam may have gone to Moses upon leaving Balak, hoping for a reward from his enemy which he did not gain from his ally. Then, on being rebuffed by Moses, Balaam would then have turned to the Midianites in his last vain attempt for payment. E. W. Hengstenberg, *A Dissertation on the History and Prophecies of Balaam,* trans. J. E. Ryland, bound with *Dissertations on the Genuineness of Daniel and the Integrity of Zechariah* trans. B. P. Pratten (Edinburgh: T. & T. Clark, 1848), pp. 512–13. The original title of this work is *Die Geschichte Bileams und seine Weissagungen* (Berlin: Ludwig Dehmigte, 1842).

Others have suggested that Balaam may have related the incidents to Israel at the time of his death. Keil writes: "At the time when he fell into the hands of the Israelites, he no doubt made a full communication to the Israelitish general, or to Phinehas, who accompanied the army as priest, concerning his blessings and prophecies, probably in the hope of saving his life; though he failed to accomplish his end." C. F. Keil, *Biblical Commentary on the Old Testament: The Pentateuch,* C. F. Keil and F. Delitzsch series, trans. James Martin, 3 vols., reprint, (Grand Rapids: Eerdmans, [n.d.]), 3:203. A refinement of this suggestion was made by Cox, who related the narration of the events to a judicial death in which there was a trial and opportunity was given for Balaam to plead in his own defense the long series of oracles. See Samuel Cox, *Balaam: An Exposition and a Study* (London: Kegan, Paul Trench, 1884), pp. 14–15. Another suggestion comes from Aalders who says, "The victorious Israelites might have found a written copy on Balaam's dead body." G. Ch. Aalders, *A Short Introduction to the Pentateuch* (London: Tyndale, 1949), p. 157.

Harrison gives a couple of suggestions, without pressing them. One is that the materials may have come to Israel through a disciple of Balaam. Alternatively, the account may have been taken from Moabite sources and then inserted into the text of Numbers "not later than the time of Samuel." Roland Kenneth Harrison, *Introduction to the Old Testament* (Grand Rapids: Eerdmans, 1969), p. 630. Allis argued strongly that the record of these events came to Moses by direct revelation from God. He uses the analogy of 2 Kings 6:12 where Elisha was said to be able to report to the king of Israel the words spoken by the king of Syria in his own bedchamber. Oswald T. Allis, *The Old Testament: Its Claims and Its Critics* (Philadelphia: Presbyterian and Reformed, 1972), p. 127. Quite another point of view is given by Segal: "The story may reasonably be considered as an imaginative representation of the actual occurrence." M. H. Segal, *The Pentateuch: Its Composition and Its Authorship, and Other Biblical Studies* (Jerusalem: At the Magnes Press, Hebrew U., 1967), pp. 68–69.

11. See again Genesis 12: 3: "And I will bless those who bless you, / But the one who condemns you I will curse." This is the point of the Balaam-Balak escapade in a moment. It is a test case for the Abrahamic covenant in its most elemental and fundamental level. Balaam was called by Balak to put Yahweh to the test, though neither Balaam nor Balak knew the nature of the roles in which they found themselves.

12. Sigmund Mowinckel, "Der Ursprung der Bil 'āmsage," *Zeitschrift für die alttestamentliche Wissenschaft,* 48 (1930): 255.

13. Norman C. Habel, *Yahweh Versus Baal: A Conflict of Religious Cultures; A Study in the Relevance of Ugaritic Materials for the Early Faith of Israel* (New York: Bookman Associates, 1964), pp. 24–26.

14. A full discussion of the oracles from an exegetical point of view is given by the writer in his dissertation, "The Theology of the Balaam Oracles: A Pagan Diviner and the word of God" (Dallas: Dallas Theological Seminary, 1973), pp. 257-331. See also *The Expositor's Bible Commentary*, ed. Frank E. Gaebelein (Grand Rapids: Zondervan, 1976—). Other studies of particular import include the following: Julius A. Bewer, "The Literary Problems of the Balaam Story in Numbers, Chapters 22-24," *American Journal of Theology*, 9 (1905): 238-40; E. F. Sutcliffe, "De Unitate Litteraria Num. XXII," *Biblica*, 7 (1926): 3-39; idem, "A Note on Numbers XXII," *Biblica*, 18 (1937): 439-42; Max Löhr, "Bileam, Num 22, 2—24, 25" *Archiv für Orient-Forschung*, 4 (1927): 85-89; Hugo Gressmann, *Mose und Seine Zeit: Ein Kommentar zu den Mose-Sagen* (Göttingen: Vandenhoeck und Ruprecht, 1913), pp. 318-34; Sigmund Mowinckel, "Der Ursprung der Bil 'āmsage, *Zeitschrift für die alttestamentliche Wissenschaft*, 48 (1930): 233-71; Eric Burrows, *The Oracles of Jacob and Balaam*, "The Bellarmine Series," III, ed. Edmund F. Sutcliffe (London: Burns Oates & Washbourne, Ltd., 1938); William Foxwell Albright, "The Oracles of Balaam," *Journal of Biblical Literature*, 63 (1944): 207-33; Joseph Coppens, "Les oracles de Biléam: leur origine littéraire et leur portée prophétique," *Mélanges Eugène Tisserant*, vol. I. '*Ecriture Sainte-Ancien Orient*, "Studi e Testi," 231 (Città del Vaticano: Biblioteca Apostolica Vaticanna, 1964): 67-80; Otto Eissfeldt, "Die Komposition der Bileam-Erzählung," *Zeitschrift für die alttestamentliche Wissenschaft*, 57 (1939): 212-42; idem, "Sinai-Erzählung und Bileam-Sprüche," *Hebrew Union College Annual*, 32 (1961): 179-90.
15. The translation of Hebrew אַחֲרִית (*'aḥărît*) as "glorious future" was suggested to me in private conversation by Bruce K. Waltke.
16. The Balaam pericope also presents an impressive use of the name *Yahweh* as well as the major appellatives of God. These issues receive discussion in the writer's dissertation, pp. 358-402. The terms include *Yahweh, Elohim, El, Shaddai, Elyon*, and *Melek*.
17. R. T. France, *The Living God* (London: Inter-Varsity, 1970), pp. 20-21.
18. C. J. Labuschagne, *The Incomparability of Yahweh in the Old Testament*, Pretoria Oriental Series, vol. 5, ed. A. van Selms (Leiden: E. J. Brill, 1966), p. x.
19. Ibid.
20. Ryrie speaks of the importance of substructural premises in the doing of biblical theology. See Charles Caldwell Ryrie, *Biblical Theology of the New Testament* (Chicago: Moody, 1959), pp. 21-22.
21. The question concerning the character and role of Balaam has been a matter of debate for centuries. Hengstenberg surveys the issue by listing a number of figures in opposing camps. He lists as supporters of the position that Balaam is to be regarded as a false prophet the following: Philo, Ambrose, Augustine, Gregory of Nyssa, Theodoret, and many Roman and Reformed theologians. Conversely, he lists those figures who have believed Balaam to be a true prophet to include: Tertullian, Jerome, Buddeus, Deyling, and Benzel. See Hengstenberg, *The History of Balaam*, pp. 340-41.
22. The question of the character of Balaam is discussed in the writer's dissertation at some length (pages 163-205). Opinions are quite varied. Only a few examples are mentioned here. Alexander Whyte regarded Balaam as a true prophet of God outside the household of Israel, to be compared with Melchizedek, Jethro, and Job as "witnesses to the profane lands in which they lived"(*Bible*

Characters: Adam to Achan, [10th ed., London Oliphants, (n.d.)] pp. 264-65). Cox similarly regards Balaam in a rather charitable light as a true prophet who proved to be false to his prophetic vocation (*Balaam,* p. 38). In the Talmud, Balaam was regarded quite negatively. The constantly recurring refrain was "Balaam, the wicked" (texts are given in my dissertation, pp. 43-51). Some modern scholars regard Balaam as a pagan mantic whom the narrator has transformed into a prophet of Yahweh. This is the view of Yehezkel Kaufmann, *The Religion of Israel: From Its Beginnings to the Babylonian Exile,* trans. and abridged by Moshe Greenberg (Chicago: U. of Chicago, 1960), pp. 84-85; and Frederick Moriarty, who avers that the historical Balaam "probably had never heard of Yahweh," but was transformed by the writer "into a devout worshiper of the Lord." See his *Book of Numbers, II: with a Commentary,* Pamphlet Bible Series (New York: Paulist, 1960), p. 6.

Perhaps the most whimsical approach to the complex problem of Balaam was taken by James Black in his book *Rogues of the Bible* (New York: Harper, 1930), pp. 59-79. He believed that there were *two* Balaams rather than one. One Balaam "knew and served the Lord Jehovah with particular fidelity, and worshipped him sincerely"; the other was a pagan, "a soothsayer or oracle-monger of the Midianites who hated Israel and tempted it to folly" (p. 67). It was the prejudice of the Jews that blended these two characters; they "did not relish the idea that their Scriptures painted such a hero as springing from a people whom they counted 'unenlightened pagans'" (p. 68). He describes the good Balaam as "a great white soul who loved the will of God to his own worldly loss. He returned to his own people with his hands empty and his heart full. Whatever he lost, he kept his lord" (p. 79).

Hengstenberg presented a mediating view respecting Balaam's character. He writes, "So kann nur eine unter beiden Extremen vermittelnde Unsicht die richtige senn" (*Die Geschichte Bileams,* p. 11). In Balaam there are elements of the knowledge of God, but never to the point of actual conversion. There are clear flashes of light by the Spirit of God, but "mann ihn den Propheten nicht beizählen darf."

One of the most famous studies of the character of Balaam is a sermon by Joseph Butler (1692-1762), Lord Bishop of Durham, entitled "Upon the Character of Balaam," *The Works of the Right Reverend Father in God, Joseph Butler, D.C.L., Late Lord Bishop of Durham,* 2 vols. (Oxford: At the University Press, 1850), 2: 74-86. In this splendid study, still worth reading, Butler comments on the complexities in the personality of Balaam: "So that the object we have now before us is the most astonishing in the world; a very wicked man, under a deep sense of God and religion, persisting still in his wickedness, and preferring the wages of unrighteousness, even when he had before him a lively view of death .... Good God, what inconsistency, what perplexity is here!" (p. 80). In Butler's view, Balaam was a pagan diviner who was used of God, but who was not rightly related to Yahweh. This is essentially the point of view taken in the present paper.

It was Samuel Daiches who pointed the way to an understanding of Balaam's role as a pagan sorcerer. This was in his article, "Balaam—a Babylonian *bārū*: The Episode of Num 22, 2—24, 24 and Some Babylonian Parallels," *Assyrisches und Archaeologisches Studien: H. V. Hilprecht gewidmet* (Leipzig, 1909), pp. 60-80. In this study Diaches points to many

magical elements noted in the narrative of Numbers 22-24 which may find
parallels in the mantic acts of the *bārū* diviner of Mesopotamia. Albright
judged these comparisons as "most impressive" ("Oracles," p. 231; Daiches's
article is discussed in my dissertation, pp. 178-85). It is particularly notewor-
thy that the *bārū* prophets were especially involved with animal divination.
Some of these elements are presented by René Largement, "Les oracles de
Bile'am et la mantique suméro-accadienne," *'Ecole des Langues Orientales
Anciennes de l'Institute Catholique de Paris: Mémorial du Cinquantenaire,
1914-1964* (Paris: Bloud & Gray, Travaux de l'Institute Catholique de Paris,
1964), pp. 37-50.

When viewed against the utter contempt and detestation that Yahweh has
for the mantic arts, and in the light of the fact that it was because of the
idolatrous-demonic mantic system that the Canaanites were to be
exterminated—the equation of Balaam with divination of the *bārū* type becomes frightfully significant. Balaam's function, that of a pagan diviner, is
loathsome to Yahweh. Yet it was this same Balaam whom God used to utter
the magnificent oracles of Numbers 22-24. It is no wonder that the personality and character of Balaam have caused such difficulties through the ages.
Who would have thought that Yahweh would use one who represents something detestable to Him? Yet that is precisely what has happened in our
narrative; this, too, is part of the wonder of our God. He ordains glory to
Himself, even of instruments such as Balaam.

As a mantic prophet of the *bārū* type, Balaam's knowledge of Yahweh
becomes understandable. He was a professional trafficker with the gods, a
craftsman in the supernatural. His claim "Yahweh my God" (Num. 22:18) is
not a statement of relationship, but is rather an attempt at manipulation.
How very little he really knew of Yahweh was to be demonstrated when he
began to curse the people of that God.

23. For a strong presentation of the demonic nature of idolatry, see Unger, *Biblical Demonology: A Study of the Spiritual Forces Behind the Present World
Unrest* (Wheaton, Ill.: Scripture Press, 1952).

24. The incomparability of Yahweh as presented in this psalm is developed by the
present writer in *Praise! A Matter of Life and Breath* (Nashville: Thomas
Nelson, 1980).

25. One of the tragedies of history has been the way in which the uniqueness of
Israel has become the instrument of cursing by those who are in fact different
from her. For a brief but eloquent account of the suffering of Israel through
the ages, see *O Jerusalem!* by Larry Collins and Dominique LaPierre (New
York: Simon and Schuster, 1972), pp. 17-32. Cf. Abba Eban, *My Country: The
Story of Modern Israel* (London and Jerusalem: Weidenfeld and Nicolson,
1972), pp. 25-45; Werner Keller, *Diaspora: The Post-Biblical History of the
Jews,* trans. Richard and Clara Winston (London: Pitman, 1971).

26. Labuschagne, *The Incomparability of Yahweh,* pp. 152-53.

27. John Bright, *The Authority of the Old Testament* (Nashville and New York:
Abingdon, 1967), p. 132.

28. Paul van Imschoot, *Theology of the Old Testament,* vol. 1, *God,* trans. Kath-
run Sullivan and Fidelis Buck (New York: Desclée, 1965), p. 69.

29. The NIV reads, "Ah, who can live when God does this?"

30. A glance at Numbers 23-24 might lead one to conclude that there are four
oracles. In fact, there are seven and each of the seven is introduced with

precisely the identical formula, "And he took up his oracle and said" (Num. 23:7*a,* 18*a;* 24:3*a,* 15*a,* 20*b,* 21*b,* 23*a*). Considering the role that the number *seven* plays in the narrative of our section and in the Torah in general, this can hardly be accidental.

31. Martin Noth, *Numbers: A Commentary,* trans. James Martin, The Old Testament Library, ed. G. Ernest Wright (Philadelphia: Westminster, 1968), p. 178.

32. Witness the reaction against literary criticism by Sandmel, who argues that modern scholars fail to understand the ancient mind when they approach the text. "A consequence is that all too often, so it seems to me, modern scholarship has so addressed itself in noting divergencies and discrepancies as to forget that there were elastic and intuitive minds behind the writings." Samuel Sandmel, "The Ancient Mind and Ours," in *Understanding the Sacred Text: Essays in Honor of Morton S. Enslin on the Hebrew Bible and Christian Beginnings,* ed. John Reumann (Valley Forge: Judson, 1972), p. 43.

33. The verb וִיכַזֵּב (*wîkazzēb*) may be taken as a potential imperfect that is negated. The Mighty is unable—unable to contradict His character, and unable to demean His excellences. The word order in the verse places emphasis on the negation. God is utterly different from man. Something that comes far too easily for many men is impossible for Almighty God: He cannot lie.

34. Van Imschoot, *Theology of the Old Testament,* 1: 55-56.

35. Ibid., p. 56.

36. Ibid., pp. 66-67.

37. This verse should be compared with the preceding context. In verse 24 of the same chapter we read, "For Yahweh your God is a consuming fire, a jealous God." Hence, in this chapter there are in close juxtaposition two aspects of the person of God that are often bifurcated in the popular imagination. The contrast is usually stated: "The God of the Old Testament is a God of wrath, but the God of the New Testament is a God of love." This is a subjective misunderstanding that needs to be addressed repeatedly.

38. Some writers have attempted to include verses 6-8 of Micah 6 as part of the conversation between Balaam and Balak that was not recorded in Numbers. Among those holding this view are Butler (*Works,* 2: 76) and Geikie (*Old Testament Characters,* pp. 115-16). Such an identification is a methodological flaw. Balaam and Balak are mentioned in verse 5 as part of a series of historical examples in Yahweh's *rib* with Israel. Verses 6-7 may be regarded as a rhetorical device whereby the prophet allows the people of Israel to speak to the prophet. His own response is given in verse 8. Compare, e.g., C. F. Keil, *The Twelve Minor Prophets,* trans. James Martin, 2 vols., reprint (Grand Rapids: Eerdmans, n.d.), 1: 492-97.

39. See, e.g., G. Ernest Wright, *God Who Acts: Biblical Theology as Recital* (London: SCM, 1952).

40. Paul D. Feinberg has criticized Eissfeldt for neglecting to see the acts of God as revelatory. See Feinberg's doctoral dissertation, "The Doctrine of God in the Pentateuch" (Dallas: Dallas Theological Seminary, 1968), p. 173.

41. Van Imschoot, *Theology of the Old Testament,* 1: 189; cf. George A. F. Knight, *A Christian Theology of the Old Testament* (London: SCM, 1964), pp. 55-56.

42. Kaufmann, *The Religion of Israel,* p. 84.

43. Leah Bronner, *The Stories of Elijah and Elisha: As Polemics Against Baal*

Worship, Pretoria Oriental Series, ed. A. van Selms (Leiden: E. J. Brill, 1968), vol. 6. See also, Kaufmann, *The Religion of Israel,* p. 13.

44. See Mowinckel, "Der Ursprung der Bil'āmsage," p. 260; Ladislas Martin von Pákozdy, "Theologische Redaktionsarbeit in der Bileam-Perikope (Num 22–24)," *Von Ugarit nach Qumran,* ed. Otto Eissfeldt (Berlin: Verlag Alfred Töpelmann, 1958), pp. 170-71.

45. Arnold M. Goldberg, *Das Buch Numeri,* "Die Welt der Bibel" (Düsseldorf: Patmos-Verlag, 1970), p. 106.

46. Kramer lists a number of Sumerian proverbs concerning the ass. He writes, "The donkey, as is well known, served as the chief beast of burden and draught animal in ancient Mesopotamia, and the Sumerians good-humoredly represented him as the slow-moving, and frequently foolish, creature that he is in European literature of a later date. His main objective in life seems to be to act contrary to the wishes of his masters: for example: . . . The donkey eats its own bedding! . . . Like a runaway donkey, my tongue does not turn around and come back! . . . I will not marry a wife who is only three years old as the donkey does!" Samuel Noah Kramer, *History Begins at Sumer* (Garden City, N.Y.: Doubleday, Anchor, 1959), pp. 132-33; cf. idem, *The Sumerians: Their History, Culture, and Character* (Chicago: U. of Chicago, 1963), pp. 224-25; J. William Whedbee, *Isaiah and Wisdom* (New York and Nashville: Abingdon, 1971), p. 40.

47. C. S. Lewis, *Miracles: A Preliminary Study* (New York: Macmillan, 1947), p. 6.

48. Ibid., p. 69.

49. Ibid., p. 14.

50. Samuel Cox, "Balaam's Ass. Numbers xxii, 28-30," *The Expositor,* First Series, 1: (1877) 397.

51. Ibid., p. 398.

52. So, e.g., Aage Bentzen, *Introduction to the Old Testament,* 2 vols. (Copenhagen: G. E. C. Gads Forlag, 1948), 1: 240-41.

53. Moriarty, *Numbers—Part 2,* p. 7; cf. D. M. Stanley, "Balaam's Ass; or a Problem in New Testament Hermeneutics," *The Catholic Quarterly* (January 1958), pp. 50-56.

54. Homer, *The Iliad,* trans. Samuel Butler, ed. Louise R. Loomis, "The Classics Club" (Roslyn, N.Y.: Walter J. Black, 1942), 19: 404-17 (p. 307). Gordon says, "The speech of Xanthus (Il. 19:404-17), the horse of Achilles, is of a piece with the talking of Balaam's ass in the Bible (Numbers 22:28-30)." Cyrus H. Gordon, *The Ancient Near East,* 3d ed. (New York: Norton, 1965), p. 110.

55. See Kenneth E. Jones, *The Book of Numbers: A Study Manual* (Grand Rapids: Baker, 1972), p. 70; cf. William W. Bass, "Theology No Issue: An Evangelical Appraisal of Rosmarin's Jewish-Christian Theological Barriers," *Journal of the Evangelical Theological Society,* 14 (Winter 1971): 7.

56. Hengstenberg, *Dissertation,* pp. 376-88; cf. J. C. V. von Hoffmann, *Interpreting the Bible,* trans. Christian Preus (Minneapolis: Augsburg, 1959), p. 35. A rather strange view was given by Irenaeus as reported by Beegle. Irenaeus usually eschewed allegorical interpretation, but he regarded Balaam's ass as a type of Christ. See Dewey M. Beegle, *The Inspiration of Scripture* (Philadelphia: Westminster, 1963), p. 107.

57. M. A. Beek, *A Journey Through the Old Testament,* trans. Arnold J. Pomerans (London: Hodder and Stoughton, 1959), p. 79. In this respect the donkey

becomes a sort of Jiminy Cricket to Pinocchio Balaam. The biblical text speaks often of internal and subjective elements. Warrant for such in our passage, however, appears to be lacking.

58. Noth, *Numbers,* p. 179. This citation should not be thought to imply that Noth believed that this miracle "really happened"; it rather demonstrates that he regards the text to be relating a miracle.

59. Merrill F. Unger, *Unger's Bible Handbook* (Chicago: Moody, 1967), p. 133.

60. Allis, *Old Testament Claims and Critics,* p. 34.

61. Wilhelm Vischer, *The Witness of the Old Testament to Christ,* trans. A. B. Crabtree (London: Lutterworth, 1950), 1: 233.

62. The miracle of the resurrection of Christ is the culmination of the grand miracle of the Incarnation. See Lewis, *Miracles,* p. 112.

63. For the term *bārū,* see above, note 22.

64. Balaam uses a vivid and arresting figure, the horns of the aurochs (the wild ox of the Ancient Near East)—a traditional image of power, but here applied to Yahweh in a dramatic fashion. The "unicorn" of the King James Version was a mistranslation from the beginning, as may be seen from the dual/plural word for horns (תּוֹעֲפֹת, *tô'apôt*) if nothing else. The word, רְאֵם (*re'ēm*) is now identified as *Bos primigenius,* the aurochs common to Mesopotamia. Cf. Michael Avi-Yonah and Abraham Malamat, eds., *The World of the Bible,* 5 vols. (Yonkers, N.Y.: Educational Heritage, 1964), 1: 228; G. S. Cansdale, *All the Animals of the Bible Lands* (Grand Rapids: Zondervan, 1970), pp. 82–84. The error concerning the "unicorn" seems to have begun with the Septuagint, which rendered the Hebrew term as *monokeros.* On this subject, see Allen Howard Godbey, "The Unicorn in the Old Testament," *The American Journal of Semitic Languages and Literature,* 56 (1939): 256–96. Some scholars prefer to identify our Hebrew word with the oryx rather than the aurochs. See F. S. Bodenheimer, *Animals and Man in the Bible Lands,* Collection de travaux de l'Academie Internationale d'Histoire des Sciences, no. 10 (Leiden: E. J. Brill, 1960), pp. 52–53.

65. Chester K. Lehman, *Biblical Theology,* vol. 1, *Old Testament* (Scottdale, Pa.: Herald, 1971), p. 115.

66. The ascription of the term *king* to Yahweh is a first in the theology of the Pentateuch (cf. Deut. 33:5). This is remarkable. One of the grandest titles of God, and one that becomes the designation of the Lord Jesus Christ, was first used by Balaam, the pagan mantic, who was used as Yahweh's tool.

67. The point seems to be that at the very moment of the enunciation of the oracle, it was evident that God was at work for Israel.

68. This is a passage that has fulfillment in the wars of conquest (holy war) of David and of successive Davidites; ultimate fulfillment is in the person of Messiah who will win final victory over the enemies of Israel, represented in this passage by Moab and Edom.

69. The use of this verse as a messianic designation at Qumran is discussed in my dissertation on pages 27–40; representative church Fathers are noted on pages 41–43.

70. On the seven-oracle pattern, see above, note 30.

71. See J. Barton Payne, *The Theology of the Older Testament* (Grand Rapids: Zondervan, 1962), p. 260, for a brief defense of the messianic intent of Numbers 24:17.

72. See above, note 16.

73. This is the assertion of Gerhard F. Hasel, *Old Testament Theology: Basic Issues in the Current Debate* (Grand Rapids: Eerdmans, 1972), p. 63; argumentation is presented in the writer's dissertation, pp. 352-58.
74. The meaning of the name *Balaam* has been the subject of considerable debate; extensive discussion is found in my study, pp. 135-45. The original form of the name likely meant "the (divine) uncle brings forth," as argued by Albright, "Oracles," p. 232; but other meanings abound (cf. Largement, "Les oracles de Bile'am," p. 38). Yet, as the word is transcribed in the Hebrew text, it receives the Hebrew connotation of "devourer of the people." This is then another example of intentional changes of names in the Hebrew Bible. In the name *Balaam* we encounter deliberate polemics against this disreputable figure, and it was so understood in the Talmud.
75. J. R. C. Perkin, "Inspiration," *The Biblical Quarterly,* 16 (1962): 275-76.
76. Ryrie, *Biblical Theology of the New Testament,* pp. 21-22.

Part II
EXEGETICAL

5

The Song of Deborah

Richard Patterson

RICHARD D. PATTERSON *(M. Div., Los Angeles Baptist Theological Seminary; Th.M., Talbot Theological Seminary; M.A., Ph.D., University of California, Los Angeles) is professor of Old Testament and biblical languages at Northwest Baptist Theological Seminary, Tacoma, Washington.*

The festive occasion that generates the articles in this book likewise evokes fond memories for this writer. How well I remember sitting together with Dr. Charles Feinberg, poring over some Hebrew, Aramaic, or Syriac passage in an attempt to ascertain clearly the precise truth of God's objective revelation. I remember, too, his admonition that one should always bring the fruits of solid scholarship to bear upon the Word of God, not as an end in themselves, but so that in knowing its message more distinctly, the lives of God's people might be touched more effectively. Recalling the example of his own faithfulness to that dictum, I am thankful for the opportunity to express some personal observations on a very difficult text, one that has defied the exegetical efforts of biblical scholars through the ages, namely, the Song of Deborah in the fifth chapter of Judges.[1]

Indeed, as Boling remarks in his own significant study on the passage, "A catalogue of full-dress studies of the Song of Deborah would read like a Who's Who in biblical research."[2] Unfortunately, such a catalogue would contain the names of but few conservatives, notable exceptions being Keil and Delitzsch and, more recently, P. C. Craigie. This article will be a further attempt to follow the admonition of Dr. Feinberg with regard to bringing the results of grammatical-historical research to bear upon the text at hand.

THE SETTING OF THE SONG

LITERARY FORM

Although some scholars view the origin of Judges 5 in an Israelite covenant renewal festival[3] or in an early war song adapted to the Yahweh cultus,[4] the *Sitz im leben* of Deborah's song actually is to be found in a victory celebration that immediately followed Israel's defeat of the confederation of Canaanite kings (Judg. 4).[5]

Such victory songs are amply paralleled in the secular literature of the ancient world. Thus, a stele in the temple at Karnak recounts the victory that Amon-Re had granted to the great pharaoh Thutmoses III. This literary genre is followed by Amenhotep III in the same dynasty, by Seti I and Merneptah in the nineteenth dynasty, and by Ramses III of the twentieth dynasty.[6] Perhaps the most notable victory song is that of Tukulti Ninurta I of Assyria (1244-08) over the Kassite king Kaštiliaš IV (1242-35).[7]

The Scriptures record other similar victory celebrations.[8] Accordingly, although it is true that Deborah's song is unique in the book of Judges, it is certainly not novel in terms either of the literature of the Ancient Near East that antedates or is contemporaneous with the biblical context of the Old Testament canon.

DATING AND HISTORICAL BACKGROUND

The dating and circumstances of the Battle of Ta'anach by the Waters of Megiddo (Judg. 5:19) and the resultant victory ode are to be sought in the complex historical details relative to Palestine's Late Bronze and Early Iron periods. In this regard, the essential trustworthiness of the biblical chronology stands vindicated. According to the stated Old Testament data, the four hundred eightieth anniversary of Israel's Exodus from Egypt occurred in Solomon's fourth regnal year (c. 967 B.C.).[9] Counting back from that date to a 1447 B.C. Exodus, and allowing eighty years for the wilderness wanderings and the activities of Joshua's day, and taking into consideration the united monarchy through Solomon's fourth year, the era of the Judges would encompass the period 1367-1044 B.C., or about 323 years.[10]

The essential accuracy of such a chronological framework was noted long ago by John Garstang, who suggested that, properly understood, the periods of rest mentioned in Judges correlated too nicely with the reigns of the strong Egyptian pharaohs following the eighteenth dynasty to be purely coincidental.[11] Following Garstang's clue and keeping Wood's chronological criteria in view, the following tabular chart reflects the details of the scriptural data.[12]

THE PERIOD FROM JUDGES TO THE DIVIDED KINGDOM

DATE	BIBLICAL DATA	JUDGE	OPPRESSOR/REST	EGYPTIAN PHARAOH
1367–1359	Judges 3:8		Aramaean/ Mesopotamian oppression in days of Aššur-uballit	
1359–1319	Judges 3:11	Othniel	REST	Horemhab (1342–14)
1319–1301	Judges 3:14		Moabites	
1301–1221	Judges 3:30	Ehud	REST	Ramses II (1301–1234) Merneptah (1234–22)
1221–1201	Judges 4:3	Shamgar	Canaanites	
1201–1161	Judges 5:31	Deborah and Barak	REST	Ramses III (1195–64)
1161–1154	Judges 6:1		Midianites	
1154–1110	Judges 8:28 9:22 10:7f.	Gideon, his sons Abimelech Tola, Jair	Ammonites	
1110–1104	Judges 12:7	Jephthah		Ramses IV–XI (1164–1085) Weak 20th Dynasty
1104–1064	Judges 13:1 15:20 16:31 1 Sam 4:18	Ibzan, Elon, Adbon Samson (ca. 1094–74) Eli (40 yrs. LXX = 20)	Philistines (I)	Divided 21st Dynasty (1085–950)
1064–1044 1044–1004 1011–971 971–931 931	1 Sam 7:2 Acts 13:21 2 Sam 5:5 1 Kings 11:42 1 Kings 12:19	Samuel Saul David Solomon Division of the Kingdom	Philistines (II)	

The context of the events delineated in Judges 4–5 falls into the times of the third, or Canaanite, oppression of the Israelites (1221–01 B.C.). As the biblical account opens, the author notes that because of Israel's apostasy, the Lord had allowed the Canaanites to afflict them for some twenty years (Judg. 4:1–3). It will be remembered that the tribe of Manasseh had failed to expel completely the Canaanites from western and northwestern Canaan (Judg. 1:27). It was in that very area that the renewed Canaanite menace had been felt.

With the death of Merneptah in 1222 B.C., the reinvigorated Canaanites were again able to press an attack against the Israelites. The head of the Canaanite coalition (Judg. 5:19) was Jabin of Hazor, who apparently had gained control of the northwestern valley areas, including the Plain of Esdraelon.[13] Jabin and his associates had as their field commander a certain Sisera[14] from Harosheth Haggoyim[15] (Judg. 4:2; 5:19). Sisera's military might included nine hundred iron chariots, which gave him a vast superiority over the Israelites (Judg. 4:3; 5:6-8).

Due to Israel's cry of repentance (Judg. 4:3), God raised up as liberators from the oppression the prophetess Deborah, from the hill country of Ephraim, and Barak, son of Abinoam of Kedesh in Naphtali (Judg. 4:4-9; 5:7-12).[16] The two succeeded in raising an army, which they assembled at Mount Tabor.[17]

When Sisera learned of the Israelite mobilization, he moved his heavy chariot division into the Plain of Esdraelon across the eastern branch of the south fork of the Kishon River, especting to move in for the kill (Judg. 4:13; 5:19).[18] In the ensuing battle, God arranged the forces of nature and the details of the campaign so that the Israelites won a crushing victory (Judg. 4:4-16; 5:19-23). Sisera himself had managed to escape. He was making his way toward Hazor and safety when a certain Jael, wife of Heber the Kenite, urged him to turn aside to her tent to rest and to hide (Judg. 4:17-18). Jael then slew him as he slept (Judg. 4:19-21; 5:24-27), presenting his slain body to Sisera's pursuers (Judg. 4:22).[19]

THE SINGING OF THE SONG

As the *Sitz im Leben* has been summarized, the song itself can now be examined. A transcription and translation of the text is given first. An analysis of the song[20] follows.

TRANSLATION AND TRANSCRIPTION

Verse

2	(This happened)	
	When volunteers enlisted willingly in Israel,	בפרע פרעת בישראל
	When the people whom the Lord had blessed offered themselves freely.	בהתנדב עם ברך יהוה
3	Hear, O kings	שמע מלכם
	Give ear, O princes,	האזן רזנם
	I to Yahweh	אנך ליהוה
	I myself will sing	אנך אשר
	I will sing to Yahweh	אזמר ליהוה
	The God of Israel.	אלה ישראל

4	Yahweh, when you went out from Seir	יהוה בצאתך משער
	When you came from the plains of Edom	בצעדך משד אדם
	The earth quaked	ארץ רעש
	Yea, the heavens dripped	גם שמם נטף
	The clouds poured down water	גם עבם נטף מם
5	The mountains shook	הרם נזל
	From before Yahweh, the One of Sinai	מפן יהוה ז סן
	From before Yahweh, the God of Israel.	מפן יהוה אלה ישראל
6	In the days of Shamgar Ben Anat	בים שמגר בן ענת
	In the days of Jael	בים יעל
	Highways ceased (so that)	חדל ארחת
	They who walked the roads	הלך נתבת
	Took circuitous paths.	ילך ארחת עקלקלת
7	Warriors ceased—	חדל פרזן
	Ceased in Israel	בישראל חדל
	Until I, Deborah, arose,	עד שקמת דבר
	I arose (as) mother in Israel.	שקמת אם בישראל
8	(When) God chose new (warriors),	יבחר אלהם חדשם
	There was not a shield in five cities	אז לחמש ערם מגן
	Nor was a spear seen	אם ירא רמח
	Among forty contingents in Israel.	בארבעם אלף בישראל
9	My heart (went out) to the leaders of Israel,	לב לחקק ישראל
	Those who offered themselves freely among	המתנדב בעם
	the people whom Yahweh had blessed.	ברך יהוה
10	(Said I:)	
	O rulers on (your) tawny she-asses,	רכב אתנת צחרת
	Sitting on saddle clothes,	ישב על מדן
	Traveling upon the road,	חלך על דרך
11	Attend the sound of those who divide	שח-ם קל מחצצם
	(the flock)	
	Among the watering troughs.	בן משאבם
	There they utter	שם יתן
	The righteous deeds of Yahweh (and)	צדקת יהוה
	The righteous deeds of (his) warriors in Israel.	צדקת פרזן בישראל
11c	Then they went down to the gates,	אז ירד לשערם
	The people of Yahweh.	עם יהוה
12	"Awake, awake, Deborah,	ער ער דבר
	Awake, awake, sing a song.	ער ער דבר שר
	Arise, Baraq,	קם ברק

	Take your captives,	ושב שבך
	Son of Abinoam."	בן אבנעם
13	Then the remnant came down	אז ירד
	to the mighty ones.	שרד לאדרם
	The people of Yahweh	עם יהוה
	Came down from among the warriors.	ירד לבגברם
14	Ephraim was mustered,	מני אפרם
	They who had rooted out Amaleq, (Set)	שרשם בעמלק
	After you, O Benjamin, with your troops.	אחרד בנימן בעממך
	Machir was mustered;	מני מכר
	(Its) leaders came down	ירד מחקקם
	And from Zebulun were those who	ומזבלן משכם
	marched with the ruler's staff.	בשבט ספר
15	But the captains in Israel	ושר בישראל
	Were with Deborah.	עם דבר
	And Issachar was assigned to Baraq;	ויששכר כן ברק
	In the plain they were deployed at his feet.	בעמק שלח ברגלו
	Among the divisions of Reuben,	בפלגת ראבן
	Great were the resolves of heart.	גדלם חקק לב
16	Why did you sit	לם ישבת
	Among the enclosures (/sheepfolds),	בן המשפתם
	Listening to the pipings for the flocks?	לשמע שרקת עדרם
	(Yea) among the divisions of Reuben	לפלגת ראבן
	Great were the searchings of heart!	גדלם חקר לב
17	Gilead	גלעד
	Remained beyond the Jordan	בעבר הירדן שכן
	And Dan,	ודן
	Why did you stay on ships?	לם יגר אנית
	Asher	אשר
	Abode by the seashore	ישב לחף ימם
	And remained on the inlets.	ועל מפרצו ישכן
18	Zebulun (was)	זבלן
	A people who scorned its soul to death	עם חרף נפש למת
	And Naphtali	ונפתל
	Went up to the heights of the (battle)field.	על מרם שד
19	The kings came, they fought.	בא מלכם נלחם
	Then the kings of Canaan fought	אז נלחם מלך כנען
	At Ta'anach by the waters of Megiddo,	בתענך על מ מגד
	(but) they took no booty of silver.	בצע כסף לא לקח
20	From heaven the stars fought	מן שמם נלחם הככבם
	From their courses, they fought	ממסלתם נלחם
	against Sisera.	עם ססרא

21	Wadi Qishon swept them away	נחל קשן גרפם
	The wadi received (/overwhelmed) them.	נחל קדמם
	O Wadi Qishon,	נחל קשן
	You did tread out the soul of the mighty one!	תדרך נפש עז
22	Then pounded the horses' hoofs	אז הלם עקב ססם
	(Together with) the wild galloping of his stallions.	דהרת דהרת אברו
23	"Curse Meroz,"	אר מרז
	Said the angel of the Lord,	אמר מלאך יהוה
	"Utterly curse its inhabitants,	אר ארר ישבה
	For they did not come to the aid of Yahweh,	כלא בא לעזרת יהוה
	To the help of Yahweh among the warriors."	לעזרת יהוה בגברם
24	Most blessed among women is Jael,	תברך מנשם יעל
	Wife of Heber the Kenite.	אשת חבר הקן
	Most blessed among women in the tent (is she).	מנשם באהל תברך
25	He asked for water;	מם שאל
	She gave him milk.	חלב נתן
	In a splendid bowl,	בספל אדרם
	She served him curds.	הקרב חמא
26	She stretched forth her hand to the tent peg,	ידה ליתד תשלחן
	Her right hand to the workmen's hammer.	וימן להלמת עמלם
	She hammered Sisera,	והלם ססרא
	Smashed his head,	מחק ראש
	Wounded and pierced his temple.	ומחץ וחלף רקת
27	Between her feet he sank down,	בן רגלה כרע
	He fell, lay prostrate.	נפל שכב
	Between her feet he sank down, falling.	בן רגלה כרע נפל
	At the (very) place where he sank down,	באשר כרע
	There he fell slain.	שם נפל שדד
28	Through the window	בעד החלן
	She peered and cried aloud,	נשקף ותיבב
	The mother of Sisera,	אם ססרא
	Through the lattice.	בעד האשנב
	"Why does his chariot	מדע בשש
	Tarry from coming?	רכב לבא
	Why do the hoofbeats of his	מדע אחר
	Chariot (horses) delay?"	פעם מרכבתו
29	The wisest of her princesses gives answer	חכמת שרתה תענן
	Yea, she herself	אף הא
	Returns her words to her:	תשב אמרהלה

30   "Are they not finding   הלא ימצא
     (And) dividing the spoil: יחלק שלל
     A maiden, two maidens   רחם רחמתם
     For each warrior (and)   לראש גבר
     Booty of dyed cloth for Sisera,   שלל צבעם לססרא
     Booty of embroidered dyed cloth   שלל צבעם רקם
     Doubly embroidered dyed cloth   צבע רקמתם
     For the neck of the spoiler?"   לצואר שלל

31   So may all your enemies   כן יאבד
     Perish, O Yahweh;   כל איבך יהוה
     But as for those who love him,   ואהבו
     (May they be) like the sun when it goes forth   כצאת השמש בגברת
        with strength.

Notes

Verse Two. בפרע פרעת (*bpr' pr't*). The Hebrew phrase has defied the best efforts of the commentators. BDB lists three roots with the same spelling. (1) "To be lofty," hence, the noun פֶּרַע (*pera'*) "leader" (from the Arabic *fara'a* "excel."[21] (2) "To sprout," hence, the noun פֶּרַע (*pera'*) "long hair," (cf. Syriac *p'ra'* "sprout," Akkadian *pirtu* "hair of the head"). (3) "Let go/loose," hence, "neglect" (cf. Syriac *p'ra'* "uncover," Arabic *farag'a* "be empty"). Coogan, building upon a proposed Ugaritic meaning for the root, translates "in the very beginning" (i.e., of the events to be enumerated).[22] Perhaps the best solution is to follow Craigie's suggestion that the word is to be related to the Arabic *farag'a,* "apply oneself exclusively," used in a sense of "volunteer for war."[23] Boling follows the lead of C. Rabin in understanding the word as a parallel to the verb in the next line.

התנדב (*htndb*) "present oneself," in a military sense "to go to war in answer to a call."[24] Thus construed, the Hebrew phrase sets the scene for the events that follow. All that Deborah would sing about had occurred at the time volunteers enlisted in Israel, offering themselves willingly.

בישראל (*bysr'l*) does double duty here; it qualifies both the preceding and following lines.[25]

Verse Three. The opening invitation to listen closely to the poet's words is common enough (cf. Exod. 15:1-2; Psalms 49:2; 143:1). Each of the major words in the verse is coupled with a standard fixed pair in parallel construction.[26]

Verses Four and Five. The theophanic material contained here is paralleled in several places in the Old Testament (cf. v. 4 with Deut. 33:

1-2*a*; Psalm 68:7 [Heb. 68:8]; Hab. 3:3; cf. v. 5 with Psalms 18:7; 68:8 [Heb. 68:9]; Hab 3:10; see also Psalms 144:5f.).[27] These verses appear to be drawn from a body of old poetic phrases and portions that depict the epic narrative of God's deliverance of His people from their Egyptian bondage, His preservation of them in the wilderness, and His triumphant leading of them into the land of promise.[28]

Although the context allows one to follow the lead of Dahood and Boling who relate the word גם (*gm*) to the Ugaritic term for thunder, since Psalm 68:7 [Heb. 68:8] reads אף (*'p*), it is best to understand it as the normal Hebrew particle, as is traditionally done, perhaps here as an untranslatable flavoring particle (cf. NIV).

The MT נָזְלוּ (*nad*e*lû*), "melted" (from נדל [*ndl*] "flow") is better taken with most ancient versions and modern commentators as a Niphal perfect from זלל (*zll*), "shake."[29]

> The four nouns in the tetracolon form two pairs arranged chiastically. Thus the earth in 4*c* is matched with the mountains in 5*a*, and the heavens and clouds are paired in 4*de*. Because the two heavenly elements "pour," the expectation is that the mountains will "shake" in 5*a* to complete the parallel with the trembling earth.[30]

The MT זֶה (*zeh*) is best seen as the old demonstrative particle *z* from **du*.[31]

Verse Six. בן ענת (*bn 'nt*). For proposed literary influence drawn from the Ugaritic Anat cycle, see P. C. Craigie and S. Dempster.[32]

חדל (*ḥdl*), "ceased," has occasioned a great deal of difficulty, with most modern English translations stressing the idea that due to the lawless times, the roads were deserted. Boling takes all that follows to be the subject of the verb. Thus, "they ceased" (i.e. the caravans and the wayfaring men who traveled the winding roads).[33] Although this makes for a smooth translation, Boling is forced to fly in the face of MT and the majority of the versions by repointing אֲרָחוֹת (*'ŏrāhôt*), "highways" as אֹרְחוֹת (*'ōr*e*hôt*), "caravans." But this word is manifestly to be translated "highways" in the following line and makes better sense as such in this line. Another possibility is to understand the Hebrew verb in the sense of "be blocked" (cf. Akk. *edlu* "locked," "impassable"), as in the Syriac version. Perhaps the solution is simply to retain the traditional Hebrew meaning of both words and understand the phrase as does P. C. Craigie, that, because of the lawless times, men could not travel the main highways but had to find circuitous routes.[34]

Verse Seven. עד שקמת (*'d shqmt*). The phrase is to be taken as a preposition followed by the old relative particle שׁ (*sh*). It is known also in

Akkadian, Amorite, and Phoenician, and the suffix conjugation of the verb קוּם (qûm) "arise."[35] The question as to whether the verb is to be taken as translated here or as the old second feminine singular is, as A. R. Hulst remarks, "tied up with the problem as to whether Deborah composed this song herself, or whether it was written by some unknown singer."[36] Because the first person seems clearly intended in verse nine, smoothness would dictate its retention here.

פרזן (przn), "warriors." The translation adopted here follows the comments of P. C. Craigie, in taking the term to be a collective noun. As Craigie notes, "The usual approach is to render [פרזות] przwt, "open land" (after the Syriac), or to understand something like "(men) of the open country" (that is, peasantry)."[37] However, the older understanding has undergone proper clarification so that the sense of the passage is greatly aided. As W. F. Albright remarks, "The word [$p^e r\bar{a}z\hat{o}n$] does not mean 'villagers,' as formerly thought, but is a collective from a Canaanite word for 'warrior,' which appears in Pap. Anastasi 1, 23, line 4."[38]

G. Garbini's attempt to equate the Hebrew word with ESA frzn(m), "iron," both here and in verse eleven is unconvincing,[39] as is P. R. Ackroyd's subsequent suggestion to view "iron" as a symbol of power.[40]

אם ('m), "Mother." S. Dempster remarks, "'Mother' need not be taken as a passive and submissive role here—an interpretation which hardly makes sense—but should mean a 'fierce protector and guardian of her people.'"[41]

Verse Eight. As Boling well remarks, "This entire verse is notoriously difficult to translate."[42] Indeed, it fairly bristles with difficulties, so that despite a basic understanding of the verse, a smooth rendition defies the efforts of the translator, as a glance at the various versions, ancient and modern, shows.

אז ('z), "then." Whereas the construct infinitive with the preposition dominates the previous two portions (vv. 1-3, 4-7), this particle is employed carefully throughout this section forming the battle narrative (vv. 8-27). The two major parts of the passage are indicated with a temporal sentence whose second clause is begun by אז ('z), vv. 8-18 emphasizing the preparation for the battle, vv. 19-27 detailing the course of the battle and its consequences. Each successive topic within these two divisions is introduced by this particle standing initially in the sentence (vv. 11c-12, 13-18, 22-27).[43] The construction here is similar to that in 2 Kings 13:19 and Job 3:13.

יבחר (ybhr) is to be read as an old preterite, a common use in older Hebrew poetry.[44]

The full line may be read in several ways:
(1) They chose new gods (KJV; cf. NIV).

(2) One chose new gods (Boling).
(3) New gods were chosen (Coogan).
(4) "God chose (chooses) new (men/things)" (cf. Craigie, Syriac, Latin).
(5) "God chose anew" (reading *ḥādāsh* and enclitic *m*; cf. Akk. *edišimma*, "anew").[45]

Against the first three is the fact that they do violence to the Old Testament prohibitions against polytheism and idolatry, for certainly the subject at hand is "Israelites." Against the last view is the fact that בחר (*bḥr*) is a transitive verb, characteristically used with substantives, which are usually introduced by the preposition ב (*b*). The latter point is also telling against view four, but since we are dealing with an adjective and because the context seems to allow nothing else, it is the view provisionally adopted here. Because "a new (thing)" is normally expressed by the feminine (cf. Isa. 43:19; 48:6; Jer. 31:22), full significance must be allowed to the masculine plural adjective here. The point, then, is that in the days when the old warriors had all but disappeared, God was choosing new ones, including the godly Deborah.

לחמש ערם (*lḥmsh ʿrm*). This division of the consonants makes for smoother sense than the usual "war in the gates," and forms a good parallelism with the following lines.[46] The last three lines of verse 8 have been viewed as interrogative sentences (Craigie) or as declarative sentences (Boling). The difficulty in viewing them as questions is that the particle אם (*ʾm*) normally is formed only with the second half of a double question, as is common also in Ugaritic (cf. UT, p. 109). On the whole, it is best to take the sentence as having been formed in accordance with the oath pattern, the particle אם (*ʾm*) having been deleted with the second member, a further example of double duty words in elliptical expressions.[47]

Verses Ten and Eleven. The ass was by no means scorned by the wealthy or those of nobility (cf. Judg. 10:3ff.; 12:13ff.; 1 Kings 1:33, 38; 2 Kings 4:22; 9:18-19; Zech. 9:9), as attested by its employment at Ugarit.[48]

צחרת (*shrt*), "tawny" (cf. Ug. shrr(t) "burn/shine"). M. Dahood suggests a comparison with *libbî ṣᵉ ḥarḥar*, "my heart is fever-racked" (Psalm 38:11,[49] G. Bush suggests that the ass in question was more probably of a rare white color.[50]

מדן (*mdn*). A difficult term,[51] it has been taken as a carpet,[52] a saddle blanket,[53] fine clothing of state,[54] a judgment seat,[55] or Midian.[56] W. F. Albright notes that Delbert Hilliers suggests that "*mdn* may be derived from a dissimilated by-form of the word which appears in Ugaritic as *mdl* (see Jonas Greenfield, 'Ugaritic *Mdl* and Its Cognates,' *Biblica*, XLV [1964]: 527-34)."[57] A final decision is difficult. As Martin points out, "The differences in verse 10 may be differences of activity or differences of social class." Since the surrounding parallel lines deal with the idea of travel, perhaps the two ideas may be combined to suggest the social status of a traveler. Thus, whether one travels by donkeyback or rides on a rich saddle cloth or walks along the roadside, he is invited to respond to Deborah's cry.[58]

The solution taken here follows the lead of NIV, which takes the second line of the verse as a further elaboration of the first, by extending this principle so as to view the third line as a still further description. Thus, the whole phrase forms the address to Israel's leaders for whom she was burdened (v. 9). If the preposition is taken with the following noun as one metrical unit, we here have another example of the common Semitic 3 + 2 + 2 tricolon.[59]

שׂחים (shh-m), "consider/attend." This verb is best reassigned to verse 11 and constructed with the m of the first word there, thus forming an example of an imperative with enclitic m.

מחצצם (mhṣṣm) has been variously rendered in modern translations as "musicians" (RSV; NIV), "archers" (KJV), "cymbals" (Boling), or simply "those who divide" (NASB). On the whole, the last suggestion is the simplest. Thus, J. Gray remarks:

> We should note E. F. C. Rosenmuller's suggestion (*Scholia in Vetus Testamentum-Judices et Ruth, 1835, ad loc.*) to retain the Hebrew text, but to take the participle *mᵉḥaṣᵉṣim* as referring to the shepherds dividing their flocks, as the writer has seen Arab shepherds do by the sound of the voice, sheep separating from goats at the troughs by the wells.[60]

יתן (ytn) has been taken by many to be related to the Ugaritic *tnn*, "repeat." However, such an equation is both difficult and unnecessary; rather, a play on the usual idiom נתן(ב)קול (ntn [b] qôl), "lift up the voice," "utter," is probably to be seen in the poet's artistic composition of the line. A Qal passive suffix conjugation from *ytn* is also not impossible.[61]

Weiser's suggestion to take the initial m on מִקּוֹל (miqôl) as a comparative,[62] thus, "louder than the voice of those who distribute water among the well-channels," is not without possibility.

אז ('z). The particle introduces the next subsection dealing with the response to Deborah's challenge.

שׁערים (sh'rm), the "gates" of the individual Israelite town that would send troops to the battle. As Martin remarks, "The city gate was the usual place of commercial and legal activity; here it seems also to be the place of local muster."[63]

Verse Twelve. שׁב שׁבך (shb shbk). The familiar phrase carries with it the idea not only of the victory procession, but the fruits of victory, as well.[64]

בן עבנעם (*bn 'bn'm*). For the familiar Hebrew and Ugaritic parallel construction: PN, son of PN, see S. Geviritz, pp. 50-52.

Verse Thirteen. אז (*'z*) again introduces the subsection, in this case dealing with the general mobilization and preparation for the coming battle.

שרד (*śrd*), "remnant," that is, those tribes who responded to the muster in distinction to the whole of Israel, some of whom did not (cf. vv. 15c-17).[65]

ירד (*yrd*), "came down," that is, from the various towns to the staging area for the campaign.

עם (*'m*), almost with the sense of "troops," as argued consistently by Boling.

גברם, אדרם (*gbrm, 'drm*) are parallel terms for Israel's mighty men who would lead her into battle.[66]

Verse Fourteen. מני (*mny*) means "number," "muster," as in 1 Kings 20:25. Here it has the old original *yodh* retained. It should be vocalized either as an imperative מְנִי (*mᵉnî*) or as a Qal passive suffix conjugation מֻנִי *muniy*.

שרשם (*shrshm*). This word is located in a difficult line. Several emendations have been suggested for it. Thus, Gray, following the LXX and RSV, redivides the word into *shārū shām*, and emends *amalek* (Amalek) to עֵמֶק (*'ēmēq*) "valley", translating the line "from Ephraim, they set out thither into the valley" (i.e., the plain at Tabor).[67] Although imaginative, the attempt rests upon sheer conjecture. Boling takes the word to be a verb meaning "take root," and translates "those of Ephraim have taken root in Amaleq" (i.e., the Ephraimites failed to respond to the summons).[68] But surely just the opposite is the case. Craigie (*Further Notes*, p. 351f.) suggests a relation with Egyptian *srs*, "take command of a corps," and, following the lead of LXX, emends "Amalek" to "valley," translating the line "from Ephraim, officers [go down] into the valley."[69] However, all of this is tenuous, at best.

Two simpler solutions commend themselves. The first possibility, granted the juxtaposition of Amalekites and Ephraimites (cf. Judg. 12:15), is to divide the word into שׁ (*sh*), the relative particle (cf. v. 7) and רשׁם (*rshm*) "to note" (cf. Syriac *resham*, "assign") in the sense of "be listed." The parallel uses of the preposition *b*, "with Amalek," and "with your troops," lends credibility to the suggestion. The Amalekites were well-known warriors (cf. 1 Sam. 27:5-7), and seemed ready and willing to join in any marauding foray for gain (cf. Judg. 3:12-14; 6:3f., 33; 7:12; 1 Sam. 30:1-6). The difficulty with this view is the general scriptural representation of Amalek as being Israel's consistent enemy (cf. Psalm 83:7). If, however, the preposition is translated "from" and Amalek is understood as a geographical entity within Ephraim, the suggestion may still have merit. The second possibility is to take the word as a denominative verb in the Piel stem, formed with an enclitic *m,* in its usual sense of "root out." Thus understood, it would form an epithetic expression of "how Ephraim had shown strength in rooting out those of the Amalekites who were in its midst."[70] On the whole, this latter is the simplest.

בעממך אחריך, (*b°mmk, 'ḥrk*) is an example of *oratio variata* with a shift from indirect to direct discourse.[71] Benjamin leads out, followed closely by Ephraim.

Since Machir was the oldest son of Manasseh (Josh. 17:1-2; cf. Num. 26:29), Machir is apparently a designation for that portion of Manasseh that lay west of Jordan. Thus, Keil and Delitzsch remark:

> This explanation of the word is required, not only by the fact that Machir is mentioned after Ephraim and Benjamin, and before Zebulun and Issachar, but still more decidedly by the introduction of Gilead beyond Jordan in connection with Reuben, in ver. 17, which can only signify Gad and eastern Manasseh. Hence the two names *Machir* and *Gilead,* the names of Manasseh's son and grandson, are poetically employed to denote the two halves of the tribe of Manasseh; Machir signifying the western Manassites, and Gilead the eastern.[72]

ספר (*spr*). The term is probably to be understood in connection with its Akkadian cognate *šapāru,* "rule," as Boling, following Tsevat, suggests.[73] However, Gray's proposal to connect the term with the scribe who recorded the conscription (cf. 2 Kings 25:19) is not without merit.[74]

Verse Fifteen. כן (*kn*) means "be arranged," "assign an order" (cf. Ug. *kn,* "(be) in order"; Akk. *kunnu,* "assigned to a position/place") as in 2 Chronicles 29:35; 35:10, 16. Here it is used in the sense of "be assigned."

שלח (*shlḥ*) means "stretch out." Here again in a Qal passive. It means "deployed."

Verses Fifteen and Sixteen. פלגת (*plgt*) means "divisions," "clans" (cf. 2 Chron. 35:5), not "water courses" (KJV).

חקק לב (*ḥqq lb*), "resolves of heart." A word play is clearly intended between this phrase and the חקר לב (*ḥqr lb*), "searchings of heart" of verse 16. Although there were many initial resolves to help Deborah and Barak, upon reflection Reuben stayed home.

למ (*lm*) is taken here and in verse 17 by Cross as an example of emphatic ל (*l*) with enclitic מ (*m*), "verily."[75]

משפתם (*mshptm*). W. F. Albright connects the word with (*sh ᵉ pattāyim*) (cf. Psalm 68:14) as a dual form of the word for hearth or fireplace.[76] Gray retains the traditional idea of "enclosures" or "sheepfolds" and remarks,

> This feature is well illustrated in Transjordan in ancient drystone sheepfolds with converging foldwalls to facilitate the coralling of flocks in the event of sudden raids from the desert.[77]

Verse Seventeen. שכן (*shkn*), "dwelt," "tabernacled." Boling (p. 112) is probably correct in seeing this as a derisive remark which emphasized that Gilead, rather than coming, remained at home beyond the Jordan.[78]

גר אניּת (*gr 'nyt*). The phrase is a difficult one. Most modern English translations follow the lead of MT here, understanding the phrase to mean "remained/lingered on/beside ships." Cross and Freedman, followed by Boling, translate "took service on ships."[79] (But note that in his *Canaanite Myth and Hebrew Epic,* Cross translates it "sojourns on ships.")[80]

J. Gray,[81] followed cautiously by P. C. Craigie[82] cites Ugaritic evidence and omits למ (*lm*), "why" (as in two Hebrew manuscripts, the Targum and the Latin Vulgate) and repoints the word for ships in accordance with the Arabic verb *'āna,* "be at ease." He translates the line "and Dan abode at ease."

Whether one views the reference to Dan as preceding (Boling, Cundall, and Keil and Delitzsch) or following (Moore, Martin, Wood) their migration northward (Judg. 17–18), the reference to ships is not without meaning. Without adequate reasons to the contrary, it would appear best to retain the traditional MT here.

מפרץ (*mprs*) is a hapax legomenon from the root *prs,* "break into/up/open." The parallel with "seashore" probably demands the meaning "bay" or "inlet."

Verse Eighteen. על (*'l*), "went up," takes the consonantal text from the verb עלה (*'lh*), "go up." This provides a better parallel structure with the preceding lines.[83] As for the heights of the (battle)field, Boling remarks that it "refers to the fact that the Esdraelon plain is characterized by undulations and hillocks which provided positions of relative advantage for the opposing forces."[84]

Verse Nineteen. אז (*'z*), "then," is here positioned in the same sequence as in verse 8.[85]

על מ מגד (*'l m mgd*) means "by the waters of Megiddo." Here it is used in anticipation of the flash flood of verses 20 and 21. Keil and Delitzsch point out that "Taanach and Megiddo were not quite five miles apart, and beside and between them there were several brooks which ran into the southern arm of the Kishon, that flowed through the plain to the north of both these towns."[86]

Verse Twenty. נלחם הכבבם (*nlḥm hkkbm*). This is a poetic description of rain activity, the thunderstorm being utilized by God as part of His standard arsenal of battle weaponry (cf. Psalms 18:8-15; 77:16-18 [Heb. 17-19]; 144:4-6; Hab. 3:10-11). The involvement of the stars in rainstorms is known from the Ugaritic texts.[87] W. F. Albright sees a further reference to stars and cosmic battles in Habakkuk 3:6.[88]

ממסלתם (*mmsltm*), "from their courses." The Hebrew verb סלל (*sll*) may be a denominative from the Akkadian *sulū*, "highway" (from the root *salū*, "throw up/off/out").[89] Although Cross and Freedman wish to emend the phrase to *mmzltm*, "from their stations,"[90] as Coogan demonstrates, such an emendation "is unnecessary in view of the phrase *hlk kkbm* in *CTA*, 19.52 etc."[91]

Verse Twenty-one. קדמם (qdmm). Although the pointing of MT: *qᵉdûmîm*, "age old" (NIC), "ancient" (NASB), is allowable, both the syntax and the sense demand a verb, hence *qiddᵉmam*, "overwhelmed them" (Boling; cf. Psalms 18:6, 19 = 2 Sam. 22:6, 19), or "confronted them" (AYP, p. 35), "barred his flight" (Martin). The force of the preceding parallel lines probably carries with it more than the idea of intercepting Sisera's fleeing forces, hence, perhaps "receive" as in Job 3:12.[92]

The repetition of Wadi Kishon is probably vocative, indicating the impassioned victory pronouncement of the poetess.[93]

תדרך נפש עז (*tdrk npsh 'z*). The "March on my soul in strength" of most modern versions seems scarcely contextually defensible. The proposal of Cross and Freedman to read the line *tdrk nprsʿz* "his mighty chargers pounded," and to take the line with the succeeding lines of verse 22, although ingenious, rests upon a purely conjectural emendation.[94] It is perhaps best to take the various words as follows: *drk*, "tread" (although Craigie's suggestion to translate the word in accordance with Ugaritic "dominate" is not without merit),[95] *npsh*, "soul" (probably not Boling's "throat" with old retained genitive ending); ʿōz, "mighty (one)"; hence, translate either "Do thou tread out the soul of the mighty one," or as a simple declaration. As such it expresses Deborah's wish for a total annihilation of the enemy or an emphatic avowal that the river had done so.

Verse Twenty-two. ססם דהרת (*ssm dhrt*). The division of consonants here is widely accepted. The word *dhrt*[96] may be plural, as MT, or an old Canaanite feminine singular in *t*.[97] The feminine gender is used to express an abstraction. The repetition of the word "serves to intensify the expression to the highest degree" (G-K, para. 123e). The final *mem* of the first line may do double duty with the second.

אבר ('br). (Cf. Ug. 'ibr, "bull"; but the parallel here demands a horse as in Jer. 8:16). The word must be translated "stallion," and as such forms a well-attested loan word in New Egyptian.[98] P. C. Craigie, following the lead of Torczyner, suggests that the word is used here as a *double entendre:*

> The galloping of "stallions" would have been a terrifying sound to the Israelite infantry, but what they experienced was the "galloping of officers" (in a poetic sense), who were reduced by the circumstances of weather to run on foot like the horses.[99]

Verses Twenty-three and Twenty-four. אר מרז ('r mrz), "curse Meroz." Although the transition is abrupt, as Boling remarks, such "coordinative ranging of propositions one after another, without expression of syntactic connection, is characteristic of oral epic."[100]

The exact location of Meroz is uncertain.[101] E. B. Smick is probably correct in following Kraeling's suggestion that it was a Canaanite city from which the Israelite forces, due to treaty stipulations, had a right to expect some help in cutting off Sisera's retreating army.[102]

מלאך יהוה (ml'k yhwh). "The Angel of the Lord," here the unseen heavenly[103] Warrior leading the Israelite forces (cf. Judg. 2:1, 4; 5:31; 6:11ff.; 13:3ff.).

אר ארר ('r 'rr) literally means "utterly curse" (NASB), but by extension it means "curse bitterly" (KJV, NIV).

מנשם (mnshm). The comparative construction functions here as a virtual superlative.[104]

Note that A. Malamat postulates that Heber is in reality a term indicating "a nomadic tribal sub-division that had broken away from the parent tribe and wandered far afield in search of pasture."[105] But since Jael is Heber's wife, the word must surely be a personal name.

Verse Twenty-Five. ספל (spl) is "a shallow bowl fit for nobles."[106] Gordon thinks that it is a huge metal vessel (cf. Ug. spl; Akk. saplu, "metal vase/bowl").[107] But a bowl of such a large size seems out of place both here and in Judges 6:38.

חמא (hm'), "curds." Bush remarks:

> ... the *hemah* of the Scriptures is probably the same as the *haymak* of the Arabs, which is not ... simple cream, but cream produced by simmering fresh sheep's milk for some hours over a slow fire. ... The butter and milk which the wife of Heber presented to Sisera ... were forced cream or *haymak,* and *leban,* or coagulated sour milk diluted

with water, which is a common and refreshing beverage in those sultry regions.[108]

Whether this act of hospitality was simply intended to lull Sisera into a false sense of security or the proffered drink also disguised a mild sedative (so Boling, cf. Josephus *Antiq.* v: 5:4) is a moot question.

Verse Twenty-Six. תשלחן (*tshlḥn*) is an energic form expressing emphatic action.[109] Contrary to Cross and Freedman,[110] the form is probably third feminine singular with resumptive pronoun in anticipatory emphasis construction.[111]

יתד (*ytd*), "Tent peg." A. Edersheim calls it, "One of the long iron spikes to which the tent-cords are fashioned."[112]

ימן (*ymn*), "Right hand," is used in cases where a specific act of emphasis, vigor, or identification is intended.[113] Dahood argues on the basis of Ugaritic examples that the parallel *yd/ymn* must mean "left hand/ right hand," listing as examples not only this passage but Psalms 21:9; 26:10; 74:11; 89:14, 26; 138:7; 139:10; and Isaiah 48:13.[114] But close scrutiny would appear to demand that of these only Psalm 89:14 is fully allowable, and the *yd* of Psalm 74:11 is most certainly not to be translated "left hand." Here, of course, if Jael has the hammer in her right hand, she obviously must be holding the peg in her left; but this scarcely demands that wherever *yd* appears in parallel construction with *ymn* it must be translated "left hand."

The left hand/right hand motif is, indeed, a familiar one and when used symbolically carries with it the ideas of totality and completeness of action, often with concentration upon a *fixed* goal (e.g., Deut. 2:27; 5:32; 17:11, 20; Josh. 1:7; 23:6; 1 Sam. 6:12; 2 Kings 22:2; Prov. 3:16; Ezek. 39:3; Dan. 12:7; Jonah 4:11). In some cases the prominence of the right hand is underscored by contrasting it with the left hand (e.g., Gen. 48:13–19; Eccles. 10:2), but in all such cases the normal word (*'sᵉm'ōl*), "left hand," is employed.

הלם, מחק, מחץ, חלף (*hlm mḥq, mḥṣ, ḥlp*), "hammered" (cf. v. 22); *mḥq*, a hapax legomenon whose meaning is usually determined by reference to the Arabic *mahaqa,* "demolish," "destroy," and its parallels, here equals *mahaṣ* "smite through," "wound" (cf. Akk. *mahāsu* ["hit," "wound," "drive (a nail/peg)"]).[115]

Bearing in mind the clear meaning of חָלַף (*ḥālap*), "pass through," "pierce," it may be that the four verbs associated with Jael's bloody deed retain a gruesome portrayal of the action: the swinging of the hammer, the penetration of the head, the inflicting of the deep wound, and the passing of the peg through the other temple and into the ground (cf. Judg. 4:21).

רקה (rqh). The word is rare. Boling follows the suggestion of Freedman, opting for the upper neck behind the lower jaw.[116] M. Pope decides for "brow."[117] However, the association with the head here would seem to demand the temple, as traditionally held. Moreover, since רַקָּה (raqqâ) is clearly differentiated from the neck in Song of Solomon 4:3-4, S. Glickman may be correct in remarking concerning Shulamite, "Her temples (which probably include her cheeks) were healthy and flushed with excitement and beauty."[118]

Although the traditional rendering has been retained here, C. F. Whitley's suggestion that שם (shm), "there," may at times best be understood as an emphatic particle with asseverative nuances may be apropos here.[119]

Verse Twenty-eight. יבב (ybb), "cry aloud." The word is a hapax legomenon. If the comparison with the Syriac *yabbēb*, "shout with joy," is allowed fully, it may indicate that Sisera's delay only heightened his mother's excitement and joyful anticipation, rather than the usual idea (followed here) that hers was a cry of forboding anxiety. The motif of the lady waiting at the window for the returning warrior is a common one in the Ancient Near East (cf. 2 Kings 9:30ff.; see ANEP, fig. 131).

פעם מרכבתו (p'm mrkbtw), literally "the hoofbeats of his chariots," with transferral of the part (the horses) to the whole (horse and chariot). The form of aposiopesis here is due to the details of the parallel member.

Verse Twenty-nine. חבמת (ḥkmt), "the wisest (of her princesses)" is probably the old Canaanite feminine singular form (cf. Syriac, Vulgate).[120] The fact that Sisera's mother had handmaidens (literally "princesses") suggests that she was a person of wealth and prominence, perhaps as Martin proposes,[121] a queen mother. If so, Sisera himself held a kingly position.

Verse Thirty. Gray well remarks:

> The imperfects and the staccato arrangement of eight words and two couplets ... convey the urgency and excitement of the questions, and the vivid imagination of the speaker, as well as the swift, ruthless action of the spoilers, which from the point of view of the speaker was not yet completed.[122]

רחם רחמתם (rḥm, rḥmtm), "a maiden," "two maidens." As to the latter word, Cross and Freedman remark:

> The use of the dual ... is archaic, and finds a parallel in the extensive use of the dual in Ugaritic. In later Hebrew the dual was restricted to parts of the body occurring in pairs, and other natural pairs.[123]

The noun itself is virtual street language, being associated with the word for womb, and depicts graphically the fate of the captive girls. As Cundall remarks,

> Elsewhere in the Old Testament it means "womb" and in the Moabite Stone it has the meaning "girl-slaves." The nearest English equivalent is "wench," and it is clear that these unfortunate captives would be used to gratify the lusts of their captors. War brings many vile effects in its train.[124]

צבעם רקם (*ṣb'm rqm*), "a pair of embroidered dyed cloths." Note the enclitic *m* within the construct change.[125]

צבע רקמתם (*ṣb' rqmtm*). Vocalize *ṣeba' rigmātayim*, "two pieces of embroidered dyed cloth."

שלל (*shll*) should be pointed as a participle: *shōlēl*, "the spoiler."

Verse Thirty-one. The genuineness of this final verse is now frequently acknowledged.[126] Boling notes that the contrasting terms "enemies" / "those who love him" are characteristically archaic and that the latter term has been shown to be part of covenantal terminology.[127]

Moreover, the phrases כצאת (*kṣ't*) (cf. v. 4) and בגברת (*bgbrt*) (cf. vv. 13, 23) tie the verse to the main body of the poem, the former word especially forming a closing prayer to the one who as in His past redemptive work in the Exodus event has once again gone before His enemies on behalf of His own (cf. v. 23). May He ever do so!

ANALYSIS

Occasion (1–3). Deborah's song of triumph over the Canaanite kings was primarily a paean of praise to God who had given the victory (cf. Judg. 4:7). In those difficult days in the last quarter of the thirteenth century B.C., a generation of Canaanite oppression had left Israel weakened and nearly defenseless. Not only her continued occupation of the northern portion of the country, but her very existence was in jeopardy. Then God marvelously intervened on behalf of His own whom He had blessed so often before. It was a critical time; the very shape of Israel's future was at stake.[128] Despite the overwhelming power and superiority of the enemy, there were those who truly repented of Israel's spiritual condition (cf. Judg. 4:3), who would willingly enlist in Israel's cause, given proper leadership. Such they had found in Deborah and Barak and ultimately (and most importantly) in God Himself. The Lord was still Israel's God.

Historical background (4–7). Having announced her intention to praise Israel's delivering God, Deborah rehearses the conditions out of which her song ultimately would arise, detailing both the past precedent for expecting God's intervention for Israel (vv. 4-5) and the present predicament that necessitated His doing so (vv. 6-7).

The great example of God's redemption *par excellence* was that of Israel's Exodus from Egypt and conquest of Canaan. That God could intervene was certain; that He would intervene was to be expected. He is that kind of a God. What a magnificent and spectacular sight had been the approach of God, in ancient times, leading His people from the south. Coming up from the Transjordanian southland, the invincible Israelites, led by God, had formed a specter of awesome power to the citizens of Canaan. In the presence of the One of Sinai, the earth had heaved convulsively so that the mountains seemed to leap from their foundations.[129] Moreover, an awesome storm front had preceded the military host.[130] A supernatural victory had followed.[131]

Deborah next tells of the chaotic conditions that permeated the land at the close of Shamgar's heroic struggles against the Philistines (cf. Judg. 3:31; 4:1-3).[132] The Canaanite oppression had been so severe that wayfarers could no longer travel the main highways for fear of property and life. Whatever traveling there was, followed circuitous routes. The reason for such precautions was apparent: military patrol of those roads was practically nonexistent, so that rapacious gangs roamed the area at will. Conditions worsened until Deborah was raised by God to be Israel's "mother."[133]

The Battle of Ta'anach by the Waters of Megiddo (vv. 8-27). This section falls into two major portions. The first (vv. 8-18), deals with Israel's preparations for the battle; the second (vv. 19-27), describes the battle and its aftermath. Verses 8-11b detail those measures that would eventuate in changed conditions in the land. Verse 8 reemphasizes the plight of the Israelites when, under Deborah and Barak, God chose new warriors. In accordance with divine direction, Deborah instructed Barak to assemble an army whose core constituency of ten thousand troops was made up of the men of Naphtali and Zebulun (representing respectively the tribe of Barak and, probably, that of Deborah; Judg. 4:6, 10). But for those newly selected troops, there was scarcely spear or shield to be found.

In such dire circumstances, Deborah's heart was full of compassion and concern (v. 9). The parallel account stresses that Barak led the ten thousand troops to Mount Tabor near Kedesh in Naphtali (Judg. 4:8-10). His initial hesitancy was overcome by Deborah's assurance that she would accompany him. Deborah also issued a general call to the tribes to join in the crucial battle for Israel's existence (vv. 10-11). She addressed herself to Israel's leadership and urged them to consider the songs sung at the watering holes, the traditional places where Israel's epic ballads were recited. There they should consider the messages of those who rehearsed the Lord's great past victories for Israel and recalled the exploits of Israel's famous heroes.

Deborah's pleas did not go unanswered. From countryside and town the people responded, their eligible men assembling at the various designated city gates, singing songs of patriotism and victorious optimism as they came (vv. 11c–12). From there they joined the advance forces already encamped at Mount Tabor (v. 13).[134]

Verses 14 through 18 relate the roll call and battle assignments of the various tribes. The tribe of Ephraim, recently victorious over the pesky Amalekites, was assigned a place in support of Benjamin. West bank Manasseh sent its contingents. The tribe of Zebulun took the lead and was accordingly assigned the privilege of bearing the royal standard.[135] The men of Issachar supported the two core armies from Naphtali and Zebulun. Isaachar's wise captains joined Deborah's command companions, whereas others were deployed with Barak as they descended into the plain below.

The exact deployment of the respective armies and the precise course of the battle itself are difficult to piece together from the details of Judges 4–5. The groupings enumerated in Judges 5 tend to indicate that (1) a group of leaders from Issachar remained with Deborah through the fighting, perhaps as advisors and personal bodyguards;[136] (2) the men from Zebulun and Naphtali together with forces from Issachar formed the core troops that would lead the charge against Sisera; whereas (3) contingents from Benjamin, Ephraim, and west bank Manasseh made up the reserve force that perhaps would follow in a second assault.[137]

Verses 16 and 17 contain a condemnation of those who did not respond to Deborah's pleading summons to send help. The Transjordanian tribes, Reuben and Gad (Gilead), are first mentioned. Reuben in particular is castigated for its vascillating spirit. Reuben preferred listening to the shepherd's flute over answering the trumpet's call to arms. Gad simply stayed home. The northern tribes, Dan and Asher, busied themselves with their maritime duties, rather than involving themselves with God's business.[138] Far better would it have been for those tribes to follow the lead of Zebulun and Naphtali who both commended themselves valorously.[139]

In the second part of the song (vv. 19–27), the battle itself is now first detailed (vv. 19–21). Learning of the Israelite mobilization, Sisera gathered together speedily the men and weaponry of the Canaanite coalition (v. 19; cf. Josh. 11:10) so that he might choose a site that would be advantageous for the utilization of his numerous chariots (cf. Judg.

4:12-13). Proceeding past Megiddo and Ta'anach and crossing the main eastern fork of the Wadi Kishon, Sisera endeavored to array his forces at a point in the eastern Esdraelon Plain that would be broad enough for his chariotry to function effectively. Sisera's goal in penetrating so deeply into the valley was either (1) by show of force to terrorize the Israelites into submission (with a consequent payment of huge tribute), or (2) to be able to fight in a spot well-situated strategically, so that the Israelites would be cut down to the last man. Goods, men, and matériel might then be taken as spoils of war (v. 19).

However, here Sisera was to make the first of three strategic miscalculations. The day was scarcely a good one for charioteers, since recent rains had left the battleground soggy (v. 20).[140] Barely had the Canaanite forces forded the river when the heavy iron chariots bogged down in the mire. Thus the enemy's strength became a liability.[141] Barak seized the initiative and swept down mercilessly upon Sisera's forces (Judg. 4:15).[142] The victory would be a total one, for "the Lord routed Sisera." Coterminous with the Israelite charge, a sudden cloudburst swelled the waterlogged wadi and the resultant flash flooding swept away Sisera's remaining and retreating troops (vv. 20-21). The few men who escaped were relentlessly pursued by Barak's men until not one escaped (Judg. 4:16).

An account of the consequences of the battle begins by noting the confusion of fleeing soldiers and the clamor of the horses frantically pawing away at the unfavorable sod.[143] Such conditions should have facilitated Meroz in cutting off Sisera's retreat. Moreover, in the whole extraordinary incident, Meroz should have recognized the hand of God and eagerly entered the fray. For its failure, it is utterly cursed (v. 23).[144]

How different the case of Jael, the wife of Heber the Kenite (cf. Judg. 4:11; 5:6, 24). When his chariot had become helplessly transfixed in the rain-soaked ground, Sisera (and doubtless most of the rest of the charioteers) had abandoned his chariot (Judg. 4:15) and fled on foot, hoping to make his way safely to friendly territory yet controlled by Hazor (Judg. 4:17). Exhausted from battle and the fright of flight, Sisera at last came to what seemed to be sympathetic territory. At the boundary of Naphtali, marked by the great oak tree "Elon be Zoananaim,"[145] lived Heber the Kenite, with whom Jabin of Hazor had amiable relations (Judg. 4:11, 17). Mazar suggests that Heber and his wife, Jael, were prominent figures, now serving as priests at the sanctuary of Arad.[146]

But the defeated general had again miscalculated the situation. As Edersheim says,

Only outward, not real peace! There is something wild and weird about the appearance of these Kenites on the stage of Jewish history.

Originally an Arab tribe, they retain to the last the fierceness of their race. Though among Israel, they never seem to amalgamate with Israel and yet they are more keenly Israelitish than any of the chosen race. In short, these strange-converts are the most intense in their allegiance to the nation which they have joined, while at the same time they never lose the characteristics of their own race.[147]

With the disarming charm of a Judith, Jael went out to the fatigued fugitive and convinced him that he would be safe in her tent (Judg. 4:18). Here Sisera would make his third and last mistake. Having received his refreshment and Jael's promise to stand watch at the door, the now concealed Sisera fell into a heavy sleep on the floor of the tent (Judg. 4:21).[148] As he lay fast asleep, Jael took a hammer and heavy iron tent stake and tiptoed to where the sleeping Sisera lay.[149] Raising the hammer, she struck him in the temple once, twice, three times (Judg. 5:17) so that the tent peg now lay embedded in the ground on the other side of Sisera's head (Judg. 4:21; 5:24-27). Her grisly deed accomplished, Jael awaited Sisera's pursuers: Edersheim remarks,

> It is not long before Barak—a "lightning" in pursuit as in battle—has reached the spot. Jael lifts aside the tent curtain and shows him the gory corpse. In silence Barak turns from the terrible spectacle. But the power of Jabin and his dominion are henceforth and forever destroyed.[150]

The battle itself ended with the mopping up exercise in which Barak pursued the fleeing forces of Sisera, overtaking them in the forested area of Harosheth Hagoim, so that the power of Jabin and the Canaanite coalition was totally broken (Judg. 4:16, 23-24). The crucial challenge had been met successfully.

Epilogue (28-31). The scene changes abruptly. The poetess depicts the mother of the fallen leader of the Canaanite forces anticipating Sisera's return. As she waited, gazing through the latticed window with eager expectation, her anticipation changed to anxiety. Why had she not heard the hoofbeats of his returning chariots? Why did he tarry so long?

Whether or not the question expected an answer or was a mere expression of Sisera's mother's heart, nevertheless, the "wisest of princesses" seized upon the question to give a comforting reply.[151] Her rhetorical question implied that Sisera's mother would agree that the Canaanite victory had been so great that they needed an unusual amount of time to gather the spoil. Since Sisera was the field commander, collecting his larger share would cause him to be even later in returning.[152] In her wise observation, the reader is perhaps treated to an example of an ancient pun, involving the use of double entendre: whatever "dyed cloth" Sisera might have managed to pick up and tie around his neck (perhaps even given to him by Jael?) would be not only stitched with brilliantly colored thread but drenched with his own blood. It would be doubly dyed.

The poem concludes with a twofold wish: as Sisera and his forces had fallen before the Lord moving in triumph before His gallant warriors, so may all God's enemies perish. As God had gone forth before His people, rising like the sun in irresistible strength, so may it ever be for His own who love Him and follow Him implicitly!

THE SIGNIFICANCE OF THE SONG

Historically. If the *Sitz im Leben* for Deborah's song has been properly ascertained, the poem breathes the air of authenticity. Its very form as a victory song has been seen to be representative of the Late Bronze Period, particularly as viewed in the Song of Tukulti Ninurta I (1244-1208 B.C.).[153] Likewise, its historical orientation in relation to late New Kingdom Egyptian correspondences has been seen to call for a late thirteenth-century date of the Israelite/Canaanite conflict.[154]

Accordingly, a correct understanding of the poem enables the reader to appreciate the thinking and activities of that crucial period in Israel's life. As Engberg noted long ago, Deborah's song must mark some extraordinary event.[155] John Garstang connects the onset of the Canaanite oppression with the withdrawal of the Egyptian forces from the area to deal with the invasion of the sea peoples during the reign of Merneptah.[156] If so, the events of Judges 4-5 were a consequence of the complex international events and movements of the late thirteenth and early twelfth centuries B.C. In those troublesome times, the Canaanites had seized the opportunity to subdue the hated Israelite intruders. Moreover, the "oppressors" of Israel had succeeded in virtually cutting off the northern and southern tribes from one another. As G. Adam Smith has pointed out, the defeat of the Canaanites was a necessity if Israel was to survive. Moreover, victory in the area would provide a strong buffer against the rising threat of the Arameans to the north.[157]

Accordingly, the battle "at Ta'anach" (and the subsequent follow-up at Hazor[158]) was of crucial historical significance, hence well worthy of commemoration. Deborah's song was more than a campfire tale filled with hyperbolic exploits; it rested in historical fact, and that of a strategic nature.

Textually. The literary antiquity and essential textual trustworthiness of Deborah's song have been conceded by writers of nearly all theological persuasions.[159] Indeed, Cross and Freedman have demonstrated that not only in literary form but in the basic elements of grammar, vocabulary, and style the Song of Deborah belongs to the corpus of earliest Hebrew poetry.[160] Its difficult text has been transmitted so carefully across the pages of time, that even Coogan admits,

> Copyists, redactors, and translators may have altered what struck them as obscure or theologically dangerous, but even after three millennia, Judg 5:2-30 exhibits a carefully constructed unity, as several recent studies have demonstrated.[161]

This study has demonstrated that far from needing conjectural emendation or the supposition of redactional activity, the preserved consonantal text is completely comprehensible, despite its antiquity. Moreover, the underlying stanzaic structure, discovered here on purely grammatical ground, assures the reader that, rather than assigning the poem to the genre of folk ballad, as Coogan must do,[162] Deborah's song can be seen as a victory ode composed soon after the event it describes. An appreciation of the historical context and a comparison with the narrative account (Judg. 4) give reassurance that the poetic account of Judges 5 is indeed an accurate and trustworthy record of a literal, historical event. These texts support and are in keeping with a verbally inspired, inerrant biblical record.

Theologically. This brief song focuses upon a number of points that bear upon biblical theology. The most obvious stress of the song is upon the sovereign nature of the God who is Israel's saving God (vv. 3, 5). This Redeemer had gone before His people in great power, bringing them from the south to the promised land (vv. 4-5).[163] A God of judgment (vv. 14-18, 23, 31) and righteousness (v. 11), He is the one who has blessed His people (vv. 2, 9, 11) and can and will come to the aid of those who willingly yield themselves to Him (vv. 2, 8, 9, 23). Israel was yet His people (vv. 2, 8, 9, 11, 13) to whom He stood in covenant relationship (v. 31).[164] Lehman well remarks,

> The books of Joshua and Judges give repeated witness to the victories gained through the power of God in the conquest of Canaan. Through these many extraordinary events Israel was learning the meaning of the providence of God. Their Lord not only foresaw coming events but He predetermined them so that His purposes would be fulfilled.[165]

Tucked almost unnoticeably into the flow of the account is the term *remnant* (v. 13). In parallel with the term *the people of the Lord,* "God's remnant" emphasizes that God's teleological ordering of the events of history is proceeding on course and on time. Rather than being an occasion for fear of annihilation, the people whom Deborah and Barak led, under God's control, should be reminded that their force constituted "a new whole which possessed all the potentialities of renewal and regeneration."[166] The very term *remnant* should have thrilled the hearts of Deborah's hearers. The term, then, reminds the spiritually perceptive that God's purposes are not thwarted and that His promise to Abraham (Gen. 12:1-3; 13:14-16; 15:4-21; 17:14-16) goes on apace.[167] The victory over Sisera should remind the believer that Canaan will yet ultimately belong to Israel and that He will curse those who curse her.[168]

One may also note that the poem calls attention to the availability of God for the believer. Even when things seem blackest (vv. 6-8), God is the one whose aid and blessing may be invoked (v. 31; cf. Judg. 4:3). There is nothing too hard for Him who longs to undertake for those who love Him (v. 31) and unreservedly give themselves to Him (vv. 2, 8, 18).

May each believer, as Deborah of old, personally praise the Lord (v. 2) and so live that he reflects the radiant splendor of Him who longs to lead him in triumph (v. 31).

NOTES

1. Note that in this paper the standard abbreviations for the scholarly periodicals as found in such sources as the *Elenchus Bibliographicus Biblicus* and *Old Testament Abstracts* will be utilized. As well, please note the following short entry citations of works frequently cited in the paper:

AB:Ps III	M. Dahood, *Psalms* III, *The Anchor Bible* (Garden City: Doubleday, 1970).
ANEP	J. B. Prichard, ed., *The Ancient Near East in Pictures* (Princeton: U. Press, 1954).
ANET	J. B. Prichard, ed., *Ancient Near Eastern Texts Relating to the Old Testament,* 3d ed. (Princeton: U. Press, 1973).
AV	Authorized Version.
AYP	F. M. Cross, Jr., *Studies in Ancient Yahwistic Poetry* (Baltimore: Johns Hopkins, 1950).
BDB	F. Brown, S. R. Driver, and C. A. Briggs, eds., *A Hebrew and English Lexicon of the Old Testament* (Oxford: Clarendon, 1907).
CAD	M. Civil, I. J. Gelb, A. L. Oppenheim, E. Reiner, eds., *The Assyrian Dictionary* (Chicago: Oriental Institute, 1960—).
CAH	I. E. S. Edwards, C. J. Gadd, N. G. L. Hammonds, eds., *The Cambridge Ancient History,* 3d ed. (Cambridge: U. Press, 1975).
Deborah and Anat	P. C. Craigie, "Deborah and Anat: A Study of Poetic Imagery (Judges 5)," ZAW, 90 (1978):375-81.

Dictionnaire   D. Cohen, ed., *Dictionnaire des racines sémitiques* (Paris: Mouton, 1970—).
Further Notes   P. C. Craigie, "Some Further Notes on the Song of Deborah," VT 22 (1972):349-59.
G-K   W. Gesenius, *Hebrew Grammar*, ed. E. Kautzsch, 2d rev. ed. (Oxford: Clarendon, 1956).
IDB(S)   G. A. Buttrick, ed., *Interpreter's Dictionary of the Bible*, 4 vols. (New York: Abingdon, 1962). *Supplementary Volume*, ed. K. Cram (Nashville: Abingdon, 1976).
KB III   W. Baumgartner, ed., *Hebräisches und Aramäisches Lexikon*, 3d ed. (Leiden: E. J. Brill, 1974).
KJV   King James Version.
NASB   *New American Standard Bible* (Nashville: Nelson, 1977).
NIV   *Holy Bible, New International Version* (Grand Rapids: Zondervan, 1978).
POTT   D. J. Wiseman, ed., *Peoples of Old Testament Times* (Oxford: Clarendon, 1973).
RSP I, II   L. R. Fisher, ed., *Ras Shamra Parallels* (Rome: Pontifical Biblical Institute, 1972, 1975).
RSV   *Revised Standard Version* (New York: Nelson, 1952).
TDOT   G. J. Botterweck, H. Ringgren, eds., *Theological Dictionary of the Old Testament* (Grand Rapids: Eerdmans, 1974—).
Ugaritic Notes   P. C. Craigie, "Three Ugaritic Notes on the Song of Deborah," JSOT 2 (1977):33-49.
UT   C. H. Gordon, *Ugaritic Textbook* (Rome: Pontifical Biblical Institute, 1965).
Williams, Syntax   R. J. Williams, *Hebrew Syntax* (Toronto: U. Press, 1976).
ZPEB   M. C. Tenney, ed., *The Zondervan Pictorial Encyclopedia of the Bible*, 5 vols. (Grand Rapids: Zondervan, 1975).

2. R. G. Boling, *Judges,* The Anchor Bible (Garden City: Doubleday, 1975), p. 105.
3. See A. Weiser, "Das Deboralied ... eine gattungsund traditionsgeschichtliche Studie," ZAW 30 (1959):67-97; J. Gray, *Joshua, Judges and Ruth* (London: Thomas Nelson, 1967), p. 214.
4. J. Blekinsopp, "Ballad Style and Psalm Style in the Song of Deborah: A Discussion," *Biblica,* 42 (1960):61-76.
5. This is affirmed despite the negative critical remarks of A. D. H. Mayes, *Israel in the Period of the Judges* (Naperville: Allenson, 1977), p. 87, who says, "Judges 4 presents a too uneven and inconsistent text for it to be used uncritically to reconstruct the nature of this event." To the contrary, P. C. Craigie, "The Conquest and Early Hebrew Poetry," TB 20 (1969):82-83, remarks: "The Song of Deborah has been recognized for a long time as an early poem, and is generally thought to be almost contemporary with the events which it describes. ... The whole Song is a Victory Song and its setting would have been in a victory celebration held soon after the event."
6. For the victory songs of Thutmoses III and Amenhotep III, see M. Lichtheim, *Ancient Egyptian Literature,* vol. 2 (Berkeley: U. of California, 1976), pp. 35-39, 43-48; for that of Seti I, see J. A. Breasted, *Ancient Records of Egypt,* vol. 13 (New York: Russell and Russell, 1962), p. 94; for Mernepthah's Hymn

of Victory, see W. F. Edgerton and J. A. Wilson, *Historical Records of Ramses III* (Chicago: U. of Chicago, 1936), pp. 111-12.

7. For the historical details of Tukulti Ninurta's battle with the Kassite foe, see J. M. Munn-Rankin, "Assyrian Military Power 1300-1200 B.C.," *CAH,* vol. 2, part 2, pp. 286-90; for a discussion of the text, especially emphasizing its biblical relevance, see P. C. Craigie, "The Song of Deborah and the Epic of Tukulti-Ninurta," *JBL,* 88 (1969):253-65.

8. See Exod. 15:1-17; Judg. 11:34ff.; 1 Sam. 18:16ff.

9. So E. R. Thiele, *The Mysterious Numbers of the Hebrew Kings* (Grand Rapids: Eerdmans, 1965), p. 254f.

10. Note that most conservative writers allow up to seventeen years more for this period. See J. B. Payne, "Chronology of the Old Testament," ZPEB, vol. 1, p. 35f. who calls for 339 years, and M. F. Unger, *Archaeology and the Old Testament* (Grand Rapids: Zondervan, 1960), pp. 180-87 and Leon Wood, *Distressing Days of the Judges* (Grand Rapids: Zondervan, 1965), pp. 10-17 who call for 340 years.

11. J. Garstang, *Joshua and Judges* (London: Constable, 1935), pp. 62-66.

12. The seven criteria of Wood, pp. 12-13 are: "First, any numbers given in the text, apart from some legitimate questions as to accuracy of transcription, should be taken as accurate.... Second, judgeships carried on in widely separated parts of Israel's total land area would more likely be contemporaneous than those in the same or closely tangent areas. Third, two or more judgeships which involved the raising of an army to effect deliverance from an oppressing enemy would not likely have been contemporaneous, due to the problem of recruitment of troops. Fourth, times of enemy oppression, which would have involved foreign armies crossing the paths of each other, would not likely have been contemporaneous, for strife between the foreign powers themselves could then be expected to have occurred. Fifth, oppressions brought by the Transjordan nations, the Moabites, Midianites and Ammonites, could hardly have been contemporaneous, or even closely following each other, because of geographic, economic, and political considerations.... Sixth, the use of the phrase, 'the land had rest' over a given number of years, appears to be significant in respect to designating that period as one of rest for the entire land, thus forbidding the thought of any oppression existing during that time.... Seventh, the order in which the respective oppressions and judgeships are listed should be taken as the historical order, since no factor in the text suggests any rationale for an order other than chronological." The consensus of current scholarship calls for periods characterized by overlapping judgeships; see for example, J. Hayes, *Introduction to Old Testament Study* (Nashville: Abingdon, 1979), p. 225.

13. Archaeological verification of the Israelite campaign comes from the excavations of Yigael Yadin at Hazor. Those excavations revealed three destruction levels associated with the late bronze Canaanite city: c. 1400 B.C., c. 1300 B.C., and c. 1230 B.C. Yadin associates the 1300 destruction with the invasion of Seti I. Because the 1400 destruction is most likely connected with Joshua's earlier campaigns, the last destruction must be linked with Barak's subsequent fighting. See M. B. Rowton, "Ancient Western Asia," CAH, vol. 1, part 1, pp. 237-39; B. Waltke, "Palestinian Artifactual Evidence Supporting the Early Date of the Exodus," *Bibliotheca Sacra* 129

(1972):42–46. Yadin's approximate date probably is about a generation too high.

14. The name *Sisera* is generally conceded to be non-Semitic, possibly Indo-European; see C. F. Kraft, "Sisera," IDB, 4:380–81; W. F. Albright, *Yahweh and the Gods of Canaan* (Garden City: Doubleday, 1969), p. 251. If, as Kraft suggests, the name is related to the Aegean world, the presence of a military leader with such a name makes the setting of Judges 4–5 historically appropriate, for Aegean sea people formed some of the chief opponents for Merneptah in the battles of his fifth year. See A. H. Gardiner, *Egypt of the Pharaohs* (Oxford: Clarendon, 1962), pp. 270–73. For proposed parallels between the Aegean world and the time of Judges, see C. H. Gordon, *Before the Bible* (New York: Harper & Row, 1962), pp. 295–98.

15. The exact site of Harosheth Haggoyim remains unknown. If it names a city, it must have lain in the narrow valley where the Kishon River flows out of the Esdraelon Plain on its way to the Mediterranean. Y. Aharoni and M. Avi Yonah, *The MacMillan Bible Atlas* (New York: MacMillan, 1965), pl. 59, have suggested on the basis of the Hebrew words that the term is a geographical one, referring to a highly forested area in central Galilee controlled by Gentile forces. For "Galilee of the Gentiles," see Isa. 9:1.

16. Y. Aharoni and M. Avi Yonah, pl. 59, 61, locate this Kedesh just off the southwestern tip of the Sea of Galilee, the site being known as Khirbet Qedesh. This city is to be distinguished from the city of a similar name in Josh. 20:17. Certainly the better known Kadesh on the Orontes River is neither in Naphtali nor close enough to be the proper city here.

17. The imagined contradiction between the two tribes and ten thousand men of Judg. 4:10 and the response of the six tribes of Judg. 5:13ff. is resolved by recognizing that Judg. 4 is simply detailing the initial muster of those tribes most closely associated with Barak, whereas Judg. 5:13ff. delineates the final roll of all the tribes that responded to Deborah's call.

The fact that Mount Tabor is mentioned only in Judg. 4 constitutes no discrepancy with Judg. 5 but merely furnishes supplementary details. Obviously, "Mount Tabor" was the staging area for the mustered Israelite troops from which their attack would be launched.

18. The excavations of Paul Lapp at Ta'anach suggests that there was little occupation there in the late thirteenth century B.C., the major settlement after the destruction by Thutmoses III in 1468 B.C. not occurring until the twelfth century. Another major destruction took place about 1125 B.C. See Paul Lapp, "The 1966 Excavations at Tel Ta'annak," BASOR 185 (1967):3; "The 1968 Excavations at Tel Ta'annak," BASOR 195 (1969): 5. Many equate the scriptural battle of "Ta'anach by the Waters of Megiddo" with the 1125 destruction (e.g., G. A. Turner, *Historical Geography of the Holy Land* [Grand Rapids: Baker, 1973], p. 123; C. F. Pfeiffer, *The Biblical World* [Grand Rapids: Baker, 1966], p. 561). Supportive evidence is usually found in that Megiddo seemingly suffered a destruction about 1140–30 B.C., so that the failure to mention Megiddo in Judg. 4–5 indicates that the battle in question took place when that city lay in ruin and Ta'anach was therefore the prominent place. See A. Negev, *Archaeological Encyclopedia of the Holy Land* (New York: Putnam's, 1972), p. 204; R. K. Harrison, *Introduction to the Old Testament* (Grand Rapids: Eerdmans, 1971), p. 687.

Actually, however, the biblical record does not state that the battle took place at Ta'anach itself, but records it as a point of reference for the battle scene. Consequently, the archaeological evidence concerning Megiddo and Ta'anach may well be inapplicable to the context of Judg. 4–5, their destruction being connected with the unsettled conditions of Gideon's day, the growing strength of the Philistines, and the upheaval occasioned by the general movement of various peoples at the end of the Late Bronze and Early Iron Periods. See further K. A. Kitchen, "The Philistines," POTT, p. 60; W. W. Hallo and W. K. Simpson, *The Ancient Near East* (New York: Harcourt Brace Jovanovich, 1971), pp. 117–20; C. Roebuck, *The World of Ancient Times* (New York: Scribners', 1966), pp. 120–21; S. Hermann, *A History of Israel in Old Testament Times* (Philadelphia: Fortress, 1975), p. 112.

19. The incident at the house of Sisera's mother, which forms part of the epilogue to Deborah's song (Judg. 5:28–31), will be discussed in the analysis.

20. The essential integrity of Deborah's song is taken to be established. Indeed, it may be shown as M. D. Coogan, "A Structural and Literary Analysis of the Song of Deborah," CBQ 40 (1978):14 remarks, "The author of the Song was disciplined and sophisticated, not primitive and naive; the metrical structure, the use of chiasm, parallelism, paronomasia, and repetition all point to a careful and self-conscious literary technique."

   In keeping with the demonstrated antiquity of the song (see AYP, pp. 27–42, 59–61), the principle of phonetic consonantism will be employed throughout the transcription.

   For the value of Ugaritic material to the understanding of the Old Testament texts, see the helpful notes and cautions of S. Segert, "The Ugaritic Texts and the Textual Criticism of the Hebrew Bible," in *Near Eastern Studies in Honor of William Foxwell Albright,* ed. H. Goedicke (Baltimore: Johns Hopkins, 1971), pp. 413–20.

21. Thus, M. Dijkstra and J. C. deMoor, "Problematical Passages in the Legend of *AQHÂTU,*" UF 7 (1975), p. 182, compares ESA *fr'* "first fruits" "optimum (crop)," to Judges 5:2 and translates "brave leadership manifested itself in Israel".

22. Coogan, p. 145.

23. Craigie, "A Note on Judges V2," VT 18 (1968):399.

24. Boling, p. 107.

25. Cf. M. Dahood, AB:Ps III, pp. 441–44. For this type of subordination, see R. J. Williams, *Syntax,* p. 540; M. Dahood, AB:Ps III, pp. 426–27; A. B. Davidson, *Hebrew Syntax,* 3d ed. (Edinburgh: T. & T. Clark, 1958), pp. 191–92. For the corresponding Akkadian construction, see W. von Soden, *Grundriss des akkadischen Grammatik* (Rome: Pontifical Biblical Institute, 1952), p. 219.

26. On the subject of fixed pairs, see S. Gevirtz, *Patterns in the Early Poetry of Israel* (Chicago: Oriental Institute, 1963), pp. 2–4, 10–14; Y. Avishur, "Word Pairs Common to Phoenician and Biblical Hebrew," UF 7 (1975):13–47, esp. p. 19. Note, however, the caution of P. C. Craigie, "Parallel Words in the Song of Deborah," JETS 20 (1977):15–22.

27. For "theophany" in ancient Israel, see Jörg Jeremias, *Theophanie: Die Geschichte einer altestamentlichen Gattung* (Neuenkirch: Neuenkirchener Verlag, 1965).

28. F. Cross and D. N. Freedman, *Canaanite Myth and Hebrew Epic* (Cambridge: Harvard U., 1973), pp. 86n, 164f.

29. See E. Lipinski, "Judges 5, 4-5 et Psaumae 68, 8-11," *Biblica* 48 (1967):195-98.
30. A. Globe, "The Text and Literary Structure of Judges 5, 4-5," *Biblica* 55 (1974):174-75.
31. Cf. Arab., *d,* Ara./Syr., Ug. d, ESA *d/dt,* Old Ara., Ph z(u/i), Geez. za. The case for the appearance of this particle in old Hebrew is well established; see W. Moran, "The Hebrew Language in Its Northwest Semitic Background," *The Bible and the Ancient Near East,* ed. G. E. Wright (Garden City, N.Y.: Doubleday, 1965), p. 69; E. Lipinski, op. cit., p. 198f.
32. "Deborah and Anat: A Study of Poetic Imagery (Judges 5)," ZAW 90 (1978):374-81 and S. Dempster, "Mythology and History in the Song of Deborah," WTJ 41 (1978):33-51.
33. Boling, p. 101f.
34. Craigie, *Further Notes,* pp. 6-7.
35. For the particle ŝ(a), see R. J. Williams, *Syntax,* pp. 25, 77-78.
36. A. R. Hulst, *Old Testament Translation Problems* (Leiden: E. J. Brill, 1960), p. 21.
37. P. C. Craigie, *Further Notes,* p. 350.
38. W. F. Albright, *Yahweh and the Gods of Canaan* (Garden City, N.Y.: Doubleday, 1969), p. 49.
39. G. Garbini, "**PARZON* 'Iron' in the Song of Deborah," JSS 23 (1978):23f.
40. P. R. Ackroyd, "Note to **PARZON* 'Iron' in the Song of Deborah," JSS 24 (1979):19f.
41. S. Dempster, p. 47.
42. Boling, p. 109.
43. *'z* after a previous clause, see KB III, p. 26.
44. See *AYP,* pp. 54-55; Williams, *Syntax,* pp. 32-33; B. Waltke, *Hebrew Syntax Notes* (Portland: Western Conservative Baptist Seminary, 1974), p. 45.
45. For enclitic *m,* see H. Hummel, "Enclitic mem in Early Northwest Semitic, especially Hebrew," JBL 76 (1957):85-107.
46. See P. C. Craigie, *Further Notes,* pp. 350-51.
47. See Dahood, AB: PS III, pp. 429-44.
48. See W. Byerlin, *Near Eastern Religious Texts Relating to the Old Testament* (Philadelphia: Westminster, 1978), p. 207; cf. O Keel, *The Symbolism of the Biblical World* (New York: Seabury, 1978), p. 280; W. F. Albright, *Archaeology, Historical Analogy and Early Biblical Tradition* (Baton Rouge: Louisiana State U., 1956), pp. 31-41. For the sense of the preposition *l* as "in" (properly "in the possession of") see Dahood, p. 395. For the interchange of *l* and *b,* see UT, pp. 92-93. For a consideration of the proper limits of prepositional equations, see M. D. Futato, "The Preposition 'Beth' in the Hebrew Psalter," WTJ 41 (1978):68-83. For *rmh* , "lance," see my remarks at Joel 3:10 in the forthcoming *Expositor's Bible Commentary,* vol. 12 (Grand Rapids: Zondervan). Boling (pp. 54-55, 110) is probably right in translating *'lp* "contingents."
49. M. Dahood, *Ugaritic-Hebrew Philology* (Rome: Pontifical Biblical Institute, 1965), p. 70.
50. G. Bush, *Notes on Judges* (Minneapolis: Klock and Klock, 1976), p. 63.
51. Note G. F. Moore's remarks in *Judges* (Edinburgh: T. & T. Clark, 1978), p. 148.
52. A. E. Cundall, *Judges* (Downers Grove, Ill.: Inter-Varsity, 1973), p. 96.

53. J. D. Martin, *The Book of Judges* (Cambridge: Cambridge U., 1975), p. 67.
54. KB III, p. 518.
55. Boling, p. 101.
56. Coogan, p. 148.
57. Albright, p. 49.
58. Martin, p. 67.
59. See further G. E. Watson, "Verse Patterns in Ugaritic, Akkadian and Hebrew Poetry," UF 7 (1975):485.
60. J. Gray, *Joshua, Judges* and *Ruth* (Greenwood, s.c.: Attic, 1977), p. 219.
61. For the Qal passive, see R. J. Williams, "The Passive *Qal* Theme in Hebrew," *Essays on the Ancient Semitic World,* ed. J. W. Weavers and D. B. Redford. (Toronto: U. Press, 1970), pp. 43-50.
62. Weiser, p. 80.
63. Martin, p. 70. For the critical importance of the ancient city gate, see R. de Vaux, *Ancient Israel* (New York: McGraw-Hill, 1961), pp. 49-50.
64. Cf. C. F. Keil and F. Delitzsch, *Joshua, Judges, Ruth,* Biblical Commentary on the Old Testament (Grand Rapids: Eerdmans, 1956), p. 318.
65. For the term as employed in the remnant motif, see G. Hasel, *The Remnant* (Berrien Springs: Andrews U., 1974), pp. 386-88.
66. For אדרם (*'drm*), "mighty ones," see *RSP,* I: 60; G. W. Ahlstrom, TDOT, 1:73-74; for גבר (*jbr*), "mighty man," "hero," see H. Kosmala, TDOT, 2:373-77. For the individual roots, see D. Cohen, ed., *Dictionnaire,* 1:10; 2:97.
67. Gray, p. 222.
68. Boling, p. 111.
69. Craigie, p. 351f.
70. So W. H. Mare, "Amalek," "Amalekites," ZPEB, 1:124.
71. Cf. A. T. Robertson, *A Grammar of the Greek New Testament in the Light of Historical Research* (Nashville: Broadman, 1934), pp. 442-43.
72. Keil and Delitzsch, p. 317f.
73. Boling, p. 112.
74. Gray, p. 223.
75. Cross, p. 235n.
76. W. F. Albright, p. 275.
77. Gray, p. 223. On the whole problem, see further P. C. Craigie, *Ugaritic Notes,* pp. 41-43.
78. Boling, p. 112.
79. Cross and Freedman, p. 28. See also Boling, p. 133.
80. Cross, p. 235n.
81. Gray, p. 224.
82. P. C. Craigie, *Ugaritic Notes,* pp. 39-41.
83. Cross and Freedman, p. 34.
84. Boling, p. 113.
85. For the chiasmatic sentence here, see A. R. Ceresko, "The A:B: :B:A Word Pattern in Hebrew and Northwest Semitic," UF 7 (1975):73-88.
86. Keil and Delitzsch, p. 320.
87. Cf. Craigie, *Ugaritic Notes,* pp. 33-38.
88. W. F. Albright, "The Psalm of Habakkuk," in *Studies in the Old Testament and Prophecy Dedicated to T. H. Robinson,* ed. H. H. Rowley (Edinburgh: T. & T. Clark, 1950).

89. See the writer's remarks on *ṣālal* in *Theological Wordbook of the Old Testament* (Chicago: Moody, 1980).
90. Cross and Freedman, p. 34.
91. Coogan, p. 150. cf. F. J. Helfmeyer, "הלך *hālakh*," *TDOT* 3:389.
92. Cf. M. Pope, *Job,* The Anchor Bible (Garden City, N.Y.: Doubleday, 1965), p. 31.
93. Cf. the writer's remarks at Joel 3:11 in the forthcoming *Expositor's Bible Commentary,* vol. 12.
94. Cross and Freedman, pp. 30, 35-36.
95. Craigie, *Deborah and Anat,* p. 378.
96. The word *dhrt* is derived from *dhr,* "dash," "gallop." Cf. Nahum 3:2 and the remarks of K. J. Cathcart, *Nahum in the Light of Northwest Semitic* (Rome: Biblical Institute Press, 1973), p. 12.
97. Cf. Williams, *Syntax,* p. 24; G-K, para. 124*d*.
98. Cf. W. F. Albright, *The Vocalization of the Egyptian Syllabic Orthography* (New Haven: American Oriental Society, 1934), p. 39. On the whole problem, see J. Gray, *The Keret Text in the Literature of Ras Shamra,* 2d ed. (Leiden: E. J. Brill, 1964), p. 49. For the root, see Cohen, *Dictionnaire,* 1:5.
99. P. C. Craigie, *Further Notes,* pp. 352-53.
100. Boling, pp. 113-14.
101. A. Negev, *Archaeological Encyclopedia of the Holy Land* (New York: Putnam's, 1972), p. 205.
102. E. B. Smick, "Meroz," ZPEB 4:193.
103. For the term itself, see G. Vos, *Biblical Theology* (Grand Rapids: Eerdmans, 1954), pp. 88-89. See further P. C. Craigie, *The Problem of War in the Old Testament* (Grand Rapids: Eerdmans, 1978), pp. 36, 94-97. For the concept of "holy war" and "Yahweh's wars," see W. Kaiser, Jr., *Toward an Old Testament Theology* (Grand Rapids: Zondervan, 1978), pp. 134-36; R. De Vaux, pp. 258-63.
104. Davidson, p. 49.
105. A. Malamat, "Mari and the Bible: Some Patterns of Tribal Organization and Institutions," JAOS 82 (1962):144-46.
106. Gray, *Joshua, Judges, and Ruth,* p. 227.
107. Gordon, UT, p. 451.
108. Bush, p. 74.
109. See UT, pp. 72-73; cf. AB: Ps III, p. 387f.; and R. J. Williams, "Energic Verbal Forms in Hebrew," in *Studies in the Palestinian World,* pp. 75-85.
110. Cross and Freedman, p. 37f.
111. Cf. *Syntax,* par. 574; for the term "anticipatory emphasis," see A. H. Gardiner, *Egyptian Grammar* (London: Oxford, 1957), pp. 114-17.
112. A. Edersheim, in *Bible History* (Grand Rapids: Eerdmans, 1956), 3: 124 calls it, "One of the long iron spikes to which the tent-cords are fashioned."
113. See H. Cremer, *Biblio-Theological Lexicon of New Testament Greek,* 4th ed. (Edinburgh: T. and T. Clark, 1954), pp. 72-73.
114. Dahood, RSP, vol. 1, p. 195f.
115. See M. Held, "*mhṣ/ 'mhš* in Ugaritic and other Semitic Languages," JAOS 79 (1958): 169-76.
116. Boling, p. 99.
117. M. Pope, *Song of Songs,* The Anchor Bible (Garden City, N.Y.: Doubleday, 1977), p. 464.

118. S. Glickman, *A Song for Lovers* (Downers Grove, Ill: Inter-Varsity, 1976), p. 16. For the use of the descriptive love song, see J. B. White, *A Study of the Language of Love in the Song of Songs and Ancient Egyptian Poetry* (Missoula, Mont.: Scholars Press, 1978), pp. 148-49.
119. C. F. Whitley, "Has the Particle *shm* an Asseverative Force?" *Biblica* 55 (1974):394-98.
120. For the use of bound structure as a substitute for a superlative, see Williams, *Syntax,* p. 78.
121. Martin, p. 76.
122. Gray, *Joshua, Judges and Ruth,* p. 228.
123. Cross and Freedman, p. 39.
124. Cundall, p. 101.
125. See D. N. Freedman, "The Broken Construct Chain, Further Examples," *Biblica,* 55 (1974):549-63; AB:Ps III, pp. 381-84.
126. Cf. Cundall, p. 101; Boling, p. 115f.
127. See further W. L. Moran, "The Ancient Near Eastern Background of the Love of God in Deuteronomy," CBQ 25 (1963):77-87; M. Fishbane, "The Treaty Background of Amos 1:11," JBL 89 (1970):313-18; P. R. Ackroyd, "The Verb Love—אָהֵב *'āhēb* in the David-Jonathan Narrative," VT 25 (1975):213f.
128. The critical nature of the time and the crucial importance of the impending battle are succinctly detailed by G. A. Smith, *The Historical Geography of the Holy Land* (New York: Harper & Row, 1966), p. 254. "On the eve of Deborah's appearance in Israel Esdraelon which had been assigned to Issachar was still in possession of the Canaanites and scoured by their chariots. This meant not only that the entrances to the hill country of Israel were in Canaanite hands but that the northern tribes Zebulun and Naphtali were cut off from the southern Manasseh, Ephraim, Benjamin and the still ineffective Judah. The evil therefore was far greater than the oppression of Issachar; it affected the national existence of Israel and its removal was a concern of all her tribes."
129. Compare Exodus 15:14-16*a;* Habakkuk 3:6*b*-7; Psalms 18:7; 68:8f. (Heb. 68:9f.); 144:5.
130. Compare Psalms 18:5; 68:8 [Heb. 9]; 77:16-18; 144:6; Habakkuk 3:10*b*-11.
131. These statements prepare the reader for the battle's outcome. Just as the earlier Canaanite kings had witnessed God's victory through Israel, so it could happen in the crucial encounter against the Canaanites of Deborah and Barak's time.
132. These, too, would be noted as "the days of Jael," another heroic figure (cf. Judg. 4:11, 17-21; 5:24-27).
133. G. Bush, p. 61, calls Deborah Israel's "benefactress."
134. Adam Smith, p. 255, points out: "It is not necessary to suppose that Barak arranged his men high up Tabor; though Tabor, an immemorial fortress, was there to fall back upon in case of defeat. The headquarters of the muster were probably in the glen, at Tabor's foot, in the village Deburieh—perhaps a reminiscence of Deborah herself—which also in Roman times was occupied by the natives of Galilee in their revolt against the foreigner who held the plain. ... Josephus (ii Wars XXI.3) speaks of a garrison at Dabaritta, as it was called in his day, to "keep guard on the great plain."
135. Zebulun's role was not merely one of color bearing, for they were to com-

mend themselves with outstanding valor in the ensuing fray, as well as the other core troops from Barak's Naphtali (v. 18).

136. J. Gray, *Joshua, Judges and Ruth,* pp. 210–11, suggests that Deborah herself may have led or sent a diversionary movement that drew Sisera's heavy chariotry into less favorable terrain; so, too, C. Herzog and M. Gichon, *Battles of the Bible* (London: Weidenfeld & Nicholson, 1978), p. 51.

137. See Y. Aharoni and M. Avi Yonah, pl. 60.

138. This writer follows Wood, (pp. 147–50,) and Martin, (p. 71,) in identifying Dan's homeland as now being in the north rather than in its original southern location. In addition to the reasons put forward by these writers, the fact that the tribes are grouped geographically in Judg. 5 argues for a northerly locale.

139. Note that the two southernmost western tribes, Judah and Simeon, are neither commended nor condemned; they simply are not mentioned. Some have suggested their geographical remoteness to the battle scene, but surely they were no more distant than Reuben who was so strongly criticized. Keil and Delitzsch (p. 319f.) are possibly closer to the truth when they postulate some early preoccupation with the Philistines. There must also have been some historical conditions that prevented the involvement of these two tribes (see A. D. H. Mayes, pp. 98–105), perhaps a preoccupation with unoccupied Jerusalem, as Cundall (p. 99), decides. There may even have been some degree of disagreement and disassociation of these two tribes from the other ten; certainly a basic tension seems to have existed between the two portions of Israel throughout its history. See S. Hermann, pp. 190–93; J. Bright, *A History of Israel* (Philadelphia: Westminster, n.d.), pp. 207–11; R. deVaux, pp. 95–99.

140. G. Adam Smith, (pp. 264–68), compares this to the similar problem encountered by the British in their Esdraelon campaign of 1918.

141. See C. F. Pfeiffer, *Old Testament History* (Grand Rapids: Baker, 1973), pp. 224–25.

142. A. Edersheim (p. 122,) points out the seemingly helpless state of the Israelites. All the more, then, Barak's ability to evaluate properly the situation and to turn the condition to one's advantage was a mark of his military capabilities, whatever faults he might have had. Compare the remarks of O. Wilcken, *Alexander the Great* (New York: Norton, 1967), pp. 240–44 concerning the generalship of Alexander of Macedon.

143. L. Wood (*The Distressing Days of the Judges,* p. 192) aptly remarks, "The meaning is best taken to be that the horses, pulling the chariots, broke ranks as the chariots became stalled in the mud, and, with wild prancing, galloped away from the helpless drivers. This put the enemy in complete disarray, and God's army won a remarkable victory."

144. De Vaux (p. 261) correctly observes, "Both the prose account and the song are close enough to the events to have given us a faithful version of what the participants thought of this war: for them it was a sacred action."

145. For the Galilean location of the scene at Jael's tent, see G. Adam Smith, pp. 256–57. Smith notes that Sisera's flight was "the same direction as the French military maps show the flight of the Turks to have taken in 1799, when Kleber's small square, re-enforced by Napoleon, broke up vastly superior numbers on the same field of Sisera's discomfiture."

146. B. Mazar, "The Sanctuary of Arad and the Family of Hobab the Kenite,"

JNES 24 (1965):297–303. It is interesting that Heber was descended from the clan from which Moses took Zipporah, his Kenite bride. For the problem of the relationship of Hobab to Moses, see S. Barabas, "Hobab," in ZPEB, 3:173.

147. Edersheim, p. 124.

148. R. Pfeiffer, *Introduction to the Old Testament* (New York: Harper, 1948), p. 329, imagines a contradiction between Judg. 4:21 and 5:27 as though in the poetic account Sisera is hit on the head "while drinking sour milk outside the tent." R. K. Harrison, (pp. 687–88), well remarks, "As in some other instances, Pfeiffer has deliberately misrepresented the content of the Hebrew, for nowhere in the Song of Deborah was Sisera spoken of as sitting outside a tent drinking buttermilk when the fatal blow was struck, nor was his condition of relative awareness mentioned in the poetic section of Judges 5:26f. Quite obviously, there is no contradiction here of the kind alleged by this sort of hypercriticism." Boling (p. 115) points out that Judg. 5:27 simply plays on the point that the very spot where Sisera collapsed in exhaustion was the place of his undoing.

149. Martin (p. 75) imagines a contradiction between the account of Sisera's death given here and that in 4:20–21, so that there are "two variant traditions regarding the death of Sisera only one of which is reproduced in the prose narrative." Actually, the two accounts are complementary: (1) Jael goes out to meet the fleeing Sisera, urging him to entrust himself to her (4:17–18); (2) he does so and she conceals him (4:18b); (3) when Sisera complains of his extreme thirst, Jael further alleviates his fears by giving him milk and curds, rather than the simple water for which he asked (4:19; 5:25); (4) having posted Jael as a sentry at the door of her tent, Sisera collapses from sheer exhaustion in its interior and falls fast asleep (4:20–21); (5) as Sisera lies in exhausted sleep, Jael, having fetched the tent peg, tiptoes to his side and drives the peg through his temple (4:21; 5:26–27). Actually 5:27 puts the whole thing in a poetic setting. Verse 27a depicts Sisera's arrival, collapse, and falling asleep. As Boling, p. 115, remarks, "27b recapitulates his arrival at the tent and his collapse in exhaustion, while 27c makes that the point of his undoing." Boling also suggests a word play between the *bên raglèhā*, "between her feet," here and the military use of *regel* in 4:10 and 5:15. Great Sisera was now "under the command of" Jael!

150. A. Edersheim, p. 124.

151. As R. B. Y. Scott (*The Way of Wisdom* [New York: MacMillan, 1971], p. 78), points out, true wisdom carries with it the ability to apply knowledge skillfully to the proper situation. See also W. L. Humphreys, "The Motif of the Wise Courtier," in *Israelite Wisdom: Theological and Literary Essays in Honor of Samuel Terrien,* ed. J. G. Gamme, W. A. Brueggemann, W. L. Humphreys and J. M. Ward (New York: Union Theological Seminary, 1978), pp. 177–90.

152. For the rhetorical use of the interrogative sentence, here demanding an affirmative reply, see R. Gordis, *The Word and the Book* (New York: KTAV, 1976), pp. 152–57. For the spoils of war, see R. de Vaux, p. 255f.

153. P. C. Craige ("The Song of Deborah and the Epic of Tukultininurta," p. 255) points out that "the content of the passage ranges from the situation before the battle to the final victory of Tulkultininurta over Kashtiliash, king of the Cassites. Whereas the Song of Deborah celebrates a victory after a

decisive battle, the epic covers what was in effect a military campaign; there was more than one particular battle."
154. See above, p. 7.
155. R. M. Engberg, "Historical Analysis of Archaeological Evidence," BASOR 78 (1940):6–7.
156. J. Garstang, pp. 291–94. The Egyptian hold on northern Syria had slipped during the reign of Ramses II. The Merneptah Stele seems to indicate that certain of the invaders were drawn into lower Canaan and there were defeated. Some may have escaped extinction, and, together with survivors from the campaign of Ramses III in his eighth year, formed the background to the later Philistine problem. See further A. H. Gardner, *Egypt of the Pharaohs,* pp. 283–87.
157. See above, p. 31. For the rising threat of Aram in the period of the Judges, see R. A. Baughman, "Arameans," in IDB, 1:192f. Note however, that nothing is mentioned of Bethshan which, as J. Bright, (p. 158) points out, may have remained out of direct Israelite contact.
158. See A. Negev, p. 204; Y. Aharoni, "Megiddo," in *Archaeological Encyclopedia of the Holy Land,* ed. M. Avi Yonah and E. Stern (Jerusalem: Israel Exploration Society and Masada Press, 1977), 3:847; A. E. Glock, "Taanach," in *Archaeological Encyclopedia of the Holy Land,* 4:1146–47.
159. See, for example, W. F. Albright, "The Earliest Forms of Hebrew Verse," JPOS 2 (1922):69–86; J. A. Bewer, *The Literature of the Old Testament* (New York: Columbia U., 1962), pp. 6–9; R. G. Boling, pp. 116–17; A. Cundall, pp. 90–95.
160. See AYP, pp. 10–11, 27–42, 51–57.
161. M. Coogan, p. 144.
162. Ibid., pp. 165–66.
163. The prose account reminds the reader that God controls history (Judg. 4:1–2, 6–7, 14, 23). This victor would appear to be the same Angel of the Lord who went before His people on other occasions (cf. Judg. 5:23, 31 with 2:1, 4; 6:11ff.; 13:3ff.). If so, the passage does take on Christological importance, although J. Borland, *Christ in the Old Testament* (Chicago: Moody, 1978), p. 21, insists that the passage itself does not contain a Christophany. Note that a passage may be Christophanic without containing a Christophany.
164. This is heightened if the covenant force in "those who love him," (see notes at v. 31) is allowed.
165. C. K. Lehman, *Biblical Theology* (Scottsdale, Pa: Herald, 1971), p. 223.
166. G. Hasel, p. 388.
167. See W. Kaiser, Jr., pp. 84–89.
168. Gen. 12:3; cf. Judg. 5:31.

6

An Exegetical and Theological Exposition of Psalm 139

Donald R. Glenn

DONALD R. GLENN *(M.A., Brandeis University; Th.M., Dallas Theological Seminary)* is associate professor and chairman of Semitics and Old Testament studies at Dallas Theological Seminary, Dallas, Texas.

Because of its profound theological insights into the nature of God and His intimate concern for man, Psalm 139 has long been one of the favorite texts of Christian theologians, exegetes, and expositors. W. A. Shelton, for example, calls it "one of the grandest psalms in the entire collection, if not, indeed, the best of them all," and says of it, "Its tone is high, and its conception of the personal and highly spiritual nature of God rises to glorious heights. . . . It is the O.T.'s highest conception of the relationship of God to the individual soul."[1]

On the other hand, due to the number of textual variants, rare words, difficult syntactical structures, and unusual figures of speech, the exegesis of several verses and their significance to the meaning of the psalm as a whole have been greatly debated. Oesterley, for example, says: "There are few psalms which present so many exegetical difficulties."[2] Unfortunately, the exegetical difficulties involve some of the most theologically significant verses in the psalm. For example, J. A. Alexander says of verse 16, which describes God's foreknowledge: "This is one of the most obscure and doubtful verses in the book of Psalms."[3]

In addition to the normal exegetical and theological concerns, modern scholarship, following the lead of Herman Gunkel[4] and Sigmund

Mowinckel,[5] has become increasingly interested in the literary form and cultural setting (*Sitz im Leben*) of this and other psalms. Though several recent works treat the psalm under the same general literary form—a psalm of innocence—and against the same cultural background—a prayer before a judicial ordeal involving the charge of idolatry—[6] I believe there are adequate hermeneutical and exegetical grounds for reexamining the identification of the form and cultural background.

It will be the purpose of this study to determine the form and purpose of Psalm 139, to develop its specific message, and to delineate its contribution to biblical theology.

STRUCTURE

Because of repeated words and motifs and progressive development of themes, few scholars would deny the unity of Psalm 139.[7] Some of these repeated words—called *inclusios* by modern scholars when they appear at the beginning and end of a work,[8] are the verbs חָקַר (*ḥāqar*), "to search" (v. 1), and יָדַע (*yāda'*) "to know" (v. 23), and the noun דֶּרֶךְ (*derek*), "way" (in vv. 3 and 24). Moreover, the word רֵעַ (*rē'a*), "purposes, intentions," is repeated in verses 2 and 17, and a semantically related word, שַׂרְעַפָּי (*śar'appāy*), "anxious thoughts," occurs in verse 23. In addition to these verbal links, several motifs link the psalm together. The anxious concern for his independence vis-à-vis the knowledge of God expressed in the figures of verse 5 finds its logical continuation in the rhetorical proposal for flight in verses 7-12. Verses 13-14 are syntactically linked to the preceding by the causal *kî* and furnish the grounds for the affirmations of verses 1-4; God knows the psalmist so thoroughly because He made him.[9]

Although there is general consensus on the unity of the psalm, there is great diversity in the treatment of its thematic structuring. In addition to the bipartite division of the psalm into verses 1-18 and verses 19-24, for which several commentators argue,[10] Harriet Lovitt lists eleven different structural groupings, ranging from the tripartite division of verses 1-12, verses 13-18, and verses 19-24 advocated by Franz Delitzsch to the division into two-line or verse groupings advocated by Bernhard Duhm.[11] It would seem that the most popular treatment of the structure is the recognition of four equal strophes of six verses each, verses 1-6, 7-12, 13-18, and 19-24.[12]

Although I would not deny the shifts in theme and mood (found in vv. 5-6, 14, 17-18, 21-22, 23-24) nor the obvious dichotomy in theme and mood between verses 1-18 and 19-24, I agree with those who divide the psalm into four equal strophes of six verses. Verses 1b-3 obviously develop the theme of God's (fore)knowledge which is illustrated in verse 4. Verses 5-6, which contain the key word דַּעַת (daʿat), "knowledge," are descriptive of the psalmist's response to the fact that God knows him so well. Verses 7-10, a rhetorical question followed by two specific examples in response, are a continuation of the theme of desiring to flee from God's knowledge implicit in the martial metaphors of verse 5 (and 6). Verses 11-12 continue this theme by describing not a proposal to flee but to hide. A major break occurs at verse 13, but as noted above, it is closely related to the preceding by the causal particle כִּי (ki) and by theme, God's formation of the psalmist in the womb, which furnishes the grounds for the affirmations of God's knowledge in verses 1-4. Verse 15b, c is rather obviously an expansion of the theme of God's formation of the psalmist (as stated in v. 13), whereas verse 16 (a description of God's foreordination of the psalmist's formation or course of life) is an expansion of verse 15a, a figurative expression of God's foreknowledge. If the Masoretic text is followed in verse 14, it also deals with the psalmist's formation, "I am fearfully and wonderfully made,"[13] giving the psalmist's response to the wonder of God's formation of him in the womb. Verses 17-18 with their emphasis on God's purposes (רֵעִים, rēʿîm) are linked conceptually to the theme of foreordination treated in verse 16.

Although it is true that there is little obvious thematic connection between verses 19-24 and the preceding verses,[14] it should be remembered that the repetitions cited above deal with just these verses. In addition, it will subsequently be argued that these verses are the climax and the key to the whole psalm, expressing in both a negative and positive manner the psalmist's loyalty to God who knows him so well, because He formed him in the womb. Verses 19-22 express with rhetorical vehemence the psalmist's desire to be disassociated from those hostile to God. The psalmist does this in verse 19a by using an imprecatory wish for God to punish them. In verse 19b he uses an imperative to express his desire for their departure from his company, and in verses 21-22 he conveys that thought by using rhetorical questions and positive expressions of his loyalty to God, even inviting God to test his loyalties and lead him.

In summary, Psalm 139 is a unified whole, expressing the psalmist's loyalty to the God who knows him perfectly because He formed him and foreordained the course of his life. Verses 1-6 affirm that God knows him perfectly, verses 7-12 affirm that it is impossible to escape from the all-knowing God, verses 13-18 ground that knowledge of God in His formation of the psalmist in his mother's womb and in the foreordination of the course of his life (all of which inspires the psalmist's grateful praise). Verses 19-24 are the climax of the psalm, expressing the psalmist's loyalty to the all-knowing God.

FORM

Although the writer's classification of Psalm 139 could perhaps be guessed from his treatment of the structure, some acknowledgment of the difficulty and great diversity of classification should be given. Bullard, for example, calls Psalm 139 the "most difficult specimen to classify."[15] One indication of the difficulty of classification is the fact that Hermann Gunkel, the father of form criticism, classified it as of mixed type, combining moods of hymn and individual lament.[16] Further indication of the difficulty of classifying it is the great diversity of classifications given to it. Siegfried Wagner notes that it has been classified as a hymn, a spiritual song, a prayer, the prayer of an accused person, a song of trust, and a song of thanksgiving as well as a psalm of mixed form.[17] In addition to those somewhat formal categories, several scholars emphasize the affinities of Psalm 139 with Job and other wisdom literature and classify it as a wisdom psalm.[18] However, judging from recent studies, this classification appears to be less formal than a classification of dominant motifs or mood. Thus, for example, Psalm 139 has been classified as a wisdom hymn[19] and a polemic against dogmatic wisdom teaching, utilizing the individual lament form.[20]

As noted above, several recent studies classify Psalm 139 as a psalm of innocence.[21] According to modern form-critical studies, the psalms of innocence are a subcategory of the individual lament, and include at least Psalms 5, 7, 17, 26,[22] and perhaps also Psalms 35, 57, 69, 94, 109.[23] Though verbal and conceptual parallels are not lacking from other psalms of this genre, the verbal and conceptual parallels between Psalm 26 and Psalm 139 are particularly striking. Common words and concepts are: the imperative of בָּחַן (bāḥan) "to test," inviting God's inspection of the psalmist's loyalties (Psalm 26:2; 139:23); the description of the hypocritical adherents of God (compare Psalm 26:4 with Psalm 139:20) as "blood thirsty men," (אַנְשֵׁי דָמִים, 'anshê dāmîm, in Psalm 26:9; 139:19); and the verb שָׂנֵאתִי (śānē'tî), "I hate," expressing the psalmist's aversion to the wicked (Psalms 26:5; 139:21–22). It is those parallels that help to clarify the relationship between verses 19–22 and verses 23–24 of Psalm 139, and suggest a purpose for Psalm 139:19–24 and for Psalm 139 as a whole. In Psalm 26 the affirmation of hatred toward the wicked (Psalm 26:5) and the invitation to God to examine him (Psalm 26:2) occur in the context of his appeals to God for vindication (Psalm 26:1) that he is loyal to God (Psalm 26:1, 3, 6–8) and has nothing to do with wicked, hypocritical, bloodthirsty men (Psalm 26:4–5); he does not wish to be judged when God judges them (Psalm 26:9). The parallel motifs suggest that the psalmist in Psalm 139:19–24 is disavowing his association with wicked, hypocritical, bloodthirsty men (Psalm 139:19-22), and affirming his loyalty to God (Psalm 139:23-24), lest he too be judged when God punishes them.[24]

Although Psalm 139 admittedly lacks the introductory petition characteristic of other psalms of innocence (cf. Psalm 5:1-2[Heb. 2-3], 7:1[Heb. 2]); 17:1, 2; 26:1, 2; etc.), and although it would indeed be wrong to categorize the mood of Psalm 139:1-18 as one of lament, as might be suggested by the fact that the psalms of innocence are a subcategory of the individual lament, it should be emphasized with some older interpreters (and with several recent interpreters), that verses 1-18 are not a detached or theoretical meditation on the attributes of God, but are the basis for the psalmist's rhetorical affirmation of loyalty in verses 19-24.[25] The psalmist readily lays himself open to God's thorough scrutiny of his loyalties (Psalm 139:23-24),[26] because—not in spite of the fact that—he is well aware that he cannot hide anything from God who knows all about him. Though this combination of somewhat hymnic motifs and petition is unique to Psalm 139 as compared to other psalms of innocence, Mowinckel has appropriately noted a parallel combination in the communal lament of Psalm 90, in which the psalmist contrasts praise of God's eternity (Psalm 90:1-2) with lamentation concerning the brevity of man's life (Psalm 90:3-10) in order to motivate his petition for God to have mercy on such a short-lived people.[27]

In conclusion, although it is admitted that Psalm 139 differs markedly both in form and mood from other psalms of innocence, it is my thesis that the category of the psalm of innocence best accounts for all the features of Psalm 139 and best explains its unity and purpose. Psalm 139 is a confession of loyalty in both negative (vv. 19-22) and positive forms (vv. 23-24) to God who knows him perfectly (vv. 1-4), because He formed him and foreordained the course of his life (vv. 13-16).

CULTURAL SETTING (*SITZ IM LEBEN*)

Because similarity of cultural setting was one of Gunkel's main criteria for identifying a literary genre (*Gattung*),[28] some might assume that the identification of the literary genre of Psalm 139 automatically determines its cultural setting. That is certainly not the case, because there is still basic disagreement regarding the cultural setting of Psalm 139 among those who identify it as a psalm of innocence.

Many of the scholars who identify it as a psalm of innocence follow the lead of E. Würthwein in seeing Psalm 139 as a (nocturnal) prayer in the Temple asking God to vindicate him in a judicial trial involving the charge of idolatry.[29] However, some see it against the background of the wisdom schools as either a wisdom teacher's defense against the charges of impiety,[30] his polemic against traditional wisdom teaching,[31] or his model prayer for his students.[32]

It may be seriously questioned whether one can be so specific about the cultural setting of Psalm 139. Though there may be little doubt that certain cases were brought to the Temple to be argued before God who delivered His decision through the lot or priestly decisions (cf. Deut. 17:8–9; 19:16–18; 1 Kings 8:31–32 and see the examples in Josh. 7:16–21; 1 Sam. 14:24–26), and though the positing of a judicial trial at the Temple may clarify certain allusions in the psalms to appeals for vindication (e.g., Psalm 26:1) and oaths of abjuration (e.g., Psalm 17:3–5 [Heb. 4–6]), there is no explicit literary evidence in either the psalms or the Israelite legal and historical books, canonical or noncanonical, linking the psalms with such a judicial trial. However, even if the allusions in the other psalms of innocence do refer to a judicial proceeding in the Temple, there are no such allusions in Psalm 139. There is no appeal for vindication in this psalm nor any explicit reference to the fact that David has been accused of any wrongdoing, much less the charge of idolatry that several scholars posit on the basis of a faulty interpretation of עֹצֶב ʿōṣeb "pain."[33] The psalmist is not protesting his innocence of any charges in this psalm; he is affirming his loyalty to God, not in external action but in internal devotion (note לְבָבִי, lᵉbābî, "heart" and שַׂרְעַפָּי, śarʿappāy, "anxious thoughts"). This could have been done at the Temple on the occasion of a judicial trial, but it could also have been done away from the Temple on other occasions (e.g., Psalm 63:1 [Heb. 2]).

AUTHORSHIP

In view of the phrase lᵉdāwid in the superscription of Psalm 139, one should also be hesitant about attributing this psalm to a teacher in the wisdom schools. Though it is true that this phrase might mean "concerning or about David" or "belonging to a Davidic collection" as well as "by David,"[34] abundant evidence exists that this phrase elsewhere refers to Davidic authorship,[35] and we should not too readily dismiss that as its meaning here unless there exists evidence against this meaning and for one of the other meanings. Scholars of many different theological persuasions have indeed denied Davidic authorship of this psalm either on the basis of its putative linguistic affinities with Aramaic and late Hebrew,[36] or on the basis of its linguistic and literary affinities with the reputedly late book of Job.[37]

Recent scholarship, however, has rightly expressed its reluctance to date a piece of literature on the basis of presumed Aramaism because of an insufficiency of linguistic information about the relationship of Northwest Semitic, Hebrew, and Aramaic in the preexilic periods.[38] Gordis has also correctly noted that there was almost constant contact between the Hebrews and the Aramaeans,[39] and Archer has pointed out that those contacts were most extensive in the time of David[40] (see, e.g., 2 Sam. 10). Archer has also legitimately noted that poetry shows a tendency to incorporate rare or dialectical forms.[41] There exists, therefore, no absolute necessity for denying Davidic authorship on the basis of reputedly late Aramaic words.

As to the arguments from linguistic and literary affinities with the book of Job, it appears methodologically unsound to use a book like Job, the dating of which is more complex and more hotly debated than almost any other book in the Old Testament,[42] to date a psalm like Psalm 139. To rule out Davidic authorship conclusively, it would be necessary first to establish a clear literary dependence of the psalm on Job, and, second, to demonstrate that Job was written after the time of David. For me, those two points are at least as doubtful as the assumption of a Davidic authorship for Psalm 139. There are, moreover, many linguistic and literary affinities with other psalms that are ascribed to David,[43] and Archer has argued that the patriarchal period is just as plausible for the date of the composition of Job as any other.[44]

In addition to the fact that there is good evidence for attributing to David many of the psalms containing the phrase לְדָוִד (l^edāwid) in their superscriptions and that the evidence for the Davidic authorship of Psalm 139 is scarcely incontrovertible, I am unconvinced that there is clear evidence for any other interpretation here. Thus, although לְדָוִד l^edāwid might conceivably mean "concerning David" or "on behalf of David" elsewhere,[45] such a meaning appears out of place in Psalm 139, which is a prayer *by* a person, not *in behalf of* or *about* a person. Likewise, though the phrase לְדָוִד (l^edāwid), like the term לַמְנַצֵּחַ (lamnaṣṣēaḥ), "for the director of music," may conceivably refer to the collector, not the author,[46] such an interpretation of לְדָוִד (l^edāwid) in Psalm 139 scarcely resolves the alleged difficulties raised by linguistic and literary affinities, unless one is prepared to ascribe to the term דָּוִד (dāwid) a titular, rather than a personal sense,[47] a sense which is difficult to establish in the psalms themselves and which is contrary to Christian and Jewish tradition.

In conclusion, although no claim is made here to have proved Davidic authorship, it is hoped that enough has been said to establish that the traditional ascription of Psalm 139 to David is as valid as any other option.

TRANSLATION

1   For the director of music. A psalm of David.

    O LORD, you search me and you know me.
2   You know when I sit and when I rise;
        you perceive my thoughts long before.
3   You discern when I travel and when I rest;
        you are familiar with all my ways.
4   In fact, before there is a word on my tongue,
        you know all about it, O LORD.
5   You surround me behind and before
        and impose on me your control.
6   Such knowledge is too overpowering for me;
        it is insuperable and I cannot prevail against it.
7   Where could I go from your Spirit?
        Where could I flee from your presence?
8   If I were to ascend into heaven, you would be there.
        If I were to make my bed in the depths, you would be there too.
9   If I were to fly with the wings of the dawn
        and alight on the far side of the sea,
10 even there your hand would guide me
        and your right hand would hold me fast.
11 If I were to say, "At least let darkness overwhelm me
        and let the light around me turn into night,"
12 even darkness would not prove too dark for you,
        but the night would be as light as day;
        darkness and light are alike to you.

13 [Iknow this] because you created my inmost being;
        you knit me together in my mother's womb.
14 I praise you because I am fearfully and wonderfully made;
        indeed I know full well that all your works are wonderful.
15 My frame was not hidden from you
        when I was made in the secret place,
        when I was woven together in the depths of the earth.
16 Your eyes saw my unformed body
        and all the days that were ordained for me
            were written in your book
            before one of them even occurred.
17 How precious are your thoughts about me, O God!
        How vast is the sum of them!

18 Were I to count them, they would outnumber the grains of sand!
    Though I awake, I am ever present before you.
19 Oh, that you would kill the wicked, O God!
    You bloodthirsty men, get away from me!
20 They speak of you with evil intent;
    your adversaries use your name for wrong ends.
21 Do I not hate those who hate you, O LORD,
    and abhor those who rise up against you?
22 I hate them with utmost hatred
    and count them as my enemies.
23 Search me, O God, and know my heart;
    test me and know my anxious thoughts.
24 See if there is any offensive way in me
    and lead me in the age-old way.

SYNTHETIC OVERVIEW

Summary: Knowing that the Lord created him and foreordained the course of his life, David acknowledges that it is impossible to hide from His thorough knowledge; so he passionately avers his loyalty to Him and asks for His guidance.

  I. David acknowledges that he is the object of God's thorough knowledge and control (vv.1-6).
    A. David acknowledges that the LORD knows him thoroughly (vv.1-4).
      1. Thesis statement: David acknowledges that the LORD knows him thoroughly (v.1).
      2. David acknowledges that the LORD knows his every action, thought, and inclination (vv.2-4).
        a) David acknowledges that the LORD knows his every thought and act (v.2).
        b) David acknowledges that the LORD is thoroughly familiar with all he does (v.3).
        c) David acknowledges that the LORD knows his every thought before he utters it (v.4).
    B. David acknowledges that such knowledge involves the control of his life (vv.5-6).
      1. David acknowledges that such knowledge restricts his independence (v.5).
      2. David acknowledges that he cannot prevail against such awesome knowledge (v.6).

II. David acknowledges that he could not escape or hide from such knowledge and control (vv.7-12).

    A. David acknowledges that he could not escape from the LORD's knowledge and control (vv.7-10).

        1. Thesis statement: David affirms rhetorically that he could not escape such knowledge (v.7).

        2. David acknowledges that he could not escape from the LORD's knowledge in either heaven or hell (v.8).

        3. David acknowledges that he could not escape from the LORD's knowledge and control regardless of how far or fast he fled (v.9-10).

    B. David acknowledges that he could not hide from the LORD (vv.11-12).

        1. David proposes hiding from the LORD in thick darkness (v.11).

        2. David acknowledges that even the thickest darkness could not hide him from the LORD (v.12).

III. David bases these conclusions on the awareness that the LORD created him and foreordained the course of his life, for which he gratefully praises Him (vv.13-16).

    A. David gratefully acknowledges that he is the product of the LORD's miraculous handiwork (vv.13-14).

        1. David acknowledges that the LORD carefully formed him in the womb of his mother (v.13).

        2. David gratefully praises the LORD for the miraculousness of his formation (v.14).

    B. David acknowledges that the LORD's oversight of his formation in the womb involved the foreordination of his life (vv.15-16).

        1. David acknowledges that the LORD oversaw his intricate development in the womb (v.15).

        2. David acknowledges that this oversight involved the foreordination of his life (v.16).

    C. This leads David to exult that the LORD's thoughts of him are vast and precious (vv.17-18).

        1. David exults that the LORD's thoughts of him are vast and precious (v.17).

        2. David exults that he is ever in God's thoughts (v.18).

IV. David avers his loyalty to this all-knowing, intimately concerned LORD by passionately disassociating himself from the LORD's enemies and asking for His guidance (vv.19-24).

A. David affirms his loyalty to the LORD by passionately disassociating himself from the LORD's enemies (vv.19-22).
   1. David disavows association with the LORD's enemies (vv.19-20).
      a) David disavows association with the wicked and petitions the LORD to kill them (v.19).
      b) David describes the wicked as enemies of the LORD who misuse His name (v.20).
   2. David affirms passionately and rhetorically that he has nothing to do with them (vv.21-22).
B. David asks the LORD to examine his loyalties and lead him in the age-old way (vv.23-24).
   1. David asks the LORD to examine his loyalties (v.23).
   2. David asks the LORD to point out his wrongs and lead him in the age-old way (v.24).

EXEGESIS

David states that the LORD knows all about him and thus essentially controls him (vv.1-6). He realizes also that he cannot escape from such knowledge and control (vv.7-12). David bases these conclusions on the fact that the LORD formed him in his mother's womb and foreordained the course of his life (vv.13-16), facts that indicate His gracious concern for him (vv.17-18) and lead to affirmations of loyalty to Him (vv.19-24).

"You know all about me." In verses 1-4 David affirms that the LORD knows him thoroughly. David affirms this first in a summary statement in verse 1, expands it comprehensively in verses 2-3, and illustrates it concretely in verse 4. In verse 1 David indicates the thoroughness of the LORD's knowledge through the term חֲקַרְתַּנִי (*ḥăqartanî*), "you search me," using a verb that elsewhere is used of men spying out a land (e.g., Judg. 18:2), prospecting for precious metal (e.g., Job 28:3), or conducting a thorough investigation into matters of fact in a legal case (e.g., Deut. 13:15). This verb is also used elsewhere of the LORD's knowledge of the secrets of men's hearts, i.e., their inner thoughts and motives (cf. Psalm 44:22; Jer. 17:10). In the context of Psalm 139:1-4, it is undoubtedly used anthropomorphically,[48] emphasizing that the LORD's knowledge of David is as thorough as though he had conducted a complete investigation of his acts, his thoughts, and his motives.

The thought of the thoroughness of the LORD's knowledge alluded to in verse 1 is explicitly specified in the verbs and their objects in verses 2-3. Using merism, a figure in which polar opposites are used to indicate the totality of all generically related acts, events, localities, and so on,[49] David states that the LORD knows everything he does, i.e., sitting and rising (v.2), traveling and resting (v.3), and every other activity related to any of these.[50] David further refers to the comprehensiveness of the LORD's knowledge of his activities by the phrase כָּל־דְּרָכָי (kol-dᵉrākay), "*all* my ways," in verse 3, a common metaphor (or hypocatastasis)[51] for a person's actions, undertakings, and moral behavior.[52] David further emphasizes the thoroughness of this knowledge by the verbs in verse 3. With the verb זֵרִיתָ (zērîtā), "you discern" (lit. "winnow"), sometimes erroneously interpreted as meaning "you measure or determine,"[53] David anthropomorphically and metaphorically compares the LORD's knowledge to the process of winnowing grain;[54] the LORD knows everything he does as though each act had been painstakingly winnowed (or sifted). In verse 3*b* he says climactically that the LORD is "familiar," or "intimately acquainted,"[55] with all his ways.

In verse 2*b* David acknowledges that the LORD not only knows his every act but his every thought and intention[56] as well. David states that the LORD knows his thoughts and intentions, מֵרָחוֹק (mērāḥôq). This phrase may have either a spatial nuance referring to the LORD's transcendence ("from afar")[57] or a temporal nuance referring to the LORD's prescience ("long before").[58] Since David's emphasis in the statements of verses 1-3 is on the thoroughness of the LORD's knowledge, and since there is no other indication of his intention to contrast this with the LORD's transcendence—as there is, for example, in Psalm 138:6 and Jeremiah 23:23-24—David is probably affirming that the LORD knows his thoughts and intentions before he himself does. That this is a reference to the LORD's prescience of his thoughts is perhaps further indicated by verse 4, which according to L. C. Allen is the reiteration of the motif of verse 2*b*.[59] Verse 4 reads literally, "There is not a word on my tongue, behold you know all of it." Though this could mean that the LORD not only knows what David says but the thoughts and intentions underlying his words, many interpreters have correctly seen that the mutuality between verse 2*b* and verse 4 is best served by seeing this as a reference to the LORD's foreknowledge of his words.[60] If this is so, David is affirming in verses 1-4 that the LORD not only knows everything he does, but everything he says and thinks, and He knows all this long beforehand.

In verses 5-6 David affirms that such thorough knowledge is overpowering and involves control of his life. Though some interpreters have seen these verses as an expression of gratitude for the LORD's protecting hand and of awe regarding the LORD's omniscience,[61] the metaphors in verse 5 and the motif of the impossibility of flight from the LORD in the following verses argue that David is here affirming that the knowledge just described limits his independence.[62] This is most clear in verse 5*b* where David affirms that the LORD hems him in "behind and before," which is a figurative way of saying "on all sides."[63] The verb that David uses here צַרְתָּנִי (*ṣartānî*), "you surround me" comes from a root that elsewhere is used of besieging a city (e.g., 2 Chron. 20:1).[64] The clear idea of control indicated by this anthropomorphic hypocatastasis (comparing the LORD's knowledge to a siege) is reiterated in verse 5*b* where David affirms that through such knowledge the LORD imposes His control on him. That the anthropomorphic phrase David uses in verse 5*b* (תָּשֶׁת עָלַי כַּפֶּכָה, *tāshet ʿālay kappekâ*, "[lit.] you put your hand on me") indicates control, not protection, is clear from its only other occurrence in Job 9:33. There it refers to Job's desire for someone to exercise authority over both himself and God so that he will be guaranteed an impartial hearing.

In the light of these metaphors referring to the LORD's control, and in the light of the following verses in which David denies the possibility of escape from the LORD's knowledge and control, verse 6 should not be understood as an expression of awe about the incomprehensibility of the LORD's knowledge,[65] but of David's awe at his inability to overcome such knowledge, that is, his inability to maintain his freedom, or independence. This suggests that the phrase פְּלִאיָה . . . מִמֶּנִּי (*pilîyyâ . . . mimmenî*)[66] means "beyond my powers, abilities" (i.e., "overpowering for me"),[67] not "incomprehensible for me,"[68] and the phrase לֹא אוּכַל לָהּ (*lōʾ ʾûkal lāh*) means "I cannot prevail against it,"[69] rather than "I cannot grasp, understand it."[70] In addition to being more in keeping with the general context of verse 5 and verses 7-10, these nuances are also more appropriate to the epithet נִשְׂגְּבָה (*niśgᵉbâ*), "it is insuperable," which is another martial hypocatastasis comparing the LORD's knowledge to the impregnable walls of a fortress.[71]

The recognition that such knowledge limits his independence and cannot be overcome (vv.5-6) leads naturally to the next section (vv.7-12) where David denies the possibility of escape from the all-knowing, LORD.

"I cannot escape from you." As in verses 1-6, David announces his theme in the introductory verse (v.7) and expands it in the following three verses (vv.8-10). In verse 7 David asks rhetorically where he can flee from the LORD's presence or run from his Spirit.[72] That this question implies a negative answer, "Nowhere,"[73] is obvious from the continuation in verses 8-10 where David uses the spatial—or to use Krašovec's terms, cosmical and geographical—merisms[74] to deny flight from the LORD. Using the vertical (and cosmical) polar opposites heaven and hell,[75] and the horizontal (and geographical) polar opposites east and west implied in the phrases "wings of the dawn" and "the far side of the sea,"[76] David denies the possibility of escaping from the LORD's presence ("you would be

there" v.8), and control[77] ("your hand would guide me and your right hand would hold me fast," v.10) anywhere in the universe. Due to the use of the zoomorphic hypocatastasis "wings of the dawn" (v.9a), in which the rays of dawn are compared to the wings of a bird and the use of the verb אֶשְׁכְּנָה (’eshkᵉnâ), "I would alight," which is used of a bird alighting after flight in Psalm 55:7, some interpreters have correctly noted that David denies the possibility of escape regardless of the most rapid flight known to him.[78] In other words though he were to take flight on the rays of dawn like a winged bird, he could not escape from the LORD's presence and control.

Some interpreters have erroneously seen verses 7-10 as David's expression of consoling thoughts regarding the LORD's comfort, protection, and guidance wherever he might be.[79] Though this could perhaps be argued from the predominant usage of the verb נָחָה (nāḥâ), "to guide" (v.10a) which refers to beneficent guidance,[80] it ignores the connection with verses 5-6 where the LORD's knowledge and consequent control are viewed as a threat to David's independence. That verses 7-10 are consolatory also runs counter to a proper interpretation of verses 11-12 where David denies that even the most oppressive darkness could hide him. The key to David's thought and mood in these verses is the main verb in verse 11a where David proposes[81] that the darkness יְשׁוּפֵנִי (yᵉshûpēnî), "[lit.] bruise me." Though this verb has commonly been emended on the basis of some of the ancient versions[82] to יְשׁוּכֵּנִי (yᵉśûkkēnî), "cover me"—a thought that would be appropriate to the idea of protection—the canons of textual criticism argue against it.[83] If the Masoretic text is thus retained in verse 11a, David is affirming that even if he were to seek escape in darkness so thick or oppressive that it would be like a heavy weight crushing him, that darkness would not prove too dark for the LORD, that is, he could not hide from Him,[84] because the LORD's knowledge, unlike man's, is not limited by darkness. Darkness and light are alike to Him.

In summary, David says that the LORD knows all about him. He knows his every thought, word, and action (vv.1-4). Moreover, David cannot escape no matter how far or how fast he tries to flee (vv.7-10), nor how hard he tries to hide (vv.11-12) from such knowledge, which limits his independence (vv.5-6). In verses 13-16 David gives the basis for the conviction that the LORD knows him so well—the LORD formed him in his mother's womb and foreordained the course of his life.

"*You created me and foreordained the course of my life.*" The connection between verses 13ff. and verses 1ff. is explicitly indicated by the conjunction כִּי (kî). Though some interpreters understand this particle as asseverative ("yes," "indeed"),[85] most correctly emphasize the causal nuance; the LORD knows him, because the LORD formed or created him.[86] That David intends this link between verses 13ff. and verses 1-4 explicitly is perhaps indicated by the repetition of the pronoun אַתָּה (ʾattâ), "you," in verses 2, 13 and the use of the object כִּלְיֹתָי (kilyōtāy), "my inmost being" (lit., "kidneys"), the most secret, inmost part of man[87] where, as A. R. Johnson notes, "the real sentiments of the elusive *ego* . . . find their expression."[88] H. W. Wolff, for example, sees the explicit connection between the LORD's knowledge of David's thoughts (vv.2b,4) and the creation of his kidneys when he states: "In the context of an examination of conscience it is understandable that the psalmist should first name his kidneys—the highly sensitive organ of self-knowledge—as being created by Yahweh (v.13a)."[89]

As in the preceding sections, David announces his theme in the introductory verse (v.13). However, the precise nuance of this introductory theme and its relation to the following verses have sometimes been misunderstood because of the confusion arising from homonymic roots underlying the two verbs in this verse. Thus, there are two possible roots for קָנִיתָ (qānîtā), meaning either "to possess" or "to create,"[90] and two possible roots for תְּסֻכֵּנִי (tᵉsukkēnî), meaning either "to cover" or "to weave together."[91] Though little misunderstanding has been caused by a failure to recognize two roots in קָנִיתָ (qānîtā)—since even here the concept of creation is commonly acknowledged[92]—great misunderstanding about the nature of his formation and the expansion of this theme in the following verses has been created by the failure to recognize that תְּסֻכֵּנִי (tᵉsukkēnî) means "you knit(or wove)me."[93] By means of this verb, which involves an anthropomorphic hypocatastasis, David is stating that the LORD took as much painstaking care over his formation as a woman laboring over a piece of tapestry. H. W. Wolff concretely applies the comparison here when he states: "Everything that grew in his mother's womb is the work of the great weaver שׂכך (śkk); skin and muscles are seen as fabric."[94] This idea, which is supported by the parallel usage of this verb in Job 10:11, is reiterated in the verb רֻקַּמְתִּי (ruqqamtî) in verse 15c where David uses another hypocatastasis to compare his formation to the work of weaving or embroidering.[95]

In addition to reiterating in verse 15 the idea of the LORD's painstaking care in his formation in his mother's womb, David emphasizes the LORD's awareness of him in this prenatal state. Though the child in the womb (cf. Eccles.11:5) is hidden from man, nonetheless God is aware of David even there. The thought of the secrecy of his development in the womb is explicitly stated in the qualification בַּסֵּתֶר (bassēter) in verse 15b, "in the secret place," and figuratively reiterated in the hypocatastasis בְּתַחְתִּיּוֹת אָרֶץ (bᵉtaḥtiyyôt ʾāreṣ) in verse 15c, where the womb is compared to the lowest parts of the earth, that is שְׁאוֹל *sh^e'ôl* (cf. Ezek. 31:14, 16, 18), because of its darkness and secrecy.[96] However, despite this secrecy, David affirms that his developing body, namely his bones or skeletal framework[97] (probably a synecdoche, a part of his body for the whole)[98] were not hidden from the LORD, when he was thus formed. Because of his use of the hypocatastasis comparing his mother's womb to the darkness and secrecy of שְׁאוֹל (*sh^e'ôl*), there can be little doubt that David intends this contrast as the basis for his earlier affirmations that he could not escape from the LORD in the heavens or the depths שְׁאוֹל (lit., *sh^e'ôl*, v. 8) nor hide from Him in the dark (vv.11-12).

The thought of the LORD's awareness of him during his formation in his mothers's womb (v.15) is reiterated in verse 16*a*, "your eyes saw my unformed body (i.e., my embryo),"[99] and expanded in the words that follow in verse 16*b-d*. In verse 16*b* David refers to a book of the LORD upon which something is written. Like several other references to a book of God in the Old Testament (compare, e.g., Isa.4:3; Ezek.2:9-10; Dan.12:1) and like the references in Ancient Near Eastern religions to a tablet of destiny,[100] this is an anthropomorphic expression referring to foreordination, that is something is as known and designed beforehand as if it were detailcd in a book.[101] U. Becker, for example, states: "The book is here [in the O.T.] a picture of God's eternal purposes for the future of his pcople, his world, or his creatures."[102] However, due to a possible ambiguity in the antecedent of the pronoun on כֻּלָּם (*kullām*), "all of them," in verse 16*b* and on בָּהֶם (*bāhem*), "among them," in verse 16*d*, there are two possibilities regarding what David refers to as foreordained. If the pronoun is understood to refer to the embryo in verse 16*a*, David is affirming that the LORD foreordained (or blueprinted) the development of his embryo in the womb.[103] If, on the other hand, the pronoun is understood to refer proleptically[104] to the word *days* in verse 16*c,* David is affirming that the LORD foreordained the days of his life, that is, either how long he would live (cf. Job. 14:5), or, by metonymy,[105] what would happen during the course of it (cf. Jer. 1:5).[106] Though a reference to the foreordination of the development of the embryo fits in well with the context of verses 13, 15, and though the lack of agreement in number between the plural, "them" and the singular "unformed substance (embryo)" is no absolute hindrance (גֹּלֶם, *gōlem* could be a collective), the broader context of verses 1-12 as well as the connection with the following verse is better served by seeing this as referring to the foreordination of the course of David's life. Thus, the reason David can affirm that the LORD knows his every thought, word, and action (and knows them beforehand מֵרָחוֹק, *mērāḥôq*, v.2*b*), and the reason he cannot escape from this knowledge and consequent control is because the LORD formed him and foreordained the course of his life. Likewise, the reason that in verses 17–18 David responds with such awe about the LORD's thought and purposes (רֵעֶיךָ, rē-'ekā), is that the LORD's foreordination of his life proves how precious and constant are the LORD's thoughts about him.

That these latter verses (vv.17–18) are an expression of awe at such intimate concern of the LORD for him and not, as often interpreted, an expression of awe at David's inability to understand God's purposes and plans[107] seems clear from the normal use of the verb יָקַר (yāqar) and its derivatives[108] and from the inner consistency of each clause in verses 17–18 referring to God's thought and purposes. Thus, מַה יָּקְרוּ (mah yāq'rû) in verse 17a means "how precious," not "how difficult, incomprehensible."[109] Likewise verse 18b refers to God's occupation with thoughts of David—"I am ever in your thought,"[110] not with David's occupation with thoughts of God—"I am ever occupied with you." David affirms in these verses that the thoughts and purposes reflected in the LORD's formation of his body in his mother's womb and the attendent foreordination of his life are precious (v.17a), are vast in number (v.17b), are beyond counting (v.18a), and are continuous (v.18b). Though this latter idea of God's continued occupation with thoughts of David seems assured because of contextual consistency and parallel usages of עִם ('im), there exists some ambiguity as to the duration of this continuance because of the difficulty of understanding the word הֱקִיצֹתִי (hĕqîṣōtî), "[lit.] I awake." Many different interpretations (none entirely satisfying) have been suggested for this enigmatic phrase, including "when I 'awake' in resurrection,"[111] "when I 'awake' from meditation,"[112] and "when I awake from sleep (induced by counting God's thoughts)."[113] I tentatively accept the second proposal, which appears to be somewhat more consistent with the concept of counting in verse 18a, that is though the count be interrupted, he is ever in God's thoughts.[114]

Before leaving this section, a word should be said about verse 14, which has often been erroneously interpreted more parenthetically than it need be. Following some of the ancient versions,[115] many interpreters see this as an hymnic aside in praise of God's greatness as manifested in His works and (following an unsupported textual emendation in v.14c, "you know my soul"[116]) in His awesome knowledge of David.[117] Though there is admittedly good textual evidence for this interpretation of verse 14a, the context appears to favor the elsewhere more reliable Masoretic text, which refers to David's praise of the LORD for the awesomeness and miraculousness of His creation against the background of the LORD's creative work in general. By repeating the root פָּלָא (pālā')[118] and modifying it by an adverbial accusative,[119] David affirms that he, like all of God's created works, is miraculous (cf. Psalms 8:4,7; 19:2), and miraculous in a way that inspires his grateful awe. This appears a more appropriate reaction to the affirmation that the LORD formed him or knit him together in the womb (v.13) than does a praise of the LORD's greatness in general.

In summary, David affirms in verses 13-18 that the LORD miraculously and awesomely formed him in the womb (vv.13-14), watched over his development (v.15), and foreordained the course of his life (v.16). David responds to this evidence of the LORD's concern for him with expressions of awe that the LORD's thoughts and purposes concerning him are so vast and constant (vv.17-18).

"*I want to be loyal to you.*" As noted above under the discussion on structure and form, verses 19-24 are the climax and key to the meaning of the psalm as a whole. Having affirmed that the LORD knows him through and through (vv.1-4), because He created him and foreordained the course of his life (vv.13-16), and having affirmed (vv.7-12) that there is no escape from this knowledge (which limits his independence, vv.5-6), David has expressed his awe of the LORD's intimate concern for him (vv.17-18). This leads naturally to an expression of loyalty to the LORD (vv.19-24). As noted above (see discussion of structure), David does this in both a negative (vv.19-22) and a positive manner (vv.23-24). Also, as noted, David affirms his repudiation of association with the wicked in the broadest rhetorical completeness. This rhetorical completeness is seen most clearly in the rhetorical question in verse 21 and the answering affirmation that follows in verse 22. In these verses the verb שָׂנֵא (*śānē'*), "to hate," occurs three times, once in the question of verse 21*a* to be followed by a slightly stronger synonym in verse 21*b* (קוֹט *qôṭ*, "to abhor"), and twice in the affirmation of verse 22*a*. As is clear from its usage elsewhere (cf. Psalms 26:5; 101:3), this verb is not to be understood as an expression of personal animosity but of repudiation of association.[120] This latter idea is also clearly seen in the apostrophe[121] of verse 19*b* where David turns from petition to God regarding the wicked to a demand that they get out of his presence. If Würthwein is correct in seeing this as equivalent to a self-curse if he were to be found associated with the wicked, then even verse 19*a*, a petition for God to kill the wicked, can be understood as a repudiation of association.[122]

Because it has sometimes been assumed that David is here addressing himself to God about his personal enemies who falsely accuse him or seek to destroy him,[123] it should be emphasized that the enemies are everywhere explicitly identified as enemies of God. They are "your adversaries" (v.20*b*),[124] "those who hate you" (v.21*a*), "those who rise up against you" (v.21*b*). They are, moreover, specifically described in the cryptic words of verse 20. If the Masoretic text of this verse is retained (and there is no good external evidence for any other),[125] they are described as hypocrites and covenant breakers, those who break the third commandment by using God's name for false or wicked purposes.[126] Nowhere are they described as David's enemies or as attacking or accusing him. Only when he has finished expressing in rhetorical fullness his repudiation of his association with them does he say, "I consider them my enemies."[127] Judging by the parallel in Psalm 26:9 (cf.vv.4–5), there does not even appear to be any necessity for seeing אַנְשֵׁי דָמִים ('anshê dāmîm), "bloodthirsty men," in verse 19b an allusion to personal attack or charge by legal opponents which would result in his death.[128] The epithets throughout are descriptive of God's enemies with whom David will have nothing to do.

From these statements of repudiation of association with the wicked, David turns in verses 23–24 to an invitation for God to test him and lead him. In verse 23a David returns to the verbs he used in verse 1 to describe the LORD's thorough knowledge of him, submitting his heart (the seat of his thought, desires, plans, and decisions, that which governs his behavior)[129] to the LORD's penetrating scrutiny. Because of the parallelism with שַׂרְעַפָּי (śar'appāy), "anxious thoughts," in verse 22b, David has primary reference to his thoughts and motivations, which he has already acknowledged as known to the LORD (v.2b). In verse 23b David uses a common anthropomorphic hypocatastasis to compare God's scrutiny of him to the testing of metals,[130] and invites the LORD to know his anxious thoughts, שַׂרְעַפָּי (śar'appāy). The use of this word elsewhere (Psalm 94:19; Job 4:13; 20:2) suggests that it deals here with a lack of full confidence in or commitment to the LORD. David thus admits implicitly his lack of complete commitment to the Lord, but asks in verse 24 for the LORD to guide him.

Some ambiguity regarding the nature of what David wants the LORD to find out and remove through His guidance arises because of the ambiguity of the word עֹצֶב ('ōṣeb) in verse 24a. Some recent interpreters take it to refer to an idol, a meaning this word has in Isaiah 48:5, and see the phrase in verse 24a as a repudiation of the charge of idolatry.[131] Older interpreters, however, related this word to one found in 1 Chronicles 4:9 and Isaiah 14:3, meaning "pain," and saw in it a reference to God's punishment for sin.[132] Buttenweiser, however, has very appropriately compared it to the use of the verb עֲצָבוֹ ('ăṣābô) in 1 Kings 1:6[133] where it is stated that David never "pained" or "offended" his son Adonijah at any time. This nuance also seems appropriate for the related noun עֶצֶב ('eṣeb) in the context of Proverbs 15:1 where a gentle answer, מַעֲנֶה־רַךְ, (ma'ăneh rak), is contrasted with an offensive or painful word (דְּבַר עֶצֶב, (d^ebar 'eṣeb). Seen against the context of David's inner thoughts, motivation, and commitment, this phrase would refer to attitude and conduct offensive to the LORD. This would be more appropriate than a reference to idolatry, especially since there has been absolutely no indication of idolatry elsewhere in the psalm.

Having implicitly admitted that his loyalty might not be totally complete (v.23*b*), and being unsure whether there might not be some grounds of offense in his thoughts, motives, and actions, David asks for the LORD to guide him, בְּדֶרֶךְ עוֹלָם (*b*ᵉ*derek* ʿôlām). Among some of the more common suggestions for this phrase have been: the way of prolonged life, the way of former times, or the way of the everlasting one, that is, God.[134] Though this phrase is without exact morphological parallels, the key to its interpretation may perhaps be sought in the semantically related phrases נְתִיבוֹת עוֹלָם (*n*ᵉ*tîbôt* ʿôlām) in Jeremiah 6:16 and שְׁבִילֵי עוֹלָם (*sh*ᵉ*bîlê* ʿôlām) in Jeremiah 18:15. Both of them refer to age-old paths, paths that God characterizes as good (Jer. 6:16), and both claim that following of those paths results in rest for the soul (Jer. 6:16), whereas abandoning them results in disaster (Jer. 18:15). In the context of concern about offending God, a reference to such a path seems very appropriate.

In summary, having repudiated association with the enemies of God who use His name for their own wicked purposes (vv. 19-22), David asks God (who knows him thoroughly, verses 1-4, because He created him, verses 13-16, and from whose knowledge there is no escape, verses 7-12) to examine his thoughts and motivations, which may not be thoroughly committed to Him (v. 23) and to see whether there is anything that would cause Him offense. If there is, it is David's desire to be guided along the ancient path of favor and blessing (v. 24).

THEOLOGICAL CONCERNS

Theology and theologians have sometimes been characterized as abstract and impersonal. This is certainly not the case with David and his treatment of the LORD's knowledge, presence, will, and control in Psalm 139. Though David speaks of these in very comprehensive terms, he sees them not in the abstract, but in the concrete, in the context of an intimate "I-You" confrontation with a God who, though awesome in knowledge and power, is intimately concerned with the object of His creation.

Thus, David does not affirm that the LORD knows everything in general, that is, that He is omniscient, but that He knows everything about him personally, his thoughts and motivations (v. 2*b*), his words (v. 4), and his deeds (vv. 2-3). Likewise, David does not affirm that the LORD knows all things possible as well as actual, but merely that He knows all about *his* (David's) thoughts, words, and deeds long beforehand (v. 2*b*), and that He knew before his birth what would transpire during each of *his* days (v.

1*b*). Likewise, though the hypothetical structure and the use of the broadest possible cosmical and geographical merisms give an abstract quality to David's denial of escape from such knowledge (vv. 7-12), it should be emphasized that David's point is not that God is everywhere present—always and at the same time—but that everywhere he turns, *he* is confronted by the LORD who knows him so thoroughly. In addition, though David acknowledges the awesomeness of the LORD's creation in general (v. 14*b*), it is the LORD's intimate concern with *his* formation in his mother's womb (v. 13) that inspires his praise (v. 14*a*). Moreover, David does not affirm that God decreed everything, but merely that He foreordained the course of *his* life (v. 16), a fact which he does not find repressive but highly precious, because he knows *he* is ever in God's thoughts (vv. 17-18). Finally, David may intimate but does not state that God will judge all men. He is, however, aware that *he* can offend Him, and is concerned that *he* walk in a way pleasing to Him (v. 24).

This is not to deny that the statements in the psalm cannot be theologically abstracted or broadened to include the fact that God is omniscient (knowing all things actual and possible), omnipresent, sovereign creator and disposer of all, and righteous judge of all men. It is, however, to say that the message of Psalm 139 has its own theological concern—an application of the omniscience, omnipresence, sovereignty, and righteousness of God to a demand for the loyalty of the individual believer to God.

Judging by the message of Paul to the Athenians (Acts 17:24-31), this message has relevance today. He made each of us, determined our times and circumstances, knows all our thoughts and our deeds, holds all of us accountable for them, and holds out to us the opportunity to turn to Him in loyalty. In David's day that loyalty was expressed through adherence to a covenant (alluded to in Psalm 139:20, 24*b*). In our day it is expressed through faith in Jesus Christ (Rom. 3:21-26).

NOTES

1. W. A. Shelton, "Psalms LXXIII-CL," in *The Abingdon Bible Commentary,* ed. F. C. Eiselen, E. Lewis, and D. G. Downey (Nashville: Abingdon, 1929), p. 595.
2. W. O. E. Oesterley, *The Psalms,* 2 vols. (London: S.P.C.K., 1939), 2:553.
3. J. A. Alexander, *The Psalms Translated and Explained,* reprint (Grand Rapids: Zondervan, n.d.), p. 540.
4. H. Gunkel, *Die Psalmen* (Göttingen: Vandenhoeck & Ruprecht, 1926), and H. Gunkel and J. Begrich, *Einleitung in die Psalmen* (Göttingen: Vandenhoeck & Ruprecht, 1933).
5. S. Mowinckel, *The Psalms in Israel's Worship,* trans. D.R. Ap-Thomas, 2 vols. (New York: Abingdon, 1962).
6. Cf. J. Holman, "Analysis of the Text of Ps. 139," *Biblische Zeitschrift* 14

(1970): 37-71, 198-227; L. C. Allen, "Faith on Trial: An Analysis of Psalm 138," *Vox Evangelica* 10 (1977): 5-23. See also M. Dahood, *Psalms III,* The Anchor Bible (Garden City, N.Y.: Doubleday, 1970), pp. 283-99.

7. Some exceptions are: Gunkel, *Die Psalmen,* p. 589, and H. Schmidt, *Die Psalmen* (Tübingen: J. C. B. Mohr, 1934), p. 245, both of whom considered vv. 19-24 as later additions by the same poet; C. A. Briggs and E. G. Briggs, *A Critical and Exegetical Commentary on the Book of Psalms,* 2 vols. (Edinburgh: T & T Clark, 1907), 2:293-94, divide the psalm into an original vv.7-12, a later addition of vv.1-6, 13-16, 23-24, a still later addition of vv.17-22, and late glosses; Moses Buttenwieser, *The Psalms* (Chicago: U. of Chicago, 1938), p. 535, thought that vv.19-22 were foreign to the psalm, vv.19-20 belonging originally to Psalm 140 and vv.21-22 to Psalm 141. More representative of scholarly opinion however, is Oesterley, 2:553, when he states: "As the subjectmatter of the psalm and the mode of its treatment from beginning to end would lead one to suppose, it is a unity."

8. See J. H. Stek, "The Stylistics of Hebrew Poetry," *Calvin Theological Journal* 9 (1974): 15-30 for definitions, discussion, illustration, and further bibliography in the area of stylistics. The definition and discussion of *inclusio* are found on p. 19.

9. For conceptual parallels linking God's knowledge to His creative activity, see Psalms 33:13-15; 94:9.

10. See, for example, E. Würthwein, "Erwägungen zu Psalm CXXXIX," *Vetus Testamentum* 7 (1957): 169,175; J. Holman, "The Structure of Psalm CXXXIX," *Vetus Testamentum* 21(1971): 298-310.

11. H. B. Lovitt, "A Critical and Exegetical Study of Psalm 139" (Ph.D. diss., Columbia University, 1964), pp. 34-35.

12. Some examples are: J. J. S. Perowne, *The Book of Psalms,* 2 vols., reprint (Grand Rapids: Zondervan, 1966), 2:438-39; A. F. Kirkpatrick, *The Book of Psalms* (Cambridge: U. Press, 1912), p. 786; A. Cohen, *The Psalms* (London: Soncino, 1945), pp. 451-55; D. Kidner, *Psalms 73-150* (London: Inter-Varsity, 1975), pp. 463-68. See also *The Ryrie Study Bible* (Chicago: Moody, 1978), p. 927, and The New American Bible (New York: P. J. Kenedy & Sons, 1970), p. 849.

13. KJV. See also *New American Standard Bible* (NASB), *New International Version* (NIV), and *New American Bible* (NAB).

14. For example, J. M. Bullard, "Psalm 139: 'Prayer in Stillness'," *Society of Biblical Literature,* 1975 Seminar Papers, 2 vols. (Missoula, Mont.: Scholars Press, 1975), 2:142, says: "There is nothing intrinsic to these almost imprecatory verses that in any way would seem to connect them logically to the great psalm (vv.1-18)."

15. Ibid., p. 141.

16. H. Gunkel, pp. 587-89.

17. S. Wagner, "Zur Theologie des Psalms CXXXIX," *Vetus Testamentum Supplement* 29(1978):358. For further discussion of the various classifications of Psalm 139 as well as bibliography, see J. M. Bullard, "Psalm 139: 'Prayer in Stillness,' " pp. 145-47, and H. Schüngel-Straumann, "Zur Gattung und Theologie des 139 Psalms," *Biblische Zeitschrift* 17(1973):39-42.

18. See, for example, C. Barth, *Introduction to the Psalms* (Oxford: Basil Blackwell, 1966), p. 18; G. von Rad, *Wisdom in Israel,* trans. J. D. Martin (Nashville: Abingdon, 1972), pp.40, 49; O. Eissfeldt, *The Old Testament, an Introduction,* trans. P. R. Ackroyd (New York: Harper & Row, 1965), p. 125.

19. See, for example, H. P. Müller, "Die Gattung des 139. Psalm," *Zeitschrift der Deutschen Morgenlandischen Gesellschaft, Supplement* 1 (1969): 354-55.

20. Schüngel-Straumann, p. 51.

21. In addition to the works listed in n. 6 see also Würthwein, pp. 165-82; P. Dri vers, *The Psalms, Their Structure and Meaning* (New York: Herder and Herder, 1964), pp. 246-47; H. J. Kraus, *Psalmen,* 2 vols. (Neukirchen Kreis Moers: Neukirchener Verlag, 1960), 2:916. Mowinckel, 2:131-32, understands the psalm under the same motif, but calls it a protective psalm.

22. See Gunkel, *Einleitung in die Psalmen,* p. 251, and C. Westermann, *The Psalms: Structure, Content and Message,* trans. R. D. Gehrke (Minneapolis: Ausburg, 1980), p.70.

23. See J. W. Rogerson and J. W. McKay, *Psalms 1-50* (Cambridge: Cambridge U., 1977), p. 14, and Drijvers, pp. 240-46.

24. For this latter thought see the exegesis under דֶּרֶךְ־עֹצֶב (*derek 'ōṣeb*) in Psalm 139:24 below.

25. For an example of an older interpreter who emphasizes this connection, see E. W. Hengstenberg, *Commentary on the Psalms,* trans. P. Fairbairn and J. Thompson, 3 vols. (Edinburgh: T. & T. Clark, 1860), 3:492-94. For an example of a recent interpreter, see Mowinckel, 2:75.

26. See the exegesis of Psalm 139:23-24 below.

27. Mowinckel, 1:24, 91; 2:75, 131.

28. See J. H. Hayes, *An Introduction to Old Testament Study* (Nashville: Abingdon, 1979), pp. 127-128.

29. See the works cited in nn. 6 and 21.

30. So J. L. Koole according to Allen, pp. 9-10. Koole's article, "Quelques remarques sur le Psaume 139," *Studia Biblica et Semitica Theodoro Christiano Vriezen Dedicata* (Wageningen: n.p., 1966), pp. 176-80, is unavailable to me. Compare Eissfeldt, p. 125.

31. Schüngel-Straumann, pp. 29-51.

32. R. Kilian, "In Gott geborgen. Eine Auslegung des Psalms 139," *Bibel und Kirche* 26(1971): 97-102.

33. See the works cited in nn. 6 and 21.

34. See, for example, the discussion of A. A. Anderson, *The Book of Psalms,* 2 vols. (London: Oliphants, 1972), 1:44-45.

35. See for some of the evidence D. Kidner, *Psalms 1-72* (London: Inter-Varsity, 1973), pp. 22-25. Among the more pertinent points are the fact that the historical books attribute poetry to David (cf. 2 Sam. 1:17-27; 23:1-7), that some psalms are specifically attributed to incidents in David's life (e.g., Psalms 7, 51), and that both the Lord and His apostles understood the phrase in certain psalms to refer to Davidic authorship, because they built arguments on this very point, arguments that have no validity if David did not in fact write the psalms in question (e.g., Mark 12:35-37; Acts 2:25-32).

36. For example: F. Delitzsch, *Biblical Commentary on the Psalms,* trans. F. Bolton, 3 vols., reprint (Grand Rapids: Eerdmans, n.d.), 3:343; Kirkpatrick, p. 786; Briggs and Briggs, 2:492-93. Commonly acknowledged Aramaic words are רִבְעִי (*rib'î*), "my lying down," in v.3, אֶסַּק (*'essaq*), "I ascend," in v.8, עָרֶיךְ (*'ārekā*), "your enemies," in v.20, and perhaps רֵעַ (*rē'a*), "intentions, purposes," in vv.2,17.

37. For example: Kirkpatrick, p. 786; Buttenweiser, pp. 541-43. For examples of linguistic and conceptual parallels compare Psalm 139:8 with Job 17:13, and Psalm 139:13 with Job 10:11.

38. See, for example, R. Gordis, *The Book of God and Man, A Study of Job* (Chicago: U. of Chicago, 1965), pp. 161-62, 334; K. A. Kitchen, *Ancient Orient and Old Testament* (Chicago: Inter-Varsity, 1966), p. 145.
39. Ibid., pp. 161-62.
40. G. L. Archer, Jr., *A Survey of Old Testament Introduction* (Chicago: Moody, 1974), p.441.
41. Ibid.
42. Ibid., pp. 457-62, for various views of the date of composition.
43. See the superscriptions of Psalms 5, 7, 17, 26 (especially Psalm 7), and note the parallels to Psalm 26 pointed out above.
44. Archer, pp. 457-62.
45. Thus possibly, though not necessarily, Psalm 20; cf. Anderson, 1:45.
46. See, for example, Rogerson and McKay, pp. 4-5.
47. See I. Engnell, *Studies in the Divine Kingship* (Uppsala: Almquist and Wiksell, 1943), pp. 176-77.
48. For similar anthropomorphic verbs see E. W. Bullinger, *Figures of Speech Used in the Bible,* reprint, (Grand Rapids: Baker, 1968), pp. 888-89.
49. See A. M. Honeyman, "Merismus in Biblical Hebrew," *Journal of Biblical Literature* 71 (1952): 11-18 (esp. p. 17), and J. Krašovec, "Die polare Ausdrucksweise im Psalm 139," *Biblische Zeitschrift* 18(1974): 224-48 (esp. pp. 230-32). An English example is: They came from far and near, i.e., from everywhere.
50. See ibid., pp. 234-35.
51. See Bullinger, pp. 745-47 for a distinction between these two terms.
52. See F. Brown, S. R. Driver, and C. A. Briggs, *A Hebrew and English Lexicon of the Old Testament* (Oxford: Clarendon, 1907), s.v. "דֶּרֶךְ (*derek*)" 5, p. 203. Henceforth referred to as BDB.
53. So, for example, L. Koehler and W. Baumgartner, *Lexicon in Veteris Testamenti Libros* (Leiden: E. J. Brill, 1958) s.v. "זָרָה (*zārāh*)" II, p. 266. Henceforth referred to as KBL. This verb never occurs elsewhere in biblical or nonbiblical Hebrew or in any of the other Semitic languages; its existence is posited on an assumed relationship to the noun זֶרֶת [*zeret*], "span."
54. For parallel usages involving the legal scrutiny of men see Proverbs 20:8,26.
55. See BDB, s.v. "סָכַן (*sākan*)," p. 698; KBL, s.v. "סָכַן (*sākan*)," p. 658.
56. See KBL, s.v. "רֵעַ (*rēʿa*)," p.898. Though this word occurs only here and in v. 17, its meaning is assured by its relation to the word רְעוּת (*rēʿût*), "longing, striving," which occurs in Ecclesiastes 1:4; 2:7, 11, 26, etc.
57. See BDB, s.v. "רָחוֹק (*rāḥôq*)" 2.*a.* (1), p. 935, and compare Psalm 138:6; Jer. 23:23.
58. See BDB, s.v. "רָחוֹק (*rāḥôq*)" 2.*b.*, p. 935, and compare Isa. 22:11.
59. Allen, p. 11. Allen points to the relation between vv.7-12 and v.5 as another example of this phenomenon.
60. See, e.g., Kirkpatrick, p. 787, and compare W. E. Barnes, *The Psalms,* 2 vols. (London: Methuen, 1931), 2:636, and note also NASB, NIV and *Revised Standard Version* (RSV).
61. E.g., Oesterley, 2:555; Anderson, 2:906-7.
62. See, e.g., Delitzsch, 3:346-47.
63. I.e., another merism; see, e.g., Krašovec, pp. 236-37.
64. See BDB, s.v. "צוּר (*ṣûr*)" II. 2, 3, p. 848. The Septuagint and Vulgate erroneously understand the verb as from צוּר (*ṣûr*) IV, "to fashion."

65. So, for example, Kirkpatrick, p 787, among many others.
66. Reading K°thib as in Judg. 13:18.
67. See BDB, s.v. "פלא (pālā')" Niph.1, p. 810, and compare Jer. 32:17 and Gen. 18:14.
68. See BDB, s.v. "פִּלְאִי (pil'î)," p. 811, and compare BDB, s.v. פָּלָא (pālā') Niph. 2, p. 810.
69. See BDB, s.v. "יָכֹל (yākōl)" 2.b, p. 408, and compare Gen. 32:25 [26].
70. So KBL, s.v. "יָכֹל (yākōl)" 3, p. 381, for this passage only.
71. See BDB, s.v. "שָׂגַב (śāgab)" Niph. 1, and compare Prov. 18:11.
72. It is doubtful whether David consciously intends a distinction in the persons in the godhead. That this passage stands at the end of a long evolutionary process whereby רוּח (rûah), "spirit" becomes equivalent to the divine presence as suggested by BDB s.v. "רוּח (rûah)" 9.f., p. 926, may, however, be doubted. B. W. Anderson is much closer to the truth when he states: "The Spirit is not identical with God but is the agency of his historical activity in the world" (cf. *Interpreter's Dictionary of the Bible,* s.v. "God, OT view of," by B. W. Anderson, 2:422).
73. See Bullinger, p. 949, for similar rhetorical questions.
74. Krašovec, p. 237.
75. See ibid., pp. 237-39, for a discussion of biblical and extrabiblical parallels; also compare Isa. 7:11.
76. Referring to the relative position of the Mediterrannean Sea in reference to Palestine. Cf. BDB, s.v. "יָם (yām)" 9, p. 411.
77. In addition to the verbs אָחַז ('āhaz), "to grasp," and נָחָה (nāhāh)," to lead," which express this clearly, note also the anthropomorphic use of "hand" in Bullinger, p. 889, and compare the discussion at v.5b.
78. See, for example, Delitzsch, 3:347, and Kirkpatrick, p. 789.
79. See, for example, Buttenweiser, pp. 536-37, and compare Hengstenberg, 3:497-99.
80. See, e.g., BDB, s.v. "נָחָה (nāhâ)" Hiph., p. 635, where it is noted: "esp. in path of blessing."
81. Though the form יְשׁוּפֵנִי (y°shûpēnî) could be either jussive or imperfect, I believe the jussive is more in keeping with the hypothetical mood of vv.7-12.
82. See, e.g., R. Kittel, ed., *Biblia Hebraica,* 3d ed. (Stuttgart: Württembergische Bibelanstalt, 1937), p. 1095, who cites the Greek version of Symmachus and Jerome's translation of the Hebrew text as support (henceforth referred to as BH₃).
83. Since the Masoretic text is supported by the majority of the ancient versions, the external evidence favors it. Moreover, the Masoretic text is decidedly the more difficult reading.
84. As may be seen in the translation above, this writer agrees with the majority of commentaries and modern translations in seeing v.11 as a compound protasis (condition) and v.12 as a compound apodosis (consequence). This syntax is similar to that of vv.9-10 and avoids the tautology between vv.11 and 12 involved in seeing v.11a as the protasis and v.11b as the apodosis (as in KJV).
85. E.g., Briggs and Briggs, 2:496.
86. E.g., H. W. Wolff, *Anthropology of the Old Testament,* trans. M. Kohl (Philadelphia: Fortress, 1974), p. 96, and Cohen, p. 453.
87. Cf. KBL, s.v. "כִּלְיָה (kilyâ)," p. 437.

88. A. R. Johnson, *The Vitality of the Individual in the Thought of Ancient Israel* (Cardiff: U. of Wales, 1964), p. 75.
89. Wolff, p. 96.
90. Cf. KBL, s.v. "קָנָה (*qānâh*)," I & II, p. 843, contra BDB, s.v. "קָנָה (*qānâ*)" 1., pp. 888-89, "get, acquire," and compare KJV "Thou hast possessed."
91. Cf. BDB, s.v. "סָכַךְ (*sākak*)," I & II, pp. 696-97, contra KBL, s.v. "סָכַךְ (*sākak*)," 4., p. 657, "keep blocked, hidden," and compare KJV "thou hast covered."
92. See, e.g., BDB, s.v. "קָנָה (*qānâ*)" 1.*a*., p. 888, where it is stated: "to get, acquire . . . of God as originating creating."
93. See, for example, Briggs and Briggs, 2:496-97, where it is denied that תְּסֻכֵּנִי (*t*ᵉ*sukkēnî*) refers metaphorically to a mode of creation and where רֻקַּמְהִי (*ruqqamtî*), "I was woven," in v.15 is emended into וְקַמְתִּי (*w*ᵉ*qamtî*), "I shall rise."
94. Wolff, p. 96.
95. See KBC, s.v. "רָקַם (*rāqam*)," and compare, for example, Exod. 26:36; 27:16; 28:39. Since there is no Piel for either this verb or the parallel עֻשֵּׂיתִי (*ʿuśśê tî*), "I was made," they should probably be identified as Qal passives, not Pual. Cf. *Gesenius' Hebrew Grammar*, ed. and enl. E. Kautzsch, ed. and trans. A. E. Cowley (Oxford: Clarendon, 1910), pp. 140-41, par. 52*e*., henceforth referred to as GKC; the same is true of יֻצָּרוּ (*yuṣṣārû*), "were (fore)ordained," in v.16*c*.
96. See BDB, s.v. "תַּחְתִּי (*taḥtî*)," p. 1066, where it is noted: "fig. of the dark and hidden interior of the womb Ps 139¹⁵."
97. The noun עֹצֶם (*ʿōṣem*) elsewhere means "might"; it is only here that BDB, s.v. "עֹצֶם (*ʿōṣem*)" 2, p. 782, and KBL "עֹצֶם (*ʿōṣem*)" II, p. 728, see the meaning "bones." Perhaps the text ought to be repointed to עֲצָמַי (*ʿăṣāmay*), the plural of עֶצֶם (*ʿeṣem*), "bone," plus first person suffix.
98. Cf. Bullinger, pp. 640 ff.
99. The word גֹּלֶם (*gōlem*) occurs only here in biblical Hebrew. Consequently, גָּלְמִי (*golmî*) is often emended to גְּמֻלַי (*g*ᵉ*mūlay*), "my actions" (e.g., Gunkel, *Die Psalmen*, p. 592, and Oesterley, 2:554) or כָּל־יָמַי (*kol-yāmay*), "all my days" (e.g., W. Gesenius, *Hebräisches und Aramäisches Handwörterbuch über das Alte Testament*, rev. F. Buhl (Gottingen: Springer-Verlag: 1915), s.v. "גֹּלֶם [*gōlem*]," p. 142; henceforth referred to as GBH). The meaning "embryo" is supported by the Aramaic word גּוֹלֶם (*gôlem*), "shapeless mass," applied to the embryo in rabbinic literature (cf. M. Jastrow, *A Dictionary of the Targumim, The Talmud Babli and Yerushalmi, and the Midrashic Literature*, 2 vols. (New York: Pardees, 1950), 1:222, s.v. "גּוֹלֶם [*gôlem*]" 1). It is also supported by the translation of the ancient versions, and seems consistent with other references to David's bodily form, e.g., kidneys (v.13*a*) and bones (v.15*a*).
100. See for a discussion of this H. Ringgren, *Religions of the Ancient Near East*, trans. J. Sturdy (Philadelphia: Westminster, 1973), pp. 108-9.
101. In view of the somewhat common occurrence of the preterite (or simple past) use of the prefixed form in poetry and the probability of its attestation within this same context (e.g., תְּסֻכֵּנִי [*t*ᵉ*sukkēnî*] in v.13*b*), it is erroneous to consider יְכָּתֵבוּ (*yikkāt*ᵉ*bû*) as a progressive or continuous present as e.g., Allen, p. 22, fn. 62. For the preterite use of the prefixed form see, e.g., R. J. Williams, *Hebrew Syntax: An Outline* (Toronto: U. of Toronto, 1976), pp. 23-33, par. 176-77.

102. *The New International Dictionary of New Testament Theology,* s.v. "Book, Read, Letter," by U. Becker, 1:243.

103. For this understanding see the translation of KJV. This assumes that the noun גֹּלֶם (*gōlem*) is a collective.

104. See GKC, p. 425, par. 131*k-n,* and compare Isa. 43:14 and Num. 24:17.

105. See Bullinger, p. 594.

106. For this understanding see the translations of RSV, NASB, and NIV and the majority of modern commentaries (e.g., Kirkpatrick, pp. 789-90, and Anderson, 2:910, among many others).

107. See, e.g., Perowne, 2:442, and Kissane, 2:296.

108. See BDB, s.v. "יָקַר (*yāqar*)," p. 429, "be precious, prize, appraised"; יָקָר (*yāqār*), pp. 429-30, "precious, rare, splendid, weighty (influential)."

109. The only biblical parallel for this nuance is the adjective יַקִּירָה (*yaqqîrâ*) in the Aramaic of Dan. 2:11.

110. See BDB, s.v. "עִם (*'im*)," 4*b,* p. 768, "in one's consciousness." For Psalm 139 BDB notes: "in thy thought and care."

111. See, e.g., D. Kidner, *Psalms 73-150,* p. 467, and Dahood, *Psalms III,* p. 296, and compare passages listed under BDB, s.v. "קִיץ (*qîṣ*)," Hiph.2.

112. See, e.g., Buttenweiser, pp. 537-40 and compare Jer. 31:26.

113. See, e.g., Delitzsch, 3:352.

114. If the verb were an imperfect rather than a perfect, the iterative idea suggested by some interpreters (e.g., Perowne, 2:442) would also be possible if not even preferable, i.e., "Were I to continue the count every morning on arising, I would be ever in your thinking." Also, if there were more evidence for it—in this psalm and other psalms of innocence—this could be a reference to David's confidence that he will be vindicated on the next morning, when he is tried for disloyalty to God (cf. Anderson, 1:152-53 on Psalm 17:15).

115. So the Septuagint, Jerome's translation of the Hebrew, the Syriac, and the Targum according to BH₃. 11 Q P's a נורא אתה (*nôr' 'th*), "you are awesome (?)" would also appear to support this reading (cf. J. A. Sanders, *The Psalms Scroll of Qumran Cave II,* Discoveries in the Judean Desert of Jordan IV (Oxford: Clarendon, 1965), p.41).

116. Reading יָדַעְתָּ (*yāda'tā*) for יְ־דַעַת (*yōda'at*); cf. BH₃.

117. See, e.g., Holman, pp. 65-69, who states on p. 69: "The flow of thought stops in vs. 14 for a contemplation of God's greatness." Many interpreters, however, connect v. 14*c* with v. 15*a* as suggested by the editor of BH₃ (see, e.g., Anderson, 2:910).

118. Though the Hebrew text of v.14*a* reads נִפְלֵיתִי (*niplêtî*), from the root that פָּלָה (*pālâ*) might mean "I am distinguished/distinct" (cf. Exod. 33:16)—a thought not at all inappropriate to the context—the majority of lexicons and commentaries see this as another example of the confusion of the III א (') and III ה (*h*) roots (see, e.g., BDB, s.v. "פָּלָה [*pālâ*]" Niph. 2. and compare Psalm 17:7 with Psalm 31:22). The parallelism is closer if the roots are the same.

119. See GKC, p. 375, par. 118*p,* and compare the Niphal participles in Psalm 65:6 and Job 37:5.

120. Thus A. E. Barnes, *Notes on the Old Testament, Psalms,* ed. R. Frew, 3 vols. (Grand Rapids: Baker, 1950), 3:298, states: "The word *hate* here . . . must be understood in the sense . . . that he did not desire to be associated with them, that he wished to avoid their society." Dahood, *Psalm I,* p. 31, is erroneous in applying it as a *terminus technicus* for repudiation of *idolatry.*

121. For this figure cf. Bullinger, pp. 901ff, and for a similar use, see Psalm 6:8 [Heb 9].
122. Würthwein, p. 173.
123. See, e.g., Allen, p. 15, and Barnes, 2:634.
124. This word, which also appears in 1 Sam. 28:16, is the Aramaic equivalent of the normal Hebrew צָר (ṣār). See BDB, s.v. "עָר ['ār]," II, p. 786. This word is often emended but without adequate textual grounds. All the ancient versions have a word implying these consonants—either "adversaries" or "cities." The Aramaic coloring of this psalm noted in fn. 36 also argues for its retention.
125. The reading יַמְרוּךָ (yamrûkā), "they rebel against you," in v.21a is supported by only one minor Greek variant, and is manifestly the easier reading. The ancient versions were generally misled by taking the word עָרֶיךָ ('ārèkā) in v.20b to refer to cities, and offer little or no help in this verse. The Masoretic text, though difficult, has the advantage of offering an understandable parallelism.
126. Understanding אָמַר ('āmar) to be used in the sense of "mention, name, invoke" as in Gen. 43:29, 1 Sam. 16:1 (cf. BDB, s.v. "אָמַר ('āmar)" 1, p. 56), and understanding the word שֵׁם (šēm), "name" to have been left out by ellipsis (cf. Bullinger, p. 8, and see BDB, s.v. "נָשָׂא (nāśā')" 1.b(7), p. 670d; cf. Exod. 20:7; Deut. 5:11).
127. Lit., "They have become enemies to me." See BDB, s.v. "1," 4, p. 512 where it is noted that הָיָה + ל (hāyâ + l) refers to transition into a new state or condition.
128. Contra Allen, p. 15.
129. See Johnson, pp. 75–80.
130. See BDB, s.v. "בָּחַן [bāḥan]," 2.a, and compare Psalm 7:10; Jer. 11:20.
131. See, among others, Würthwein, pp. 173-74; Dahood, *Psalm III*, p. 299; Allen, p. 16. These interpreters also point out that this was the interpretation of the Targum. See BDB, "עֹצֶב ('ōṣeb)," II., p. 781.
132. See Bullinger, p. 536, and cf., e.g., Delitzsch, 3:354, and Cohen, p. 455. See BDB, s.v. "עֹצֶב ('ōṣeb)" I, p. 780.
133. Buttenwieser, p. 545.
134. See Delitzsch, 3:354, who refers to all of these.

7

An Exegetical and Theological Study of Daniel 9:24-27

Paul D. Feinberg

PAUL D. FEINBERG *(M.A., Roosevelt University; B.D., Th.M., Talbot Theological Seminary; Th.D., Dallas Theological Seminary; Ph.D. candidate, University of Chicago) is professor of biblical and systematic theology at Trinity Evangelical Divinity School, Deerfield, Illinois.*

Serious Bible students have always realized the importance of Daniel 9:24-27. Desmond Ford says that "chapter 9 is not only the devotional heart of the book but also contains 'the crown jewels' of Old Testament prophecy."[1] Guinness's comments are even stronger: "Of all the prophecies in the Bible, Daniel's of the 'seventy weeks' is the most wonderful and the most important. It stands erect among the ruins of time like the solitary and colossal obelisk amid the mounds of Heliopolis."[2] Gruenthaner speaks of its difficulty as well:

> There is probably no passage of the Old Testament upon which so much labor and ingenuity has been expended as the striking prophecy of the seventy weeks which closes the ninth chapter of the Book of Daniel. Many of the Fathers and not a few Catholic apologists down to our time consider it a Messianic prophecy accurately defining the time of Christ's redemption.[3]

It is therefore entirely fitting that an essay on this text be offered in honor of my father, Charles Lee Feinberg, because the issues raised in it have been central concerns of his life and ministry. This is a passage with both messianic and eschatological implications.

The Context of the Prophecy

Although the context is always an important determinant in the interpretation of any passage, it is unusually so here because the prophecy of the seventy weeks came to Daniel in answer to his prayer recorded in the early verses of the chapter.

With the accession of Darius the Mede, Daniel observed in the writings of Jeremiah the prophet that the desolation of Jerusalem was to last seventy years (Jer. 25:11-12; 29:10), so he prayed regarding the time of completion (Dan. 9:2). In Daniel 9:3-19 we have one of the great prayers of the Bible. The prophet confesses the sins of the people and entreats God to fulfill His promises. He reminds God that Jerusalem is a reproach to all those around. He asks God to forgive the sins of His people and to restore the city and the people.

Gabriel was sent by God to Daniel in answer to the prayer. He brought instruction that the prophet might understand God's purposes for His people (Dan. 9:20-23). Views concerning the relationship of this instruction (Dan. 9:24-27) to the preceding context fall into three general groups. Some commentators think that Jeremiah's seventy years had passed without the restoration of the people to the land and the rebuilding of city and sanctuary, and that Gabriel brought the message that the return was *not* imminent. Daniel was told that another 490 years had been decreed upon his people and city. There was, as it were, an extension of the exile.[4]

One can safely say that this is not the meaning of the prophecy of seventy weeks. God does not make promises and then go back on His word. The Scriptures tell us that God's prophet must bring a word that comes to pass (Deut. 18:22), because God does not lie (Titus 1:2). Furthermore, we know from history that Cyrus did allow the Jews to return to their land and rebuild their Temple and city (2 Chron. 36:22-23; Ezra 1:1; Isa. 44:28; 45:13). Thus, God used Cyrus to end the seventy years of captivity spoken of by Jeremiah.

Some other writers see no need for the prophecy of Jeremiah to be clarified. Daniel was simply praying for a quick fulfillment to the promise. Gabriel came to Daniel to assure him that the prophecy would be realized, and that the restoration of people and land would actually occur.[5] I would not want to quarrel with this interpretation. I just think there is more.

Still other commentators think Daniel was not sure when the seventy years of captivity were concluded. That was because Nebuchadnezzar had laid seige to the city of Jerusalem three times. Only the third time did the city fall into his hand, and he destroyed the Temple and took its vessels to

Babylon. However, he took captives during each seige. Therefore, it would be only natural for Daniel to inquire of God as to which of the three deportations marked the beginning of the seventy years of exile.[6]

God's response through Gabriel was interesting indeed. There is no specific answer to the exact time of the end of captivity. We know that in the year the prophecy of Daniel 9 was given, Cyrus freed the Jews, ending their captivity. The seventy *years* of captivity are the clue to a prophecy of seventy *weeks*. In the seventy years of captivity God put an end to idolatry, which had been a besetting sin prior to God's judgment. The new prophecy of seventy weeks foresees a time when *all* transgression, sin, and iniquity will be done away with in Israel. Then the nation will no longer be "thy [Daniel's] people" and Jerusalem "thy city" but God's people and God's city.

THE COMMENCEMENT OF THE SEVENTY WEEKS

The question of the beginning of the seventy weeks is sometimes called the terminus a quo of the prophecy. Whatever is meant by the seventy weeks of Daniel's prophecy, they begin with the "going forth of a command." There is, however, no consensus on which command and corresponding date. As a matter of fact, two commonly defended dates are nearly 100 years apart (538–36 B.C. and 445–44 B.C.). It should be noted that the word *commandment* is not the usual Hebrew word מִצְוָה but דָּבָר. It is the same word used in 9:23 of God's command to Gabriel to go to Daniel. For this reason some have thought that the command was God's decree, not that of a human ruler.[7] However, Pusey seems to be right in observing that although the decree was God's, nevertheless it came through a man and was made effective by him.[8] The word for "command" is far more commonly used for a message, a declaration, or prophetic prediction.[9]

There are four widely suggested starting points, each of which we shall now examine.[10]

THE FIRST YEAR OF CYRUS

The decree of Cyrus has wide support among Bible students. The date for this decree varies. Hoehner sets it as October 29, 539 B.C.[11] Pusey, on the other hand, thinks that it was given in 536 B.C.[12] By far the most common date given for this edict is 538–37 B.C.[13] At any rate this first year of Cyrus is found in a number of places in Scripture (2 Chron. 36:22–23; Ezra 1:1–4; 6:3–5). Moreover, the importance of this decree is attested to by the fact that Cyrus is prophesied of more than one hundred years before his birth (Isa. 44:26–28; 45:1–5, 13).

The support for this date is as follows. The first year of Cyrus was a year of great change. It was the year of the edict of liberation, the termination of captivity and exile, marked by a formal decree (Ezra 1:1-4). Daniel 9:25 simply says that the period begins with the "going forth of the command," not its actual accomplishment. The decree of Cyrus speaks explicitly of going to Jerusalem and rebuilding the Temple, which constituted the first step in rebuilding the city. Therefore, the initial command to restore Jerusalem was unquestionably given by Cyrus. It is a matter of record that the exiles who returned under Zerubbabel did not finish the task, but the unfinished task was not because of failure to have permission to pursue the work.[14]

Although the decree of Cyrus is not without support or defenders, the following considerations lead me to think that it is not the intended terminus a quo. The edict related to the Temple and not to the city. Young, who defends this date, replies:

> It is not justifiable to distinguish too sharply between the building of the city and the building of the temple. Certainly, if the people had received permission to return to Jerusalem to rebuild the temple, there was also implied in this permission to build for themselves homes in which to dwell. There is no doubt whatever but that the people thus understood the decree (cf. Haggai 1:2-4). The edict of Cyrus mentions the temple specifically, because that was the religious center of the city.[15]

Young goes on to argue that Ezra pictures the city of Jerusalem as existing in some restored form (Ezra 4:12; 9:9).

Each of the references cited by Young is open to challenge. Although Haggai's prophecy *does* tell of Jews living in houses, they apparently were *not* in Jerusalem. Moreover, the Temple had not been rebuilt, and it was the prophet's task to exhort the people to do so. It was a disgrace for some to be living in luxurious houses and for the Temple to be in disrepair. Furthermore, the question as to whether or not Jerusalem had been rebuilt is answered in the graphic description of Nehemiah, which details the utterly devastated condition of the city (Neh. 2:12-15).[16]

Both passages in Ezra (4:12; cf. 4:13, 16; 9:9) refer to Artaxerxes' reign (465/4-423 B.C.), not to Cyrus's.[17]

Nevertheless, one who defends this date might reply that the passage refers only to the going forth of the command, not its completion.

Hoehner criticizes this view because it does not distinguish between the *rebuilding* of the city and the *restoration* of the city to its former state. Even though it might be argued that the rebuilding of the city began in the time of Cyrus, the city was not restored until a much later time.[18] I find Hoehner's objection unconvincing because it seems that the restoration of the city is to be completed after the first seven weeks, not at the time of the giving of the decree.

There is, however, a decisive reason for rejecting this date if one takes these weeks to be weeks of years (490) and this to be a prophecy of the coming of the Messiah (both points to be discussed below). There is no reasonable date for the birth of the Messiah that will allow only 490 years to have elapsed between 538-37 B.C. and the date of birth.[19]

THE THIRD YEAR OF DARIUS HYSTASPES

The decree of Darius would place the commencement of the seventy weeks in 519-18 B.C. The decree grows out of the question of Tattenai, governor of Judah, regarding the right of the returned exiles to rebuild the Temple (Ezra 5:3-17). In response to this request, Darius made a search for Cyrus's decree, and then issued one of his own (Ezra 6:1-12).[20]

This date for the start of the seventy weeks has never been very popular. Every objection directed against the decree of Cyrus holds with equal force against this view. Furthermore, this decree is not a new one but simply a confirmation of Cyrus's earlier command.

THE SEVENTH YEAR OF ARTAXERXES

A third date suggested for the terminus a quo is the seventh year of Artaxerxes, 458-57 B.C. At this time Ezra was commissioned and sent home with a new group of exiles. As a result of this decree, Temple worship was established and civil leaders were appointed (Ezra 7:11-26).

The support for this date is as follows. Pusey argues that of the four proposed dates, only two are major decrees. The decree of Darius is simply a confirmation of Cyrus's earlier edict. Moreover, the command of Artaxerxes in 445-44 B.C. is a renewal and enlargement of the existing decree. Because of the importance given Artaxerxes' decree in Daniel 9:25, it would seem to be one of the two major edicts. Therefore, Pusey takes 458-57 as the date for the beginning of the seventy weeks.[21]

Wood relates this date to the rebuilding of the city in seven weeks, or forty-nine years (Dan. 9:25). He asks if we can place the rebuilding of the city at or about 409 B.C. Even though there are no hard historical details, there are some indications that, he thinks, point in that direction. God gave Ezra and Nehemiah the task of rebuilding the city. Although Nehemiah did return to Babylon from Jerusalem, he came again to the city and remained there the rest of his life. Therefore, it is not totally without justification to take the first group of seven weeks as setting off the period of rebuilding and restoring the city under Ezra and Nehemiah.[22]

The chief objection to this date is that the decree deals with the rebuilding of the Temple, not the city. Therefore, this cannot be the terminus a quo.

Those who defend this date answer the aforementioned objection in three ways.

First, it is pointed out that the decree seems to allow unlimited freedom, because Artaxerxes allowed the Jews to use the leftover gold and silver for the Temple (Ezra 7:18). He also allowed them to appoint civil leaders (Ezra 7:25). Those who reject this date will be unconvinced because neither of those freedoms had to do with the restoration of the city of Jerusalem.[23]

Second, it is argued that this command did involve the rebuilding of Jerusalem in a moral or spiritual sense, even if one grants that it did not directly relate to the city itself.[24]

Finally, it is argued that it is not wise to distinguish too sharply between the rebuilding of the Temple and the restoration of the city. If permission was granted to restore the Temple, it is very unlikely, in view of the many enemies who tried to hinder the work, that the Jews would have expended great effort to accomplish the task while at the same time leaving it unprotected. Moreover, Ezra 4:12 and 9:9 seem to indicate that people were living in houses during this period and that some kind of wall, even if it was not a defensive military wall, had been built.[25]

THE TWENTIETH YEAR OF ARTAXERXES

The final date that we shall consider is that of 445-44 B.C., which was the twentieth year of the reign of Artaxerxes (Neh. 2:1-8). The decree came at the request of Nehemiah to return to Jerusalem. Nehemiah requested letters be given to him for the governors beyond the river.

In support of this view it is most frequently claimed that this decree, and this decree *alone,* deals with the city, the walls, and the gates. This kind of decree is required by Daniel 9:25. The former decrees were all concerned with the Temple.[26] The king even wrote a letter to Asaph to provide the materials to be used in the construction of the walls.

This view also would fit nicely with two other aspects of Daniel 9:25. The work was to be completed in seven weeks, or forty-nine years. This period would have elapsed shortly after 400 B.C. The indications that the city had been restored by this time have been presented above. Furthermore, the work would have been done in troubled times (Ezra 4:7-23).[27]

It will be enough simply to record the major problems with this position, as I will give a more detailed treatment of the latter two dates below. As has been implied, a number of commentators reject this date because they think the decree is not a major one. It simply reaffirms an earlier existing edict and enlarges upon it. Further, if we take 445-44 as the beginning of the seventy weeks, then the first sixty-nine weeks will come to a close in either A.D. 32 or A.D. 33. Because Daniel 9:26 demands that Messiah will be "cut off" after sixty-nine weeks, we have a late date for the crucifixion. Finally, this date relies for its calculations on a prophetic or 360-day year.[28]

A word of summary and conclusion may be helpful here. I have set forth, along with their major objections, the four views concerning the terminus a quo of the seventy weeks. Two, 538-37 B.C. and 519-18 B.C., seem unlikely dates for, at a minimum, they do not reach to the time of the Messiah. The dates 458-57 B.C. and 445-44 B.C. seem more promising. Further judgment should be held until the conclusion of the seventy weeks has been discussed.

THE CONCLUSION OF THE SEVENTY WEEKS

Differences of opinion on the conclusion, or terminus ad quem, of the seventy weeks of Daniel are even more diverse than the views of the terminus a quo. It is even possible to suggest schools of interpretation based upon the time that one sees the prophecy as fulfilled. Although there are numerous differences within each school, I think it is helpful to divide the schools of interpretation into three groups: Maccabean interpretations, Roman interpretations, and eschatological interpretations. The name for each school comes from its understanding of the time of the fulfillment of the seventieth week (Dan. 9:27).

THE MACCABEAN INTERPRETATIONS

A group of interpreters sees the seventieth week as having transpired in the Maccabean period. Of the three schools of interpretation there is most agreement here.

The central point of agreement among those who hold this view is that the events of the seventieth week relate to the terrible persecutions of Antiochus Epiphanes (170-164 B.C.). The seventy weeks have been divided into three periods: seven weeks, sixty-two weeks, and one week. The most common starting points for the seven-week period is 587-86 B.C., although some interpreters would begin the period as early as 606-5 B.C. The first period is forty-nine years long and ends with the appearance of an anointed one. The anointed one who ends the first period is different from the one who concludes the second period. By far, the person most commonly identified with the first anointed one is Cyrus. He appeared in 538–36 B.C., so he would fit the forty-nine-year conclusion. Other suggestions include Joshua, the high priest (Zech. 3:1), and Zerubbabel, the governor of Judah (Hag. 1:1). The period itself covers the time of the Exile.[29]

The second period, sixty-two weeks, or 434 years, begins in 536 B.C. and ends in 171–70 B.C. with the "cutting off" of an anointed one who is a prince. It is a period that deals with the rebuilding of the city of Jerusalem. During this time, Jerusalem will stand complete with marketplace and moat.

The candidates for the anointed prince who is cut off are numerous. The most common view takes Onias III as the person referred to here. Some think he may be the "prince of the covenant" in Daniel 11:22. Whatever the case be, he was disposed of by Antiochus in 175 B.C. at the instigation of his brother Jason. In turn Jason succeeded him to the office, and served in that capacity for three years. He was replaced by Menelaus. During this period, Onias retired to a place of safety outside of Antioch. About 171–70 B.C. Menelaus was called to Antioch to explain why tribute to the king was in arrears. While in Antioch, Menelaus convinced the king's regent, Andronicus, that Onias should be murdered, as he was implacably opposed to the Hellenizing regime in power. The disgust that the murder of Onias aroused among the faithful is recorded in 2 Maccabees 4:7–9, 23–38. On this understanding of the text, "he shall have nothing" means that the city and its oversight were no longer his. Having moved to Antioch, Onias was not even in the city of Jerusalem.[30]

Daniel 9:26 also prophesies the destruction of the city and the Temple. Defenders of a Maccabean interpretation think that this is a reference to the plundering of the Temple in 169 B.C. (1 Macc. 1:20–28; 2 Macc. 5:11–16) or 167 B.C. (1 Macc. 1:29–35; 2 Macc. 5:22–26).[31]

The last or seventieth week is a reference to Antiochus Epiphanes and the renegade Jews who followed him in his attempts to Hellenize the Jews (171/70–164 B.C.). Daniel 9:27, then, would parallel Daniel 7:7–8, 23–26; 8:8–25; 11:28–39 (cf. 1 Macc. 1:10–15). In the middle of the week Antiochus proscribed the Jewish worship. The end of "sacrifice and oblation" is the usual way to express the cessation of all worship (cf. Psalm 40:6). The end to sacrifice would be accompanied by a horrible abomination (cf. Dan. 7:25; 11:31). Usually, the term *abomination* has reference to an idol. The very difficult second half of Daniel 9:27 is thus interpreted to mean that an idol, most likely a statue of Zeus Olympus (1 Macc. 1:54–59; 2 Macc. 6:1–2), was placed on a high porch of the Temple, desecrating it.

Idols replaced sacrifices. The author of the prophecy thought that the profanation of the Temple would last three and a half years.[32]

Even though this interpretation of the prophecy is quite old[33] and widely held among interpreters, particularly of a liberal theological persuasion, there are some decisive reasons for rejecting it. The first and most obvious is that it cannot adequately account for the second period of sixty-two weeks, or 434 years. The period from 586 B.C. to 538-36 B.C. is forty-nine years, or seven weeks, and 171-70 B.C. to 164 B.C. is seven years or one week. But if one begins the second period in 538 B.C. and runs it to 170 B.C., there are only 368 years.[34]

The problem of the missing years is compounded by the fact that most of those who hold this view believe that the author of Daniel 9 lived in the Maccabean period and was writing primarily history. Typical of this position is the statement of Hartman and Di Lella:

> Therefore, our author's prediction that the desecration of the temple would end three and a half years after it had begun was not a *prophetia post eventum,* but a genuine prediction, which slightly overshot its mark. By observing the progress that the Maccabean forces were making in their war against the Syrian armies, our author could foresee that Judas Maccabeus would soon gain control of the temple area in Jerusalem.[35]

If we assume for the sake of argument that Daniel 9:24-27 is fundamentally a case of prophecy after the event, then one wonders why the author was not more careful to get the details *correct.* What he said would then have been far more convincing.

A second reason for rejecting this interpretation is related to the prayer that precedes the prophecy of the seventy weeks. That prayer is *not* of Maccabean origin. Had it been, it would have invoked the wrath of God against those who were persecuting God's people. Rather, there is meek submission to what has happened and an acknowledgement that the punishment is just. Ford states it well: "Those who compare this prayer with the apocryphal writings of the last pre-Christian centuries—those of Baruch, Ecclesiasticus, Judith, the noncanonical additions to Daniel— find a 'great gulf fixed.' "[36] The apocryphal prayers are wordy and self-serving. Daniel's prayer is neither of these.

A third reason that this is not the correct view is that the events of the Maccabean period do not fit Daniel 9:26-27. The Temple was to be destroyed, according to Daniel. Antiochus Epiphanes stopped sacrificial worship and profaned the altar by having a pig offered on it. However, he did not destroy the Temple. Furthermore, 9:27 speaks of a "firm coven-ant" that the oppressor was to make with the Jews. Again, Antiochus made no such covenant. There were some opportunistic and renegade Jews who did support Antiochus and his policies, but such support never took the form of even an informal agreement.

Finally, Josephus in his writings took this passage to be a prediction of the destruction of the Temple by the Romans.[37] Moreover, Jerome relates a Jewish interpretation that understood 9:24-27 to be about events in the Roman period.

Few Bible students will be satisfied with Porteous's resolution of the matter:

> That the end predicted by the author of the book of Daniel did not come, any more than the expectation of the early Christians of the imminent return of Christ was literally fulfilled, presents us with a challenge in our interpretation of the Bible, but need not affect our faith in the power of God to save to the uttermost.[38]

ROMAN INTERPRETATIONS

A second general group of interpretations puts the fulfillment of the seventieth week in the Roman period. Interpretations here may be fur-ther divided between Jewish views and messianic views.

Jewish views. The first Jewish interpretation is found in Jerome's *Commentary on Daniel.* The Jews were not impressed by Daniel's division of the period into three periods: seven, sixty-two, and one, respectively. It is common to put the smaller number first, and then the larger. As an example of this phenomenon, Abraham and his age is cited. His age is not given as 175 years, but five, seventy, and one-hundred. Jerome appeals to Genesis 25:7 for this order. Such an order, however, is not found in either the Masoretic text or the Septuagint. It could be that the reference is either to a paraphrase of Josephus or to Genesis 12:4, where it does say five and seventy.[39]

On the basis of the aforementioned consideration, it is held that the fulfillment of the seventy weeks does not follow the actual order of the text. All that is necessary is that the sum of the years total 490.

According to Jerome, the Jews began the seventy weeks with the de-cree of Cyrus. In a short time they thought the nation would return, Jerusalem would be rebuilt by Ezra and Nehemiah, and the Temple would be restored. Although it is not explicitly stated, all these things seem to be a part of the first sixty-two weeks. Before the sixty-two weeks are complete, Christ will be born, ending prophets and prophecy.[40]

It appears that the sixty-two weeks are followed by one week in which Christ is slain. Further, the seven weeks, or forty-nine years, cover a period from Vespasian to Hadrian, although this is stated ambiguously. Braverman's comments are enlightening:

> The phrase 'upon his [Vespasian's] death the seven weeks or forty-nine years were complete' is most ambiguous. Judging from the continuation of the above phrase, the *terminus ad quem* of the entire seventy-week period is the establishment of Aelia upon the ruins of Jerusalem and the crushing of the Jewish revolt by Hadrian and his general, Tinus Rufus. Since we have already accounted for sixty-three weeks, there must be a seven-week or forty-nine year period from the death of Vespasian to the Hadrianic persecutions.[41]

Braverman's hypothesis is substantiated by our modern knowledge of the chronology of that period. Vespasian died in A.D. 79. Hadrian followed Trajan in A.D. 118 and was responsible for provoking the Bar Kochba rebellion in 132. Thus, forty-nine years after A.D. 79 would have approximately marked the end of the era of Hadrianic persecutions (A.D. 128). This particular interpretation is further supported by the comments of Jerome upon the Jewish tradition.[42]

Jerome, however, gives an alternative interpretation about the single week (Dan. 9:27). It is that Vespasian and Titus concluded a peace with the Jews for three years and six months, as did Hadrian. There are two problems with this alternative tradition. First, the two halves of the single week do not follow one another successively, as the verse states, but they are interrupted by a period of approximately sixty-five years. Second, this view demands a peace with both Vespasian *and* Titus. We do know that Titus was not involved in Judea in A.D. 66.[43]

In evaluating this view one must first judge its authenticity. This is the longest tradition that Jerome records in his commentary, and one of the longest in any of his works. But it cannot be found in toto in any existing rabbinic literature. Parts, on the other hand, are well known. Moreover, Jerome declares that he is presenting a paraphrase in order to bring out the sense more clearly. This is the only time Jerome says he is giving a paraphrase. There are at least two places where the paraphrase is evident. The first is the reference to the Messiah. Jerome's handling is definitely for Christian consumption. The Jews used *anointed* for the Hebrew מָשִׁיחַ, whereas the Christians used the term *Christos*. This latter designation was unpleasant to the Jews. It is, however, found in Jerome.[44] A second place where a Christian interpretation is interjected is seen in Jerome's understanding of וְאֵין לוֹ. He takes this to mean: "... and the nation who shall reject him shall go out of existence." This is a reference to the Jews and their rejection of Jesus.[45]

If one allows for the fact that this is a paraphrase, the general authenticity of the tradition need not be questioned. On the other hand, there are conclusive reasons for rejecting it. Besides the general objections that can be brought against Roman and non-Messianic interpretations, this particular view fails in that the time from the decree of Cyrus to A.D. 70 is 656 years, not the 483 years, or sixty-nine weeks. Moreover, the treatment of the three divisions in an order different from that in the text counts against this view. Although a number or an age might be stated by giving the smallest division first, the examples cited have nothing to do with the prophecy of seventy weeks. In Daniel we have more than the simple statement of a number. That number is divided into three groups, with events that mark the commencement and conclusion of the period.

The oldest rabbinic tradition for Daniel's seventy weeks is *Seder Olam Rabbah,* ch. 28. Most subsequent rabbinic and medieval Jewish commentators follow this approach. Near the end of the chapter an anonymous interpretation is offered. The first seven weeks are related to the exile and the return to the land. The next sixty-two weeks are spent in the land. The final week predicts a period that is partially spent in the land and partially spent in exile.[46]

After the anonymous chronology, there is the statement of Rabbi Jose, the author of *Seder Olam Rabbah.* He attempts to establish the beginning of the seventy weeks with the destruction of the first Temple and the end of the period with the destruction of the second Temple. Jose completely ignores the seven, sixty-two, one division of the seventy weeks. He declares that there are 70 years of the first Temple's destruction, and 420 years of the second Temple's existence. An immediate problem with such an interpretation is that the terminus a quo would be before the vision is given to Daniel. In answer, Jose cites instances of retroactive decrees.[47]

Jose's chronology has little to do with Jerome's. The chief point of agreement is that both see the period as lasting 490 years. However, Jose begins the period 51 years before the tradition recorded in Jerome and ends it 65 years before Jerome's fall of Betar. Thus, any objection against the interpretation presented in Jerome holds with almost equal force against Jose's *Seder Olam Rabbah.*

It is worthy of note that Josephus is unusually evasive in his handling of Daniel 9:24-27. He does not directly refer to the prophecy, nor does he give his interpretation. This is significant because he gives more attention to Daniel than to any other prophet.[48] There is a complete picture of the prophet's life, as well as references to verses in chapters 1-6 and 8, but there is no clear reference to chapter 9. At best, there is an oblique allusion in *Antiquities* 10.276.

Jerome does cite Josephus in support of two points. He appeals to *Jewish Wars* 6.93 in corroboration of the cessation of sacrifice at the time of the destruction of the second Temple. Josephus specifically mentions that sacrifices ceased prior to the destruction of the Temple because of a lack of lambs during the siege of Titus.

Jerome cites Josephus to the effect that Vespasian and Titus made a peace with the Jews for three and a half years. In the extant works of Josephus there is no record of such a statement. The closest that one can find is Josephus's record of a long speech by Titus telling of his humanitarian nature and detailing, over and over again, how he and his father, Vespasian, offered peace to the Jews.[49]

Messianic view. This view finds the seventieth week fulfilled in the Roman age, but it differs from the preceding interpretations in one important aspect. Each of the commentators holding this view thinks that Daniel's prophecy gives a clear prediction of the coming of the Messiah. As such, they are distinctively Christian.

Messianic interpretations accept differing beginning points for the seventy weeks. For instance, E. J. Young would commence the period with the decree of Cyrus in 538–37 B.C., whereas G. W. West thinks that 445–44 B.C. is correct. B. F. C. Atkinson defends 457 as the terminus a quo.[50] The reason for the wide diversity of opinion here is that Young thinks the seventy weeks, with its three divisions, is to be understood in symbolic fashion. One is mistaken to try to find an exact calculation. The figures of seven, sixty-two, and one should only be taken as showing the comparative length of each period.

Where these various messianic interpretations converge is in their identification of מָשִׁיחַ נָגִיד of Daniel 9:25. Rather than identifying the personage with some priest or civil leader (who would have been anointed), it is argued that this is reference to the Messiah. The Messiah and His work must be meant, because of the things that are to be accomplished in the period (Dan. 9:24). Moreover, the Messiah alone has the requisites called for in Daniel 9:25. It is true that the Hebrew מָשִׁיחַ had not yet attained the status of a technical term, Messiah. And further, it is a fact that both priests and kings were anointed in the Old Testament.[51] However, many of those suggested could not possibly qualify. Cyrus has been advanced, but he was not a theocratic king. As a matter of fact, he was a heathen, even though chosen by God for a specific purpose. Nor is Onias satisfactory, since he was only a priest. Therefore, the only person who fits the description is Jesus (Psalm 110:4; Zech. 6:13; John 4:25).[52]

Daniel 9:25 simply says "until Messiah the Prince." This is sufficiently ambiguous to allow the terminus ad quem of the sixty-nine weeks to be any of these: Christ's birth, His baptism, or His crucifixion. I shall discuss how one arrives at one of these as correct, when I deal with eschatological interpretations.

Although there is difference in detail, those who fall within this school of interpretation agree that the events of verses 26 and 27 relate to the Roman period, in particular the crucifixion of the Messiah and the destruction of the city of Jerusalem and the Temple. Verse 26 says it is *after* sixty-nine weeks that the Messiah will suffer. However, it does not say whether it is *immediately* after or some time *later*. The "cutting off" of Messiah indicates a violent death. The Hebrew word is used of making a covenant, involving the death of a sacrificial animal (Gen. 15:10, 18). The word is used of the death penalty (Lev. 7:20) and always of an unnatural, violent death (cf. Isa. 53:8).[53]

In Daniel 9:26 there is a second event predicted. It is the destruction of the city and the sanctuary by "the people of the prince." West identifies this prince with the Messiah, and the people who destroy the city and sanctuary then are the Jews. The prince of verse 26 is the same as in verse 25, just as the anointed one, or Messiah, of verse 26 is the same as in verse 25. But did the Jews destroy the city and Temple? West answers yes: "Messiah is cut off and the people of Messiah, by their iniquity, destroy the city and the Sanctuary."[54]

The more common understanding of the prince is Titus (A.D. 70). This prediction deals with the events that surrounded the destruction of the city and Temple. It is the people, not the prince, that accomplish the ruin. The figure of a flood may mean either an invading army (Isa. 8:7-8; Dan. 11:10, 22, 26) or the wrath or judgment of God in general (Psalm 32:6; Nah. 1:8). Both are applicable here. "The end" may be of either the city or the prince. Ford thinks that the Hebrew is intentionally ambiguous, because first it is the city and later the prince.[55]

Now we come to verse 27. Those who take this interpretation see this verse as fundamentally parallel to verse 26. Although Messiah is to be cut off after sixty-nine weeks, Daniel 9:26 does not say how long after the period is complete that the cutting off will occur. This matter is the subject of 9:27. It is to occur in the middle of the seventieth week. Thus, it is the Messiah who causes the covenant to prevail. Jesus Christ is the subject of the beginning of verse 27. "Sacrifice and grain offering" refers to the entire worship under the old economy. By His death He causes the sacrificial system to cease.[56]

The last half of Daniel 9:27 is taken in two ways. First, there are those who take the abomination and destruction to be a reference to Titus and

A.D. 70.[57] Second, other commentators see this as going beyond the fall of Jerusalem and the ruin of the Temple to a final climactic judgment.[58] Thus, on this last account, 9:27b is eschatological in its character.

The interpretation of verse 27 is the crucial point of difference between a Roman interpretation and an eschatological interpretation. The former view is defended in the following ways. It is common to claim that the six items of Daniel 9:24 were accomplished at Christ's first coming, and therefore the seventy weeks are complete. J. Barton Payne gives the most original and thorough attempt to establish this point. He tries to show that each of the infinitival phrases of verse 24 is related to an event predicted in 9:25-27, and that they were fulfilled in Christ's first coming.[59]

Meredith G. Kline gives an extended argument in favor of a Roman period fulfillment based upon the identity of the covenant of 9:27. He argues that the covenant cannot be an agreement between the Antichrist and the Jews, but must be a covenant between the Messiah and His people. A summary of Kline's position follows. The language of Daniel 9 is thoroughly redemptive. It is the only chapter in the book where the covenantal name of God, Yahweh, is found (9:2, 4, 10, 13, 14, 20). The prayer is the Todah, or confessional prayer. It includes the confession of sin and the acknowledgement of the justice of God's actions. This is preparatory to the renewing of the covenant and restoration of the blessing.[60]

Thus, when a covenant is introduced in Daniel 9:27, Kline asks:

When, therefore, we find a covenant mentioned in verse 27, there should be no doubt as to its identity. The whole context speaks against the supposition that an altogether different covenant from the divine covenant which is the central theme throughout Daniel is introduced here at the climax of it all.[61]

Kline distinguishes between the "making" of a covenant and the "ratifying" of a covenant. It is the latter that is in view here. A new covenant is not inaugurated here, but an already existing covenant is caused to prevail. The former would be indicative of an agreement between the Antichrist and his followers, whereas the latter fits the Messiah and His redemptive covenant.[62]

Kline finds further support for his view in that the word *prevail* (or "firm") in 9:27 also is used of the Messiah in Isaiah 9 and 10, particularly Isaiah 9:6 where He is called the "mighty God." All of this leads Kline to conclude that the Messiah is the sole subject of Daniel 9:26-27. Even the prince of 9:26b is the Messiah, and the destruction of the city of Jerusalem is done by a divine army (Matt. 22:2ff., esp. v. 7).[63]

To the already-mentioned reasons for a Roman period fulfillment E. J. Young adds these. It is his contention that an eschatological fulfillment of any of these events is contrary to the messianic character of the passage. Unlike Kline, who identifies the prince of 9:26 with Christ, Young thinks that this is a reference to Titus. Thus, the initial "he" of 9:27 cannot have as its antecedent the prince of 9:26. The correct antecedent must be the Messiah of 9:26a. Young defends this view on the grounds that the prince is in a subordinate position in the verse—he is not even the subject. Even the people are given more prominence than the prince. Finally, Young thinks that the prince of 9:26 must be Titus, not some future prince, as those who defend an eschatological view of this text would see it. It makes no sense to talk about people who belong to a prince who is more than 1900 years hence.[64]

Even though a Roman period fulfillment is not without some support, there do seem to be considerations that lead me to reject it. Because some of these reasons are connected with the superiority of the eschatological interpretation and I do not want to be unduly repetitious, one should read the discussion of the eschatological view as well.

Is spite of Payne's attempt to identify the goals of the seventy weeks (9:24) with events of the period (9:25-27), I remain unconvinced that these goals were fulfilled at Christ's first advent. Johnson expresses the point well:

The basic questions of sin and righteousness were certainly settled when Christ hung on Calvary. . . . It is equally true that the results of Christ's redemption have not yet been fully applied in this world. If Daniel is speaking only of the *provision* made for sin and righteousness, the decisive act that will in time bring an end to the kingdom of Satan and of man, then indeed, this prophecy may be said to be fulfilled. But if his words are to be taken as referring to that *actual* restraint and judgment of sin and the ushering in of the righteousness of God which shall bring everlasting peace and blessing, then they still await their consummation in the return of the Lord [italics added].[65]

Second, although one can appreciate the insights of Kline into the connection between Daniel 9 and God's redemptive and covenantal purposes, one may still wonder if every word must have a direct relation to that covenant. Why is an eschatological interpretation any less related to God's covenantal and redemptive purposes than is Kline's? God is dealing with the sins of His people. God will make a final end of their disobedience after they have committed a gross transgression by entering into an agreement with one who is the very antithesis of Christ, Antichrist. God often allows sin to run its course to show its utter heinousness. Such is the case here.

Furthermore, there are a number of questions that one may raise about Kline's (and others') interpretation of 9:27. Commentators of various persuasions note that Daniel does not use the usual idiom for "making a covenant." Kline and Young take this as an indication that Daniel is not speaking of the *initiation* of a new covenant, but the *ratification* of an existing one. Payne draws support for this position from the fact that the word *new* is omitted from some Greek texts of Matthew 26:28. But all of this seems quite tenuous. Payne overlooks the fact that the adjective *new* is in Luke 22:20 and 1 Corinthians 11:25, and the new covenant is quoted twice in Hebrews.[66] Moreover, I wonder if the distinction between initiating a covenant and ratifying a covenant is a good one. One wonders where we have biblical examples of this; none are cited. Possibly the distinction could be made with respect to the covenant God made with Abraham. In Genesis 12 there is the initiation of the covenant, whereas in Genesis 15 we have the ratification of the covenant. If this be the case, Kline's argument is lost because the normal idiom is found here (Gen. 15:18). Suppose that one takes Genesis 15 as the initiation of the covenant, and subsequent covenantal renewals as ratifications. This problem of undue distinctions still remains. In Genesis we have the sacrifice of animals at the initiation of the covenant, whereas with the covenant of Daniel 9:27 the sacrifice is at the ratification. Why the unusual designation for the making of a covenant? I think it is to show that it is *not* a covenant initiated by God; it is an agreement between the Antichrist and his people.

There are some additional matters that deserve comment with regard to this covenant. Why does Christ's death result in His covenant prevailing for only *one week?* Does not Christ's covenant prevail eternally for those that are His? Furthermore, the unusual verb used in "to make a firm covenant" carries with it the implication of forcing an agreement upon someone because of superior strength.[67] If this be so, such an action would be more in accord with the prince rather than the Messiah.

Is an eschatological fulfillment out of keeping with the messianic character of the prophecy, as Young claims? I think not. Remember Messiah has *two* comings. Thus, an eschatological fulfillment in connection with Messiah's coming would in no way detract from the messianic character of the passage. Rather, it would retain it.

The "cutting off" of Messiah is in a period after sixty-nine weeks (Dan. 9:26), but there is no *clear* indication that it takes place in the seventieth week. A more normal way to express an action occurring in that period would be to precede it with "during" or "in the midst of" as in Daniel 9:27.[68] The placing of the crucifixion of the Messiah in the seventieth week, then, rests on the establishment of the parallel character of 9:26–27. The "cutting off" of Messiah is identical with His "making a firm covenant," a view I have already criticized.

Although Christ's death did make sacrifice unnecessary, it did not cause it to cease, as is required by 9:27. Sacrifice and offering did not cease until the events surrounding the fall of Jerusalem in A.D. 70, about forty years later.

There is a problem with the identity of the prince of Daniel 9:26. Those who see a Roman fulfillment usually identify him with Messiah or Titus. If the prince of 9:26 is the Messiah, neither he nor his people destroyed the city and the Temple in any physical sense. To claim that the Jews destroyed the city by their disobedience is to attempt to avoid the obvious meaning of the text. If on the other hand the prince is Titus, then one is faced with these problems. First, the prince seems to be future to the people who do the destroying ("of the prince who is to come"). Furthermore, if Titus is referred to in 9:26, one wonders why he is even mentioned. Young refuses to allow him to be the antecedent of the "he" in 9:27, and notes correctly that the prince has a subordinate position even in 9:26b. It is the *people* who do the destruction. Why, then, does Daniel even mention Titus? Why not simply say that a people will come and destroy Jerusalem and the Temple?

Finally, there is a problem with the terminus ad quem of the seventieth week. For some, like Young, the problem is not as acute because they do not take the weeks as weeks of years, but only as symbolic of periods of time. I shall examine the acceptability of such a view shortly. However, for those who do try to understand the seventy weeks as weeks of years, the difficulty is immense. The two most likely dates for the crucifixion of Christ are A.D. 30 and 33. If this takes place in the middle of the week, then the seventy weeks must be over at the latest by A.D. 37. This will not even allow the period to run to the destruction of the Temple in A.D. 70. One must close the period with the stoning of Stephen or the spread of the gospel to the Gentiles.[69] One wonders what in the text warrants this view. Further, on what basis is one justified in claiming that the destruction of the Temple is *outside* the seventy weeks, or that the latter half of verses 26 and 27 take us to the consummation of all things?[70] The switch is sudden indeed, given the understanding of the text to that point.

ESCHATOLOGICAL INTERPRETATIONS

We now come to the last group of interpretations. I have called them eschatological because at least a part of the seventieth week will have its fulfillment in the events that surround the second advent of Christ. It should be noted that although I have not called these interpretations messianic, as I have the ones immediately preceding, they are messianic in at least two senses. First, all adherents of these views believe that Daniel 9:25 contains a prediction of the first advent of Christ. Second, the events of the seventieth week are related to the second advent of Christ and His final disposition of sin and establishment of righteousness.

It will be helpful to divide this group of interpretations into two further groups: symbolic, or schematic, views and interval views.

Symbolic, or schematic views. The defining characteristics of this method of interpretation are that the sevens are taken symbolically, or schematically, and that the seventieth week reaches to the consummation of all things. The most noted defenders of this position are Kliefoth, Keil, and Leupold.

Leupold claims that *week* has three possible meanings: a week of days, a heptad of time, or a week of years. This latter meaning is never found in the Bible. It is found only in intertestamental literature. Therefore, Leupold concludes: "We hold that of the three possibilities just mentioned the second alone is exegetically sound and correct."[71]

These groups, or heptads, of time are to be understood symbolically. The symbolism, however, is important. The numbers seven and ten ($7 \times 7 \times 10$) are symbolic of perfection and completion. This symbolism is in keeping with the six statements of God's purposes for men. They cover the perfect consummation of Messiah's work, which will be experienced at His second advent and the consummation of all things.[72]

The three divisions of the seventy weeks (seven, sixty-two, and one) set off God's activities in general seasons. Therefore, the exact dates for commencement and conclusion are not so crucial. The first period begins with the decree of Cyrus to allow the Jews to return to their homeland and build their city and Temple. This period comes to a close with the appearance of an important person called "an anointed one, a prince." This is none other than the Messiah, our Lord Jesus Christ. The fact that there is no article is easily explainable, because the emphasis is on the quality of the terms described.[73]

The second period begins with the Messiah's first advent. The great achievement of the second group of heptads is that spiritual Jerusalem will be rebuilt. This means that in the period subsequent to the coming of the Messiah, the church will be built. This will be accomplished in spite of opposition ("in distressful times"). The contrast between seven and sixty-two is to be understood symbolically. The second period is to be a good deal longer than the first.[74]

Daniel 9:26-27 deals with the third period. The period of the building of the church comes to a close with the "cutting off" of the anointed one. This is not a reference to the crucifixion. It is to be understood in parallelism with "and he shall have nothing." The Messiah will not have what we would expect from Him. He will lose His followers and influence. "The season of the successful building of the city and sanctuary is at an end. As far as the Messiah is concerned, Messiah shall be a dead issue. His cause will seem to have failed."[75]

Why should this be? The one who brings the setback for the Messiah is the Antichrist. The objects of his hatred will be the city and the Temple, the very things that had been built during the previous sixty-two heptads. This last heptad is expanded in 9:27. The Antichrist, trying to imitate Christ, makes a covenant with his followers. The climax of his seeming success is that he will bring a halt to the *totality* of the cult, or worship. It takes him some time ("the middle of the week") to gain his objectives, but his end is sure. A destined destruction will be poured out on him.[76]

There are a number of difficulties with this position. First, the "cutting off" of Messiah is simply a loss of followers and influence, whereas, as has been pointed out previously, this word means a violent death, often being used for the death penalty (Lev. 7:20; Isa. 53:8).

Second, this interpretation takes Jerusalem and the sanctuary in a symbolic or typical way. The building of city and sanctuary is a reference to the building of the church. There is, however, no indication in the text that a typical or symbolic interpretation is intended. Moreover, such an interpretation seems to wrench the text from its historical context, hardly an appropriate application of historical-grammatical hermeneutics.

Third, this view takes 9:26 as parallel with 9:27. The events of verse 26 are said to have occurred *after* the completion of sixty-nine weeks, but the first mention of the seventieth week is found in 9:27. I shall argue below that the seventieth week does not begin until 9:27.

Fourth, clearly the crucial claim of this position is related to the acceptability of taking the weeks as symbolic. The feature that makes these weeks difficult to understand is that Daniel is the only place in the Old Testament where the plural is שָׁבֻעִים instead of שָׁבֻעוֹת. This form is found in Daniel 9:24, 25a, 26; 10:2b, 36). Nevertheless, the following considerations lead me to think weeks of years are meant:

1. Often the word means weeks of days (Gen. 29:27-30; Dan. 10:2-3). However, 490 days are insufficient to finish the prophecy, but 490 years do make sense.[77] In other words the context determines whether days or years are meant. A similar case can be seen in עָשׂוֹר. In most occurrences the word means ten days, but three times it has reference to a ten-string instrument.[78]

2. The Jews were acquainted with weeks of years (Lev. 25; Deut. 15).

The context has been dealing with multiples of seven, or years (10 × 7, Dan. 9:1–2).[79]

3. The most convincing reason is that Daniel has been thinking about seventy years of captivity (Jer. 25:11; 29:10). Every year of exile represented a cycle of seven years in which the seventh year, the sabbatical year, had not been observed. Thus, the 70 years of captivity were the result of having violated seventy sabbatical years. This would have been done over a period of 490 years. Daniel now is given a prophecy of units of seven concerning another 490 years (2 Chron. 36:21; cf. Lev. 26:33–35; Jer. 34:12–22).[80]

4. The only other occurrence of שָׁבֻעִים in Daniel (10:2–3) is followed by the designation "days," showing that the unit of sevens is different in the two passages.

5. If the seventieth week (Dan. 9:27) is eschatological, as I shall argue further on, and if this seventieth week is related to Daniel 7:25; 12:7; and Revelation 12:14, then the division of the week into two halves of three and a half years, forty-two months, or 1260 days confirms the week of years view.[81]

6. Even though Daniel's usage in Scripture is unique, there are extra-biblical uses of weeks of years.[82]

Interval views. By far the most common view in the eschatological school of interpretation of the seventieth week is that there is an interval between the end of the first sixty-nine weeks and the beginning of the seventieth week. This seventieth week is, of course, fulfilled eschatologically.

The first formulation of an interval interpretation is that of Robert C. Newman.[83] I shall call his position the *sabbatical year view.* Newman takes his cue from the relationship of the captivity with the sabbatical cycles. Furthermore, he cites the Talmud as having a remark about the coming of the Messiah that is associated with a seven-year cycle. Thus, the weeks are not to be converted into years (e.g., sixty-nine weeks into 483 years). They are to be counted as sabbatical cycles. He determines that the sixty-ninth cycle would have fallen between A.D. 27 and 34. These dates would accommodate any seriously held view for the date of the crucifixion. If one counts backwards from the sixty-ninth sabbatical year, 455 B.C., which Newman thinks is the seventy weeks' terminus a quo, falls within the first sabbatical cycle. The result of counting sabbatical years rather than actual years is that one has a cushion of six years at either end (in the first and sixty-ninth sabbatical year). There does seem to be a problem, because Daniel 9:26 says that Messiah will be cut off *after* sixty-nine weeks. On Newman's account, the Messiah is crucified *during* the sixty-ninth week. His response is that the Jews use *after* three days (Matt. 27:63; Mark 8:31) and *on* the third day (Matt. 20:19; Mark 9:31) interchangeably, which solves the problem. The final sabbatical cycle is future. An interval is justified on the grounds that the Temple is destroyed in 9:26, but sacrifices are spoken of in 9:27, presupposing a rebuilt Temple.[84]

Newman does present us with an ingenious solution, but in the end I think there are two reasons for rejecting his interpretation. First, the seventieth week does not just seem to be a sabbatical cycle. As I have shown above, it is divided into two three-and-a-half-year periods. The last half is specified in terms of months and days. There does not seem to be the flexibility that Newman suggests, at least not in the last week. But maybe such is the case only with the last week.

Second, even if we accept Newman's resolution to the problem of the crucifixion, we are still left with the question of the destruction of Jerusalem and the Temple. There are *two* events, not one, spoken of in Daniel 9:26. Either both are *on* the sixty-ninth sabbatical year or *after* it. But Newman must have one occurring *on* the sixty-ninth cycle and one *after* it.

A second interval interpretation is presented by Allan A. MacRae.[85] His position might be called the *double interval view*. This designation comes because he has an interval after the first as well as the second division of the seventy weeks. The seventy weeks of Daniel begin with Cyrus's decree in 538 B.C., if they are to begin with a human command. "Not only is this the only edict to rebuild Jerusalem of which we have historical evidence; it is so important that it is directly quoted twice in the Bible."[86] It is quoted in Ezra 1 and 6, as well as being confirmed by Darius.

MacRae, however, suggests that the first period began, not with a human command, but with God's decree to rebuild Jerusalem in 587 B.C. (Jer. 32:44). There are three precise periods, but there are unmentioned and unspecified intervals between each period. The first period was forty-nine years, and was concluded in the time of Daniel. The anointed one at the end of seven weeks was Cyrus. This fulfillment would have given Daniel confidence that the rest of the weeks also would be accomplished.[87]

There is no mention concerning any event that marks the beginning of the second period. According to MacRae, an unmentioned interval of about one hundred years would intervene, taking us to about 436 B.C. Somewhere in this period Jerusalem would stand. It would be before Messiah is cut off, because the cutting off would take place after the conclusion of the sixty-two weeks.[88]

There would follow again an unmentioned interval of many centuries until the appearance of the Antichrist. This final week is eschatological and relates to the rule of the Antichrist.[89]

MacRae offers these considerations in support of his position. It takes into account the fact that the command is God's command. Further, the prophecy is a general rather than exact prediction of the coming of the Messiah. The prediction of the general time of Messiah's coming is more in accord with the nature of biblical prediction. Moreover, this interpretation follows the pointing of the Masoretes. Their pointing separates quite clearly the three periods and makes it necessary that there be two anointed ones. Finally, the identification of the first anointed one with Cyrus is in accord with the overwhelming number of times that the Hebrew מָשִׁיחַ does not refer to the Messiah.[90]

In spite of my agreement with many of the aspects of this interpretation, I think there are two decisive reasons for at least modifying this view. First, the terminus a quo of the period has already begun some forty-nine years before the prophecy ever came to Daniel. This is unusual to say the least. Second, the introduction of two intervals is problematical. I shall argue shortly that there are indications that justify an interval between the close of the sixty-ninth week and the commencement of the seventieth week. But similar indications are entirely lacking for an unmentioned interval between the first and second divisions of the prophecy. Furthermore, there are alternative interpretations that handle the text as well or better, which do not require the introduction of a second interval.

I now turn to the two most common interval views. They are essentially the same. The point at which they differ is over the kind of year that one is to use in calculating the prophecy. One uses a solar year, whereas the other a prophetic year.

Let me first examine the *solar year view.* Proponents of this view take the terminus a quo for the seventy weeks to be the seventh year of Artaxerxes in 458-57 B.C. The seventy weeks are divided into three groups of seven, sixty-two, and one. Usually, however, there is a rejection of the Masoretic punctuation that would demand the appearance of an anointed one at the end of *both* the seven-week period and the sixty-two-week period. Rather, the seven weeks are set off as the period of the rebuilding of the city of Jerusalem and the Temple.

The justification for rejecting the Masoretic pointing is as follows. The Masoretes added pointing and punctuation in the ninth and tenth century A.D. Their work is not a part of the inspired text. Although the athnach is often the principal break in the sentence, it is not invariably so. Moreover, the Masoretes often put an athnach where it would be unexpected. A particularly clear example of such punctuation is to be found in Numbers 28:19, but there are other cases (e.g., Gen. 7:13; 25:20; Exod. 35:23; Lev. 16:2; Isa. 49:21; 66:19). Finally, if we accept the Masoretic punctuation, there is great difficulty in making sense out of the passage. It would seem that it took 434 years to build the plaza and moat.[91]

For reasons already given, 9:25-26 are references to the Messiah. Thus, the terminus ad quem of the sixty-nine weeks is some event in the life of Christ. It cannot be the crucifixion, because 9:26 says that that is after the conclusion of the sixty-nine weeks. Three events have been suggested for the end of the sixty-nine weeks: Christ's birth, His baptism, or His triumphal entry. If one begins with the 458 B.C. date and figures 483 solar years, he will reach A.D. 26 (Remember, it is just one year from 1 B.C. to A.D. 1.) Interestingly enough, A.D. 26 is the most commonly accepted date for the baptism of Christ and His entrance into His ministry. Moreover, it allows us to accept the most widely defended date for the crucifixion, A.D. 30 because that would be after sixty-nine weeks.[92]

In Daniel 9:26 two events are related that occur after sixty-nine weeks have elapsed, but before the seventieth week has commenced. The Messiah will die a violent death, and the city of Jerusalem and its Temple will be destroyed (A.D. 70). Thus, these two events transpire in an interval between the sixty-ninth and the seventieth week.

Because the idea of an interval is so central to this view, it is well to examine the evidence for such a break.

1. As has been stated before, the six goals of the seventy weeks as given in Daniel 9:25 have not been fulfilled as yet.

2. Intervals in the fulfillment of prophecies are a common Old Testament phenomenon (e.g., Luke 4:18-19; cf. Isa. 61:1-2).

3. The seventieth week is treated separately from the first sixty-nine. Although the final week is divided, it is nevertheless a unit unto itself.

4. The crucifixion of the Messiah and the destruction of the city and Temple are after sixty-nine weeks (Dan. 9:26). The first mention of the seventieth week is made in 9:27, allowing for the possibility that there may be an interval.

5. The difficulties already discussed in giving an adequate interpretation of 9:26-27, when the seventieth week follows immediately after the first sixty-nine, count against this view.

6. Daniel 9:27b fits well with what we know elsewhere about the events of the last half of the Tribulation period (e.g., Dan. 7:25; 2 Thess. 2:3ff.; Rev. 12, 13, 19).[93]

7. The idea of an interval can be seen in Daniel 7, 8, and 11. "The rationale for such a gap is simply that there was a need to speak of times relative to both advents of Christ, and there was no need to speak of the history between them."[94]

8. Jesus speaks of the abomination of desolation as yet future (Matt. 24:15; Mark 13:14). The value of this consideration will depend on whether or not one sees the Olivet discourse as having been fulfilled in the destruction of Jerusalem in A.D. 70.

Having cited the reasons for believing that there is an interval between the sixty-ninth and the seventieth week, I am ready to turn to a discussion of the final week as described in Daniel 9:27. This is oftentimes called the week of the Antichrist. It is the time of domination by the prince that will come, the end-time world ruler. The "he" of 9:27, then, has as its antecedent "the prince" of 9:26. In support of this description of the seventieth week, the following considerations may be advanced:

1. "The prince" of 9:26 is the nearer antecedent.

2. The prince is said to be a Roman (9:26), which is in accord with 7:8, 23-24, where a little horn arises out of the fourth kingdom, Rome.[95]

3. An article before the participle "who shall come" indicates that this one has been previously mentioned and is known to the readers (e.g., 7:8, 23-24).[96]

4. The rest of the verse fits the activities of the Antichrist well.

5. Titus is an unlikely candidate because he is not that important a figure in history to warrant such extensive treatment. There really would be no reason to mention both the people and the prince unless they both had biblical significance.[97]

Briefly, then, the Antichrist will make an agreement with his followers for seven years. This will allow the rebuilding of a Temple and the reinstitution of sacrifices. In the middle of this agreement the Antichrist will go back on his word and cause the entire Temple worship to cease. Even though the last half of Daniel 9:27 is difficult indeed, it seems to say that Antichrist will establish some kind of idol worship (cf. 2 Thess. 2:3ff.; Rev. 13) in place of Temple worship. However, his end has been decreed by God, and he shall be removed by divine judgment.

The objections to this interpretation of the seventieth week fall into three general classes. First, such an understanding of Daniel 9:27 demands that the Antichrist make a covenant with his followers. This cannot be the case, it is asserted, because the text says nothing about making a covenant, only ratifying it. Nowhere else in the Bible do we find a statement that Antichrist will make a covenant.[98] I have already answered the question about the making of a covenant. However, let me respond to the claim that this is the only statement of a covenant involving the Antichrist. One may genuinely contest that claim, but let us assume it is correct just for the sake of argument. If Daniel 9:27 is the only place in the Bible that teaches such a covenant, that is *enough*. To demand otherwise is to require that every truth in Scripture be confirmed somewhere else in the Bible.

Second, there is dissatisfaction with the identification of the "he" of 9:27 with "the prince" of 9:26. I have already discussed this matter, so I will not do so again. There is, however, an extension of this objection by Young that merits consideration. He thinks it is untenable to separate the people and the prince of 9:26 by thousands of years.

> It therefore follows, upon this view, that the people belong to a prince who will not appear for years (nearly 2000 have already elapsed) after they themselves have perished. But how can this be? How can the Roman armies of Titus possibly be regarded as belonging to a prince who has not yet appeared?[99]

Young goes on to say that it is not enough that the prince simply be a Roman; he must rule over the people so he can say they are his.[100]

The response to Young is direct and simple. Why should anyone accept Young's demands? All that is required is that the people are related to the prince in some way. They are. They are of the same nationality. To require more is to require more than the text does.

Finally, the idea of an interval is objected to. It is argued that the interval is already longer than the entire period (nearly 2000 years versus 490 years). There is no gap between the first and the second period. There is no hint of a gap in the text. One must evaluate these objections in light of the evidence presented earlier for the interval. If there is justification for it and if such an interval gives the best sense to the passage, this understanding is to be preferred even though that interval has already lasted nearly 2000 years.

There is an objection by Mauro that also must be answered. He claims that *numbers* are never interrupted in their successive fulfillment. It may be the case that there are intervals between the first and second advent in the fulfillment of prophecies, *but* these prophecies do not contain numbers in them. Thus, the usual examples of intervals do not apply here.[101]

Tatford tries to answer Mauro in this way. God's method of computation is not that of man's. God only counts when Israel is subject to God and not serving heathens.[102] The immediate problem with Tatford's view is that he cannot explain why the seventieth week counts. On his view it should not, for "the many" are in league with Antichrist. But Tatford may have the right idea. The progression of the seventy weeks could be related to Israel's presence in the land. But what seems sure to me is that Mauro's objection is not decisive against an interval. I think two things justify my claim. First, there are indications in the text that an interval is expected. These indications are lacking in Mauro's examples. Second, the seventy weeks are unique in that we have not only a number, *but* we also have that number divided into three smaller numbers. This, again, is unlike any example that Mauro cites.

An alternative interpretation to the solar year view is the *prophetic year view*. The structure of the two views is essentially the same. They diverge at two points. First, those who defend the prophetic year view begin the seventy weeks of Daniel with the decree in the twentieth year of Artaxerxes, 445–44 B.C. Second, a year is not a solar year, but a prophetic year of 360 days. Thus, the 483 years between the decree and the Messiah will number 173,880 days. If one begins with the first of Nisan (March 14) 445–44 B.C. and counts off 173,880 days, taking into account years that have an extra day due to leap year, one will find that the sixty-nine weeks came to a close on either April 6, A.D. 32 or March 30, A.D. 33 depending on whether one takes the decree to have been issued in 445 or 444 B.C. Both of these dates happen to be Palm Sunday, so Christ's cruxifixion would have been one week after the conclusion of the sixty-nine weeks.[103]

In support of the 360-day prophetic year these considerations are offered. First, although we can accurately measure the length of a year because of our sophisticated instruments (a year is 365.24219879 days, or 365 days, 5 hours, 48 minutes, and 45.975 seconds), this has not always been possible. Therefore, people in the past had different calendars, many of which had 360 days.[104] Second, this 360-day calendar is used in the Bible with respect to prophecy (Dan. 7:24–25; 12:7; Rev. 12:14; 13:5; cf. Rev. 11:3; 12:6 [1260 days] and 11:2 [42 months]). As a matter of fact, a majority of the passages just cited bear upon Daniel 9:27 because they relate to the time of tribulation.[105] Third, in Genesis 7:11 (a nonprophetic passage) is it recorded that the Flood began on the seventeenth day of the second month, and Genesis 8:4 says that it ended on the seventeenth day of the seventh month. Both Genesis 7:24 and 8:3 specify that this was 150 days (this shows that there were thirty-day months).[106]

Of the three arguments just given, the second is by far the most impressive. One may question if the first argument has a bearing on the debate. The third argument does not cover a whole year, and thus may omit various schemes to add days to make the ancient year more like ours.

There are three further problems that one may raise with the prophetic year view. First, some think the Jews used a year of 360 days. Justification for this is found in the prophetic year. But the Old Testament connects the Feast of Passover (the middle of the first month) with the offering of the first ripe grain (Lev. 23:6–14). Thus, the Jewish calendar was tied to the seasons.[107] As a matter of fact, from Qumran calculations we know that although the Jews had thirty-day months, they had methods for correcting the calendar to the seasons and the sun.[108] Second, if one commences the first sixty-nine weeks in 445 B.C., then there was an A.D. 32 crucifixion, a very unlikely date. On the other hand, if the decree was issued in 444 B.C., then the death of the Messiah took place in A.D. 33, a much more likely date but still not the most widely accepted.[109] Finally, those who follow this interpretation must begin the calculations on the *first* of Nisan (we are not told the exact day of the decree). But if the decree was issued even one week later, then it would be impossible to end the 483 years, even granting a prophetic year, before the cutting off of Messiah.[110]

CONCLUSIONS

In this chapter I have sought to examine Daniel's prophecy of seventy weeks, particularly as its teaching touches upon the Messiah and eschatology. We may summarize my conclusions as follows:

1. Whereas Jeremiah's prophecy of the seventy years of captivity came to cure Israel of the sin of idolatry, Daniel's prophecy promises his people that in a period set apart by God, He will finally remove their transgression and establish everlasting righteousness.

2. Although there are four decrees that might serve as the terminus a quo of this period, either 458-57 or 445-44 B.C. seem to make the most sense of the passage. One's preference will in some measure depend on which view of calculating the period he chooses, solar or prophetic year.

3. The prophecy covers a period from the time of Daniel until the second advent of Christ. As such, it is eschatological. Its seventieth week predicts the reign of Antichrist.

4. Daniel's prophecy is messianic as well. It contains a prediction of the coming of the Messiah (His baptism or triumphal entry, depending on whether the solar year or the prophetic year is used) and His death. It is also messianic in that it looks forward to that time when the Messiah shall return to put an end to the forces of wickedness and bring in His reign of righteousness upon the earth.

NOTES

1. Desmond Ford, *Daniel* (Nashville: Southern Pub. Assoc., 1978), p. 198.
2. Henry C. Guinness, *The Divine Programme of the World's History* (London: Hodder & Stoughton, 1888), p. 329.
3. Michael J. Gruenthaner, "The Seventy Weeks," *Catholic Biblical Quarterly*, 1 (1939): 44.
4. Norman W. Porteous, *Daniel: A Commentary* (Philadelphia: Westminster, 1965), pp. 139-40. See also E. W. Heaton, *The Book of Daniel: Introduction*

and Commentary (London: SCM, 1956), p. 210, and Frederick A Tatford, *The Climax of the Ages: Studies in the Prophecy of Daniel* (London: Marshall, Morgan & Scott, 1953), p. 159.

5. Meredith G. Kline, "The Covenant of the Seventieth Week" in *The Law and the Prophets: Old Testament Studies Prepared in Honor of Oswald Thompson Allis.,* ed. John H. Skilton (Nutley, N.J.: Presby. and Ref., 1974), pp. 454-55.

6. Leon Wood, *A Commentary on Daniel* (Grand Rapids: Zondervan, 1973), p. 247. See also Edward J. Young, *The Prophecy of Daniel: A Commentary* Grand Rapids: Eerdmans, 1949), pp. 195-96, and Harold W. Hoehner, *Chronological Aspects of the Life of Christ* (Grand Rapids: Zondervan, 1977), pp. 115-16.

7. Allan A. MacRae, "The Seventy Weeks of Daniel" (Paper delivered at the Evangelical Theological Society, Deerfield, Ill., 1978), p. 3. See also George W. West, *Daniel the Greatly Beloved* (London: Marshall, Morgan & Scott, n.d.), p. 78.

8. E. B. Pusey, *Daniel the Prophet* (Minneapolis: Klock & Klock, 1978), p. 186.

9. MacRae, p. 3.

10. Wood, p. 252. See also Young, p. 202.

11. Hoehner, p. 121.

12. Pusey, p. 187.

13. See Ford, p. 229; Wood, p. 252; Ronald S. Wallace, *The Lord is King: The Message of Daniel* (Downers Grove, Ill.: Inter-Varsity, 1979), p. 168.

14. Phillip C. Johnson, *The Book of Daniel* (Grand Rapids: Baker, 1964), p. 71. See also Young, p. 202.

15. Young, p. 203. See also Ford, pp. 229-30.

16. John F. Walvoord, *Daniel: The Key to Prophetic Revelation* (Chicago: Moody, 1971), p. 226.

17. Hoehner, p. 122.

18. Ibid., p. 123.

19. See M. McNamara, "Seventy Weeks of Years," *The New Catholic Encyclopedia* (New York: McGraw-Hill, 1967), 8:142; Porteous, p. 141; H. C. Leupold, *Exposition of Daniel* (Columbus, Ohio: Wartburg, 1949), pp. 422-23; Young, p. 193; Ford, pp. 199-200; Andre Lacocque, *The Book of Daniel,* trans. David Pellauer (Atlanta: John Knox, 1979), pp. 195-6; Heaton, p. 213; Clyde T. Francisco, "The Seventy Weeks of Daniel," *Review and Expositor,* 57 (April 1960): 134.

20. Hoehner, p. 124. See also Wood, p. 252.

21. Pusey, pp. 188-89.

22. Wood, p. 254.

23. Hoehner, p. 125.

24. Wood, p. 253.

25. Gleason L. Archer, *Commentary on Daniel,* in *The Expositor's Bible Commentary,* (Grand Rapids: Zondervan, forthcoming).

26. Sir Robert Anderson, *The Coming Prince* (London: Hodder & Stoughton, 1895), pp. 51 ff.; G. W. West, p. 75; Tatford, p. 164; S. P. Tregelles, *Remarks on the Prophetic Visions in the Book of Daniel* (London: Bagster, 1864), p. 101; Alva J. McClain, *Daniel's Prophecy of the Seventy Weeks* (Grand Rapids: Zondervan, 1940), p. 17; Walvoord, p. 225; Renald E. Showers, "New Testament Chronology and the Decree of Daniel 9," *Grace Journal* 11

(1970): 30; Robert C. Newman, "Daniel's Seventy Weeks and the Old Testament Sabbath-Year Cycle," *Journal of the Evangelical Theological Society,* 16 (Fall 1973): 232; Robert D. Culver, *Daniel and the Latter Days.* Rev. ed. (Chicago: Moody, 1977), pp. 151 ff.; Hoehner, p. 126.

27. Hoehner, p. 126.
28. For a defense of the A.D. 32 date see Showers and for an A.D. 33 date see Hoehner. See Newman for a date in the sabbatical year between A.D. 27-34.
29. McNamara, p. 142; Lacocque, p. 195; Porteous, p. 141. Pusey, p. 202, also records these suggestions: Nebuchadnezzar, Alexander, Seleucus Philopater.
30. Heaton, p. 215; L. F. Hartman and Alexander A. Di Lella, *The Book of Daniel,* The Anchor Bible (Garden City, N.Y.: Doubleday, 1978), p. 252. See also C. G. Ozanne, "Three Textual Problems in Daniel," *The Journal of Theological Studies,* 16 (October 1965): 446.
31. Hartman, p. 252; Heaton, pp. 214-15; Porteous, p. 143.
32. McNamara, p. 142; Porteous, pp. 143-44; Heaton, p. 216; Hartman, p. 253.
33. L. E. Knowles, "The Interpretations of the Seventy Weeks of Daniel in the Early Fathers," *Westminster Theological Journal,* 7 (May 1945): 159. See also Gleason L. Archer, *Jerome's Commentary on Daniel* (Grand Rapids: Baker, 1958), pp. 95ff.
34. Pusey, p. 205; Ford, p. 199; Hartman, pp. 252-53.
35. Hartman, p. 253.
36. Ford, p. 199.
37. Josephus, *Antiquities* 10.11.7.
38. Porteous, p. 144.
39. Jay Braverman, *Jerome's Commentary on Daniel: a Study of Comparative Jewish and Christian Interpretations of the Hebrew Bible,* in *The Catholic Biblical Quarterly Monograph Series No. 7* (Washington, D.C.: Catholic Biblical Assoc. of Amer., 1978), p. 104. See Josephus *Antiquities* 1.256.
40. Braverman, p. 105.
41. Ibid., pp. 105-6.
42. Archer, *Jerome's Commentary,* p. 109.
43. Braverman, p. 106.
44. Samuel Krauss, "The Jews in the Works of the Church Fathers," *Jewish Quarterly Review,* 6 (1894): 243-44, esp. n. 3 on p. 244.
45. Ibid.
46. *Seder Olam Rabbah,* ch. 28.
47. Ibid.
48. Josephus, *Antiquities* 10.186-281.
49. Josephus, *The Jewish Wars* 6.333ff.
50. Young, p. 205; G. W. West, p. 79; Basil F. C. Atkinson, *The Times of the Gentiles* (London: Protestant Truth Soc., n.d.), p. 67.
51. Joyce G. Baldwin, *Daniel: An Introduction and Commentary* (Downers Grove, Ill.: Inter-Varsity, 1978), p. 170.
52. Young, pp. 203-4.
53. Baldwin, p. 171.
54. G. W. West, p. 88. See also Kline, pp. 463-64.
55. Ford, p. 233.
56. Ibid., p. 234; Young, p. 217; G. W. West, p. 94.
57. John Calvin, *Commentaries on the Book of the Prophet Daniel,* trans.

Thomas Myers (Grand Rapids: Eerdmans, 1948), pp. 224-26 (by A.D. 70). Atkinson, p. 70, suggests that the seventieth week may end with Acts 10 and the third Pentecost. This would make the destruction of the Temple after the end of the seventy weeks. Young, pp. 218-19, ends the period with A.D. 70, as does J. Barton Payne, "The Goal of Daniel's Seventy Weeks," *The Journal of the Evangelical Theological Society,* 21 (June 1978): 97-115. Young also suggests that the period may end with the death of Stephen (p. 213).

58. G. W. West, p. 97, connects the latter part of 9:27 with 2 Thessalonians 2:11 and Revelation 13. Ford, pp. 201-2. Kline, p. 489, claims that the prophecy reaches to the consummation of all things.
59. Payne, pp. 97-115.
60. Kline, pp. 452-62.
61. Ibid., p. 463.
62. Ibid. See also Ford, pp. 233-34; Young, p. 209.
63. Kline, pp. 466-67.
64. Young, p. 211.
65. Johnson, p. 70.
66. Robert H. Gundry, *The Church and the Tribulation* (Grand Rapids: Zondervan, 1973), p. 189.
67. Baldwin, p. 171.
68. Hoehner, p. 131.
69. See n. 57 above for various solutions to this problem.
70. See n. 58 above for views that include an eschatological element.
71. Leupold, p. 406.
72. C. F. Keil, *Biblical Commentary on the Book of Daniel,* trans. M. G. Easton (Grand Rapids: Eerdmans, 1949), pp. 399-402.
73. Leupold, p. 421.
74. Ibid., pp. 423-24.
75. Ibid., p. 427.
76. Ibid., p. 433.
77. Wood, p. 247.
78. Hoehner, p. 215.
79. Wood, p. 247.
80. Hoehner, p. 215; Wood, p. 247.
81. Hoehner, p. 218.
82. Hoehner, p. 135, nn. 63-66. See also Roger T. Beckwith, "The Significance of the Calendar for Interpreting Essene Chronology and Eschatology," *Revue de Qumran,* 38 (May 1980): 167-202.
83. Newman, pp. 229-34.
84. Ibid., p. 231.
85. MacRae, pp. 1-9.
86. Ibid., p. 6.
87. Ibid., p. 8.
88. Ibid., pp. 8-9.
89. Ibid., p. 9.
90. Ibid., pp. 3-7.
91. William Wickes, *A Treatise on the Accentuation of the Twenty-one So-called Prose Books of the Old Testament* (Oxford: Oxford U., 1887), pp. 40-41. See also Hoehner, p. 130 and Young, p. 204.

92. Wood, pp. 252–53.
93. Edward Dennet, *Daniel The Prophet: and the Times of the Gentiles* (Orange, Calif.: Ralph E. Welch Foundation, 1967), p. 157; Nathaniel West, *Daniel's Great Prophecy: Its Twelve Chapters Explained* (London: Prophetic News, n.d.), pp. 69–70.
94. Wood, p. 260.
95. Ibid., p. 258.
96. N. West, p. 70; Wood, p. 258.
97. Wood, p. 258.
98. Ford, p. 201; Young, p. 210; N. West, p. 69.
99. Young, p. 210.
100. Ibid., pp. 211–12.
101. Philip Mauro, *The Seventy Weeks and the Great Tribulation* (Boston: Hamilton, 1923), pp. 95–99.
102. Tatford, p. 173.
103. For A.D. 32 see Anderson, Culver, McClain, Showers, and Walvoord. For A.D. 33 see Hoehner.
104. See n. 83 above.
105. Hoehner, p. 136.
106. McClain, p. 16; Hoehner, p. 136.
107. Newman, p. 230.
108. Beckwith, p. 167.
109. Hoehner, p. 137, cf. Wood, p. 253.
110. Newman, pp. 230–31.

Part III

TEXTUAL AND LINGUISTIC

8

A Reassessment of the Value of the Septuagint of 1 Samuel for Textual Emendation, in the Light of the Qumran Fragments

Gleason L. Archer

GLEASON L. ARCHER *(L. L. B., Suffolk University; B. D., Princeton Theological Seminary; M. A., Ph.D., Harvard University) is professor of Old Testament and Semitic languages at Trinity Evangelical Divinity School, Deerfield, Illinois.*

INTRODUCTION

Ever since the 4QSam[a] fragments were published in BASOR (132, December 1953), renewed interest has been directed towards the value of the LXX version of Samuel in solving problems of textual corruption in those two books. The reason for this heightened prestige is found in the frequent instances in which the Qumran fragments seem to favor the presumed *Vorlage* of the LXX as over against the Masoretic text. The case for this heightened preference was indicated by F. M. Cross in the article just cited, as well as in the follow-up article on the 4QSam[b] fragments published in JBL no. 74 (1955) and the *New American Bible* discussion of all of the 4Q fragments, which appeared in 1970. This increased interest in the textual witness of the Septuagintal 1 Samuel prompted me at last to make a careful examination of 1 Samuel as a whole, in order to review the trustworthiness of this version from a somewhat broader standpoint than its relationship to the Qumran fragments alone. The relationship of those fragments to the proto-Septuagintal family is hardly to be denied, but a reexamination of the three traditions needs to be undertaken in order to put the LXX in the right perspective in relation to the MT.

A COMPARISON OF THE LXX, THE MT, AND THE QUMRAN FRAGMENTS

It should be pointed out that in his reconstruction of the text, Professor Cross inserted a great many words that were not preserved in the fragments themselves. (See Figure 1.) For example, only two words actually appear in column 1, line 9, out of the nine that are contained in Cross's reconstructed text. In line 10 there is only one word out of eight; only one in 1. 11 out of eleven; only one in 1. 12 out of the nine; and in 1. 13 not a single word is preserved in the manuscript fragments, even though Cross has supplied ten words for that line. If we inquire as to the basis on which the editor reconstructed these missing words, we find that in most instances they consist of a translation from the Septuagint back into Hebrew.

Before I was quite aware of the distinction between the 4Q text and those words that were supplied in brackets by Dr. Cross, I was greatly impressed by the striking similarity between 4Q and the LXX that came through again and again where the MT differed from the LXX. But after I became fully cognizant of the force of the brackets, I came to see that the editor's own presuppositions had greatly influenced his choice of words supplied. But when all of the bracketed portions have been deleted from the primary data, the evidence of relationship between 4Q and the LXX is greatly reduced. In other words, this reconstructed text is largely the product of circular reasoning: the missing portions must be Septuagintal, since some of the preserved Qumran readings resemble the Septuagint more than the Masoretic text. Even though all such readings are clearly presented as merely conjectural, the student must be on guard against being overly affected in his assessment of the solid, objective evidence afforded by these fragmentary portions from Qumran 4. In my subsequent discussion, therefore, I shall discuss only those passages that do in fact appear in the 4Q material, rather than that which has been supplied by Dr. Cross's scholarly intuition.

PASSAGES IN WHICH 4Q RESEMBLES THE LXX RATHER THAN THE MT

Col. 1 (see Figure 2):

(1) 1:22   Perhaps *met' autou* agrees with an *'immō*^{w}, which may possibly have appeared in the lacuna of 4Q; at any rate the MT lacks such an *'immō*^{w} after *lō' 'ālata*.

(2) 1:23   "May the LORD establish," *hayyōṣē' mippīkā* (4Q), agrees with the LXX *to exelthon ek tou stomatos sou*, as over against MT, which has simply *'et-d^{e}bārô* ("His word").

(3) 1:24   ". . . and she went up with him to Shiloh" (*watta'al 'ō*^{w}*tō*^{w} *šīlō*^{h})

Figure 1

Relative position of characters on fragments of 4Q Samᵃ

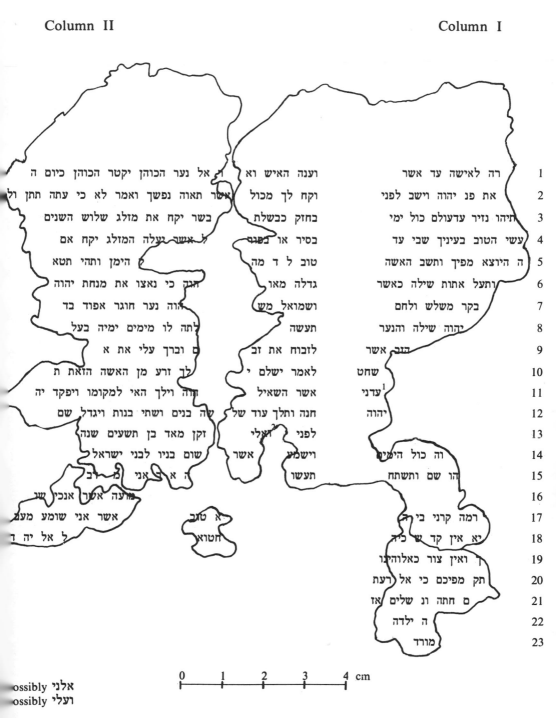

Column II		Column I	
אל נער הכוהן יקטר הכוהן כיום ה	וענה האיש וא	רה לאישה עד אשר	1
אשר תאוה נפשך ואמר לא כי עתה תתן ול	וקח לך מכול	את פנ יהוה וישב לפני	2
בשר יקח את מזלג שלוש השנים	בחזק כבשלת	חיהו נזיר עדעולם כול ימי	3
אשר יעלה המזלג יקח אם	בסיר או בפרנ	עשי הטוב בעיניך שבי עד	4
הימן ותהי תטא	טוב ל ד מה	ה היוצא מפיך ותשב האשה	5
הנה כי נאצו את מנחת יהוה	גדלה מאו	ותעל אתות שילה כאשר	6
הוה נער חוגר אפוד בד	ושמואל מש	בקר משלש ולחם	7
לתה לו מימים ימיה בעל	תעשה	יהוה שילה והנער	8
ם וברך עלי את א	לזבוח את זב	הזב אשר	9
לך זרע מן האשה הזאת ת	לאמר ישלם י	שחט	10
זה וילך האי למקומו ויפקד יה	אשר השאיל	עדני	11
חנה ותלך עוד של שה בנים ושתי בנות ויגדל שם	לפני העלי	יהוה	12
זקן מאד בן תשעים שנה	וה כול הימינ		13
שום בניו לבני ישראל	וישמע אשר	וה כול הימינ	14
ה א אני מ יב	תעשו	הו שם ותשתח	15
מעה אשר אנכי שמ			16
אשר אני שומע מעב	א טוב	רמה קרני בי ה	17
ל אל יה ד	חטוא	יא אין קד ש כיה	18
		ואין צור כאלוהינו	19
		תק מפיכם כי אל רעת	20
		ם חתה ונ שלים אז	21
		ה ילדה	22
		מורד	23

0 1 2 3 4 cm

אלני possibly

ועלי possibly

Figure 2

4Q Samᵃ as Reconstructed by F. M. Cross	Masoretic Text of I Samuel 1:22-2:6, 2:13-25	Septuagint Text of I Samuel 1:22-2:6, 2:13-25
COLUMN I	COLUMN I	COLUMN I

Septuagint — COLUMN I

1:22 καὶ Αννα οὐκ ἀνέβη μετ᾽ αὐτοῦ, ὅτι εἶπεν τῷ ἀνδρὶ αὐτῆς· "Εως τοῦ ἀναβῆναι τὸ παιδάριον, ἐὰν ἀπογαλακτίσω αὐτό, καὶ ὀφθήσεται τῷ προσώπῳ κυρίου καὶ καθήσεται ἐκεῖ ἕως αἰῶνος.

1:23 καὶ εἶπεν αὐτῇ Ελκανα ὁ ἀνὴρ αὐτῆς Ποίει τὸ ἀγαθὸν ἐν ὀφθαλμοῖς σου· κάθου, ἕως ἂν ἀπογαλακτίσῃς αὐτό· ἀλλὰ στήσαι κύριος τὸ ἐξελθὸν ἐκ τοῦ στόματός σου. καὶ ἐκάθισεν ἡ γυνὴ καὶ ἐθήλασεν τὸν υἱὸν αὐτῆς, ἕως ἂν ἀπογαλακτίσῃ αὐτόν.

1:24 καὶ ἀνέβη μετ᾽ αὐτοῦ εἰς Σηλωμ ἐν μόσχῳ τριετίζοντι καὶ ἄρτοις καὶ οιφι σεμιδάλεως καὶ νεβελ οἴνου καὶ εἰσῆλθεν εἰς οἶκον κυρίου ἐν Σηλωμ, καὶ τὸ παιδάριον μετ᾽ αὐτῶν.

1:25 καὶ προσήγαγον ἐνώπιον κυρίου, καὶ ἔσφαξεν ὁ πατὴρ αὐτοῦ τὴν θυσίαν, ἣν ἐποίει ἐξ ἡμερῶν εἰς ἡμέρας τῷ κυρίῳ, καὶ προσήγαγεν τὸ παιδάριον καὶ ἔσφαξεν τὸν μόσχον. καὶ προσήγαγεν Αννα ἡ μήτηρ τοῦ παιδαρίου πρὸς Ηλι

Figure 2 (continued).

1:26 καὶ εἶπεν Ἐν ἐμοί, κύριε· ζῇ ἡ ψυχή σου, ἐγὼ ἡ γυνὴ ἡ καταστᾶσα ἐνώπιόν σου ἐν τῷ προσεύξασθαι πρὸς κύριον·

1:27 ὑπὲρ τοῦ παιδαρίου τούτου προσηυξάμην, καὶ ἔδωκέν μοι κύριος τὸ αἴτημά μου, ὃ ᾐτησάμην παρ' αὐτοῦ·

1:28 κἀγὼ κιχρῶ αὐτὸν τῷ κυρίῳ πάσας τὰς ἡμέρας, ἃς ζῇ αὐτός, χρῆσιν τῷ κυρίῳ.

2:1 Καὶ εἶπεν Ἐστερεώθη ἡ καρδία μου ἐν κυρίῳ, ὑψώθη κέρας μου ἐν θεῷ μου· ἐπλατύνθη ἐπὶ ἐχθρὸν τὸ στόμα μου, εὐφράνθην ἐν σωτηρίᾳ σου.

2:2 ὅτι οὐκ ἔστιν ἅγιος ὡς κύριος, καὶ οὐκ ἔστιν δίκαιος ὡς ὁ θεὸς ἡμῶν· οὐκ ἔστιν ἅγιος πλὴν σοῦ.

2:3 μὴ καυχᾶσθε καὶ μὴ λαλεῖτε ὑψηλά, μὴ ἐξελθάτω μεγαλορρημοσύνη ἐκ τοῦ στόματος ὑμῶν, ὅτι θεὸς γνώσεων κύριος καὶ θεὸς ἑτοιμάζων ἐπιτηδεύματα αὐτοῦ.

2:4 τόξον δυνατῶν ἠσθένησεν, καὶ ἀσθενοῦντες περιεζώσαντο δύναμιν·

2:5 πλήρεις ἄρτων ἠλαττώθησαν, καὶ οἱ πεινῶντες παρῆκαν γῆν· ὅτι στεῖρα ἔτεκεν ἑπτά, καὶ ἡ πολλὴ ἐν τέκνοις ἠσθένησεν.

2:6 κύριος θανατοῖ καὶ ζωογονεῖ, κατάγει εἰς ᾅδου καὶ ἀνάγει·

*A doubtful reading; should be אוד; Photograph is not clear.

Figure 2 (continued).

4Q Sam[a] as Reconstructed by F. M. Cross	Masoretic Text of I Samuel 1:22-2:6, 2:13-25	Septuagint Text of I Samuel 1:22-2:6, 2:13-25
COLUMN II	COLUMN II	COLUMN II

Septuagint Text (COLUMN II)

2:13 καὶ τὸ δικαίωμα τοῦ ἱερέως παρὰ τοῦ λαοῦ, παντὸς τοῦ θύοντος· καὶ ἤρχετο τὸ παιδάριον τοῦ ἱερέως, ὡς ἂν ἡψήθη τὸ κρέας, καὶ κρεάγρα τριόδους ἐν τῇ χειρὶ αὐτοῦ,

2:14 καὶ ἐπάταξεν αὐτὴν εἰς τὸν λέβητα τὸν μέγαν ἢ εἰς τὸ χαλκίον ἢ εἰς τὴν κύθραν· πᾶν, ὃ ἐὰν ἀνέβη ἐν τῇ κρεάγρᾳ, ἐλάμβανεν ἑαυτῷ ὁ ἱερεύς· κατὰ τάδε ἐποίουν παντὶ Ισραηλ τοῖς ἐρχομένοις θῦσαι κυρίῳ ἐν Σηλωμ.

2:15 καὶ πρὶν θυμιαθῆναι τὸ στέαρ ἤρχετο τὸ παιδάριον τοῦ ἱερέως καὶ ἔλεγεν τῷ ἀνδρὶ τῷ θύοντι Δὸς κρέας ὀπτῆσαι τῷ ἱερεῖ, καὶ οὐ μὴ λάβω παρὰ σοῦ ἑφθόν ἐκ τοῦ λέβητος.

2:16 καὶ ἔλεγεν ὁ ἀνὴρ ὁ θύων Θυμιαθήτω πρῶτον, ὡς καθήκει, τὸ στέαρ, καὶ λαβὲ σεαυτῷ ἐκ πάντων, ὧν ἐπιθυμεῖ ἡ ψυχή σου. καὶ εἶπεν Οὐχί, ὅτι νῦν δώσεις, καὶ ἐὰν μή, λήμψομαι κραταιῶς.

2:17 καὶ ἦν ἡ ἁμαρτία τῶν παιδαρίων ἐνώπιον κυρίου μεγάλη σφόδρα, ὅτι ἠθέτουν τὴν θυσίαν κυρίου.—

2:18 καὶ Σαμουηλ ἦν λειτουργῶν ἐνώπιον κυρίου παιδάριον περιεζωσμένον εφουδ βαρ,

Figure 2 (continued).

ומעיל קטן [8]תעשה [לו אמו והע]לתה לו מימים ימימה בעל[ותה את אישה] [9]לזבוח את זב[ח הימי]ם	2:19	וּמְעִיל קָטֹן תַּעֲשֶׂה־לּוֹ אִמּוֹ וְהַעַלְתָה לוֹ מִיָּמִים יָמִימָה בַּעֲלוֹתָהּ אֶת־אִישָׁהּ לִזְבֹּחַ אֶת־זֶבַח הַיָּמִים׃	καὶ διπλοΐδα μικρὰν ἐποίησεν αὐτῷ ἡ μήτηρ αὐτοῦ καὶ ἀνέφερεν αὐτῷ ἐξ ἡμερῶν εἰς ἡμέρας ἐν τῷ ἀναβαίνειν αὐτὴν μετὰ τοῦ ἀνδρὸς αὐτῆς θῦσαι τὴν θυσίαν τῶν ἡμερῶν.
וברך עלי את א[לקנה ואת אשתו] [10]לאמר ישלם י[הוה] לך זרע מן האשה הזאת תח[ת השאלה] [11]אשר השאיל[ה לי]הוה וילך האיש למקומו	2:20	וּבֵרַךְ עֵלִי אֶת־אֶלְקָנָה וְאֶת־אִשְׁתּוֹ וְאָמַר יָשֵׂם יְהוָה לְךָ זֶרַע מִן־הָאִשָּׁה הַזֹּאת תַּחַת הַשְּׁאֵלָה אֲשֶׁר שָׁאַל לַיהוָה וְהָלְכוּ לִמְקֹמוֹ׃	καὶ εὐλόγησεν Ηλι τὸν Ελκανα καὶ τὴν γυναῖκα αὐτοῦ λέγων Ἀποτείσαι σοι κύριος σπέρμα ἐκ τῆς γυναικὸς ταύτης ἀντὶ τοῦ χρέους, οὗ ἔχρησας τῷ κυρίῳ. καὶ ἀπῆλθεν ὁ ἄνθρωπος εἰς τὸν τόπον αὐτοῦ,
ויפקד יה[וה את] [12]חנה ותלך עוד שלושה בנים ושתי בנות ויגדל שמ[ואל] [13]לפני יהוה	2:21	כִּי־פָקַד יְהוָה אֶת־חַנָּה וַתַּהַר וַתֵּלֶד שְׁלֹשָׁה־בָנִים וּשְׁתֵּי בָנוֹת וַיִּגְדַּל הַנַּעַר שְׁמוּאֵל עִם־יְהוָה׃	καὶ ἐπεσκέψατο κύριος τὴν Ανναν, καὶ ἔτεκεν ἔτι τρεῖς υἱοὺς καὶ δύο θυγατέρας. καὶ ἐμεγαλύνθη τὸ παιδάριον Σαμουηλ ἐνώπιον κυρίου.
*ואלי זקן מאד בן תשעים שנה [14]וישמע [את] אשר [יע]שום בניו לבני ישראל	2:22	וְעֵלִי זָקֵן מְאֹד וְשָׁמַע אֵת כָּל־אֲשֶׁר יַעֲשׂוּן בָּנָיו לְכָל־יִשְׂרָאֵל וְאֵת אֲשֶׁר־יִשְׁכְּבוּן אֶת־הַנָּשִׁים הַצֹּבְאוֹת פֶּתַח אֹהֶל מוֹעֵד׃	Καὶ Ηλι πρεσβύτης σφόδρα· καὶ ἤκουσεν ἃ ἐποίουν οἱ υἱοὶ αὐτοῦ τοῖς υἱοῖς Ισραηλ,
ויאמר להם למה] [15]תאשון] כדברים האל]ה א[ש]ר אני [שו]מ[א מפי כול] [16]עם יהוה	2:23	וַיֹּאמֶר לָהֶם לָמָּה תַעֲשׂוּן כַּדְּבָרִים הָאֵלֶּה אֲשֶׁר אָנֹכִי שֹׁמֵעַ אֶת־דִּבְרֵיכֶם רָעִים מֵאֵת כָּל־הָעָם אֵלֶּה׃	καὶ εἶπεν αὐτοῖς Ἵνα τί ποιεῖτε κατὰ τὸ ῥῆμα τοῦτο, ὃ ἐγὼ ἀκούω ἐκ στόματος παντὸς τοῦ λαοῦ κυρίου;
אל בני כי לוא טובה הש]מועה אשר אנכי שו[מע אל] [17]תעשון כן כי לו]א טוב[ות השמועות] אשר אני שומע מעב [18]עם אלהים	2:24	אַל בָּנָי כִּי לוֹא־טוֹבָה הַשְּׁמֻעָה אֲשֶׁר אָנֹכִי שֹׁמֵעַ מַעֲבִרִים עַם־יְהוָה׃	μή, τέκνα, ὅτι οὐκ ἀγαθὴ ἡ ἀκοή, ἣν ἐγὼ ἀκούω· μὴ ποιεῖτε οὕτως, ὅτι οὐκ ἀγαθαὶ αἱ ἀκοαί, ἃς ἐγὼ ἀκούω, τοῦ μὴ δουλεύειν λαὸν θεῷ.
ואם] חטוא [יחטא איש לאיש]ל אל יהוה [ואם]	2:25	אִם־יֶחֱטָא אִישׁ לְאִישׁ וּפִלְלוֹ אֱלֹהִים וְאִם לַיהוָה יֶחֱטָא־אִישׁ מִי יִתְפַּלֶּל־לוֹ וְלֹא יִשְׁמְעוּ לְקוֹל אֲבִיהֶם כִּי־חָפֵץ יְהוָה לַהֲמִיתָם׃	ἐὰν ἁμαρτάνων ἁμάρτῃ ἀνὴρ εἰς ἄνδρα, καὶ προσεύξονται ὑπὲρ αὐτοῦ πρὸς κύριον· καὶ ἐὰν τῷ κυρίῳ ἁμάρτῃ, τίς προσεύξεται ὑπὲρ αὐτοῦ; καὶ οὐκ ἤκουον τῆς φωνῆς τοῦ πατρὸς αὐτῶν, ὅτι βουλόμενος ἐβούλετο κύριος διαφθεῖραι αὐτούς.

*The photograph seems to read ע, not א; read עלי.

in 4Q agrees with LXX *eis Sēlōm,* rather than omitting the destination altogether, as MT does. (Note that in this instance 4Q uses a perversion of *'ēt* as the word for "with", rather than the *'im* of the MT. *'ōᵂtōᵂ* was seldom used for *'ittōᵂ* prior to Jeremiah.)

(4) 1:24   4Q's *bāqār mᵉshallēsh* ("three-year-old cattle") agrees with LXX's *en moschōi trietizonti* as over against MT's *bᵉpārîm shᵉlōshâh* ("with three bullocks").

(5) 1:24   With LXX the 4Q Ms inserts after the aforesaid words the additional "and bread" (*wᵉleḥem*) omitted by MT altogether.

(6) 1:25   4Q agrees with LXX in making the verb not plural, as MT has it, but singular—"he sacrificed" rather than "they sacrificed" (*wayyishḥaṭ* rather than *wayyishḥāṭû.*

(7) 1:28   The length of the lacuna in 4Q seems to favor a reading *lᵉYahweʰ. wattōʾmer,* corresponding to LXX's *kai eipen,* rather than MT's *wattitpallēl Ḥannâh wattōʾmar* ("and Hannah prayed and said . . .").

Col. 2 (see Appendix, p. 229):

(8) 2:2   With LXX the 4Q inserts a *kīy* missing in the MT (= *hoti*) before *'ên qadôsh* ("there is none holy").

(9) 2:4   The vestiges in 4Q indicate *qešet gibbōrīᵛ mḥattāʰ* ("He has shattered the bow of the mighty"), in approximate agreement with LXX's *toxon dunatôn ēsthenēsen* ("He has enfeebled the bow of the mighty," as over against MT's *qeshet gibbōrîm ḥattîm* ("the bow of shattered mighty-men")—which is grammatically difficult or impossible in the MT, since the latter demands a predicate adjective agreeing with *qeshet,* the subject.

(10) 2:16 4Q agrees with LXX in inserting "all" before "that thy soul desires," as over against MT, which omits the "all."

(11) 2:17 4Q reads ". . . because they despised the offering of Yahweh" (*kīᵛ niʾᵉṣūᵂ 'et-minḥat Yahweh*) in agreement with LXX (*hoti ēthetoun tēn thysian Kyriou*) as against MT, which inserts "the men" (*hāʾᵃnāšîᵛm*) as subject of "despised."

(12) 2:20 The MT may possibly have omitted a *lamed* in *yāsēm Yahweh lᵉkā zeraʿ* ("May Yahweh grant offspring to you," which 4Q gives as *yᵉšallēm Yahweh lᵉkā zeraʿ* ("May Yahweh reward you with offspring")—note the resemblance between ישלם and ישם—in conformity with LXX: *'apoteisai soi Kyrios sperma.*

(13) 2:20 4Q reads the singular in *wayyēlek hāʾîᵛš* ("And the man went . . ."), in agreement with LXX: *kai apēlthen ho anthrōpos.* MT reads " . . . and *they* went . . ." (*wᵉhālᵉkūᵂ*).

(14) 2:21 LXX's *kai 'epeskepsato Kyrios* ("*And* the Lord visited . . .")

agrees with 4Q's *wayyipqōd,* rather than with MT's *ki*[y]*-pāqad* ("*Surely* He visited . . .").

(15) 2:21 As the object of God's gracious visitation the 4Q specifies Hannah, and then continues: "and she *again* gave birth" (*wattēled 'ō*[w]*d*). So also the LXX: "*tēn Annan kai eteken eti.*" MT inserts after *Hannah:* "and she *conceived and* gave birth" (*wattahar wattēled*) omitting the word "again" ('*ō*[w]*d*).

(16) 2:22 4Q has no "all" before the relative pronoun in: *wayyišma'* ('et-) '*ašer ya'*[a]*sū*[w]*m*); likewise LXX: *kai ēkousen ha epoioun* ("and he heard what they were doing"). But, the MT does insert an "all": '*et kol-'ašer ya'*[a]*sū*[w]*n*; note the 4Q-m ending, which may be the object pronoun "them," resumptive for the relative '*ašer;* MT uses the nun-paragogic for this verb form.

(17) 2:22 After this verb comes the subject: *bānā*[y]*w lib*[e] *nē*[y] *Yisrā'ēl,* i.e., "all that which his sons were doing to the sons of Israel." So reads the 4Q, just like the LXX (*epoiuoun hoi huioi autou tois huiois Isrāēl*). But MT inserts "all": "all that which his sons were doing to all Israel"—omitting "the sons of."

(18) 2:22 The MT continues after this last clause with the following disgraceful report concerning Samuel's sons: *w*[e] '*et-'ašer yiškē-bū*[w]*n 'et-hannāšī*[y] *m haşşōb*[e] '*ō*[w]*t petah 'ōhel mō*[w]'*ēd* ("and that they used to lie with the women who served at the doorway of the tent of meeting"). LXX omits this entirely, and apparently 4Q did likewise, judging by the space allowed by the very few letters that have survived between the lacunae.

(19) 2:25 The 4Q preserves only a single word, *ḥāṭō*[w]', but this is sufficient to support the distinctive reading of the LXX, *ean hamartanōn hamartēi (anēr eis andra)*—"If a man sinning sins against a man . . ."—as against MT, which omits this infinitive absolute and reads simply: "If a man sins against a man. . ."

These nineteen examples of agreement between the Qumran fragments and the LXX serve to establish that the *Vorlage* of the Septuagint was fairly close to that of 4Q, despite a few rather startling dissimilarities, which will be discussed. But of the discrepancies between the Septuagint and the Masoretic text described above, the greatest number (nine) consist of the insertion of a single word in the 4Q-LXX tradition that does not appear in the MT—generally a dispensable, inconsequential word (1, 3, 5, 7, 8, 10, 15A, 19). Next most frequent (four) are instances where 4Q-LXX omit a single word occurring in the MT (11, 15B, 16, 17). In two instances (6, 13) there is disagreement in the number of a verb form (i. e., singular for a plural, or vice versa). In two instances a different particle is used (12, 14). In one case (4) a synonymous phrase in LXX-4Q is used for a single word in MT. In another (9) the same word is used in two different forms. In one instance the MT includes a long clause not found in 4Q-LXX (i. e., 18). This last is probably the most significant discrepancy in the entire section just reviewed.

PASSAGES IN WHICH 4Q DIFFERS FROM BOTH MT AND LXX

1:22 4Q reads "And he will dwell before (Yahweh)"—$w^e y\bar{a}\check{s}ab\ lipn\bar{e}^y$ (Yahweh). But here LXX agrees with MT in reading kai kathēsetai ekei = $w^e y\bar{a}\check{s}\check{s}ab\ \check{s}\check{s}\bar{a}m$: "and he will live before Yahweh."

1:22 After that same clause, 4Q inserts another clause entirely missing from both MT and LXX: ($w^e n\bar{a}tatt\hat{i}^y w\ n\bar{a}z\hat{i}^y r\ {}^{\circ}ad\ {}^{\circ}\bar{o}^w l\bar{a}m\ ko^w l\ y^e m\bar{e}^y\ (hayy\bar{a}^y w)$), i.e., "and I will make him a nazirite permanently all his days."

2:16 4Q inserts "And the man answered" ($w^e {}^{\circ}\bar{a}n\bar{a}^h\ h\bar{a}{}^{\circ}\hat{i}^y \check{s}$) before "and said." But MT has simply "And the man said to him," which is quite close to LXX: kai elegen ho anēr (but without $aut\bar{o}^i$ "to him").

2:18 4Q shows a qal active participle in $na{}^{\circ}ar\ h\bar{o}^w g\bar{e}r\ {}^{\circ}ep\bar{o}^w d$ ("a youth wearing an ephod"), whereas MT uses the passive participle: $na{}^{\circ}ar\ h\bar{a}g\bar{u}^w r\ {}^{\circ}ep\bar{o}^w d$, as does LXX: paidarion periezōsmenon ephoud.

2:21 4Q omits the word for "youth" before Samuel's name: wayyigdal $\check{S}^e m\bar{u}^w {}^{\circ}\bar{e}l$ ("and Samuel became great"; but LXX agrees with MT in the insertion of to paidarion, i.e., $hanna{}^{\circ}ar$, before "Samuel".)

2:22 4Q supplies a specific number of years after the statement that Eli had become very old: $z\bar{a}q\bar{e}n\ m^e {}^{\circ}\bar{o}d\ ben\ ti\check{s}{}^{\circ}\hat{i}^y m\ \check{s}\bar{a}n\bar{a}^h$ (i.e., 90 years old); but this does not appear in either MT or LXX.

Two other deviations are to be quite clearly inferred despite the presence of lacunae in the text of 4Q. They are:

2:16 MT reads $w^e {}^{\circ}im$-$l\bar{o}{}^{\circ}\ l\bar{a}qaht\bar{i}^y$ ("And if not, I will take. . .)—as does also LXX: kai ean mē lēmpsomai . . . But 4Q has space only for ${}^{\circ}att\bar{a}^h\ titt\bar{e}n$ ("you shall give now") before $w^e l\bar{a}qaht\bar{i}^y$ ("then I shall take. . .").

2.14 This involves the addition of a clause not appearing in either LXX or the MT: $t\hat{o}^w b\ l^e bad\ meh($. . . $\check{s}\bar{o}^w\ q\ hayy\bar{a}m\bar{i}^y n$ ("good except for . . . the right foreleg"). LXX and MT end off with ". . . the priest would take hold of it. . ." (elambanen heautōi ho hiereus—yiqqah hakkōhēn $b\bar{o}^w$), before finishing the verse with "thus they used to do to all Israel who came there to Shiloh" (a clause missing entirely in 4Q, which continues with verse 17 right after $hayy\bar{a}m\bar{i}^y n$).

This brings up the most startling aberration to be found in all of the 4Q fragments, and that is the transposition of verse 13 (lacking three words) to a position right after verse 16. To this was added an interpolation before verse 17 that corresponds to neither MT nor LXX, namely, the statement about the right foreleg just cited above. It should be noted that

LXX follows the MT order completely in verses 13 and 14, and fur-thermore it includes verse 15, which seems to have been omitted entirely from 4Q. The lacunae leave no room for even a trace of this verse: "And before the fat was offered up in smoke the priest's servant would come and say to the man who was sacrificing, 'Give the fat to the priest, and do not take for yourself that which is cooked [MT:"only what is raw"] out of the pot'" (a phrase not found in MT). Admittedly, there are some de-viations of a minor sort between LXX and MT in this verse, but they mainly agree as to the order and content of these verses, 14–17, and 4Q is grossly deviant. A passage like this raises serious questions as to the closeness of relationship between 4Q and the Hebrew *Vorlage* of the LXX.

PASSAGES IN WHICH MT, LXX AND 4Q ALL DIFFER FROM ONE ANOTHER

1:22 MT reads: "But Hannah did not go up [LXX adds: "with him"], for she said to her husband, 'Until the lad is weaned—then I will bring him and he shall appear before Yahweh and dwell there perma-nently.'" LXX inserts, "Until the lad goes up" before "I wean him." This appears to be a change of position for the sequence of ideas, but at any rate, LXX omits MT's "then I will bring him" (*wah ᵃbiʾōtîw*). As for 4Q, it may or may not have included "with him" after "did not go up"—there is a lacuna there. But it certainly deviates from both in inserting a *lipnē ᵛ* (*Yahweh*) right after *w ᵉyāšab* ("and he shall dwell").

1:24 MT reads: "And she brought him up with her" (*wattaʿălēhû ʿimmāh*); LXX has "And she went up with him" (*met' autou*), rather than using the transitive hiphil of the verb and making him (the lad Samuel) its object. 4Q omits "with her/him" altogether, although it makes "him" the object of "and she brought up" (*wattaʿal ʾō ʷtō ʷ*).

1:28 MT ends as follows: ". . . he has been lent *šāʾûl* to Yahweh; and they worshipped Yahweh there." But LXX ends quite differently: ". . . (the days which) he shall live [reading *hōye ʰ* or *yiḥ ʰ* for MT's *hāyā ʰ*], as a loan to the Lord." The final MT clause ("and they wor-shipped Yahweh there") is altogether missing. 4Q shows only the letters for:—*ēhū ʷ wattištaḥū ʷ* . . . ," but this is enough to establish that it read: ". . . him, and she worshipped." This is clearly much closer to the MT than to the LXX, despite minor variants.

2:16 MT reads: "And the man said to him. . ."—the antecedent being clear enough from the preceding context. But 4Q fills it in explicitly, saying: "And he said to the servant of the priest. . ." The LXX differs from both in omitting the dative altogether: "And the man would say. . ." (*Kai elegen ho anēr,*) followed by the direct quote.

2:16 In the direct quote itself, the MT words it, "Let them certainly offer the fat up in smoke today" (*qaṭṭēr yaqṭī^y rū^{w}n kayyō^{w}m haḥēleb*). The 4Q conforms quite closely to this, but omits the infinitive absolute, saying: "Let the priest offer up the fat in smoke"—apparently omitting "today" (*kayyō^{w}m*). But the LXX reads the infinitive absolute as an agential participle, saying: "Let *him who sacrifices* offer up the fat in smoke, as is fitting. . ."—a phrase that apparently replaces *kayyō^{w}m*.

2:20 MT reads: "'May Yahweh grant thee offspring from this woman in recompense for the loan which he (sic) has lent (*šā'al*) to Yahweh.' And they went to his (sic) place (*lim^{e}qômō^w*)." As for the 4Q, after a lacuna it reads; ". . . which she (?) has lent to Yahweh.' And the man went to his place." Thus it relieves the grammatical difficulties of the MT, either because it has preserved the more original wording, or because it decided to bring about grammatical harmony by altering its *Vorlage*. The LXX words it: "'. . . may the Lord grant to thee offspring from this woman, in recompense for the loan which thou hast lent to the Lord.' And the man (i.e., Elkanah) went to his place." This last clause conforms completely with the 4Q reading as against the MT, but all three differ as to the subject of the word for "loan." MT has "*he* has lent," LXX has "thou has lent," and 4Q has "she has lent" (or at least, if there was no following hē in the lacuna, 4Q used a hiphil for "he" instead of the improbable qal form of the MT (*šā'al*).

2:21 Where the MT has *wayyigdal hanna'ar Š^{e}mū^{w}ēl 'im-Yahweh* ("And the lad Samuel grew before Yahweh", 4Q has: *wayyigdal Š^{e}mū(^{w}ēl)-lipnē^y Ya(hwe^h)—hanna'ar* being omitted, and *lipnē^y* used in place of *'im* before *Yahwe^h*. LXX includes *paidarion* (= *hanna'*ar) but probably favors *lipnē^y* with its *enōpion* before *Kyriou* (although conceivably *enōpion* might have been used for *'im* in this case, rather than *meta* or *pros* with the accusative) before *Kyriou*. Thus each supports the other only in part. The LXX wording was: *kai emegalynthē to paidarion Samouēl enōpion Kyriou*.

SUMMARY OF THE RELATIONSHIP BETWEEN 4Q, LXX AND THE MT

The fragmentary condition of the 4Q document compels the analyst to resort to extrapolation and inference as he attempts to establish the relationship between the three traditions. But enough data have been preserved to draw several significant conclusions.

1. The 4Q is by no means in the same tradition as the Septuagint, although there are strikingly numerous affinities to be observed. Of these the commonest is the insertion of nonessential words like "all" (a-10,

a-22) on the part of 4Q-LXX, or vice versa, as in a-17. Similarly they insert "the sons of Israel" where MT reads "Israel" alone (a-17); or a prepositional phrase like "with him", where MT lacks it (a-1). Similarly, a strengthening infinitive absolute is added before the main verb, where MT has none (a-19); or else an adverbial particle like "again," which does not appear in MT, though it is implied by the context (a-15). On the other hand, MT inserts a dispensable verb immediately before another verb, such as "she *conceived and* gave birth," where 4Q and LXX omit this traditional pairing (a-15). The insertion of such superfluous words for the sake of greater clarity or heightened emphasis is somewhat reminiscent of the distinctive technique of lQIs[a] (the complete scroll of Isaiah) and other second-century copies of a popular, nonliturgical type.

2. On the other hand, 4Q-LXX may omit a noun-subject easily inferrable from the context where MT inserts it (a-7, a-11). Yet MT omits a noun-subject in one instance where 4Q-LXX insert it (a-13).

3. There is at least one instance where 4Q-LXX use a plural verb in place of MT's singular form (a-6). Or else there is a slightly different ending to the verb that hardly changes the sense (a-16).

4. 4Q-LXX may employ a phrase that expands the single word employed by the MT, such as "that which comes forth from thy mouth" in place of "his word" (note the difference in pronoun here), as in a-2.

5. A different introductory particle, "For" instead of "And" (*Kî* instead of *wa*) may be employed (a-21).

6. In one case there is a phrase used by 4Q-LXX ("that which comes forth from thy mouth"), which expands upon the single word ("His word") in the MT—with a significant difference in the suffix pronoun (a-2).

7. A more substantial variant may be found, which involves a different treatment of the same root (a-4). That is, MT's "three bullocks" appears in 4Q-LXX as "three year old cattle" (the noun is different in each case).

8. In at least one case it looks as if a medial letter missing in the MT has been preserved in the 4Q-LXX tradition, i. e., "May Yahweh *grant*" appears as "May Yahweh *reward* you" (y[e]šallēm in place of yāsēm)—a-12). Similarly, a verb that appears in 4Q as qal perfect (ḥattā[h]) replaces a grammatically impossible passive adjective (ḥattī[y]m) in the MT. LXX has a different verb from that of 4Q, but at least it holds to the same basic structure of the clause.

9. Only one case was noted of a significant additional phrase present in 4Q-LXX but missing in MT: 4Q tells us that Hannah and Elkanah went up "to Shiloh," whereas LXX gives it as *Sēlōm* (probably intended to refer to the same city, with an -m ending, like the Pool of *Siloam* as an equivalent to *Shīlo[a]ḥ*).

10. Attention has already been called to the MT sentence in 1 Samuel 2:22, which is of real importance in the context, but has not been preserved at all in either the LXX or the 4Q fragments.

In section *b* we found that there were nine instances in which the 4Q fragments differed significantly from both the MT and the LXX, where the latter two agreed with each other in reading the adverb "there" instead of 4Q's "before Yahweh" (b-1), or, in the introduction of a direct quote, 4Q uses "*answered* and said," whereas MT and LXX have merely "he said" (b-3). Again, 4Q uses an active participle where both MT and LXX have it as a passive (b-4). Or it inserts a noun subject lacking in both MT and LXX (b-5). Or it may supply specific information, such as Eli's actual age, where MT and LXX simply state that he was "very old" (b-6). But on the other hand, 4Q may omit a subordinate clause in a dialogue, where MT and LXX both preserve it (b-7). In another case the 4Q inserts a clause (partly lost in a lacuna) not found in MT-LXX, but then proceeds to omit the closing sentence in that same verse, which both MT and LXX preserve (b-8). The strange transposition of 2:13 and verse 14 to a position after verse 16 (according to MT and LXX) has already been discussed at length (b-9). All of these examples serve to underline the observation that the affinity of the Qumran fragments to the Septuagint should not be overemphasized, for the peculiarities occasionally found in 4Q indicate that its tradition was somewhat complicated if not actually erratic.

As to the list of seven instances in which all three traditions differ from one another, some of them involve minor insertions or deletions that do not materially affect the sense of the passage (c-1, c-2, c-5, c-7). 4Q may specify by inserting the noun referred to only by a pronoun in the MT (c-4), or omitted altogether in LXX. In one instance 4Q clears up grammatical problems involving gender of the subject or of the possessor, which are presented by the MT, whereas LXX clears this up by using still different pronouns from either 4Q or MT (c-6).

From all of the preceding data we may draw the conclusion that 4Q represents a somewhat different text-tradition from that which underlies the MT, and in a majority of instances it favors the LXX where it differs from the MT. For the most part, however, the deviations from the MT do not necessarily demonstrate a closer fidelity to the presumed original text than the MT does. In other words, there is little to indicate that LXX or 4Q are textually superior to the MT itself. Yet on the other hand, there is a small number of cases where 4Q and LXX agree in a reading that seems definitely superior to that of the MT where the latter presents a definite problem. In such cases, a carefully controlled use of the 4Q-LXX data may lead the textual critic to a valid and helpful correction of the MT reading. Yet it should be borne in mind that the LXX did not originate until the

third-century B.C., and the 4QSam^a fragments appear in a first-century
hand. (The 4QSam^b fragments may have been copied down in the third
century.) Therefore, the focal point of manuscript data from non-
Masoretic (or non-Sopherim) sources is not early enough to help us to
establish improved readings where mistakes crept into the Masoretic
tradition earlier than the third century. Thus, in the much-discussed
textual problem of 1 Samuel 13:1, where the numeral is completely missing from Saul's age when he became king, neither 4Q nor LXX (apart
from one uncertain figure of "30" that may have stood in the Lucianic
recension) furnish any compensation for this loss. (Origen's Hexapla
omits this verse altogether; some Lucianic witnesses do the same, and the
Syriac Peshitta gives the figure as "21.") Therefore, we should not expect
either the 4Q tradition nor that of the Septuagint to deliver more correc-
tive insight for MT textual problems that would have been retrievable by
the third century B. C. Nor is it justifiable to grant the prima facie pre-
sumption in favor of the LXX where it differs from the MT, as some
text-critics seem inclined to do—that is, where the Septuagintal reading
pleases them personally more than the wording of the Masoretic text.
This type of criterion is altogether unscientific, and the Qumran data do
not furnish any real support for such a cavalier procedure.

GENERAL SURVEY OF THE TYPES OF DISCREPANCY BETWEEN MT AND LXX

APPARENT MISUNDERSTANDING OF HEBREW WORDS, OR IGNORANCE OF THEIR MEANING

Passing from a detailed consideration of the relationship to the 4Q
fragments, we should point out certain definite characteristics of 1
Samuel in the Septuagint suggesting that its textual witness should be
treated with considerable caution and reserve. One factor that occasionally comes to the fore is the imperfect acquaintance shown by the
Alexandrian Jewish translators toward the Hebrew vocabulary of this
book.

1:24 The word *nēbel* (which probably referred to a ten-stringed harp) is
not translated but merely transliterated as *nebel* in the Greek. Conceivably, this was a loan word adopted into Hellenistic Greek from Hebrew,
and as such it may have found its way into the everyday usage of Greek-
speaking Jews. This would be analogous to our employment of the
Ashkenazic Hebrew term *kosher*. Similarly, we find in 5:4 the Greek
transliteration *ammapheth* for the Hebrew *hammiptān* ("the threshold").
Yet it should be noted that this word is preceded by *ta emprosthia*, which
means "the front parts," and may therefore have been intended as the

translation of *hammiptān,* followed by the transliterated Hebrew word itself, as if intended to be put in parentheses. This would constitute a type of gloss adopted right into the text itself.

As for examples of words that were seriously misinterpreted, we have in 7:16 the description of Samuel's activity—that he used to judge Israel *en pasi tois hagiazomenois toutois* ("in all these holy [places ?]"). This may possibly suggest a different Hebrew word in the *Vorlage,* but the MT has *hamm ͨqāmō ʷt haʾēlle ͪ,* which means "all these places"—possibly referring to cultic centers. (Cf. the Arabic *maqāmun,* "shrine"). A similar ambiguity arises in connection with 8:3, where the MT's *wayyiṭṭū ʷ . . . àh ͨ rē ʸ habbeṣa ͨ* ("And they turned away after gain") appears in LXX as "They inclined after the completion" *(eklinan opisō tēs synteleias). Synteleia,* "end" or "completion," makes no sense at all in this context. J. F. Schleusner *(Lexicon in LXX,* ii. 194) suggests that it means here a sum of money lent out at interest, on the analogy of the Arabic *biḍā ͨatun* ("goods, merchandise"), but it is extremely doubtful whether any reader, Hebrew or Arab, would ever have gotten such a meaning out of *beṣa ͨ* or its Arabic cognate. As for the word *mō ʷ ͨēd* in 9:24, the Septuagint rendering of *kî ʸ lam-mō ʷ ͨēd* as "testimony" *(martyrion)* is clearly impossible. *Mō ʷ ͨēd* is derived from the root *yā ͨad* ("appoint"), not from *ͨū ʷd* ("be a witness"). In the case of 5:10, where the Lord is said to have afflicted the Philistines of Gath *ba ͨpōlī ʸ m* ("with tumors"), the LXX rendering of *eis hedras* (on their *seats*")—whether this referred to their anuses or not—is certainly wide of the mark. (Oddly enough, The LXX verse goes on to interpolate: *kai epoiēsan hoi Geththaioi heautois hedras* ("And the Gittites made seats for themselves"—which would normally mean that they proceeded to build a new set of chairs for them to sit on!)

THE SEPTUAGINTAL TENDENCY TOWARD EXPANSION OR INTERPOLATION

In a sense, the wording of this heading involves a prejudgment in favor of the superior accuracy of the MT, and it must be admitted that it is theoretically possible in some of these cases that it is the MT that has failed to include words that were contained in the autographon, but which have been preserved in the LXX. But a careful survey of all such instances leads to an overall impression that the LXX has resorted to embellishment or dramatic emphasis at a later, secondary level.

In some cases this point may seem arguable, as in 1:11, where Hannah is quoted by the LXX as saying, *Adōnai kyrie elōai sabaōth* ("O Lord, Lord, my God, Sabaoth"), as over against the MT's less ostentatious *Yahwe ͪ ṣ ͤ bāʾōt* ("O Yahweh of hosts"). Note that in 1:20 another *Sabaōth* appears after "Lord," whereas the MT has simply *kî ʸ mēYahwe ͪ š ͤʾltī ʸw* ("For from Yahweh I have asked for him").

Occasionally there is a tendency on the part of the LXX to insert a participle for emphasis, equivalent to the Hebrew infinitive absolute, where such is lacking in the MT. The example of *ḥāṭō'* in 2:25 was already noted in a-19, where it found support from the 4Q. But in the clause following, where the MT has simply, "For Yahweh was pleased (*ḥāpēṣ*) to put them to death," the LXX again slips in a participle: *hoti boulomenos ebouleto Kyrios diaphtheirai autous* ("For the Lord firmly purposed to destroy them").

In other cases there are entire phrases or clauses added to the text that may go back to a tradition akin to that of the 4Q manuscript. For example, in 5:5 there is a rather awkwardly worded statement concerning the avoidance of setting foot on the threshold of the temple of Dagan in Ashdod: "For they step clear over it" (*hoti hyperbainontes hyperbainousin*) when they enter that sanctuary for worship. Again, in 6:1, after the words "... six months", the LXX gives this interesting bit of information (inferrable from vv. 4-5): "and their land bred mice/rats." In 7:14, after mentioning the stone that Samuel set up midway between Ekron and Gath (which the LXX records as "Ashkalon and Azob"), the Greek version adds, "... and Israel got back their boundary from the hand of the Philistines." Then the sentence finishes with a clause that agrees with the MT.

As already noted in connection with the discussion of the 4Q fragments, the LXX occasionally inserts the antecedent noun where the MT is content with a mere pronoun. Thus in 9:24 the MT reads: "And he set (it) before Saul, and he said, 'Behold, the portion-set-aside (*hanniš'ar*) has been set before you.'" The LXX construes the pronouns as follows: "And Samuel said to Saul, 'Behold the portion-set-aside (*to hypoleimma*), set it down before you and eat!"

Another type of expansion involves a gloss that is absorbed right into the text itself. Thus in 10:5 the MT reads: "... the hill where the garrison (or "pillars"?) of the Philistines is" (*gibᵉ'at'ᵃ šer-šām nᵉṣīᵘ bēᵘ Pᵉlištīᵘm*). For this the LXX reads: "... the hill where the monument (*anastēma*— reading it as singular!) of the Philistines is, there is Nasib the Philistine." In other words, the transcription *Nasib* from the Hebrew, *nᵉṣīᵘb* or *nᵉṣīᵘbēᵘ*, has been preserved along with the translation equivalent, "monument." This trait strongly indicates a later, interpretive form of the text rather than an original, independent *Vorlage*.

THE SEPTUAGINTAL UNCERTAINTY AS TO THE SPELLING OR VOCALIZATION OF NAMES

It seems quite certain that the Alexandrian Jews who translated 1 Samuel were quite uncertain of the proper reading of many of the names of people and places occurring in the historical narrative. Furthermore, their uncertainty often suggests a most imperfect grasp of the etymology

of those names bordering upon an unscholarly grasp of Hebrew nomen-
clature such as one might expect of mere tyros who had no Hebrew background. Sometimes a proper name is mistakenly derived from a common
noun (as in the case of the Nasib just cited above), for we find in 5:4 an
Amapheth in the LXX that does not appear as a name in the MT, but
seems rather to have been garbled from *hammiptān* (the doorsill)—for
which there is also the glossated equivalent *emprosthia*. Or else there is a
confusion between consonants that resemble each other in shape, such as
Sared for Hebrew *ṣᵉrōʷr* (*rēsh* confused with *daleth*). Or else, there is a
more serious garbling from a good Semitic pattern into a non-Semitic
barbarism, such as *Selkha* for *Shᵉlīshah* in 9:4 (in this case the Alexandrinus reads correctly as *Salissa*). *Baithōn* in 13:5 and 14:23 is perhaps
understandable from the Hebrew spelling of *Bēʸt ʾĀwen* (only the *aleph*
and its vowel have been lost), but *Melkhol* is a markedly unsemitic deviation for *Mīykal* in 14:49, and *Ephermem* is an egregious garbling of
ʾEpes-dammīʸm in 17:1. For the name of the Philistine king of Gath,
Ākīʸš, LXX comes up with the surprising form *Ankhous* (which conceivably could go back to an authentic oral tradition, provided the Hebrew
yodh should have been *waw*). But *Messara* for *Mᵉṣādōʷt* in 23:19 is a
rather unsemitic variant resting upon another confusion between *resh*
and *daleth*. It is interesting that the same name is spelled *Maserem* five
verses before (v. 14). But *Sadaiem* in 24:3 is hopelessly garbled for *ṣūʷrēʸ*
hayyᵉ ᶜelīʸm (be it noted that in this case the Vaticanus reads *Eddaiem,* the
Alexandrinus *Aeiamein,* and Origen's fifth column *Abialeim*; the LXX is
hopelessly corrupt in each of these witnesses). So important a personage
as *ʾAbigayil,* the wife of David, is regularly referred to as *Abigaia* in
LXX, as if the final *lamed* was completely forgotten by the Alexandrian
translators.

The point of all of these examples (which could be multiplied many
times over in the later chapters of 1 Samuel) is that the LXX shows such a
careless or uncertain transmission of proper names in the case of at least
a fifth of the total list of names discoverable in the entire book, as to
suggest that it is somewhat unreliable as a witness to the non-Masoretic
Hebrew text tradition from which it was derived. Therefore, it will usually require some corroboration from other sources or from some special
linguistic factor to serve as a reliable basis for correction of the Masoretic
text. In 1 Samuel, then, as for the other books of the Old Testament it will
be best to adhere to the MT reading wherever it makes good sense in the
context, even though a deviant Septuagintal reading might also seem
plausible. Only where the MT reading shows an obvious difficulty or
confusion should an apparently more trouble-free reading in the LXX be
adopted—and even then, only if the surrounding context of the LXX
seems to be perfectly straightforward and free of confusion.

9

The WAW-Consecutive with "Imperfect" in Biblical Hebrew: Theoretical Studies and its Use in Amos

Thomas J. Finley

THOMAS J. FINLEY (M.Div., Talbot Theological Seminary; M.A., Ph.D., University of California, Los Angeles) is associate professor and chairman of Semitics and Old Testament at Talbot Theological Seminary, La Mirada, California.

The versions, both ancient and modern, often use a variety of tenses for the same Hebrew verb form. In Psalm 3:4 [Heb. 5a] the verb אֶקְרָא (’eqrā’), an imperfect, is followed by וַיַּעֲנֵנִי (wayya‘ănēnî), a waw-consecutive with imperfect.[1] The Syriac translates both with perfect forms.[2] The Septuagint uses the aorist for both verbs, whereas the Vulgate uses the future tense in both instances. Similar differences exist among modern versions. The King James Version reads, "I cried . . . and he heard me." The New English Bible has, "I cry aloud . . . and he answers me," but the New American Standard Bible translates, "I was crying . . . and He answered me." This variety of translations emphasizes the controversy over the nature of the Hebrew verb system that has continued into modern times.[3]

Some recent studies of the Hebrew verb have demonstrated that a variety of factors are important in the determination of verbal function. In addition to verb morphology there are factors such as word order,[4] the use of particles,[5] the lexical content of the verb,[6] and literary genre (poetry versus prose). Also important is a consideration of diachronic and synchronic studies. Ideally, the synchronic study seeks to describe the linguistic nature of a corpus of texts that is homogeneous with respect to time. This means that the entire Old Testament, which covers a span of at least a millennium, is scarcely ideal for synchronic study. A diachronic

241

study then takes the results of synchronic studies of various periods and reconstructs a linguistic history.

The restricted environment of the *waw*-consecutive with imperfect (hereafter generalized as *wayyiqtōl*) makes it a convenient form for study. It has a distinct form and occurs in initial position within its clause. In prose it normally occurs in the sequential narration of past events. In this article we hope to demonstrate that insight into the nature of *wayyiqtōl* can elucidate the various functions of Hebrew verbal forms. More explicitly, we will attempt to align the form *wayyiqtōl* with the perfect (suffix conjugation) form in terms of its function. That function can be most generally described as "perfective aspect," a term that will be defined later in the chapter.

MORPHOLOGY

A major insight into the form *wayyiqtōl* that has resulted from studies in both comparative Semitics and in Hebrew verb morphology and syntax is that the *yiqtōl* part of *wayyiqtōl* has a separate origin from the ordinary imperfect without the conjunction. That is, there were actually two distinct forms of the verb constructed with pronominal prefixes. One developed into the ordinary imperfect, and the other was used with *wayyiqtōl*. Divergence of form would lend support to a theory of divergence of function. So at the outset it can be seen that even though the form *yiqtōl* has imperfect function, *wayyiqtōl* may or may not have that function. Three lines of argumentation support this contention. First, the form *wayyiqtōl* is often distinct from the ordinary imperfect, not only because of the conjunction but also because the prefixed verbal part itself is often different. Second, comparative Semitic studies, especially in Akkadian and early Canaanite, point to the existence of a second prefix conjugation (see n. 1) in those languages with similarities to *wayyiqtōl* in form and function. Finally, a form of the imperfect without the conjunction is used in early Hebrew poetry in contexts with no imperfect functions associated with it.

MORPHOLOGY OF THE PREFIX CONJUGATION

From a morphological viewpoint, there are actually three forms of the prefix conjugation (PC). These may be described as "simple," "short," and "long." Many verbs do not have all three forms (because of formal overlap), but the Hiphil stem of the regular verb contains all three and may be used as a model: (1) simple—יַקְטִיל (*yaqtîl*); (2) short—יַקְטֵל (*yaqtēl*); (3) long—אַקְטִילָה (*ʾaqtîlâ*). Short forms are normally limited to the third singular and the second masculine singular. They occur regularly with the Hiphil stem, in the Qal and Hiphil stems of *ayin-waw/yod* roots (middle weak), and in all stems of *lamed-he* roots (final weak) except the Pual and Hophal. The long form may occur with the first person of any class of verb except *lamed-he* (where it overlaps the simple form).[7]

In terms of function, the following general statements may be made: (1) The short form is used for jussive meaning in the third person. (2) The *wayyiqtōl* form is almost always constructed with a short form whenever one is available.[8] (3) The long form is used for cohortative meaning. (4) The long form may rarely combine with *wayyiqtōl* in the first person (resulting in וָאֶקְטְלָה [*wā'eqtᵉlâ*]).[9] (5) The form *wayyiqtōl* is never used for jussive or cohortative meaning. (6) The simple form has the functions that are traditionally classified as "imperfect."

A morphological study of the prefix conjugation reveals, then, that when used with *wayyiqtōl* it differs in form from that used for imperfect functions. The short form of the prefix conjugation serves for both *wayyiqtōl* and the jussive, though *wayyiqtōl* never functions as a jussive. Another factor to keep in mind for the discussion that follows is that Hebrew *wayyiqtōl* occurs most frequently (though not always) in a past narrative context.

COMPARATIVE SEMITICS

The use of comparative Semitics to understand the Hebrew verbal system owes much to Hans Bauer. His reconstruction of the history of the Semitic verbal system in 1910 casts a long shadow on contemporary discussions.[10] W. Gross in 1976 could state that Bauer's reference to the "archaic style" of the form *wayyiqtōl* has been thoroughly confirmed by the Ugaritic texts.[11] In light of the importance of Bauer's study, his main results will be presented here.

At one point in proto-Semitic, according to Bauer, a prefix conjugation (**yaqtul*) functioned as a perfect participle and a suffix conjugation (**qatala*) functioned as a present participle. In a later stage of West Semitic (including Arabic, Ethiopic, Canaanite, and Aramaic) a reversal of functions developed. The form **yaqtul* was used for the present, future, and imperfect; **qatala* served as a perfect (largely past functions and the "perfective" aspect; see below for further definition). But when the *waw*-consecutive form is used, whether with the prefix conjugation or with the suffix conjugation, the more archaic functions are preserved in Hebrew. Therefore the form *wayyiqtōl* has functions that can be described as "perfect," resulting from a development of the ancient **yiqtol* as perfect participle.[12]

COMPARISON WITH AKKADIAN

G. R. Driver, the son of S. R. Driver, expanded on Bauer's views.[13] For him, however, the different Hebrew forms were not proto-Semitic versus West Semitic but West Semitic versus East Semitic (Akkadian). The use of *waw*-consecutive, according to Driver, is due to the composite nature of Hebrew from its earliest stages. That is, it represents a combination of East Semitic and Northwest Semitic elements. *Waw*-consecutive with the suffix conjugation is the same as the Akkadian conjunction *u* plus a suffix conjugation known as the "permansive,"[14] and *wayyiqtōl* is equivalent to the Akkadian enclitic *-ma* suffixed to a verb plus a following preterit form (a prefix conjugation).[15] Driver seized upon the preterit function of Akkadian *iprus* and its formal similarity to the Hebrew prefix conjugation to posit similarity of function for the Hebrew *wayyiqtōl*. That is, they both have preterit (narrative past) function, and they both consist of a pronominal element prefixed to a verbal root with a vowel between the second and third root letters.

COMPARISON WITH OLD CANAANITE

Akkadian is only distantly related to Hebrew. Especially in the verb, Akkadian shows strong divergences from all of the other Semitic languages. More weighty comparisons can be made between Hebrew and its close relative, old Canaanite as reflected in the Ugaritic texts and the Amarna letters.[16]

Ugaritic has a prefix conjugation (*yqtl*) and a suffix conjugation (*qtl*). The form *yqtl* is marked for different moods by vocalic endings: *-u* for indicative; *-a* for subjunctive; and no ending (zero ending) for a form that functions as the jussive in the third person but that occurs in all three persons.

With reference to verbal function, a division is made by both Cyrus Gordon and S. Segert between nonliterary prose and literary texts. For the prose texts these scholars agree that the distinction between the verbs is basically that of tense, *yqtl* for the present/future and *qtl* for the past.[17] For the poetic texts, however, the same tense oppositions do not hold true. As Gordon stated: "In fact *yqtl* is the regular narrative form [in poetry] and we shall often translate it as a historical present . . . ."[18] He adds, "It seems that *yaqtul* was also used to indicate the past [in poetry] as well as the jussive."[19] Gordon's illustrative example is based on a final weak root. Such forms presumably had a *-y* or *-w* (the third root letter) when the form ended in a vowel (*yaqtulu* or *yaqtula*), but the *-y* or *-w* was elided for the *yaqtul* form. Segert also lists a number of cases from poetic texts of final weak verbs without final -*y* which occur in a past narrative context and cannot be jussives. An example is *ybk,* normalized as *yabki,* which can be translated as a historical present, "he weeps" (I Aqht 173, Gordon's numbering).[20]

D. Rudolf Meyer went so far as to call Ugaritic *yaqtul* a "preterit/ jussive." He then went on to relate the preterit function of *yaqtul* to Hebrew *wayyiqtōl*.[21] That is, both are short forms of a prefix conjugation. Ugaritic *yaqtul* is short compared to *yaqtulu,* and Hebrew *wayyiqtōl* uses the short form of the prefix conjugation if it is available. The syntactic connection between the Ugaritic and Hebrew forms would consist in the use of the short form in both for jussive and past narrative (preterit) functions.

The main difficulty with Meyer's analysis is that both Ugaritic *yaqtul* and *yaqtulu* may express the past narrative in poetic contexts.[22] It is still unclear for Ugaritic exactly how these forms differ in past context.

The Amarna letters also offer some important insights into old Canaanite. However, two things must be kept in mind. First, there are dialectal differences within the Amarna letters.[23] Second, the language of these letters is neither fully Canaanite nor fully Akkadian. It was a language that arose through the need for political and commercial contact between various states with different spoken languages. An additional point, which is not always stated clearly, is that the Amarna letters contain more than simply Canaanite "glosses" (explicit Canaanite forms inserted next to Akkadian forms). They also contain many elements of Canaanite structure. Nevertheless, one cannot assume automatically that a given form is pure Canaanite rather than a hybrid.

Moran and Rainey have done the most extensive work with regard to the verbal system of the Amarna letters, especially in terms of Canaanite or Northwest Semitic reflections.[24] Their conclusions are: (1) the verbal form *yaqtulu* is used for present-future or past iterative; (2) *yaqtul* is used for the jussive or preterit; and (3) *yaqtula* is used for what Moran calls the "emphatic jussive" (probably a form which is related to the Hebrew cohortative). Whether the scribe used a form with doubled second root letter was irrelevant.[25] The only factor that determined tense was the contrast between the short form (*yaqtul*) and the long form (*yaqtulu*).

Here there is apparently good evidence for a Canaanite preterit-jussive *yaqtul* that contrasted with a long form used for present-future or past iterative functions. However, the cautions expressed above must be remembered. This is especially true since the "preterit-jussive" overlaps Akkadian *iprus* in form. Nevertheless, the Amarna materials do give additional evidence for a comparison between Hebrew, early Canaanite, and Akkadian of the following type:

	Short Prefix Conjugation	Long Prefix Conjugation
Hebrew	וַיִּקְטֹל (*wayyiqṭōl*)	יִקְטֹל (*yiqṭōl*)
Akkadian	*iprus*	(*iparras?*)
Ugaritic	*yaqtul*	*yaqtulu*
Amarna	*yaqtul*	*yaqtulu*

POETIC SYNTAX

The Hebrew prefix conjugation without *waw* can be used in certain poetic texts in past context without any idea of frequentative or habitual action.[26] Most recently this has been demonstrated by David Robertson. His method was to take poetic sections with clearly past context and analyze the use of the prefix and suffix conjugations (e.g., in Exod. 15 and Amos 2:9–12).[27]

What Robertson has shown is that in isolated poetic passages the Hebrew prefix conjugation without *waw* may have the same functional relationship to old Canaanite *yaqtul* as Hebrew *wayyiqṭōl*. However, one aspect that Robertson did not consider was the distinction between simple and short forms of the Hebrew prefix conjugation. Gross attempted to correct this deficiency in Robertson's analysis. He showed that the short forms tend to occur at the beginning of a clause, whereas the simple forms tend to occur within a clause. For example, the short form is used in Deuteronomy 32:8, "He fixed (יַצֵּב, *yaṣṣēb*) the boundaries of peoples." Two temporal clauses precede the clause in question, but within its own clause the short verbal form (the simple form would be יַצִּיב, *yaṣṣîb*) occurs first. Contrast this with Deuteronomy 32:14, "and blood of grapes *you drank* (תִּשְׁתֶּה, *tishteh*) for wine." The simple form (the short form would be תֵּשְׁתְּ, *tēsht*) follows the object. Gross found no exceptions to this tendency for the simple forms, but he did find one case of a short form that was not in first position (Deut. 32:18). Gross cautiously proposed that the simple prefix conjugation in non-initial position be described as something like a "historical imperfective aspect." The short form in initial position, on the other hand, should be connected with *wayyiqṭōl*, a form to which Gross assigned perfective function (see below for a definition of the term "perfective").[28]

EVALUATION OF THE EVIDENCE

There is a morphological distinction within the Hebrew prefix conjugation that corresponds to a similar situation in Akkadian, Ugaritic, and some of the Amarna letters. At least from a formal viewpoint we are justified in positing a historical relationship. In Akkadian and old

Canaanite the formal distinction is matched by a syntactic or functional distinction. It would seem likely that there is also a functional distinction between the short and simple forms in Hebrew, a distinction that goes beyond the generally recognized jussive (short)/indicative (simple) distinction. That is, the non-jussive use of the short prefix conjugation in *wayyiqtōl* or without *waw* in some early poetry contrasts with the simple prefix conjugation in syntactic function.

One weakness of presentations that merely assume that the simple form and the form *wayyiqtōl* express the same "imperfect" function is their failure to account for the historical data. For example, S. R. Driver felt it necessary to explain *wayyiqtōl* by the idea of "nascent" action in the imperfect. A form such as " . . . וַיֹּאמֶר [*wayyō'mer*] is then properly not *and he said*, but *and he proceeded-to-say*."[29] But Driver did not offer any syntactic evidence for this statement, although he did attempt to account for the formal distinctions within the "imperfect" (prefix conjugation) as historical development within Hebrew. He saw the short form *wayyiqtōl* as developing from recession of the accent due to the "heavy prefix [*waw* plus *dagesh*]."[30]

Naturally, the establishment of a formal similarity between Hebrew *wayyiqtōl*, Akkadian *iprus*, and old Canaanite *yaqtul* does not establish the function of the Hebrew form. In fact, it does not even establish that there was not an assimilation of function in originally distinct forms occasioned by the similarity in morphology (in many forms the morphological distinction between short and simple is neutralized). The function of *wayyiqtōl* can be established only by syntactic analysis of individual texts.

STRUCTURAL ANALYSIS

It is important to remember that elements of a language form part of a larger structure. A form like *wayyiqtōl* must not be studied in isolation but in terms of its relationship to the rest of the system.

BASIC OPPOSITIONS

Much of the controversy about the Hebrew verb still concerns the basic oppositions expressed by the suffix and prefix conjugations. That is, do these forms differ in terms of past/non-past, completed action/incomplete action, or in some other way?

It is crucial to analyze exactly the different functions that might be present in the various Hebrew verb forms. Three terms that are frequently applied to studies of the Hebrew verb are tense, aspect, and the German term *Aktionsart*, or "kind of action." Careful definition of these terms will clarify exactly what sorts of oppositions are being proposed by various grammarians. Actually, part of the problem with many studies of the Hebrew verb is the lack of explicit definitions.

TENSE

Tense relates situations (actions, events, or conditions) in terms of time. If a situation is related to the moment of speaking, absolute tenses such as past, present, and future are used. A relative tense, such as the English present participle, relates a situation to another situation besides the moment of speaking ("when *walking* down the road, I often meet Harry").[31]

ASPECT

The term *aspect* is often used rather loosely. In this chapter we will follow the definition given by Comrie: "Aspects are different ways of viewing the internal temporal constituency of a situation."[32] By this definition, aspect is a subjective category. The speaker may wish to view a situation from the outside. That is, he may desire to simply state the action as a whole without referring to its progress or course (internal temporal constituency). For this viewpoint or aspect, Comrie uses the term *perfective*. On the other hand, the speaker may desire to view an action from the inside, observing its various stages in progress. In this case, the aspect is called *imperfective*. A crude analogy might be made between a snapshot and a motion picture. If it were possible to capture an entire situation over a period of time on a snapshot, that would be a perfective view. A motion picture of the same situation would provide an imperfective view of it. Comrie gives the following example: "John read that book yesterday; while he was reading it, the postman came."[33] The verb "read" simply states the totality of what happened and could be described as perfective, in opposition to the progressive form "was reading." The latter verb inserts the speaker into the same situation and is imperfective. Aspect is subjective in the sense that the viewpoint chosen depends on the speaker. This is not to say, of course, that there are not objective factors that help determine the speaker's choice. In the above example, the desire to relate the action of reading to the arrival of the postman determined the use of the progressive form.

Comrie deliberately used the term *perfective* as opposed to *perfect*. The latter term is used by grammarians of both English and Greek to refer to "the continuing relevance of a previous situation" and therefore expresses "a relation between two time points."[34] Hence the perfect, which includes the past perfect, the present perfect, and the future perfect, is technically not an aspect as defined above. Comrie gives a good illustration of how the perfect relates two time points: "Thus one of the possible differences between *John has arrived* and *John arrived* is that the former indicates persistence of the result of John's arrival, i.e., that he is still here, whereas the second does not."[35] In the remainder of the chapter the term *perfect* will refer to this special sense, while the term *perfective* will be saved for the aspectual distinction discussed above.

AKTIONSART

Whereas aspect is a subjective category, *Aktionsart,* or "kind of action," refers to an objective description of the actual situation. Brockelmann introduced this important distinction into Semitics in 1951.[36] According to P. Kustár, *Aktionsart* (which he calls *Aktio*) refers to the perception of an event in terms of its beginning, its continuation, or its completion, and specifies the change of the action during its occurrence in relation to objective time.[37] That is, if a situation is divided into beginning, middle, and end, *Aktionsart* refers to the objective perception of one of these points or the relation between them. For example, the categories of ingressive ("he began to sing") and frequentative ("he used to sing every day") are categories of *Aktionsart.*

INTERRELATIONSHIPS

Tense, aspect, perfect, and *Aktionsart* are not mutually exclusive for the Hebrew verb, though one of them may be primary. An example of the relationship between tense and aspect is seen in some African languages with aspectual markers. The imperfective forms are interpreted as present tense when there is no contextual reference to time, whereas the perfective is interpreted as past.[38]

Aktionsart has an important relation to aspect. Comrie refers to the "inherent meaning" of a verb. The inherent meaning determines various categories of *Aktionsart,* which can be expressed by a given aspect. For example, some verbs can be described as "punctual" in that they do not describe situations that have a duration in time. The verb *cough* can express such a situation. "He coughed," could mean a single cough. But an imperfective form, "he was coughing," could only mean a series of individual coughs. It could not refer to the inside of a single cough, because the individual cough is a point action.[39] The speaker can still choose to describe the situation from the outside ("he coughed five times") or from within ("he was coughing"), but the inherent meaning of the verb determines the *Aktionsart* expressed by the aspect (imperfective aspect for iterative *Aktionsart*).

Sometimes the contrast between the Hebrew suffix conjugation and prefix conjugation is described in terms of "completed" or "incompleted" action.[40] Actually, this distinction applies only to situations that include a process that leads up to a specific terminal point. Comrie describes such situations as "telic." The sentence "John is singing" is not telic, because it does not imply a specific point at which John will finish singing. "John is singing a song," however, has as its terminal point the end of the song and is therefore a telic situation. The perfective aspect used for a telic situation implies the completion of the process, whereas the imperfective aspect implies that the process is not yet finished.[41] Because of this interaction of aspect, *Aktionsart,* and inherent meaning, it can be only partially true to describe the opposition between prefix and suffix conjugations in Hebrew as one of completed versus incompleted action. For situations that are not telic, the contrast would have to be different. For example, stative verbs in the suffix conjugation do not imply completed action. The form יָדַעְתִּי (*yādaʿtî*) can be translated "I know" or "I knew," but even the latter translation does not imply that at some point I ceased to know.

APPLICATION TO THE HEBREW SYSTEM

Despite much evidence to the contrary from biblical passages, several scholars still prefer to describe the Hebrew system as basically one of tense. Blake was able to restrict the form *wayyiqtōl* to the past only by textual "correction" of numerous passages.[42] M. Silverman's statement that "the simple past [suffix conjugation] and the *waw* past [*wayyiqtōl*] always refer to past tense in the broadest sense" and that "the simple future [prefix conjugation] and the *waw* future [*waw* with suffix conjugation], correspondingly, always refer to present or future time in the widest sense" has to be very "wide" indeed to encompass the multitude of apparent contradictions.[43] Tense does seem to be a factor on the basis of secondary functions or on the basis of contextual factors, but many interpreters have had a hard time with classifying the system as fundamentally one of tense.

C. Brockelmann applied aspect to Semitic languages in general. He used the term "cursive" for the imperfective and "constative" for the perfective. In his application of aspect to biblical Hebrew itself, he pointed out a tendency for the aspectual system to develop into a tense system in a later stage, largely under Aramaic influence.[44] S. Segert also proposed a historical development within biblical Hebrew from an aspectual to a tense system.[45] Naturally, such historical development can be verified only by detailed studies in passages clearly differentiated by date of composition and literary genre (poetry versus prose).

Two recent studies that are based on a structural approach to language have also taken an aspectual approach to the Hebrew verb system. F. Rundgren's book *Das althebräische Verbum; Abriss des Aspektlehre* is a theoretical study that places the various forms of the Hebrew verb within a structural system. For Rundgren, Hebrew *wayyiqtōl* expresses the perfective aspect along with the suffix conjugation. Stylistic reasons determine the choice between *wayyiqtōl* or the suffix conjugation.[46]

Rundgren's definition of aspect is based on a principle that he terms "privative" oppositions. Two terms are in a privative opposition if one of the terms contains a characteristic lacking in the other. The term that contains the characteristic is "marked," whereas the other term is "unmarked."[47] The terms *man* and *woman* would form a privative opposition in English. *Man* may imply the male gender, or it may be used in a generic sense to include both man and woman. *Woman,* on the other hand, always implies the female gender. *Man,* when used in the sense of male may then be considered the negative member of the opposition. Its gender is non-female. "*Man*" in the generic sense is the neutral member of the opposition.

For Rundgren, the imperfective aspect is marked because of its implicit reference to the internal development of a situation. A punctual situation (see above) expressed by the perfective aspect is the negative member of the opposition (non-imperfective), because it is characterized by a lack of internal development. But there is also a neutral value for the perfective aspect in that it may simply state a verbal idea with no reference one way or the other to its internal development. Since the perfective has both a negative and a neutral value with respect to the imperfective, it is the unmarked member of the opposition whereas the imperfective is marked.[48]

Rundgren attempted to show that *wayyiqtōl,* like the suffix conjugation, has both a negative and a neutral value, and is therefore to be classified as perfective in aspect.[49]

A second structural study is the recent work by W. Gross, which is based on an examination of *wayyiqtōl* in poetic passages.[50] An important distinction that Gross makes is between "individual" and "general" circumstances. Individual circumstances refer to specific, individual acts, whereas general circumstances refer to general situations.[51] "He is eating his supper" would be an individual circumstance; "he eats three meals a day" would be general. Gross points out that *wayyiqtōl,* like the suffix conjugation, cannot be used to designate individual circumstances in present time. The only exceptions are with a special subclass of verbs that express emotions, or feelings (e.g., *'bl* "to mourn").[52]

Inherent meaning is obviously important here. A specific situation can be viewed from the outside most naturally when it is past with reference to the speaker. To look at it from within is to make it present to the speaker. Emotions would form an exception, since they can be conceived of more as conditions than actions that have an unfolding development. A general situation, on the other hand, lends itself to a summary statement in the perfective, regardless of its time point in relation to the speaker. It follows that Gross's conclusion, if valid, is evidence for classifying the suffix conjugation and *wayyiqtōl* as perfective.

Further, Gross shows that the specific functions of *wayyiqtōl* are aligned with the suffix conjugation in opposition to the prefix conjugation. There are a few restrictions on *wayyiqtōl*, however, that do not apply to the suffix conjugation. First, if progress or sequence from one action to another is emphasized, the form *wayyiqtōl* must be used. Progress is a frequent though not a necessary feature of *wayyiqtōl*. Second, *wayyiqtōl* cannot be used at the beginning of a section (וַיְהִי *way*ᵉ *hî*) being an exception, as in Esther 1:1 and the first verse of numerous other books, or for previousness to a past, present, or future situation. The usage of *wayyiqtōl* may be described, then, as follows:[53]

1. It designates individual past circumstances, mostly with progress, in the perfective aspect. Even when there is no progress it must be used if the verb occurs in a syndetic clause (the conjunction *waw* in *wayyiqtōl* makes the clause syndetic) in first position.

2. It can probably be used for "coincidence" (instantaneous action—see Num. 31:50).

3. In syndetic clauses with the verb in first position it can designate the present perfect (see Isa. 2:7).

4. It may stand for general present circumstances in situations of general experience if the verb is in first position in a syndetic clause (see Prov. 20:20). If there is progress, *wayyiqtōl* is obligatory. Examples occur only in poetry.

5. Expression of individual present circumstances is possible only for a small class of verbs such as those that express an emotion (see 2 Sam. 19:2).

Drawing on those studies that see aspect as basic to the Hebrew verbal system, we may outline the structure as follows:[54]

Perfective Aspect	*Imperfective Aspect*
Suffix Conjugation (SC)	Prefix Conjugation (PC)
waw +SC (?)	simple *waw* +PC
wayyiqtōl	*waw* +SC (?)

In the absence of context to the contrary, the perfective implies past time and the imperfective present or future time (non-past). The imperfective may express functions such as frequentative or progressive action. The perfective may be used to relate two time points in the sense of continuing relevance (past perfect, present perfect, future perfect). These conclusions will be tested by the analysis of an extended passage from one biblical author, namely the book of Amos.

SYNCHRONIC ANALYSIS OF AMOS

The book of Amos was chosen as a convenient section for synchronic study, yet it is not without its problems. Numerous interpreters have proposed that various sections of Amos are later additions, especially the "doxologies" (4:13; 5:8-9; 9:5-6), the concluding message of salvation (9:8b-15), and the third person narration of Amos's encounter with Amaziah (7:10-17). Such proposals are based on internal criteria that are somewhat subjective.[55] There is no substantive external evidence for the proposed additions. The doxologies may have come from hymns, which Amos incorporated into his work, so they may be chronologically prior to Amos.[56] H. W. Wolff proposed that 7:10-17 was added by a contemporary of Amos.[57] There is no insurmountable objection to saying that Amos composed the passage personally. In any case, a large portion of it quotes Amos directly. As for 9:8b-15, Soggin notes that "until a few years ago the text was usually explained as a late addition, but today there are many authors who argue for its authenticity."[58] It forms a fitting conclusion to the prophecies of judgment against both kingdoms (see 2:4-16), with ultimate salvation under the Davidic Messiah.

In order to understand the function of *wayyiqṭōl* in Amos, a study was made of the oppositions between the suffix conjugation (SC), the prefix conjugation (PC), *wayyiqṭōl, waw* with the suffix conjugation (W+SC), and simple *waw* with the prefix conjugation (W+PC). The oppositions will be presented in terms of word order, verbal functions, and clause relationships.

WORD ORDER

One fact that stands out about the use of verb forms in Amos is their distribution in terms of clause position. The results may be summarized as follows:

1. PC—never in clause-initial position.
2. SC—clause-initial position reserved for the beginning of a new syntactic section; otherwise SC never in clause-initial position.
3. *wayyiqṭōl*, W + SC, W + PC—always in clause-initial position.

The SC in clause-initial position occurs at the beginning of a new division in the text (marked by new paragraphs in the *New American Standard Bible* at 5:10, 21; 6:8; 8:7; and 9:1), in a direct quotation after its introductory phrase (5:2; 7:10; 8:2), with the resumption of narrative after a quotation (4:2; 7:3), and with two parallel expressions ("she has fallen" // "she lies forsaken," 5:2). In 4:10 there is an example of two SC forms in initial position, the second being asyndetically related to the first and followed by a clause with *wayyiqṭōl* (SC–SC-*wayyiqṭōl*). In this case the first two clauses are independent with no stress on which event happened first ("I sent a plague ... [and] I slew ... "). The third clause, however, reports a result of both events ("and I made the stench ... rise up").

VERBAL FUNCTIONS

The functions of the various verb forms will be examined by reference to the past, present, or future contexts in which they occur.

THE PREFIX CONJUGATION

The PC occurs mostly in a future or a present context (see 3:2, 7). It is also used for nonindicative concepts such as the prohibitive (2:12) and the subjunctive after telic conjunctions (5:14). The form W+PC also has nonindicative functions (only five examples—4:1; 5:14, 24 [jussive]; 8:5; and 9:1).

There is only one context that contains PC forms in the past, 4:7-9. All five PC verbs in this passage have a frequentative function, as recognized by the translations (e.g., the NASB and the NEB).

THE SUFFIX CONJUGATION

The SC may occur in a past, present, or future context. The results of the present study are as follows:

1. Past—very frequent
   a) Individual past action—"I saw" (9:1)
   b) Repeated action viewed as a whole—"they did not keep" (2:4)
   c) Present perfect—"have we not taken?" (6:13)
   d) Past perfect—"which you had made" (5:26)
2. Future—only one example, which is either a prophetic perfect or possibly a future perfect ("they will/will have cast forth," 8:3)
3. Present—not common
   a) With stative verbs—"know" (3:10; 5:12), "love" (4:5), "hate" (5:10, 21)
   b) General condition viewed as a whole—after a participle: "and

(who) turns deep darkness to mourning and *darkens* day to night,"
(5:8);[59] "harassers of the righteous, takers of a bribe, and the poor
in the gate *they turn aside*" (5:12).

WAW WITH THE SUFFIX CONJUGATION

The form W+SC is, like the PC, mostly limited to a future (1:4) or a
present context (6:1). Certain instances remain of the form in a past
context, and there are some uncertain contexts as well.

W+SC forms in a past context may be analyzed as follows:
1. Frequentative—"and I would send rain" (4:7); "and they would stag-
   ger" (4:8)
2. Ingressive—"and it began to consume" (7:4; Amos' response in verse
   8, "Please stop!" supports the ingressive interpretation)
3. Uncertain
   a) Individual past—"and he stifled" (1:11); "and it came about" (7:2)
   b) Progressive past—"and he was stifling" (1:11; see also 9:5).

The example in 7:2 is unusual in that the form וַיְהִי (*wayeḥî*) rather than
וְהָיָה (*weḥāyâ*) might have been expected. Also, the conjunction אִם (*'im*),
which follows normally, means "if" rather than "when". The closest
parallel to the meaning "when" occurs in Psalm 78:34. Wolff proposed
that these two forms are part of a gloss that extends from 1b to 2a, but
there is no textual support.[60]

Another uncertain context is 9:5, one of the doxology passages. There
are three verbs with W+SC form. If the "touching of the earth" refers to
some past event, the forms could be either for individual past events or for
progressive or frequentative action. If the initial participle refers to any
time that God touches the earth, then the W+SC forms would stand for a
general present situation. The context of 1:11 is clearly past, but the form
וְשִׁחֵת (*weshiḥēt*) could be taken as either an individual past ("and he
stifled") or a progressive past ("and he was stifling").

WAYYIQṬŌL

As for *wayyiqṭōl*, it may always occur in a past context in Amos, though
there are some uncertain instances. It can be demonstrated that the form
is always compatible with perfective rather than imperfective functions.
Examples of *wayyiqṭōl* for individual past situations are frequent (2:4 and
often throughout the chapter). Some specific passages require further
comment.

In 1:11 the verb וַיִּטְרֹף (*wayyiṭrōp*) is followed by לָעַד (*lā'ad*), which may
be translated "continually." Does this indicate progressive function for a
wayyiqṭōl form? In the following clause, which is in poetic parallelism, the
parallel expression has an SC form with the modifier נֶצַח (*neṣaḥ*), "per-

petually." The perfective aspect simply considers the situation as a whole, regardless of how long it continued.

The verb וַתַּגִּישׁוּן (wattaggîshûn) in 6:3 follows a participle and has been interpreted as a present.[61] The wayyiqtōl form might rather indicate a present perfect function, "(Woe) to (you) who thrust from your minds the calamitous day [the day of the LORD, 5:18-20], and you have brought near a rule [lit. "seat"] of violence."[62] The interpretations are similar in that analysis as a present perfect would allow for persistent results.

A similar situation applies to the first occurrence of a wayyiqtōl form in 9:5. If the preceding participle is taken as general, "He who touches the earth," then the wayyiqtōl form would also have to be a general present, "so that it melts." The reference may also be to a specific situation such as the earthquake mentioned in 1:1 ("He who touched the earth and it melted").[63]

A participle followed by wayyiqtōl occurs with exactly the same wording in both 5:8 and 9:6 (הַקֹּרֵא ... וַיִּשְׁפְּכֵם [haqqōrē᾽ ... wayyishpᵉkēm]). The phrase could refer to God's general activity of producing rain, with wayyiqtōl for a general present viewed as a whole. However, the use of the term שָׁפַךְ (šāpak) rather indicates a sudden and overwhelming action, and the reference is probably to the Noahic Flood.[64] The sense is then, "He who summoned the waters of the sea and then poured them out over the earth."

Two wayyiqtōl forms occur after a series of verbless clauses in 7:15. Amos reacted against the idea that he practiced prophecy as a profession in the sense that he did it according to the bidding of man.[65] There is no stress on past or present in his words, which may be paraphrased, "I am not now nor ever have been making my living by prophesying." The wayyiqtōl forms that follow stress the unique, divine aspect of his call. The LORD had commanded him to prophesy. How could he follow orders from Amaziah? "But the LORD took me ... and said to me." The grammatical relation is well-stated by Wolff: "In 7:15 an event of the past is referred to solely because it determines the present."[66]

It is important to consider not only what precedes a verb form but also what follows it. In 2:11-12 there is a verbal series consisting of (1) wayyiqtōl ("and I raised up"), (2) wayyiqtōl ("and you caused to drink"), and (3) non-initial SC ("and ... you commanded"). Verb (2) is sequential to (1), and (3) is sequential to (1); but (2) and (3) are reversible (see below for the notion "reversible") with respect to each other. There is no emphasis on whether the people caused the Nazarites to drink wine before they told the prophets not to prophesy. The emphasis of wayyiqtōl on sequence led to a change to non-initial SC for the reversible situation.

CLAUSE RELATIONSHIPS

Clauses that are independent in the sense that they begin a new unit or section are attested only with a clause-initial SC (see above), with non-initial SC or PC (see 7:1, 17), and uniquely with וְהָיָה (w^{e}hāyâ, (6:9; 8:9) and וַיִּשְׁלַח (wayyishlah, 7:10). The form וְהָיָה (w^{e}hāya, "and it will come to pass") is commonly recognized as a special case of W+SC used independently.[67] The wayyiqtōl in 7:10 may be connected with the broader narrative strand of the chapter, representing an action subsequent to the vision of 7:1-9. Otherwise, wayyiqtōl, W+SC, and W+PC are always related syntactically with what precedes.

An important distinction is whether the relationship is one of simple addition or of temporal or logical sequence. A basic test is to ask whether the clause under consideration is reversible with the preceding clause. That is, is the sequence of the clauses significant, or are two events merely juxtaposed so that except for possible stylistic reasons it does not matter which event is placed first? For Amos, all examples of wayyiqtōl and W+PC are irreversible, but there are many cases of W+SC that are reversible. We may consider the passage 3:14-15, with six W+SC forms. These are: (1) וּפָקַדְתִּי (ûpāqadtî), (2) וְנִגְדְעוּ (w^{e}nigd$^{e^c}$û), (3) וְנָפְלוּ (w^{e}nāp^{e}lû), (4) וְהִכֵּיתִי (w^{e}hikkêtî), (5) וְאָבְדוּ (w$^{e^o}$āb^{e}dû), and (6) וְסָפוּ (w^{e}sāpû). Forms (1), (4), (5), and (6) are all in main clauses after a temporal clause: "When I punish Israel's transgressions *then I will punish* the altars ... ; and *strike* the winter home ... ; *and* the houses of ivory *will perish; and* the great houses *will come to an end.*" There is relationship with the initial temporal clause, but the W+SC clauses do not emphasize sequence among themselves; there are simply different aspects to God's judgment against Israel. Number (2) gives a specific instance or result of (1): "*Namely/so that* the horns of the altar will *be cut off.*" Finally, (3) is in sequence with (2), "*and they will fall* to the ground."

Additional relationships expressed by W+SC are result ("*therefore I will make* you *go into exile*," 5:27), objective ("*that* the great house *be smashed to pieces,*" 6:11), explanatory ("*and* the high places *will be desolated,*" 9:9), summarizing ("*so they will go into exile,*" 1:5), and apodosis to a conditional sentence ("*then they will die,*" 6:9).

Sequence in time is most often indicated by wayyiqtōl ("then I said," 7:8), but explanatory ("*namely I destroyed* his fruit," 2:9) and simultaneous relationships are also attested. An example of the latter is 7:5 where Amos speaks וָאֹמַר, wā^{o}ōmar) just when the fiery judgment begins to consume the land of Israel. After a participle or verbless clause, wayyiqtōl may also indicate something like simultaneous action. In 9:1 Amos sees the LORD "standing" (נִצָּב, *niṣṣāb*) when at some unspecified moment "He spoke" (וַיֹּאמֶר, *wayyōʾmer*). See also the analysis of 7:15 above.

The form W+PC normally expresses purpose ("that we may drink," 4:1), but in one case it expresses a contrastive relationship ("*but let* justice *roll down*," 5:24).

CONCLUSION

In the verbal system in Amos the first opposition is between the PC with or without simple *waw* and the SC. An aspectual opposition is indicated by the use of the PC for frequentative action in the past and of the SC for a general present situation viewed as a whole. The PC may therefore be assigned imperfective function and the SC perfective function. The use of the SC for the future is too restricted for definite conclusions. In the absence of contextual indications that the PC is in a past context, it is interpreted as present or future. Also the SC is interpreted as past, unless there is specific context to indicate a present or future situation. The SC also occurs in situations where there are abiding results (present perfect, past perfect, and possibly future perfect) and for stative verbs in a present context. These functions of the PC and SC are all compatible with the PC as imperfective aspect and the SC as perfective aspect.

The aspectual function of W+SC is unclear. Its use for the frequentative in the first of a series of frequentative actions, some of which are expressed by the PC, would argue for an imperfective interpretation. It is also in complementary distribution with the PC in non-initial position. Some examples may occur in a past context with no imperfective emphasis, however. Probably it developed into an imperfective form by way of analogy with its opposition to *wayyiqṭōl,* a perfective form, within the system. Originally it may have simply expressed a neutral value with respect to an imperfective context.

The usage of *wayyiqṭōl,* taken in correlation with its clause position, points to its function as a perfective aspect. There is a complementary distribution of SC in non-clause-initial position and *wayyiqṭōl* in clause-initial position when the clause is syntactically related to a preceding clause. When the clause begins a new section, only the SC can occur initially with perfective meaning. Some other observations support the perfective interpretation of *wayyiqṭōl.* One is its use for the perfect. Another is the possible use of the form for a general present situation viewed as a whole. Finally, there is the instance of two actions in sequence with a previous action but reversible with respect to each other. In this case the first is expressed by *wayyiqṭōl* but the second by a non-initial SC, implying similarity of function for SC and *wayyiqṭōl.*

SUMMARY AND IMPLICATIONS

Three approaches to the form *wayyiqṭōl* emphasize its functional association with the "perfect" or suffix conjugation rather than with the "imperfect" or prefix conjugation. First, morphological analysis points to a prefixed verb form used with *wayyiqṭōl*, which should be kept distinct from the prefix conjugation without *waw*-consecutive. Comparative Semitics and syntactic analysis of early Hebrew poetry confirm the morphological distinctness of the two forms, even though some leveling has occurred as a result of historical development. Second, two independent structural analyses of the Hebrew verbal system also showed the connection of *wayyiqṭōl* with the suffix conjugation. Finally, my own synchronic study of verbal oppositions in Amos led to the same conclusion.

There are several important implications to this conclusion. The first concerns terminology used in the teaching of biblical Hebrew. The terms *imperfect* and *perfect* as used in most present grammars represent a misleading mixture of form and function. It would be much better to use formal terminology, such as *prefix conjugation* and *suffix conjugation*, and to teach syntactic function separately. Second, there is a need for more synchronic studies of individual books or portions of the Hebrew Old Testament so that diachronic development in the verbal system may be discerned. Finally, the natural result of improved understanding of Hebrew grammar can only be an improved understanding of the revealed Word of God through exegesis, translation, and preaching.

NOTES

1. Traditionally the form of the Hebrew verb that is based on the addition of personal-prefixes is called the "imperfect." Another form based on the suffixing of personal endings is called "perfect." As will become clear in the course of the chapter, these terms are imprecise. The main problem is that they refer to function rather than form. This is especially a problem for the term *waw-consecutive with imperfect* because it prejudges the issue of function. Later in the chapter the terms *prefix conjugation, suffix conjugation,* and *wayyiqṭōl* (וַיִּקְטֹל) will be introduced as substitutes. These alternate terms refer exclusively to form. An introductory grammar that uses the first two is John F. A. Sawyer, *A Modern Introduction to Biblical Hebrew* (Boston: Oriel, 1976).
2. The perfect (a suffix conjugation) is used for past narrative in Syriac. See Carl Brockelmann, *Syrische Grammatik* (Leipzig: VEB Verlag Enzyklopädie, 1976), par. 208.
3. See W. Gross, *Verbform and Funktion. wayyiqtol für die Gegenwart?* (St. Ottilien: Eos Verlag, 1976), p. 18, n. 6, for a summary of viewpoints since 1951. He lists no less than ten distinct views about the basic oppositions between the prefix and suffix conjugations in Hebrew, though some of the views have simi-

lar features. Research before 1951 is summarized in C. Brockelmann, "Die 'Tempora' des Semitischen," *Zeitschrift für Phonetik* 5 (1951): 133-54.

4. See Gross, p. 12.

5. See James A. Hughes, "Another Look at the Hebrew Tenses," *Journal of Near Eastern Studies* 29 (1979): 12-24.

6. The distinction between stative verbs (which express a state or condition) and fientive verbs (which express an action or event) is commonly accepted as important for the Hebrew verbal system.

7. See Frank R. Blake, *A Resurvey of Hebrew Tenses* (Rome: Pontificiums Institutum Biblicum, 1951), pp. 6-8. Blake's study emphasizes exceptional cases. It must be used with caution; each reference needs to be checked carefully.

8. For exceptions with *Lamed-he* roots see Blake, p. 46.

9. Blake, p. 14, wrongly interpreted S. R. Driver, *A Treatise on the Use of the Tenses in Hebrew*, 3d ed. (1892; reprinted. Oxford: Clarendon, 1969), par. 69, as classifying the long form as "regular" with *wayyiqṭōl* in the first person. My own study of twenty-two high frequency verbs fully supported the contention of P. Paul Joüon that these forms are secondary (*Grammaire de l'Hébreu Biblique* [Rome, 1923], par. 47*d*). Occurrences are not limited to late books but are more common in Daniel and the postexilic books. See also Joshua Blau, "Studies in Hebrew Verb Formation," *Hebrew Union College Annual* 42 (1971): 133-34.

10. Hans Bauer, "Die Tempora im Semitischen," *Beiträge zur Assyriologie und semitischen Sprachwissenschaft* 8 (1912): 1-53.

11. Gross, p. 16.

12. Bauer, pp. 13-18, 35. See also Hans Bauer and Pontus Leander, *Grammatik des Biblisch-Aramäischen* (Hildescheim: Georg Olms Verlagsbuchhandlung, 1962), par. 77.

13. G. R. Driver, *Problems of the Hebrew Verbal System* (Edinburgh: T & T Clark, 1936). See also G. R. Driver's note in J. Weingreen, *A Practical Grammar for Classical Hebrew*, 2d ed. (Oxford: Oxford U., 1959), pp. 252-53.

14. The Akkadian system is often explained as a tense system based on three prefix conjugations—the preterit (*iprus*), the present/future (*iparras*), and the perfect (*iptaras*). See Wolfram von Soden, *Grundriss der akkadischen Grammatik* (Rome: Pontificium Institutum Biblicum, 1969), par. 77-80. The suffix form, which is called "permansive," is really more nominal than verbal in nature. See G. Buccellati, "An Interpretation of the Akkadian Stative as a Nominal Sentence," *Journal of Near Eastern Studies* 27 (1968): 1-13. See also David Marcus, "The Stative and the *Waw* Consecutive," *Journal of the Ancient Near Eastern Society of Columbia University* 2 (1969): 37-40 for the criticisms of Driver's application of Akkadian to the problem of the Hebrew suffix conjugation with *waw*.

15. G. R. Driver, pp. 85-97.

16. The classification of Ugaritic as Canaanite is accepted by the writer as tentatively valid linguistically. For a recent discussion see Joshua Blau, "Hebrew and North West Semitic: Reflections on the Classification of the Semitic Languages," *Hebrew Annual Review* 2 (1978): 21-44. A full discussion is also given in a forthcoming grammar by Stanislav Segert, *A Grammar of the Ugaritic Language* (University of California Press, Berkeley).

17. Cyrus H. Gordon, *Ugaritic Textbook,* Analecta Orientalia 38 (Rome: Pontificium Institutum Biblicum, 1965), p. 68; Segert, *Grammar,* par. 64.41.

18. Gordon, pp. 68–69.
19. Ibid., p. 72.
20. Segert, *Grammar,* par. 54.675.3.
21. D. Rudolf Meyer, *Hebräische Grammatik,* 4 vols. (Berlin: Walter de Gruyter, 1966–1972), 3:41–44.
22. See Gordon's examples, pp. 71–72.
23. See the author's doctoral dissertation, *Word Order in the Clause Structure of Syrian Akkadian,* University of California at Los Angeles (Ann Arbor, 1979), chaps. 2–4, for evidence of three distinct dialect areas in the Amarna letters from Syria-Palestine. (Available through University Microfilms.)
24. See especially W. L. Moran, *A Syntactical Study of the Dialect of Byblos as Reflected in the Amarna Tablets,* Ph.D. Dissertation, Johns Hopkins University (Ann Arbor, 1950), pp. 24–52 (available through University Microfilms); "The Hebrew Language in its Northwest Semitic Background," in *The Bible and the Ancient Near East,* ed. G. E. Wright (London: Doubleday, 1961), pp. 63–66; and A. F. Rainey, "Morphology and the Prefix-Tenses of West Semitized El-'Amarna Tablets," *Ugarit Forschungen* 7 (1975): 395–426.
25. That is, the Akkadian *iprus/iparras* contrast. See n. 15 above.
26. It is commonly recognized that the Hebrew prefix conjugation as imperfect can be used in a past context to express actions that occur repeatedly or habitually. See Ronald J. Williams, *Hebrew Syntax; An Outline,* 2d ed. (Toronto: U. of Toronto, 1976), par. 168.
27. David A. Robertson, *Linguistic Evidence in Dating Early Hebrew Poetry,* SBL Dissertation Series 3 (Missoula, Montana: Soc. of Bib. Lit., 1972), pp. 17–55.
28. Gross, pp. 143–46.
29. S. R. Driver, *A Treatise on the Use of the Tenses in Hebrew,* pp. 71–72 (emphasis his). Two more recent examples of this approach are J. Wash Watts, *A Survey of Syntax in the Hebrew Old Testament* (Grand Rapids: Eerdmans, 1964), pp. 60–69; and O. L. Barnes, *A New Approach to the Problem of the Hebrew Tenses and its Solution without Recourse to Waw-Consecutive* (Oxford: J. Thornton, 1965).
30. S. R. Driver, p. 76. Of course, in 1892 the evidence of Ugaritic was unavailable to Driver, and Akkadian and the Amarna letters were only partially understood.
31. See Bernard Comrie, *Aspect; An Introduction to the Study of Verbal Aspect and Related Problems,* Cambridge Textbooks in Linguistics (London: Cambridge U. Press, 1976), pp. 1–2; the example is Comrie's.
32. Ibid., p. 2.
33. Ibid., p. 4.
34. Ibid., pp. 52, 56.
35. Ibid., p. 56.
36. C. Brockelmann, "Die 'Tempora' des Semitischen," *Zeitschrift für Phonetik* 5 (1951): 134.
37. Péter Kustár, *Aspekt im Hebräischen* (Basel: Friedrich Reinhardt Kommissionsverlag, 1972), pp. 29–30.
38. Comrie, pp. 82–83.
39. Ibid., pp. 41–44.
40. For example, J. Weingreen, *A Practical Grammar for Classical Hebrew,* 2d ed., p. 56.
41. Comrie, pp. 44–48.

42. Blake, pp. 48–50, 79.
43. Michael H. Silverman, "Syntactic Notes on the *Waw* Consecutive," in *Orient and Occident; Essays Presented to Cyrus H. Gordon* . . . , ed. H. A. Hoffner, AOAT 22 (Neukirchen-Vluyn: Neukirchener Verlag, 1973), p. 175. The "perfect of experience" and the "frequentative imperfect" are two categories that seem to be aspectual rather than tense related. See Williams, par. 163, 168.
44. C. Brockelmann, pp. 134, 146–50.
45. S. Segert, "Verbal Categories of Some Northwest Semitic Languages: A Didactic Approach," *Afroasiatic Linguistics* 2:5 (May 1975): 9–10.
46. Frithiof Rundgren, *Das althebräische Verbum; Abriss der Aspektlehre* (Stockholm: Almqvist & Wiksell, 1961), pp. 84–104.
47. Ibid., p. 35.
48. Ibid., p. 90.
49. Ibid., pp. 94–97.
50. Gross; see n. 3.
51. Ibid., p. 11.
52. Ibid., pp. 121–22.
53. Ibid., pp. 163–65.
54. The place of *waw* +SC is unclear. Probably an originally perfective sense that had a neutral value after *waw* developed into an imperfective by analogy with *wayyiqtōl*. This, however, is problematic.
55. Cf. J. Alberto Soggin, *Introduction to the Old Testament,* The Old Testament Library (Philadelphia: Westminster, 1976), pp. 243–44; J. D. Smart, "Amos," in *The Interpreter's Dictionary of the Bible* (New York: Abingdon, 1962), 1:118–20; J. M. Ward, "Amos," in *The Interpreter's Dictionary of the Bible,* Supplementary Volume (New York: Abingdon, 1976), pp. 22–23; and Hans Walter Wolff, *Joel and Amos,* Hermeneia (Philadelphia: Fortress, 1977).
56. Smart, p. 119, thought they were characteristic of Amos's style.
57. Wolff, pp. 308–9.
58. Soggin, p. 244.
59. There may be a reference here to Genesis 1, with its repetition of "and there was evening and there was morning." At creation God established the regular alternation of day and night. See Gross, p. 101, for the view that the SC here functions as a general present in the sense that God continually changes day into night.
60. Wolff, pp. 291–92.
61. C. F. Keil, *Minor Prophets, Commentary on the Old Testament in Ten Volumes* (Grand Rapids: Eerdmans, 1973), 1:297.
62. The NASB took the initial participle with an interrogative rather than the article. The form is the same in either case, but the interpretation of the prefixed *he* as the article goes back to the Septuagint and seems to fit the context better.
63. See Gross, pp. 102–3.
64. See Gross, pp. 103–4; and Keil, 1:281.
65. Keil, 1:312–13.
66. Wolff, p. 313.
67. See E. Kautzsch, ed., *Gesenius' Hebrew Grammar,* 2d Eng. ed. trans. A. E. Cowley (1910; Oxford: Clarendon, 1970), par. 112x, Rem. 1.

Part IV
INTEGRATIVE

10

The Value of Archaeological Studies for Biblical Research

Charles Lee Feinberg

CHARLES LEE FEINBERG (M.A., Southern Methodist University; Ph.D., Johns Hopkins University; Th.B., Th.M., Th.D., Dallas Theological Seminary) is dean emeritus and professor emeritus of Semitics and Old Testament at Talbot Theological Seminary, La Mirada, California.

It is a commonplace among students of archaeology that the study of archaeology has suffered as much from its friends as from its foes. This has been true because of mistaken conceptions as to the exact nature of the evidence to be expected from archaeological discoveries. Some have asked too much of archaeology; others have expected too little; still others have asked in the wrong manner. S. R. Driver, discussing the relevance of archaeology for biblical studies, has pointed out that the testimony of archaeology may generally be divided into two large categories: that which is direct and that which is indirect. It has been stated that where the evidence of archaeology is direct, it is of the greatest possible value and usually determines the issues in question. When it is indirect and of a precise nature, it makes the suggested solution possible.[1]

USES AND ABUSES OF ARCHAEOLOGY

At this point it is appropriate to consider both the uses and abuses of archaeological research, for there are right and wrong uses of this discipline. It must never be forgotten that archaeology cannot and does not "prove" the doctrinal content of Scripture. Although biblical truth rests on historical data, in the very nature of the case biblical truth is fundamentally religious and spiritual in character, that is, it treats of the Person of God and of man and their relationships. The tangible discoveries of archaeology cannot prove or disprove such spiritual truth. That is not to suggest that there is no way to confirm or refute the doctrines of Scripture, but only that the discoveries of archaeology do not provide direct evidence for or against such claims. On the other hand, it must be remembered that the Bible is set for the most part within the framework of history. It is with reference to the history-based truth of the Scriptures that one may seek confirmation from archaeology. This area is vital for the Bible's spiritual truth. Israel's faith in their God was grounded on the interpositions of their God in their history.[2] At the same time, precisely because they are mute, the finds of archaeology are able to illuminate, supplement, and even control the written documents.[3]

Unfortunately, there have also been many abuses of archaeology, intentional and otherwise. Doctoring the evidence or "salting a dig" is not the only offense. Too many times archaeology has been pressed into service for other legitimate ends. There are five obvious abuses: (1) One is the carrying out excavations for the benefit of European museums and private collections. Although this practice was more common in the early days of archaeological research, it has not been entirely eliminated to this day. (2) There is still neglect of stratigraphic observations so important to the historian. Such practice can vitiate the entire endeavor. (3) Even in this century, as earlier, archaeology has been used to hide the activities of intelligence services of certain world powers, gathering data clearly unrelated to science. (4) In our day in all the countries of the Near East it is known that archaeology is employed to promote certain nationalistic aims. It is made to establish connections with the past and thereby promote the possession of certain territories. (Even in these cases there are some positive results. Much material has been brought to light and saved from possible destruction.) (5) Occasionally, archaeology is employed to accomplish what it does not have the capability to do. This is done even by scholars of competence and integrity. In other contexts, these same scholars would condemn the unwarranted use of archaeology. It is easy to fall prey to these unrealistic expectations because of the perennial and unabated interest in the excavations of the Bible lands. It will be seen later that "proving" the Bible and confirming it are two distinct functions and that archaeology has a role in relation to the latter but not in regard to the former.[4]

LIMITATIONS OF ARCHAEOLOGY

It is never inappropriate to underscore the limitations of archaeology, for if it steps outside the realm of its functions, it can be ineffective at best and detrimental at worst. In addition to being unable to verify spiritual truth,[5] archaeology has other limitations. For example, R. de Vaux, veteran in these areas, has issued some warnings. He has shown that just because archaeology has to do with *realia*, it is unwise to conclude that it is more objective and nearer to historical truth. Actually, the finds cannot be incorporated into any historical frame of reference until they have undergone interpretation. Archaeology provides the historian with mute documents only.[6] Moreover, because archaeology can alleviate to a certain degree the silence of texts now in hand, it is not to be assumed that the absence of archaeological evidence is sufficient to throw doubt on statements of the written sources and writers. In short, rejection of the historicity of the accounts by the archaeologists themselves who have carried out the digs at certain sites becomes a serious matter.[7]

It is too strong a conclusion to propose that, because interpretations of finds differ on occasion, the confirmation of the biblical narrative is seldom without ambiguity. De Vaux goes so far as to declare that "in certain cases the value of the archaeological evidence and the significance of the text which it is supposed to clarify have both been exaggerated."[8]

G. E. Wright has evaluated the evidence more positively. He fully recognizes that there is an interpretation of faith that is not dependent on historical confirmation or corroboration. In the Scriptures is to be found an interpretation of both events and experience that is not susceptible per se to historical or archaeological substantiation. The archaeologist cannot "prove" the Bible, "but he can and has illuminated the historical setting, the events and the cultural background with which biblical faith is concerned."[9]

It must not be considered a weakness that archaeology needs and utilizes hypotheses. It is no more a derogation for archaeology than it is for historical and literary criticism. In common with all advancing branches of scholarly study, archaeology must resort to hypotheses. Such need is inherent in all research because of the recognized incompleteness and fragmentariness of the evidence thus far available to us. But hypotheses can never be given the same confidence as facts until they are clearly substantiated by the same.[10]

Yet many, not well acquainted with the issues or the difficulties involved, express surprise that problems in archaeology have not yet been solved. The situation is not that simple. Problems inevitably remain, because available evidence, from both the side of archaeology and the Bible, is insufficient to lead to a definitive resolution of the problem. As tantalizing as it may be, interpretation must wait patiently for more information and light. On more than one occasion the interpretation of the archaeological evidence, or the biblical as well, is not the only valid or defensible one.[11] Dogmatism needs to be restricted severely, for one is aware of the many problems archaeology can raise for the student of the Scriptures. Witness the question of origins in the creation accounts, the Flood, the relationship between Ras Shamra and the Mosaic code, and others.[12] Perhaps the dictum of William G. Denver is too strong when he affirms that "the pace of discovery is such that a dozen new questions are raised for every old question which is answered."[13] Van Beek of the Smithsonian Institution is more reserved in his pronouncements. He does not believe that the finds of archaeology support or confirm all the minutiae of biblical history, but he sees the discrepancies as minor and explicable in one of several possible ways. However, he readily admits that some problems are serious and cannot find resolution easily. Furthermore, with the increasingly favorable light thrown on the Scriptures in recent years, scholars are now more willing to deal with major discrepancies with a good deal more caution than formerly, and are as a rule amenable to withholding final judgments until more evidence is available.[14]

VALUES OF ARCHAEOLOGY FOR BIBLICAL INTERPRETATION

DISCERNMENT OF AUTHENTIC TEXT

Now we shall turn our attention to the vital concern of the value(s) of archaeology for biblical interpretation. The first and indispensable step in the understanding of the Bible is to ascertain the exact text written by the authors. Those who have expected archaeologists to unearth one of Paul's epistles or the scroll written by the amanuensis Baruch at the dictation of Jeremiah the prophet have not yet had their expectations rewarded. However, manuscripts older than those extant in libraries and museums have been unearthed again and again. About the middle of this century the greatest number of manuscripts and fragments ever found came to light at Qumran. These are significant for the determination of the correct text. Noncanonical works have also been found, but not in such quantities as the canonical. An example of such a find is the discovery of part of the original Hebrew of the noncanonical Ecclesiasticus. It tends to warn us against relying too heavily on the Septuagint in the matter of accuracy.[15]

Because of the limitations of this study it will be best to treat at some length three discoveries: the Ras Shamra tablets, the Dead Sea Scrolls, and the Ebla tablets. The finds from Ras Shamra (Ugarit) in Syria from 1929 opened up a new epoch in Old Testament studies with the light they shed on Canaanite and Phoenician religion. Invaluable has been the help of the Ugaritic texts in demonstrating the early use of poetry, as in the songs of Miriam and Deborah, the final blessing of Israel by Moses, the oracles of Balaam, the use of meter, parallelism and other poetic forms. The material has served to curb the tendency of some scholars to amend the text of the Bible in order to bring it into conformity with some preconceived, rigid, and invalid patterns.[16] Wiseman states it even more forcefully:

> One obvious product of this growth in the number of available Semitic texts, of a type and date contemporary with the Old Testament records and from a closer geographical proximity to the scene of the events, is an increased understanding of the Hebrew and Aramaic languages. In particular the texts from Ras Shamra, but no less those from Mari and Alalakh, have enabled progress to be made towards a historical study of Hebrew, its vocalisation, orthography, dialects, grammar, and syntax.[17]

Suffice it to say, these aids have demonstrated that many previously offered emendations for the Masoretic text are unnecessary. Many helps in lexicography and a clearer understanding of individual words and phrases have come from the sources now under consideration. After decades of assiduous research in the Ugaritic materials, Albright could conclude:

> Ugaritic and other Northwest Semitic parallels enable us to explain the consonantal text of hundreds of passages in the Psalter and the Prophets, and sound new interpretations are now accumulating so fast that their number has been multiplied many times over within the past decade.[18]

Between the summer of 1947 and 1956 what some have called the greatest manuscript(s) discovery of modern times was made. It would be safe to say that this discovery has revolutionized certain entrenched positions of literary criticism. Called the Dead Sea Scrolls, they were discovered by Bedouin goatherds in a cave in the cliffs at the northern end of the Dead Sea. The most important of the ancient scrolls was the entire scroll of the book of Isaiah.[19] How vast have been the finds can be seen from the fact that researchers have found forty thousand fragments, composing almost five hundred documents; about one hundred are biblical texts comprising fragments of all the Old Testament canon except Esther. The dates involved, based on palaeographical and archaeological data, are from the late third century B.C. to A.D. 68.[20] Bruce concurs with Wiseman that more than one hundred copies of Old Testament books in

Hebrew or Aramaic have been found. The majority have been recovered in fragments only, but some copies are fairly complete. Among the finds are the already-mentioned Isaiah Scroll and copies of Leviticus and Psalms in good condition. Not only are all the books of the Hebrew canon (except Esther) among the finds at Qumran, but also some parts of the Greek translation of the Old Testament, the LXX, have been recovered. Additional information on the Old Testament text is afforded by commentaries on several biblical books or portions of them. The finds, thus, confirm the accepted limits of the Old Testament canon (apart from Esther).[21]

Elaborating on the importance of the discoveries for the Old Testament, Bruce holds that "they [the Qumran finds] do indeed give the deathblow to those eccentric theories which would date certain parts of the Law and the Prophets as late as the middle of the second century B.C."[22] As far as interpretation of the Old Testament text is concerned, the biblical commentaries from Qumran are of significance, not because they illuminate the original meaning of the books treated, but rather because of the light they afford on the theological tenets of the commentators and their followers/coreligionists.[23] In conclusion, Andersen has shown:

> These [DSS] have revolutionized our knowledge of the history of the transmission of the text of the Old Testament by supplying examples of texts actually in use in the time of Christ. They also include sectarian writings used by the men of Qumran. These throw light on the religious developments within Judaism at the time of the rise of Christianity.[24]

Since we have thus far been dwelling on the value of archaeological research for the ascertainment of the exact text of Scripture, it is time to consider how the discoveries stand in this respect. Scholars of varying theological persuasion are agreed that the majority of the texts agree with and confirm the consonantal text of the traditional Masoretic text apart from the much freer use of vowel letters.[25]

Because so much of archaeological study is centered upon and occupied with Old Testament areas, it can be easily overlooked that the discoveries aid tremendously in New Testament studies. Their value for New Testament studies can readily be seen in the information they present concerning a Jewish sectarian community in the desert of Judea about the time of the earthly ministry of Christ. Furthermore, that persistent tendency of attempting to interpret the New Testament in the framework of Greek and Persian thought is being modified because of the discovery of a native Palestinian-Jewish influence especially in the fourth gospel, Paul's letters, and the epistle to the Hebrews.[26] Indeed, it now appears that not a single New Testament book is not receiving light from the Qumran finds. Great strides have been made in understanding the Judaism of the New Testament era with long-needed background material for a study of the history of the origins of the Christian faith. In a definite sense the four hundred silent years between the two testaments have found their voice in the Qumran literature.[27]

A word of caution is in order at this point. It is known that when certain parallels to the corpus of truth embodied in the New Testament are found in extrabiblical materials, there are always some of the comparative religion school who soon (by extrapolation) see only homogeneity when heterogeneity is abundantly obvious.[28] The witness of reliable scholars will suffice to put the picture in correct perspective. F. F. Bruce, for example, has commented:

> While the importance of the Qumran discoveries for Old Testament study is high, their importance for New Testament study may be even higher. Until the mass of the available literature is published, any report such as this must have an interim character. But when all the possible comparisons and contrasts have been drawn and duly evaluated, one paramount fact will become even more apparent than it is already. What above everything else distinguishes Christianity from the Qumran movement, or any other movement, is the person and work of Jesus. The Qumran Teacher of Righteousness was a great man, but he was neither Son of God nor Saviour of the World. We do not know how he died, but he certainly did not rise again from the dead, and no one ever believed that he had done so.[29]

No less direct is the evaluation of W. F. Albright, when he contrasts Christianity and Essenism (referring to the religious system indicated in the DSS). Albright notes the superiority of Christianity to both Essenism and Gnosticism.[30]

If the Ras Shamra tablets and the Dead Sea Scrolls have caused revolutions in biblical studies, less cannot be said for the latest find, the Ebla tablets. A *Los Angeles Times* editorial, which appeared on April 24, 1979, speaking about the discoveries made by Professor Paolo Matthiae of Rome University (who had been excavating the site since 1964) and Professor Giovanni Pettinato (an epigrapher from the University of Rome) at a place called Tell Mardikh in Syria, reads thus:

> More than 17,000 clay tablets have been unearthed at Ebla, where a Semitic civilization flourished about 4,500 years ago. A number of these tablets reportedly contain references and allusions to persons and

places that figure prominently in the Bible. Among the persons mentioned are Abraham, Esau, Saul, Ishmael, and David. Among the places mentioned are Salem, Hazor, Megiddo, Gaza, Sinai and Jerusalem.[31]

Scholars believe that, because the links with the history of the Jewish people are so patent, Syrian authorities have placed a clamp on information concerning the tablets for political reasons, while they claim the archive throws light on "proto-Syrian history."

It is far too early to make any sweeping statements on the finds, especially since few scholars have seen the tablets, and not even a clear picture of a tablet with biblical references is available. But what facts are at hand show numerous geographic names (260 of them in one text alone). Literary texts, rituals of polytheism, ceremonies for the anointing of the king, and sacrificial systems, familiar to us from many Near Eastern sources, are mentioned. Because most of the tablets treat of economic matters, such as tariffs, tributes, and treaties, the conclusion is inescapable that Ebla was the hub of a great trade empire that reached out across the Fertile Crescent. Grammatical texts, containing 114 Sumerian Eblahite vocabularies, have been found. The language is of the Northwest Semitic group, closely related to Hebrew and Phoenician. Because of indisputable proof of early documentation in the Scriptures, the critical documentary hypothesis, which leaned heavily on oral tradition, must be rejected and considered invalid. The early documents of the Old Testament can no longer be denied Mosaic authorship—a fact attested many times over through the finds of archaeology. Authenticity is written large over the early records of the Bible.[32]

INTERPRETATION AND INERRANCY OF THE TEXT

Assuming that the correct text has been ascertained,[33] the next task is to interpret it. This necessitates a thoroughgoing understanding of the languages in which the text was written.[34] The monuments from Bible lands have shed streams of light on the languages of the Orient that are related to the Hebrew or touch upon Bible times, such as Babylonian, Assyrian, Aramaic, Sumerian, that of the Hittites, those of Ras Shamra (the principal one being Canaanite), Eblahite, and others.

There has probably never been a generation since the time of the Bible when some have not dogmatically claimed that the Scriptures contain errors of one kind or another. Without equivocation, archaeology has laid to rest a great number of alleged errors in the Bible. Wiseman has met this challenge to the veracity of the Bible in a forthright manner:

When due allowance has been paid to the increasing number of supposed errors which have been subsequently eliminated by the discovery of archaeological evidence, to the many aspects of history indirectly affirmed or in some instances directly confirmed by extra-Biblical sources, I would still maintain that the historical facts of the Bible rightly understood find agreement in the facts culled from archaeology equally rightly understood, that is, the majority of errors can be ascribed to errors of interpretation by modern scholars and not to substantiated 'errors' of fact presented by the biblical historians. This view is further strengthened when it is remembered how many theories and interpretations of Scripture have been checked or corrected by archaeological discoveries. Moreover, the specific viewpoint of the respective historians represented by the Biblical and non-Biblical sources must also be weighed in assessing the relative value of their sources.[35]

G. E. Wright has touched upon basic and indispensable considerations when he has related archaeology to the knowledge of God and history. He has maintained:

The intensive study of the biblical archaeologist is thus the fruit of the vital concern for history which the Bible has instilled in us. We cannot, therefore, assume that the knowledge of biblical history is unessential to the faith. Biblical theology and biblical archaeology must go hand in hand, if we are to comprehend the Bible's meaning.[36]

With such conclusions we can heartily concur.

Some overly timid souls have feared that to place the Bible alongside archaeology in the milieu of the Ancient Near Eastern world would detract from its solitary dignity or uniqueness. As a matter of fact, the exact opposite has been the case. Frank correctly claims:

Contrary to destroying the originality of Holy Writ, archaeology tends to highlight the uniqueness of its thought. Many of the forms are the same, but what they enshrine is quite different. Thus not only has the earlier historical skepticism been discredited, but the religious affirmations of the Bible stand out more clearly than ever.[37]

But the values of archaeology for biblical studies are not fully indicated yet. Of inestimable value have been the document discoveries that are coeval with the biblical records. The discovery and publication of about a quarter of a million documents from Syria, Anatolia, Mesopotamia, and Egypt in the last fifty years "have now the cumulative effect of providing a detailed historical development of literature contemporary with the . . . biblical documents."[38] Until the ancient world came alive through archaeological research, it could not be imagined how fully biblical literature dovetailed with all ancient Semitic literature, an irrefutable proof of authenticity and historicity. The treaties or covenants that find such a large place in the biblical records, whether they were transacted between countries or individuals, find their parallels among the "covenant" forms found in all ancient Semitic writings. For example, suzerainty (Exod. 19-24; Josh. 24; Deut.) and parity (Gen. 21, 26, 31; 1 Kings 5) treaties are found repeatedly in the ancient Semitic world. Wiseman is undoubtedly right in his evaluation of the phenomenon when he says, "As with the laws any undisputed similarity between texts of this class [he was speaking of the Wisdom Literature] and the Old Testament can be explained as the dependence of both on a common Near Eastern stock of expressions."[39]

It is the consensus of all students of archaeology of whatever theological persuasion that for background material of the ancient world, that is, as a basic tool in the study of history, there is no more indispensable discipline than that of archaeological research. For example, Albright claims that "we can now draw on established fact to tell whether an episode or allusion to life and customs is characteristic of a given period or environment. We can generally fix the language and period to which an ancient Oriental name belongs."[40]

CULTURAL AND HISTORICAL BACKGROUNDS

It would appear at times that the background help from archaeology is interminable. Not only is the biblical text itself made more clear, but the finds explain many laws, social customs, religious ideas and practices of the Bible whose meanings were not fully understood.[41] Great have been the gains in our knowledge of the history of Palestine. It is freely admitted that the Bible's historical material is not primarily political or economic in orientation, but rather religious. For this reason many areas are touched on only briefly. Here archaeological research has greatly aided in supplementing the biblical record. For example, 1 Kings 14:25-26 and 2 Chronicles 12:2-9 are greatly clarified (with reference to the invasion of Judah in Rehoboam's day by Shishak of Egypt) by the Karnak inscription with its list of captured towns in Judah and Israel as well. Likewise, Ahab's reign (1 Kings 16:29—22:40) and his alliance with Benhadad of Syria and Irhuleni of Hamath and their war against Shalmaneser III of

Assyria are found in the Shalmaneser Inscriptions. Well known are the digs at Samaria and their disclosure of the advanced material culture of Israel during the reign of Ahab.

Many details of biblical history have been confirmed by archaeology, e.g., the historicity of the exile in Babylon, which C. C. Torrey claimed at one time was a fabrication.[42] Now hear Van Beek:

> Every Judean site excavated to date, which was inhabited at the end of the seventh century B.C., is found to have been destroyed in this period and either reoccupied only after a gap of at least several decades or never inhabited again. The dearth of occupied sites in Judah during most of the sixth century B.C. indicates a depopulation of the country, which agrees perfectly with the biblical account of the Exile.[43]

The power and wealth of Solomon (1 Kings 2:12—11:43 and 2 Chron. 1-9) have been illustrated by excavations at Megiddo, Ezion-geber, and other sites. They attest to a complex national organization, an advanced material culture, and a flourishing economy in Israel. So "it is now clear that during Solomon's reign, Israel comprised the greatest and most prosperous land empire in the ancient Near East and indeed enjoyed a Golden Age."[44] And what has already been set forth for certain periods of Israel's history could be verified for other periods of Israel's history.

CONSENSUS OF SCHOLARS

After indicating the relevance of archaeology in interpretation under the three headings—the confirmation of biblical history, the provision of background, and the illumination of text and language—Blaiklock states:

> The first essential must always be to determine what the writer originally sought to communicate and to whom he first directed his communication. That is why all information which provides contemporary comment on social, political, or cultural backgrounds, which elucidates literary form and convention, explains language, or throws light on habits of thought and speech is relevant to interpretation. In the case of the OT, such information is chiefly archaeological. Around the whole sweep of the Fertile Crescent, the remains of peoples, cities and empires, epigraphical, architectural, artistic, and of every other sort of which archeology takes widening and increasingly expert notice, have elucidated and illuminated the text of Scripture from Genesis to the minor prophets.[45]

In concluding this portion of our treatment of archaeology's value in furnishing background material for the biblical records, we cannot do better than present the compelling words of G. E. Wright:

> We can now see that though the Bible arose in that ancient world, it was not entirely of it; though its history and its people resemble those of the surrounding nations, yet it radiates an atmosphere, a spirit, a faith, far more profound and radically different than any other ancient literature. The progress of archaeology, of textual, literary, and historical criticism has never obscured the fact that the biblical writers were the religious and literary giants of ancient times, though they themselves would never have said so. They claimed that they were simply bearing witness to what God had done, and that whatever was accomplished through them was God's work, not their own.[46]

Even those who are now in reaction against what they call "biblical archaeology" have to concede certain values of archaeology for biblical studies. J. Maxwell Miller admits that archaeology (1) has provided a sorely-needed check against some of the hypercritical speculative views relative to Israel's origins and history that held sway during the early years of this century, (2) has furnished a growing source of helpful information with reference to biblical times, (3) and has occasionally had direct bearing on particular biblical passages.[47]

H. F. Vos underscores eight areas where archaeology has done notable service: (1) helping us to understand the Scriptures, (2) disclosing what life was like in those days, (3) clarifying the meaning of obscure passages of the Bible, (4) illuminating the historical narratives and context, (5) confirming the accuracy of the biblical text and its contents, (6) revealing the falsity of higher critical theories of interpretations, (7) aiding in establishing the accuracy of the Greek and Hebrew originals, and (8) showing the remarkable accuracy with which the biblical text has been transmitted.[48]

Among the galaxy of witnesses to the value of archaeology for biblical interpretation is Francis Ian Anderson who writes:

> Archaeology is vital for Biblical study because of the importance of history [and we may add, geography] in the Biblical revelation. . . . The truth of the Bible as the Word of God does not need evidence from archaeology for support. But those who believe the Bible have their faith strengthened and their understanding enriched by the new knowledge now available.[49]

If possible, an even stronger position is that of Van Beek, who assures us:

> No one can understand the Bible without a knowledge of biblical history and culture, and no one can claim a knowledge of biblical history and culture without an understanding of the contributions of archaeology. Biblical events have been illustrated, obscure words defined, ideas explained, and chronology refined by archaeological finds. To say that our knowledge of the Bible has been revolutionized by these discoveries is almost to understate the facts.[50]

In his treatment Van Beek strikes a note that is seldom, if ever so expressed. He claims that archaeology has greatly helped the biblical interpreter to overcome the feeling of estrangement from the past. Whenever a biblical student seeks to project himself into biblical times, there is an almost inevitable feeling of unfamiliarity because of the barriers of time and culture. However, through the discoveries of archaeology much of the barrier is broken. The feeling of intimacy with the past that is available to the biblical student through archaeological studies would be unattainable if one had to depend solely on the written word.[51]

Although at times he appears more modest than necessary, the venerable Roland de Vaux sounds a clarion note on the values of archaeology for studies of the Scripture. He has stated:

> Archaeological research in the Near East during the past one hundred years has completely reshaped our understanding of those countries mentioned in the Bible with which the ancient Israelites had contact. . . . In short, we are now able to reconstruct—not without many remaining lacunae—the human milieu, both intellectual and spiritual, in which the Bible was composed and was first heard and read.[52]

Speaking directly to the radical claims of former years, G. E. Wright has written, "For the most part archaeology has substantiated and illumined the biblical story at so many crucial points that no one can seriously say that it is little but a congeries of myth and legend."[53]

THE EXAMPLE OF W. F. ALBRIGHT

Often when dealing with great and comprehensive themes the rule is to avoid the personal and concrete and dwell only on the concepts or principles and the abstract. But it is refreshing and compelling to view these same principles enfleshed and embodied in a human life. Such an example is available to us in one whose life and work have spanned the greater part of this century and whose odyssey parallels the fortunes of archaeology at home and abroad. I refer to William Foxwell Albright, under whom it was my privilege to study at Johns Hopkins University during the World War II years of 1943–45.[54] To comprehend the method of procedure and the results achieved thereby, it is essential to sort out the main characteristics of his thinking and how they were influenced.

After graduation from Hopkins and studies under Paul Haupt, he arrived in Jerusalem in 1919. Almost at once he began a program of coordination of archaeological data, geographical studies, philological and linguistic materials from extrabiblical sources with the text of the Bible. In the first decade of his residence in Jerusalem, by dint of the data, he found himself placing greater confidence in both the prose and poetic portions of the Scripture for the purpose of historical reconstruction. Along with this conviction he found by diligent study that there was a valid basis for the early dating of a good number of poems in the Bible. To solidify his conclusions he branched out into an almost incredible array of disciplines, which he was able to control from primary sources.

Another determination that moved him throughout his life was to discover the actions of men that brought about the traditions now transmitted to us.[55]

DILEMMA IN PENTATEUCHAL INTERPRETATION

With decades of archaeological research bombarding the old accepted positions of the higher critical approach to the Old Testament, propounded and propagated by the Graf-Kuenen-Wellhausen school, there was bound to come an impasse in the interpretation of the Pentateuch. Rolf Rendtorff of the University of Heidelberg has put it succinctly:

> This is where the dilemma of more recent Pentateuchal criticism appears. Most of all it lies in the fact that two modes of questioning have been combined which cannot be combined. More and more, literary criticism has shown the lack of unity within the 'sources' [which were supposed to underlie the Pentateuchal material]. Nevertheless, these same entities undergo examination of the basis of their supposed unified theological conception. Correspondingly, the result is unsatisfactory, as is shown by the fact that recent writers have presented quite different answers to the question of what the theology of the 'Yahwist' was. Obviously, that is a question to which the accepted method of enquiry can give no plain answer.[56]

Albright's contention was:

The tendency toward earlier dating of much Pentateuchal prose and Hebrew verse in general found increasing support among Old Testament scholars. This tendency has been powerfully reinforced by a flood of new archaeological data which have affected every possible approach to Pentateuchal problems.[57]

When we come into the specific period of the patriarchs, Wright's observations (echoed by Andersen) are particulary timely and apropos. Wright declares:

The material within it [that is, the patriarchal time] was passed down orally for many generations before it was committed to writing, and it is necessary for us to recover its original background if we are to answer the historian's questions. This can only be done by archaeological investigation, the results of which we must carefully sift and use because we have no other means of getting into the period in question.[58]

When we study the practices of the Hurrians as reflected in the Nuzi tablets, the remarkable resemblance to patriarchal customs is beyond dispute. Customs as these are long lasting as a part of the general background of culture in Mesopotamia. There is thus agreement with the tradition that the progenitors of the Israelite people came originally from that area. Furthermore, marriage and inheritance practices of the patriarchs fit into the framework of that same place and period.[59]

Edward F. Campbell, Jr., a student of Albright, rightly castigates the recent critics of Albright on his historical reconstructions of Old Testament records, especially with reference to the patriarchal period. Writes Campbell:

As I read the current burst of literature on the Patriarchal period and on the other areas where Albright sought for a coherent synthesis, it seems to me that the segments on the archeological data are at many points the weakest and the most vulnerable. I believe Albright's critics need to define more clearly the ground rules for archeological reconstruction. Among Albright's heirs, on the other hand, there is an equally serious problem: the current diatribe against the idea of doing 'biblical archeology' is hell-bent to deliver us into compartments where no one person will be trying to build compelling syntheses which do both biblical critical study and archeology justice. I wish we could bury this 'biblical archeology' controversy [wishful thinking] and get back to doing our work comprehensively.[60]

It is strange that this offensive comes at a time when the subject of the controversy can no longer defend his positions, which he did innumerable times when alive. Moreover, it is actually not the syntheses and reconstructions of Albright versus his critics' positions that constitute the burr in the saddle, but the basic presuppositions of Albright in studying the evidence over against the contrary presuppositions of his antagonists. The end result looks more like a rearguard skirmish than an effective vanguard assault. Battles and wars, military or theological, are not won by such ineffective tactics.

J. Maxwell Miller, who opposes Albright's positions, speaks confidently:

> Many of the positions developed and championed by Albright are encountering serious challenge at the moment, and it is doubtful [a prejudgment] that they will survive intact. This is true especially of his views regarding Israel's premonarchical history, which involved correlations of biblical and archeological data.[61]

In spite of these complaints against Albright, Miller claims that the greatest strength of Albright's method of historical reconstruction was his overall perception of the way in which Scripture and archaeology should be used in relation to each other in doing historical reconstruction.[62] To say the least, it is a strange form of logic that can evaluate a scholar's thinking as right in general and wrong in regard to the particulars.

Conservative scholar Donald J. Wiseman has disclosed the reason, at least in large part, for the present reaction against Albright by scholars such as Miller.[63] He has shown that

> The comparison of ancient documents with the patriarchal and later narratives has led to a radically different conception of all periods of Israelite history to that commonly accepted fifty years ago. It has also led to a state of flux [mark this] in Old Testament studies generally since there has been a departure by nearly all historians from the old critical consensus of the Wellhausen school hypothesis without any adequate replacement.[64]

It is well known that reactions are difficult to contain within certain limits; they have a mushrooming effect. Thus, the reaction against Albright and his well-supported positions has had peripheral consequences. Specifically, we are witnessing an unhappy distaste for biblical archaeology. Could it be because of the yeoman service it has done in reinstating the Scriptures into a position of deserved respectability and credibility after years of unwarranted suspicion leveled against it from the adherents of the Wellhausen School? J. Maxwell Miller affirms:

> We are experiencing a reaction against the "Biblical Archeology" movement at the moment, with some going so far as to suggest that biblical scholars and archeologists should each do their own thing [a suggestion of tunnel vision if there ever was one] and not try to work both sides of the fence.

But he admits that "many of the really interesting questions about the human past can be approached only from an interdisciplinary perspective."[66]

W. G. Denver and J. Alberto Soggin add their voices to the derogation of biblical archaeology. Denver assures us that "the chief justification for reviving the old debate on the contribution of archaeology to biblical studies is that the issues were never resolved."[67] That is highly subjective. When discussing the Tell Mardikh tablets (a subject too early for final adjudications), he contends throughout it is not valid to claim that comparisons between Israel and her neighbors "confirm the essential historicity" of the biblical traditions. He prefers to assert that the material can be used as "a helpful analogy" and that comparative studies have scarcely begun.[68] Soggin treats of another era:

> Archaeological evidence for the Davidic and Solomonic period is fragmentary and, on the whole, disappointingly scarce. Only a limited number of sites have been adequately excavated and the materials obtained are differently interpreted by the competent archaeological scholars.[69]

ARCHAEOLOGY AND HIGHER CRITICISM

Now that we have considered the nature of the evidence from archaeology and its value, there remains the important task of correlating this material with the positions held by higher criticism. Has archaeology confirmed or modified the literary criticism of the Old Testament? Because of the discoveries it has presented, has it thereby been able to pass verdicts on critical positions? There is considerable difference of opinion as to what extent archaeology has the right to pass judgment on the findings of higher criticism. The debate on the question has not been without emotional as well as rational factors. The subject was ably handled years ago in two fine articles in *The American Scholar*.[70] There it was pointed out that the Wellhausen school of criticism was swayed by the Hegelian concept of historical development. This view posited in its reconstruction of Israel's history a thesis (preprophetic), an antithesis (prophetic reaction), and a synthesis (legal or nomistic phase). Archaeological research has the value of proving the untenableness of all Hegelian and neo-Hegelian systems, even when such systems are modified by a Croce or caricatured by a Marx or Spengler.

It is artificial in the extreme and opposed to all analogy so to circumscribe the Hebrew religion in the limits of time and circumstance permitted by Wellhausen and his followers. It can be demonstrated that the "thought patterns" and conceptual life of Egypt, Syria, and Mesopotamia are in direct contrast to the picture protrayed for us by the critical school. It is well known now that Wellhausen exaggerated the resemblance between the Hebrews of the Mosaic period and the pagan Arabs who lived nearly two thousand years later. He held that primitive elements in Israelite culture meant a generally primitive state of culture; this is quite unhistorical, because primitive beliefs and advanced concepts are found side by side in the Near East. The assumption that "pious fraud" was common in Israel is without parallel in the pre-Hellenistic Orient. The opposite is true: there was a superstitious veneration for the written word and oral tradition. In Greek times matters changed in this respect.

Literary critics are quick to come to the defense of Wellhausen and claim that his failure was relative and not absolute. However, even here literary critics are willing to concede (it is a big concession and vital) that Wellhausen's view that religious development in Israel proceeded from polytheism through henotheism to a monotheism fully developed in the postexilic age is too simplistic. Evolutionary principles work no better in theology than in biology.

Where does the truth lie? The position of the archaeologist is that the picture of the literary critics relative to the history and religion of Israel is distorted and erroneous. It must be modified and revised to bring it into conformity with the findings of archaeological research. The contention of the literary critic is that, although archaeology has cleared up some difficulties and obscure passages and has modified critical assumptions or presuppositions in certain instances, the reconstruction of Israel's history set forth by literary criticism from Wellhausen on remains inviolate. Its basic postulates are untouched. This is strange logic, for you cannot eat your cake and have it, too. If the basic presuppositions of the critical view are shown to be erroneous by the force of the evidence from biblical lands, then how can the theory built on those same presuppositions stand?

Let us now indicate the specific lines along which the evidence from archaeology has modified the entire Wellhausen position. One of the basic tenets of the critical school is that in the historical development of the religion of Israel, the primitive came first and was followed in process of time by that which was more advanced, all the elements in the development proceeding along uniformitarian, unilateral, evolutionary lines. With this postulate in mind, the first accounts in Genesis, those of Creation and the Fall, were considered folk tales and legendary. But the longer archaeologists study the creation account in Babylonian and Assyrian literature (with their prototype in the Sumerian), the more they are convinced of the unique nature of what is found in Genesis 1. Albright says:

> It undoubtedly reflects an advanced monotheistic point of view, with a sequence of creative phases which is so rational that modern science cannot improve on it, given the same language and the same range of ideas in which to state its conclusions. In fact, modern scientific cosmogonies show such a disconcerting tendency to be short-lived that it may be seriously doubted whether science has yet caught up with the Biblical story.[71]

As for the stories of Eden and the Fall of man, in the light of our information of the Ancient Near East and its intellectual life, we can only conclude that when radical criticism relegates them to the realm of the folk tale and compares them with the myths of contemporary primitive people, "they actually diverge farther from the truth than did Philo Judaeus, nearly two thousand years ago."[72]

Another claim of the critical school has been that, because of the lateness of written records in Israel, the reliability of the narratives could not be maintained. Passage after passage was declared to be a literary forgery, and the charge of pious fraud was heard again and again. It has been shown that patriarchal traditions, as well as those of a later period, reveal authentic customs, names, places, and concepts. Furthermore, archaeology has confirmed the testimony of the Bible to the decline of the material prosperity of Palestine in the eighth and seventh centuries when the land was repeatedly overrun by the imperial powers of that day. Not until some three centuries later did the land experience anything like its former prosperity.

The critical view has long indicated that the development of Israel's religion proceeded from animism to polytheism through henotheism with the climax in explicit ethical monotheism, an achievement of the sixth and fifth centuries in its purest form. If archaeologists have learned anything of the religion of the Near East, it is that by the time of the patriarchs all parts of the Fertile Crescent were far removed from the animistic stage of religion. If we are to judge alone from the analogies of the religions of the ancient world, there is no basis for speaking of a tribal or national God in the records of Israel. Even the polytheists of those days granted their deities unlimited power and imposed on them no geographical limitations. The assertion that Israel's religion was much like that of Canaan is absurd. Canaanite religion was far removed from what is found in the Old Testament. There is no evidence of female deities or mythology in Israel, although there is no doubt, based on Old Testament records themselves, that syncretism was introduced into the religion of Israel. But this synthesis/amalgamation, which was contrary to the mainstream of Israel's tradition and faith, never displaced the unique worship of Israel's God. There was in Israel from earliest times the preeminence of the concepts of election and covenant that gave the nation a distinctive religious outlook. This was never lost; it was not invented by the prophets, but rather reiterated and reemphasized by them. Archaeology, thus, has taught us that the Graf-Wellhausen approach has greatly oversimplified, and thus distorted, the picture of the religion of Israel.

ARCHAEOLOGY AND NEW TESTAMENT STUDIES

Although archaeology is often spoken of in reference to the Old Testament its researches have been very valuable for New Testament studies as well (see our earlier discussion of the DSS). Here the situation is entirely different from that of the Old Testament but archaeology has done notable service again. The differences arise because the Old Testament covers a period of history of more than a millennium, whereas the New Testament touches less than a century. In the Old Testament the historical writings deal with material both national and international in scope and outreach; in the New Testament, the range of events narrated is drastically restricted. Too, the Graeco-Roman period of history had been much better known than the ancient oriental era before modern excavations began. That is not to imply at all that archaeology has no importance for New Testament studies.

In the first place, the manuscript discoveries of New Testament portions have dealt a crushing blow to the radical critical views of the Tübingen School, which allowed less than six New Testament books to the first century A.D., and placed the fourth gospel as late as the second half of the second century. With the force of the new discoveries, even some radical scholars are prepared to place John as the earliest gospel instead of the latest.[73] Second, the findings of archaeology have done much to confirm the uniqueness of early Christianity. The position had been taken that Christianity was but one of many different sects, of the same or similar character, that flourished in the eastern area of the Roman Empire about the first century A.D. The discoveries give no encouragement to any such position. Now "Christianity thus appears in the light of archaeology as a unique historical phenomenon, like the faith of Israel, which preceded it."[74]

CONCLUSION

Without controversy the service of archaeological studies for the interpretation of the Bible is invaluable. The help of archaeology by way of interpretation of the text together with the finding of more ancient texts than previously available, explanation of difficulties, illumination of hitherto obscure passages, provision of much new material for new tools of interpretation in the way of lexica, grammars, and commentaries, and orientation of the entire political, cultural, and religious background of the Scriptures with emphasis on the uniqueness of their spiritual truth, cannot be gainsaid, and for it we are deeply grateful to those who have borne the burden and heat of the day.

NOTES

1. D. G. Hogarth, ed., *Authority and Archaeology: Sacred and Profane* (London: J. Murray, 1899), p. 143. How Driver puts these principles into practice can be seen from his Schweich Lectures (British Academy, 1908, published in 1909), *Modern Research as Illustrating the Bible.*
2. Roland de Vaux, "On Right and Wrong Uses of Archaeology," *Near Eastern Archaeology in the Twentieth Century* Essays in Honor of Nelsen Glueck, ed. James A. Sanders (Garden City, N.Y.: Doubleday, 1970), p. 68.
3. Ibid., pp. 69–70.
4. Ibid., pp. 66, 68.
5. Van Beek has argued this point well in G. W. Van Beek, "Archaeology," IDB (New York: Abingdon) 1: 205. He writes: "Archaeology does not and cannot prove the Bible. The Bible deals with man's relationship to God, and is, therefore, beyond the proof of archaeology or any other discipline. While archaeology confirms many details of history and lays bare the environment of the Bible, the history and environment with which it deals is human, not divine. It can neither confirm theology nor open the realm of faith."
6. de Vaux, p. 69. He adds: "These documents have the advantage, over texts, of being contemporary with the events to which they witness and of having escaped the accidents of oral or written transmission and the changes introduced by successive interpreters. But they have the greater disadvantage of being mute, and thus they require interpretation" (ibid.).
7. For example, Kathleen Kenyon on Jericho; Judith Marquet-Krause on Ai (Joshua 7 and 8 are labeled "part of a legend"); and J. B. Pritchard on Gibeon ("... we have reached an impasse on the question of supporting the tra-

ditional view of the conquest with archaeological undergirding,") in J. P. Hyatt, ed., *The Bible in Modern Scholarship* (Nashville: Abingdon, 1965), p. 319. Cf. de Vaux, pp. 70, 75.

8. de Vaux, p. 77. His work, always of great value and perspicuity, seems to me to be in this instance disappointing, overly negative, and diffident. Hear these conclusions: "But the biblical tradition exists. It may have overstressed the role of Joshua and the extent of the first conquests, but it cannot have completely invented the story that groups of Israelites entered into Palestine at that time and established themselves at least partly by violence." And further: "Archaeology does not confirm [sic] the text, which is what it is [meaning?], it can only confirm the interpretation which we give it" (de Vaux, pp. 77-78).

9. G. Ernest Wright, *Biblical Archaeology* (Philadelphia: Westminster, 1962), p. 18. Tersely stated, "The vast majority of the 'finds' neither prove nor disprove; they fill in the background and give the setting for the story" (ibid., p. 27). Harry T. Frank has well summed up the alternatives: "Of course, had the findings of archaeology tended to indicate that the events spoken of in the Bible were fabrications, there would be ground for suggesting that the faith of biblical men was a pious fiction and not a worthy basis for confidence today.... The certainty of faith does not rest upon the conclusions of science, historical or otherwise.... Faith, the absolute assurance of man's meaningful dependence upon the activity of God, is hardly dependent upon the transitory methodologies of science" (Harry T. Frank, *Bible Archaeology and Faith* [Nashville: Abingdon, 1971], p. 341.

10. Donald J. Wiseman, "Archaeology and Scripture," *Westminster Theological Journal* 33 (1970-71):133.

11. Ibid., p. 151.

12. Howard F. Vos, "Archaeology," in *Wycliffe Bible Encyclopedia* ed. Charles F. Pfeiffer, Howard F. Vos, and John Rea (Chicago: Moody, 1975), 1:125.

13. William G. Denver in his discussion of early Israelite traditions, in John H. Hayes and J. Maxwell Miller, eds., *Israelite and Judaean History* (Philadelphia: Westminster, 1977), p. 74.

14. Van Beek, p. 204.

15. M. Burrows, "How Archaeology Helps the Student of the Bible," *The Biblical Archaeologist,* May 1940, pp. 13-14. See also F. Kenyon, *The Bible and Archaeology* (New York: Harper, 1940), pp. 280-281; W. F. Albright, *The Archaeology of Palestine* (Harmondsworth, England: Pelican, 1949), especially chapters 7, 10, and 11; Charles L. Feinberg, "The Relation of Archaeology to Biblical Criticism," *Bibliotheca Sacra* 104 (April-June 1947): 170-81. H. M. Orlinsky comes to a similar conclusion in his "Current Progress and Problems in Septuagint Research," *The Study of the Bible Today and Tomorrow,* ed. H. R. Willoughby (Chicago: U. of Chicago), pp. 144-61.

16. Wiseman, p. 145.

17. Ibid., p. 147.

18. W. F. Albright, *History, Archaeology, and Christian Humanism* (New York: McGraw-Hill, 1964), p. 35. Francis Ian Andersen concurs thus in his appraisal: "Pride of place for Old Testament research belongs to the tablets from Ugarit (Ras esh Shamra), written in alphabetic cuneiform. The language of these texts is a northern dialect of Canaanite, closely akin to ancestral Hebrew. The literary traditions of Ugarit are very close to those of the Israelite writings, especially

poetry. These discoveries have equipped us with exciting new tools for research on the language of the Old Testament. They have solved hundreds of old problems involving the meaning of words and have clarified numerous obscure grammatical constructions. It is not an exaggeration to say that every page of the Old Testament stands in new light as a result of these discoveries; but most of the results have not yet reached the general public" ("The Archaeology of the Bible," in *New American Standard Bible* (New York: Holman, 1977), p. 1362).

19. Basic for the study of the DSS are *The Dead Sea Scrolls of St. Mark's Monastery,* ed. Millar Burrows, Vol. I: *The Isaiah Manuscript and the Habakkuk Commentary* (New Haven: ASOR, 1950). Vol. II, Fascicle 2: *Plates and Transcription of the Manual of Discipline* (New Haven: ASOR, 1951). Cf. also M. Burrows, *The Dead Sea Scrolls* (New York: Viking, 1955) and *More Light on the Dead Sea Scrolls* (New York: Viking, 1958). For the steady stream of information on this intriguing find see the 1948, 1949, as well as subsequent numbers of *The Biblical Archaeologist* and *The Bulletin of the American Schools of Oriental Research. Revue de Qumran,* issued in Paris from 1958 on, is helpful in many ways, particularly in bibliographic matters. Hundreds of articles and books for the scholar and the general public have already been published. Research on the scrolls, especially its variant readings, with implications for Old and New Testament studies, goes on to this hour.

20. Wiseman, p. 134. He adds: "These provide the earliest extant copies of the Hebrew Old Testament and afford important evidence for the transmission of the text" (ibid.).

21. F. F. Bruce, "New Light from the Dead Sea Scrolls," in *New American Standard Bible* (New York, N.Y.: Holman, 1976), p. 1281. He concludes: "The Qumran discoveries, in fact, do not add appreciably to our knowledge of the history of the Old Testament canon" (ibid.).

22. Ibid.

23. Ibid., p. 1287.

24. Andersen, p. 1362.

25. Wiseman, p. 134. Bruce, p. 1282, has put it well: "The general Bible reader, it was plain, could go on using the familiar text with increased confidence in its essential accuracy. There was already good reason to believe that the Jewish scribes of the first thousand years A.D. carried on their work of copying and recopying the Hebrew scriptures with the utmost fidelity. The new discoveries bore impressive testimony to this fidelity." Bruce has further taken a firm stand (p. 1285), when he declares: "They [the DSS] have greatly extended our knowledge of the state of that text in the centuries before A.D. 70. But they also make it plain that the text which was standardized by Rabbi Akiba and his colleagues about A.D. 100 [contra certain opposing voices recently raised], the text which passed through the hands of the Masoretes and is basic to all the principal versions of the English Bible, was the most accurate type of text available then or subsequently."

26. Wiseman, pp. 137–38. W. F. Albright summed it up when he stated "We can now set the books of the New Testament against the actual Jewish background of the Herodian age" (*History, Archaeology, and Christian Humanism,* p. 39).

27. Bruce, p. 1289.

28. Witness the ill-conceived (later retracted) position of A. Dupont-Sommer (*The Dead Sea Scrolls* [Oxford: Blackwell, 1952]), which was taken up by Edmund Wilson and widely circulated in "A Reporter at Large: The Scrolls from the Dead Sea," *The New Yorker* (14 May 1955), pp. 45–121.

29. Bruce, p. 1289.

30. Albright, *History, Archaeology, and Christian Humanism,* p. 46. An interesting note on the spread of Gnosticism immediately before and after the inauguration of the Christian era is that about the time of the finding of the first Qumran MSS., the first of some thirteen codices from Nag Hammadi in Upper Egypt came to light. The material is the work of Egyptian Gnostics. Cf. ibid., p. 39.

31. *Los Angeles Times,* 24 April 1979.

32. Clifford Wilson, *Ebla Tablets: Secrets of a Forgotten City* (San Diego: Master Books, 1977), pp. 20, 33, 106, 118, and 121 especially. Dr. Wilson is an Australian archaeologist who for some years was director of the Australian Institute of Archaeology and area supervisor at Gezer, Israel, in 1969. In 1977 he was connected with Monash University, Victoria, Australia.

33. Bruce, p. 1282, affirms: "But the field in which these Biblical manuscripts have revolutionized our knowledge is the history of the Old Testament text."

34. E. M. Blaiklock has tersely stated that archaeology "has illuminated the meaning of words and established text integrity" ("Archeology," *The Zondervan Pictorial Encyclopedia of the Bible,* Merrill C. Tenney, ed., 5 vols. [Grand Rapids: Zondervan, 1974], 1:284). On the same page, he added: "The conclusion is that the Isaiah Scroll, by and large, demonstrates the astonishing accuracy of the text which has been transmitted."

35. Wiseman, pp. 151–52.

36. Wright, p. 17. On the same page he states: "In the biblical sense there is no such thing as a knowledge of God apart, or somehow separated, from the real events of this human scene and from the special responsibilities he has given us with it. Faith and knowledge in the Bible are founded in a complete commitment to the God who rules history and in the loyalty, obedience and hope which are anchored in him but which necessitate one's personal and responsible involvement in, not retreat or removal from, the events of history." H. T. Frank has similarly viewed the nexus between history and the knowledge of God. He observes: "The religion of the man whose faith is rooted in the Bible is a *historical religion* as well as a *religion with a history*. At its very heart is the confession that God reveals himself and fulfills his purposes precisely in history. Faith is trusting this kind of God. It is little wonder, therefore, that archaeology—a historical discipline par excellence—is of considerable importance for the understanding of the Bible" (p. 339). Moreover, "The weight of evidence showed that there were few reasons to doubt the essential correctness of the narrative history in the Old Testament" (ibid., p. 340). Whether in general fashion or specific manner, archaeology has demonstrated beyond cavil that biblical statements and interpretations do rest on actual events.

37. Frank, p. 340.

38. Wiseman, p. 138. He quotes W. W. Hallo: "Without this basic knowledge, all higher criticism remains hopelessly hypothetical. With it, the foundations are laid for a comparative approach to biblical criticism" (ibid.).

39. Ibid., p. 143.

40. W. F. Albright, "Moses in Historical and Theological Perspective," in *Magnalia Dei, the Mighty Acts of God, Essays on the Bible and Archaeology in Memory of G. Ernest Wright,* ed. Frank M. Cross, Werner E. Lemke, and Patrick D. Miller, Jr. (Garden City, N.Y.: Doubleday, 1976), p. 121. See also Wiseman, p. 133, for the importance of archaeology to the study of the history of the ancient world. Furthermore, Albright, "Moses," p. 122, cites the Old Assyrian tablets (19th and 18th centuries B.C.), the Mari tablets (18th century B.C.), the Nuzi tablets (15th century B.C.), and the Alalakh tablets (mainly 17th and 15th centuries B.C.) as illuminating social organization and commercial relations of the early Hebrews. The evidence is abundant in the tens of thousands of tablets unearthed from the sites already studied. Moreover, Albright, "Moses," p. 123, notes that there is now independent evidence for the close connection of the Hebrews with Tanis (biblical Zoan and Rameses). On p. 123, he also asserts: "It was once thought by most critical scholars that the name of persons mentioned in Exodus and Numbers were mostly fictitious. Now this cannot be said any longer, since the names of Israelites contemporary with Moses are nearly all typical of the people and period." Albright instances the names of Shiphrah and Puah (Exod. 1:15). Even more, he claims: "The Midianite adventure of Moses is one of the most controversial episodes in biblical history. It is now also one of the best supported traditions in the earlier books of the Old Testament" ("Moses," p. 124). The superiority of the biblical material is definitely underscored. As to the moral and social emphases of the Mosaic legislation, he affirms, "In this respect Mosaic law is not only very ancient but more advanced than any comparable material in the ancient world" (ibid., p. 130).
41. Van Beek, p. 204. The relation between Eliezer and Abraham (Gen. 15:2–4) is clarified by the Nuzi tablets, where the arrangement was common among childless couples.
42. Cf. Elihu Grant, ed., *The Haverford Symposium on Archaeology and the Bible* (New Haven: ASOR, 1938), p. 63.
43. Van Beek, p. 204.
44. Ibid.
45. Blaiklock, p. 281. He comments further: "It is to be observed in all these cases that archeology underlines the essential truth and soundness of the biblical record. It therefore enables the historian to tread with firmer foot where reliance on the bare statement of Scripture lacks extraneous support or amplification" (ibid.). And again, there are "examples of archeological discovery which throw light on fact or practice, which elucidate culture or exemplify the application of Biblical fact or custom, without providing the direct confirmation of statement" (ibid.). Cf. legal codes.
46. Wright, p. 27.
47. Cf. Edward F. Campbell, Jr., and J. Maxwell Miller, "W. F. Albright and Historical Reconstruction," *Biblical Archaeologist* 42 (Winter 1979):42–43. At the other end of the spectrum are the enthusiastic remarks of J. A. Thompson in "The Importance of Re-assessing Archaeological Interpretations in the Light of New Evidence," *Abr-Nahrain* 15 (1974–75):125.
48. Vos, p. 125.
49. Andersen, p. 1365.
50. Van Beek, p. 203.
51. Ibid., pp. 204–5.

52. de Vaux, p. 64. See also de Vaux, p. 65.

53. Wright, *Biblical Archaeology*, pp. 17–18. Thus, it is not overstated to claim as Frank (p. 341) does: "Archaeology has provided a different orientation for understanding the Bible than was possible a century, or even a generation, ago. In general it has confirmed the narratives."

54. His life story can be found in L. G. Running and D. N. Freedman, *William Foxwell Albright: A Twentieth-Century Genius* (New York: Morgan, 1975). When asked as to the Christian commitment of Dr. Albright, I have invariably referred the questioner to the last sentence of his magnum opus, *From the Stone Age to Christianity*. He was indeed the dean of biblical archaeologists.

55. Campbell, pp. 38–44. Albright himself indicates what happened: "I became increasingly 'liberal' after beginning my Oriental studies [at Hopkins under Haupt]. . . . I might have remained a 'liberal,' had it not been for two unforeseen developments. The first was the cumulative effect on me of archaeological confirmation of Biblical tradition and increasing disproof of the isolationist theory of Israelite history held by critical scholars . . ." (*History, Archaeology, and Christian Humanism*, p. 320). He who would understand Albright's thought and work must read this volume, especially the autobiographical sketch in pp. 301–27. How Albright's changes struck others can be seen in the statement of Stanley Eugene Hardwick: "In Albright's work changes toward a more radical position are exceedingly rare. Nearly all of his changes . . . represent a shift toward a more conservative position" (*Change and Constancy in William Foxwell Albright's Treatment of Early Old Testament History and Religion, 1918–1958* [Ann Arbor: U. Microfilms, New York University doctoral dissertation, 1965], p. 570).

56. Rolf Rendtorff, "The 'Yahwist' As Theologian? The Dilemma of Pentateuchal Criticism," *Journal for the Study of the Old Testament* 3 (1977):2–10, especially 5.

57. Albright, "Moses," p. 121. Andersen, p. 1364, has carried the position down to specifics. For example, he claims that Exodus preserves an accurate description of the Tabernacle used in the desert by Moses. The dimensions of the Arad temple along with its well-preserved altar are the same as the dimensions of the altar in the wilderness Tabernacle (Exod. 27:1). Moreover, the construction is identical to the design revealed to Moses on Sinai.

58. Wright, *Biblical Archaeology*, p. 17. See also Anderson, pp. 1361 and 1363 for an echoing and elaboration of Wright's position.

59. Andersen, p. 1363.

60. Campbell and Miller, p. 45.

61. Ibid., p. 37. See also p. 40 for an even more dogmatic statement of the position.

62. Ibid., p. 41. If our statement be considered too strong, then hear Miller again: "Much of what Albright claimed as archeological evidence confirming or clarifying biblical history was not that at all, but rather hypothetical constructs which he himself produced by playing biblical and archeological evidence off against each other" (ibid., p. 43). It is left to the reader to judge whether Miller grants Albright the benefit of honest scholarship.

63. Some who have reacted negatively to Albright (besides Miller) are William G. Denver in John H. Hayes and J. Maxwell Miller, eds., *Israelite and Judaean History* (Philadelphia, 1977), p. 72 (he believes we cannot be definite on patriarchal tradition); Denver, p. 77 (he expresses his point of reference on

the debate in the 1960s between archaeologists and literary critics of the Bible); and T. L. Thompson in Hayes and Miller, p. 98 (he expresses his view that archaeology and history of the early second millennium have nothing to offer that would help in handling the traditions about Abraham, Isaac, and Jacob). Furthermore, Miller (pp. 252-61) disputes identifications of sites and chronologies. Such reactions have been engendered as a result of statements by Albright ("Moses," p. 122) such as, "There can no longer be any reasonable doubt as to the antiquity of the Patriarchal tradition," and, "It is no accident that the three cities most intimately connected with Patriarchal tradition, Ur, Haran (Harran), and Nahor, are specifically mentioned as caravan centers in early cuneiform tablets."

64. Wiseman, p. 149. See above the position of R. Rendtorff in agreement.
65. Campbell and Miller, p. 46.
66. Ibid. But not many men can be called "universals," who are at home in a multiplicity of disciplines. Thus, Campbell answers Miller well: "For my own part, I am not ready to agree that Albright's syntheses lie in ruins" (ibid., p. 47).
67. Hayes and Miller, p. 77.
68. Ibid., p. 116.
69. Ibid., p. 340. Cf. also pp. 340-43.
70. The first article, entitled "Archaeology Confronts Biblical Criticism," was written by W. F. Albright and appeared in volume 2, 1938, pp. 176-88. The second article, "Higher Criticism Survives Archaeology," was by W. C. Graham and also appeared in volume 2, 1938, pp. 409-27.
71. W. F. Albright, "The Old Testament and Archaeology," *Old Testament Commentary,* ed. H. C. Alleman and E. E. Flack (Philadelphia: Muhlenberg), p. 135.
72. Ibid., p. 137.
73. Cf. W. F. Albright, *The Archaeology of Palestine,* pp. 238-40.
74. Ibid., pp. 248-49.

11

Preaching from the Old Testament

W. A. Criswell

W. A. CRISWELL (D. D., Baylor University; Th.M., Ph.D., Southern Baptist Theological Seminary; D.S.T., Western Conservative Baptist Seminary) is pastor of the First Baptist Church, Dallas, Texas.

Expository preaching has been a declining phenomenon in the American pulpit in recent years. Some have turned to topical preaching, and many have turned away entirely from biblical preaching. There is nothing wrong with topical preaching, but it is not worthy as a steady diet for any congregation. The expository sermon is the best method of preaching. God's people need to hear His Word. They need the authority of "Thus saith the Lord." The world of lost humanity cries out for what only the Word of God can supply. There is a great need today for preaching the Word of God. A preacher ought to take the Bible and preach it. He should preach it verse by verse, chapter by chapter, book by book. This is the method God has most blessed and honored in the years of my ministry.

Over a period of seventeen years and eight months, I began in Genesis 1:1 and preached through the Bible to the last verse in Revelation. God honored those efforts by building one of the finest congregations on the face of the earth. God honors this kind of preaching because the people want to know what God has to say, and expository preaching allows Him to speak through the preacher.

THE DECLINE OF EXPOSITORY PREACHING

Perhaps the most neglected area of the Bible in modern preaching is the Old Testament. If the Old Testament is used at all, it is often only the text for some topical treatise that soon departs from its context. As a consequence, Genesis, Psalms, and perhaps Proverbs are the only parts of the Old Testament with which most Christians are familiar. The Old Testament is an area that is ripe for the study and proclamation of the whole counsel of God. If a man is willing to study and to invest the time and sacrifice needed to give birth to expository messages from the Old Testament, he will discover a marvelous thing. God will bless the message. God will bless the preacher. God will bless the people.

A man honors God when he preaches from the Old Testament, because in its pages are the foundational truths of the gospel. The New Covenant is built on the Old Covenant. If one is to understand and to appreciate the New, one must read, study, preach, and teach the Old. The Old Testament contains Christ, as Jesus explained to the disciples on the road to Emmaus. "Beginning at Moses and all the prophets, he expounded unto them in all the scriptures the things concerning himself" (Luke 24:27). How could a man improve on that? What a blessed privilege to stand and preach the unsearchable riches of Christ from the pages of the Old Testament.

The words that Erasmus wrote in the preface to his Greek New Testament, the Textus Receptus, published in 1516, seem appropriate:

> These holy pages will summon up the living image of His mind. They will give you Christ himself, talking, healing, dying, rising, the whole Christ in a word. They will give him to you in an intimacy so close that he would be less visible to you if he stood before your eyes.

This beautiful tribute was written concerning the New Testament, but it is equally appropriate for the Old Testament.

There is one great theme in the Word of God. The theme is constant from beginning to end. That theme is Jesus. He is on every page, in every event, in every type, in every book. Someone once asked the famed Charles Haddon Spurgeon of the Metropolitan Tabernacle in London, "Why do your sermons all sound alike?" Spurgeon replied, "Because, I take a text and make a beeline to the cross." The entire Bible presents Jesus, and the man who wants to proclaim Christ must do so by preaching from all of the Word of God.

The decline in expository preaching in general and in preaching from the Old Testament in particular can be attributed to six distinguishable factors.

1. Modern higher critical attacks on the inspiration of the Bible have centered primarily on the Old Testament. The shift from an infallible, inerrant Bible to one that the higher critics consider both fallible and

errant, has contributed much to the decline in biblical preaching. If the
Scriptures are not really the Word of God, then they are like any other
piece of fine literature. The literature may be uplifting, but it is still
human origin. It is man's opinion. People today are looking for something
more, a word from God.

The teaching of the documentary theory of origins for the Old Testament in general and the Pentateuch in particular has destroyed the confidence of many in the truth of God's Word. The authenticity and historicity of the book of Daniel have suffered mercilessly at the critic's pen.
Daniel has been discredited as fictional by some, while others have attributed its composition to some unknown writer who lived at least 450
years after Daniel.

Whether these claims are true or not, they cannot fail to have their
effect on the uninformed. These critics stand guilty of preaching and
teaching doubts rather than exuberantly proclaiming the certainties. The
Bible, however, is the infallible, inerrant Word of God. It has endured all
the attacks of skeptics through the ages. John Clifford's poem "The Anvil
of God's Word," says it well:

> I paused last eve beside the blacksmith's door,
>   And heard the anvil ring, the vesper's chime,
> And looking in I saw upon the floor
>   Old hammers, worn with beating years of time.
> "How many anvils have you had" said I,
>   "To wear and batter all these hammers so?"
> "Just one," he answered. Then with twinkling eye:
>   "The anvil wears the hammers out, you know."
> And so, I thought, the anvil of God's Word
>   For ages skeptics' blows have beat upon,
> But though the noise of falling blows was heard
>   The anvil is unchanged; the hammers gone."

2. Because of the lack of confidence in the Old Testament, the contemporary seminarian often finds that he receives little or no training in it.
There are few courses that deal with Old Testament books. Further,
Hebrew is dropped from the course of study as unnecessary. When sermons from the Old Testament are encouraged, they are of necessity topical in nature, possessing little depth of scriptural content or context.

A failure to preach the *whole* counsel of God is in direct violation of
the mandate of 2 Timothy 4:2, "Preach the word; be instant in season, out
of season; reprove, rebuke, exhort with all longsuffering and doctrine." It
is prophetic that the call to expository preaching would precede the warn-

ing that follows in verse 3, "For the time will come when they will not endure sound doctrine; but after their own lusts shall they heap to themselves teachers, having itching ears."

3. A third reason for the decline in preaching from the Old Testament is that its value for the New Testament believer is not always clear. The first two factors were more theoretical, whereas this problem is practical. The Old Testament and its world seem to some to be so removed from, different from, and irrelevant to the present world and the needs of modern man. Therefore, it is very difficult to make the material of the Old Testament speak to today. In its pages are well over two thousand years of history. Moreover, its thirty-nine books are of a widely divergent character (e.g., history, poetry, prose, allegory, narrative, prophecy). Even here the difficulties do not end. There is also the problem of balancing the Old Testament theology and teaching on law, life after death, works and rewards, faith and practice, with New Testament theology and faith and practice.

These can and do constitute problems for the interpreter of the Old Testament. However, the two testaments are not at odds with one another, even if it does require diligent study on the part of the preacher to explain and illustrate their compatability. The failure to expend this effort leads to a paucity of good biblical exposition from the pulpit with the resultant fact that the average layman is woefully inept in his knowledge of Old Testament books. Therefore, the preacher who would preach the whole counsel of God will necessarily be required to expend the time to learn the background and context of the Old Testament.

4. A fourth reason for a decline in the preaching of the Old Testament is a disbelief in the miraculous in Scripture. If one does not believe the miraculous, it will be difficult to preach convincingly on passages such as the miraculous preservation of Noah (Gen. 6), the birth of Isaac (Gen. 21:1-8), the plagues of Egypt (Exod. 7-12), the conquest of Jericho (Josh. 6), Daniel's deliverance from the den of lions (Dan. 6:14-28), and so forth. An attitude of confidence in the Scripture allows one to preach with conviction all matters pertaining to faith and practice. The miraculous confirms and undergirds the life and ministry of the chosen men of God. The prophets were anointed with the power to perform the miraculous, and God will bless with power and reward all those who proclaim the miraculous in the Word.

5. A fifth objection that some may have against preaching from the Old Testament is that it bores their listeners. Several years ago when I announced that I was going to preach through the Bible, there was an obvious foreboding on the part of some who feared that the congregation would be ruined. They said that no one would show up to hear long

passages in the Old Testament that were unfamiliar and had never been discussed or preached. The prognostication was one of inevitable failure and doom. But the opposite happened. As I continued to preach through the Bible, God continued to bless. The church continued to grow, and heaven came down to attend us in the way. Our auditorium was filled to capacity and overflowing, and it is still filled three times every Lord's Day. People hunger and thirst for the Word, and our church continues to increase numerically and spiritually. God honors the preaching of the Word.

6. A final reason for a decline in preaching from the Old Testament is the lack of good, current exegetical and expositional commentaries on many of the books of the Old Testament. For instance, preparing sermons from Leviticus, Numbers, or Song of Solomon is both difficult and discouraging. There are very few solid evangelical works available on these books. This leaves the serious preacher with little opportunity to learn in many areas of Scripture. There is no easy solution to this problem, but God will bless your efforts and crown your work if you will pursue these difficult sections with diligence.

PREACHING THE VALUES OF THE OLD TESTAMENT

Are the critics right? Is the Old Testament unreliable, fallible, errant, and unworthy of the preacher's time and efforts? No! No! Never! The value of preaching and teaching has been proved logically, theologically, and practically a thousand times over in the years of my ministry. There is so much in the Old Testament that commends itself as a worthy source for biblical exposition and expository proclamation. Consider the following.

1. Preaching from the Old Testament is of value because it is as much a part of Scripture as the New Testament. All the Word of God is profitable and valuable for our proclamation of salvation (2 Tim. 3:16-17). The Bible minus the Old Testament would be woefully incomplete. It was the Bible used by our Lord Jesus. When he began his public ministry, he did so by reading Isaiah 61:1-2 (cf. Luke 4:16-22) and then expounding it.

The Old Testament is just as inspired, infallible, and inerrant as the New Testament. God gave it to us in revelation without error or mistake. It is dynamic, plenary, verbal, and supernatural in its writing. There can be no doubt of this fact if one takes seriously the words of the apostle Peter:

> For we have not followed cunningly devised fables, when we made known unto you the power and coming of our Lord Jesus Christ, but were eyewitnesses of his majesty. . . . We have also a more sure word

of property; whereunto ye do well that ye take heed, as unto a light that shineth in a dark place, until the day dawn, and the day star arise in your hearts: knowing this first, that no prophecy of the scripture is of any private interpretation. For the prophecy came not in old time by the will of man: but holy men of God spake as they were moved by the Holy Ghost. [2 Pet. 1:16, 19-21]

Therefore, Jesus proclaimed that not one "jot" (the smallest Hebrew character) or one "tittle" (a small projection on some Hebrew letters) would pass away (Matt. 5:18). Scripture is *supernatural* in its origin. It is a gift from the throne of God's marvelous grace. No man could originate its blessed teachings. No man could roll back the veil of history and see the future. But God can, and He does so in His book. Thus, the apostles regarded the Old Testament as the very Word of God. They taught it, preached it, and practiced it. Therefore, we ought to follow their good example and preach, teach, and practice the Old Testament.

The preaching of Peter on the Day of Pentecost was saturated with Scripture. In his message he quoted directly from Joel (Joel 2:28-32; cf. Acts 2:17-20) and Psalms (Psalm 16:8-11; cf. Acts 2:25-28). The apostle Paul was well versed in the Scripture. As he preached in the synagogue he no doubt made masterful use of his knowledge of Holy Scripture. That fact is revealed in his writings. In Romans 9, for example, he discussed the relationship between the Jew and the gospel. He quoted from Exodus, Hosea, and Isaiah (cf. Rom. 9:15, 17, 25-29; Exod. 5:2; 7:3; Hos. 1:10; 2:23; Isa. 1:9; 10:22, 23).

Preaching from the Old Testament honors Christ. He did not come to abolish the Old Testament Scriptures, only to fulfill them (Matt. 5:17-20). Whenever preaching honors the Old Testament as the Word of God, it honors Christ.

2. Preaching from the Old Testament is of value today because it is the foundation upon which New Testament doctrine and faith is built. The precepts of the New Testament did not arise in a historical and theological vacuum. Jesus came in the *fulness of time*. The Word of God had already laid the foundation for his coming. Galatians 4:4-5 says that "when the fulness of the time was come, God sent forth his Son, made of a woman, made under the law, to redeem them that were under the law." In preparing the way for that redemptive work, the Law fulfilled an important function in that it was our schoolmaster which brought us unto Christ (Gal. 3:24).

Because foundational precepts of the faith are found in the Old Testament, it should be no surprise that the New Testament is saturated with the Old Testament passages. Do away with the Old Testament and you will destroy the New Testament. More than thirteen hundred passages in the New Testament are direct quotations from the Old Testament. One cannot hope to understand the ideas contained in the New Testament without referring to their Old Testament antecedents. In the same way, preaching from the Old Testament allows the preacher to present the whole counsel of God. In proclaiming the Old Testament, the preacher is building a secure foundation for New Testament faith.

One may preach that Christ our passover is sacrificed for us (1 Cor. 5:7). However, without a careful exposition of Exodus 12 and 13, those words are void of their full impact. One may preach that Christ is our great High Priest. Without a careful study of Leviticus and Numbers, one cannot understand the true nature of Christ's priestly work and office. When we preach passages such as the great Day of Atonement (Lev. 16) or the Passover (Exod. 12), we honor Christ and our preaching calls forth the foundational truths of New Testament faith and practice.

3. Preaching the Old Testament is of value because it constitutes the backdrop for the ministry of our blessed Savior. For example, there are numerous types that illuminate the Person and work of our Lord. Paul explained their significance in his letter to the Corinthians.

> Moreover, brethren, I would not that ye should be ignorant, how that all our fathers were under the cloud, and all passed through the sea; and were all baptized unto Moses in the cloud and in the sea; and did all eat the same spiritual meat; and did all drink the same spiritual drink; for they drank of that spiritual Rock that followed them: and that Rock was Christ. . . . Now these things were our examples, to the intent we should not lust after evil things, as they also lusted. [1 Cor. 10:1-4, 6]

So then we know that the water from the rock (Exod. 17:1-7; Num. 20:2-13) was a type of Christ. The manna (John 6:31-52; Exod. 16:12-36) and the lifting of the serpent in the wilderness (Num. 21:4-9; John 3:14-15) looked forward to Christ. The sacrificial lamb and the atoning blood were types of Christ (Lev. 16:1-34; 17:10-12). Christ fulfilled all the moral precepts of the law (Matt. 5:17). Christ was the fulfillment of the Levitical priesthood (Heb. 10:7). Without the preaching and teaching of these great truths, the full implications of Jesus' redemptive work would remain an enigma.

4. Preaching from the Old Testament is of value because many attributes and activities of God are clearly demonstrated. The New Testament tells us that God is a holy God. But it is in the Old Testament that we learn about the nature of a holy God (Exod. 15:11; Psalm 47:8; 48:1; Amos 4:2). The Pentateuch teaches the law of God. It tells us that a holy God

can and does make moral demands of men. Joshua shows that the power
of God can conquer any foe. Judges warns of the consequences of sin. Ruth
reveals the kinsman-redeemer concept. Samuel presents the coming ideal
king and kingdom. Kings shows the fate of men and nations that forsake
God. Chronicles tells what happens when the devotion of men and nations
to God waxes cold. Esther shows us the providential care of God. Ezra and
Nehemiah proclaim the faithfulness of God to his promises. Job reveals
the blessedness of God's testing. Psalms teaches us how to worship and
pray. Proverbs teaches us how to live. The prophets teach us that God
knows our sin and desires our repentance.

Or what should I say about Israel. The place of Israel in redemptive
history cannot be understood without looking carefully at passages such
as Genesis 12:1-3; Exodus 19:1-6; Joshua 24:1-29; Isaiah 54:1-17; 66:1-
24; Ezekiel 34:11-16; 36:1-38; 37:1-28; and Zechariah 12:1—13:6.

What beauty! What richness! What exquisite majesty! To turn away
from the pages of the Old Testament in willful neglect surely is to sin.
How blessed is that man who lives by every word that proceeds from the
mouth of God (Deut. 8:3). How blessed is that preacher who proclaims the
precepts of the Holy Word.

> Thank God for the Bible,
> Whose clear, shining ray
> Has lightened our path
> And turned night into day.
>
> Its wonderful treasures
> Have never been told
> More precious than riches
> Set round with pure gold.
>
> Thank God for the Bible
> In sickness and health
> It brings richer comfort
> Than honor or wealth.
>
> Its blessings are boundless
> An infinite store.
> We may drink at the fountain,
> and thirst nevermore.
>
> Thank God for the Bible.
> How dark is the night,

Where no ray from its pages
Sheds forth its pure light.

No Jesus, no Bible
No heaven of rest,
How could we live,
Were our lives so unblessed?
Anonymous

5. Preaching from the Old Testament is of value, because it provides rich illustrative material. Many pastors have shelves of books on illustrations, but neglect the Old Testament. How foolish! What better illustration can one find of the consequences of anger than that seen in the story of Cain and Abel? There is no better illustration of true friendship than that of David and Jonathan. The law of divine retribution is beautifully illustrated in the story of Ahab and Naboth. Ahab desired Naboth's vineyard, but Naboth refused to sell or exchange it. This infuriated Jezebel, and she plotted to have Naboth executed. Because of the treachery of her action, God promised the extinction of Ahab's line. Ultimately, Jehu killed the last descendant of Ahab's line, Jehoram, on the property of Naboth (2 Kings 9:14–32). Judgment on the very spot of transgression. Where is there a better example of retribution?

METHODS OF PREACHING FROM THE OLD TESTAMENT

I have been preaching for more than fifty years. If I could start all over again, I would go back to my seventeenth birthday when I began to preach, and I would preach the Bible. If I could not get a message from a verse, I would take a paragraph. If I could not get a message from a paragraph, I would take a chapter. If I could not get a message out of a chapter, I would take a book. If I could not get a message out of a book, then I would take a Testament. But I would preach the *Bible*.

Expository preaching is often very narrowly defined. There are, however, a number of ways in which the preacher may employ exposition in a God-honoring way in preaching from the Old Testament. The following list represents some of the ways that God has blessed in the preaching of the Old Testament through the years of my ministry.

1. The preacher can give an exposition of a shorter section of Scripture. Sometimes this is called textual preaching. This kind of sermon may deal with a verse or part of a verse. The purpose of such a sermon is to give an exposition of the central idea(s) of the verse or passage. There are many such worthy passages and verses. Numbers 32:23 is one of these. "Be sure

your sin will find you out." This part of the verse tells us that the judgment of God on sin is certain, inevitable, universal, and personal. The
context of this chapter also shows that judgment could have been avoided.

2. A chosen topic may be explored through selected verses or passages
from the Word of God. Topical preaching of this kind is both expositional
and biblical. The kind of topical preaching that is all too common has
departed from its scriptural base to be nothing more than human opinion
or the mind of the preacher on a given subject.

If he chooses a topic, the preacher should be very careful to give an
exposition of the various passages. Recently, I preached a message on the
signs attending the second coming. I selected nine of them, and each came
directly from the Word of God. They are as follows:

a. The gathering of nations in the Middle East (Rev. 16:12-16)
b. The return of the Jews to the land in unbelief (Ezek. 36:24)
c. The revival of the Hebrew language (Jer. 31:23)
d. Rosh, Meshech, and Tubal at Armageddon (Ezek. 38:1-2; 39:1)
e. Persia (Iran), Ethiopia, and Libya aligned with Russia (Ezek. 38:5)
f. Egypt and Israel becoming friends (Isa. 19:18-25)
g. Increased knowledge and rapid transportation (Dan. 12:4)
h. Preaching of the gospel to the entire world (Matt. 24:14)
i. A great falling away among believers (2 Thess. 2:3)

The preacher can give an exposition of extended passages, even entire
books of the Bible. The advantages of this method are many. It is extremely versatile in forms that may be used—didactic, narrative, or even
dramatic. Moreover, it allows the preacher to touch on a number of topics
that his congregation needs to hear. And it allows him to fulfill his responsibility to teach while he is preaching. Remember the office of pastor
is presented as pastor-teacher in Ephesians 4:11, where God introduces
his gifts to the church. The preacher is God's gift to the church as a
proclaimer and teacher of the Word. Preaching the Bible allows him to
fulfill both of these responsibilities.

These extended expository sermons may take many forms. This is particularly true in the Old Testament where the material is so varied. The
following list represents some of the possible forms.

a. The survey or synopis sermon. On occasion there can be profit in
preaching an entire sermon on a whole book of the Old Testament. This is
easier and especially effective with some of the smaller books such as
Ruth, Obadiah, Jonah, or Nahum. This approach is particularly helpful
in that it helps the listener to grasp an *overview* of a book. One sermon on
a book helps to introduce people to it, and hopefully this will excite them
to study it more thoroughly.

b. The analytical sermon. In the analytical sermon the preacher preaches through a book paragraph by paragraph and verse by verse. As I have previously stated, I preached through the Bible in this manner. It took me seventeen years to do it. This method gives the hearer a good knowledge of the content of the Bible. It also has many advantages for the preacher in that it is systematic and gives him clear guidance on topics as he prepares his next sermons.

c. The biographical sermon. This is a simple yet God-blessed way to make the pages of the Old Testament come alive for people. The end results are most rewarding and well worth the challenge. Think of a series of expository messages on Genesis focused on Adam, Seth, Noah, Abraham, Isaac, and Jacob. But do not neglect the lesser known men and women of Scripture. Preach a series on Lot, Eliezer of Damascus, Achan, Caleb, or Gehazi. One can relate the character to a significant event in his or her life, or to a defining character trait or attribute.

Let me list some sermon topics and titles and the Bible characters I have related to them.

Lot: Living with Homosexuals
Ishmael: Islam and the Oil Slick
Achan: The Sin We Are Afraid to Confess
Elkanah: Household Heartaches
David: Sexual Drives
Ahab: Forty Years with the Wrong Woman
Malachi: When a Parent Has No Partner (God and Divorce)

d. The special occasion sermon. The preacher should not fail to capitalize on the special days of both the secular and sacred calendar. Often there are people listening to preaching on those occasions who are not there at any other time. Most of these times are obvious: New Year, Easter, Fourth of July, Thanksgiving, Christmas. Do not overlook other special occasions, such as an anniversary of the founding of the church, completion of a new building, establishment of a mission, inauguration of a new program, and so forth. The exposition should be relevant to the needs of the listeners and true to the selected passage.

e. The doctrinal sermon. Expositional preaching from the Old Testament may be enhanced by preaching some of the great doctrines of the faith. A series of such messages might include a sermon on the sovereignty of God. Nowhere is God's sovereignty more clearly defined than in the Old Testament (Isa. 55:8-9; Jer. 18:1-17). God's holiness is a doctrine that is clearly defined in the Old Testament (Exod. 28:36; 39:30; Lev. 11:44; Psalms 47:8; 89:35; Isa. 6:1-8) and is worthy of proclamation. Many other doctrines would be of preaching merit, such as the sinfulness of man, the redeeming grace of God, life after death, Spirit of God, angels, Messianic hope, and so forth.

f. The Christological sermon. Nothing will be more blessed of God than proclaiming Christ from types in the Old Testament. One may do this by preaching on many of the obvious types of Christ such as the Passover (Exod. 12), the Tabernacle (Exod. 25:8), the manna (Exod. 16), the kinsman-redeemer (Ruth 2:20), Noah's ark (Gen. 6). There are other more subtle ways that also lend themselves to proclaiming Christ in the Old Testament, such as proclaiming the ministry of the angel of the Lord (Gen. 16:7), the work of the high priest (Exod. 29:38-40), the feasts of the Lord (Lev. 23), the offerings of the Lord (Lev. 1-7).

g. The prophetic sermon. Another fruitful area for preaching is the special prophetic portions of the Old Testament. Passages that contain messianic prophecy are rich, such as Genesis 3:15, the proto-evangelion; Isaiah 7:14, the virgin birth; Isaiah 53, the suffering Savior; Psalm 22, the crucifixion, to name a few. Prophetic passages related to the end time will be a blessing to preach. A few of these are Isaiah 60-66, the future glory of Israel; Daniel 9:20-27, the vision of the seventy weeks; Ezekiel 38-39, Gog and Magog; Zechariah 9:9-17, the coming of the great king to Zion.

h. The topical series. One can even preach a series of expository sermons on a given theme or topic. This was done very effectively by my predecessor, Dr. George W. Truett. Recently, I preached a series on the theme "God Speaks to America." The series was as follows:

"Is War in the Will of God?"
"The Red in Our Flag Is Blood"
"The Cancer That Consumes Us"
"Slavery or Freedom"
"The Saving of the Nation"

In preaching from the Old Testament it is important to vary the kind of sermon. Vary your method of preparation, your method of presentation, and your method of proclamation in order to avoid stagnation. The smart farmer rotates his crops for better yield.

CONCLUSION

There is so much to commend the preaching of the Old Testament that one cannot help but wonder why more do not do it. In spite of the issues that have contributed to the decline of biblical preaching, there ought to be more sermons from this neglected portion of the Word of God.

Here is a secret that I trust will encourage the preaching of more expository messages from the Old Testament. If a man will let the Lord lead him into the Word, if he will study with diligence, the listener will rise up to call him blessed. Any man who makes the sacrifice necessary to preach from the Old Testament will find this reward. The people who hear him will consider him to be far above the average preacher of the Word. When a preacher opens this rich section of the Word to his listeners, they will respond warmly with gratitude to God.

One may stand on a firm foundation when he stands to preach the Word. It is not human opinion that will transcend time and eternity but rather the Word of God. Isaiah 40:8 is my favorite verse, and it is a faithful reminder to all who preach, "The grass withereth, the flower fadeth: but the word of our God shall stand for ever."

> The earth shall pass away some day
> But my Word shall not pass away.
> The sun may fade, the moon decay,
> But God's Word lives forever.
>
> The flags of nations may be furled,
> The mountains to the seas be hurled,
> One thing will still outlast the world,
> God's Word shall live forever!
>
> Author Unknown

SCRIPTURE INDEX

INDEX OF SUBJECTS

INDEX OF NAMES